PROBLEMS *for the* CRIMINAL LAW

Mark Findlay

OXFORD
UNIVERSITY PRESS

OXFORD

UNIVERSITY PRESS

253 Normanby Road, South Melbourne, Victoria 3205, Australia

Oxford University Press is a department of the University of Oxford.
It furthers the University's objective of excellence in research, scholarship,
and education by publishing worldwide in

Oxford New York

Athens Auckland Bangkok Bogotá Buenos Aires Cape Town
Chennai Dar es Salaam Delhi Florence Hong Kong Istanbul
Karachi Kolkata Kuala Lumpur Madrid Melbourne Mexico City
Mumbai Nairobi Paris Port Moresby São Paulo Shanghai Singapore
Taipei Tokyo Toronto Warsaw

with associated companies in Berlin Ibadan

OXFORD is a registered trade mark of Oxford University Press
in the UK and certain other countries

National Library of Australia
Cataloguing-in-Publication data:
Findlay, Mark.
  Problems for the criminal law.

  Bibliography.
  Includes index.
  ISBN 0 19 550833 5.

  1. Criminal law—Study and teaching—Australia.
  2. Criminal law—Australia. 3. Criminal justice,
  Administration of—Australia. I. Title.

345.94

Edited by L. Elaine Miller of Otmar Miller Consultancy Pty Ltd, Melbourne
Cover designed by Racheal Stines
Typeset by Desktop Concepts Pty Ltd, Melbourne
Printed through Bookpac Production Services, Singapore

Contents

Acknowledgments

The structure of this book and its commitment to problem-solving as a context for teaching and learning is in many respects the product of the team enterprise which has been the teaching of criminal law at the University of Sydney over the past decade. The critical legal theory approach was championed by Julia Tolmie and Miranda Kaye. The foundation in substantive law and process was the work of Brent Fisse, Bron McKillop, and David Fraser. My immeasurable benefit from team teaching was drawn from the enlivening experience with Julia, Miranda, Catherine Dauvergne, Lynne Barnes, Fiona Borthwick, Kristin Savell, and Laurence MacNamara.

Several of the problems, particularly in the areas of domestic violence and sexual assault, as well as the justifications and defences, are the contributions of Julia and Miranda. Both their problems and my own were amended and developed through the constructive criticisms of the team and of our students.

My view about how to construct an understanding of the criminal law has been moulded by the insights in the writing of Alan Norrie, Andrew Ashworth, David Brown, and David Weisbrot. I tested and refined these views through writing and teaching in transitional jurisdictions such as Hong Kong and the South Pacific.

There has been a burgeoning of critical writing on criminal law in Britain and Australia in recent years. My debt to the scholars responsible for this development in taking criminal law seriously is recognised throughout the text.

I have explored my comparative interests in criminal justice institutions, from my early experience of the prison struggle in New South Wales through my years of researching the jury with my friend and colleague Peter Duff. Ugi Zvekic ignited and maintained my commitment to informal mechanisms of crime control. David Garland gave me a passionate respect for theory and theorising. More recently Ralph Henham has shared my new interest in international and comparative criminal procedure.

The hundreds of 'victims' of criminal justice and their supporters in the profession have revealed the real impact of what we teach and the imperative of context.

My long-suffering commissioning editor at OUP, Jill Henry, deserves all my best wishes for her sensitive encouragement, interest, and perseverance. Wayne Findlay was a meticulous critic of the text. The anonymous reviewers provided encouragement when it was most needed and insights which have improved my work.

My students have explored the course with me over the years and provided a willing experimental environment for testing its commitments. I am very grateful to them all, even those who resisted its intent.

This book is a critique of criminal justice. It is intended as a companion to the work *Australian Criminal Justice* with Stanley Yeo and Stephen Odgers. No doubt we will continue to argue over some of its directions.

In claiming the possibility of justice as the central reason for most of what I do, I recognise the inspiration of Jack Grahame and the late and great George Petersen.

The book is dedicated to my wonderful children James, Nicholas, and Alice, who give meaning to all my effort.

Mark Findlay
Sydney
November 2000

Introduction

Essentially this is a book for the undergraduate study of criminal law. What makes it different is its problem-centred approach. This is especially relevant for the understanding of criminal law and its process within contemporary social settings. As a teaching strategy it reflects the practice in successful law programs throughout Australia.

The structure of the book advances two main themes: law in context; and the contested process of criminal trial. The problem focus enables the teacher and student to analyse issues of context and process within a critical framework. In addition, structuring the primary topics of study around 'life-problems' allows a clear understanding of the practical applications and consequences of the criminal law.

Students are attracted to criminal law because it represents a significant and early expectation of how the law operates in practice. A powerful popular image of the law is the criminal trial. Therefore, to teach criminal law effectively and in a convincing fashion, the trial should form a framework for the presentation of ideas about substance and process that confirm or challenge the student's appreciation of crime and justice.

This project draws from a variety of analytical perspectives and a range of disciplines in order to reveal the operational reality of criminal justice in Australian jurisdictions.[1] It is essentially a critical endeavour and one which recognises that the study of law is neither contained within considerations of consistent rules and principles, nor limited by the examination of procedure.

---

1   While examples from various Australian jurisdictions are used when they are relevant, and in certain discussions there is coverage of the law in several jurisdictions, this book does not endeavour to be comprehensive of the criminal law in Australia. In addition, there is a more significant reliance on the law in common law jurisdictions (both across and beyond Australia) in recognition of the form of law and process in the jurisdiction in which this program originated.

The book develops in three parts. First, there is a contextualisation of the criminal law and criminal justice, which is crucial for the appreciation of problem-centred learning and issues of substantive law and process on which it relies. Next is a discussion of problem-centred learning for the criminal law. In particular, problem-solving skills are made available, and applied. Finally, issues of law and process are examined, with a topic focus which develops in a fashion similar to the progress of the criminal trial.[2] This section opens with a critical discussion of legal principles and an analysis of criminal capacity, which is crucial to the determination of criminal liability.

This book is not a substantive reference text on the criminal law in Australia.[3] Nor is it a sourcebook of cases and materials. It is a teaching/learning tool for law students and their instructors. It may be used as a companion to introductory texts such as Findlay, Odgers and Yeo, *Australian Criminal Justice*,[4] thereby expanding its utility. Important theoretical, substantive and teaching texts in criminal law,[5] cited throughout this book, would make useful supportive reading. These are not always cross-referenced on the expectation that students will be made familiar with them within the wider teaching environment.

The jurisdictional coverage is not always comprehensive or complete. The skills developed through the use of problem-centred learning texts

---

2   The treatment of these topics suggests cohesion in the criminal law and criminal justice that centres on the trial. Although the vast majority of criminal justice issues are resolved before or outside the trial, it is the context for many important doctrines and procedures. Both symbolically and practically, the option of a trial drives many criminal law problems to a resolution. It presents a useful learning framework against which all other discretionary criminal justice outcomes can be measured. The trial also clearly identifies the obligation of participants, and the expectations of the community for the process. The trial here should not be simply equated with best-practice models. While time will be spent discussing fair trial and the impediments to it, the trial structure is utilised in a manner where its structural and institutional deficiencies (and challenges to justice) may be a feature of criminal procedure in practice.

   In addition, evidentiary issues which might be viewed as central to the existence, nature, and operation of the criminal trial will only be dealt with here either as they highlight general issues of discretion (see Chapter 2) or when they prepare the context for a discussion of more general substantive concerns such as the rights of the accused.

3   As the reader will note, it is deliberately under-referenced in order not to detract from its essentially introductory purpose.

4   M. Findlay, S. Odgers and S. Yeo, *Australian Criminal Justice*, Oxford University Press, Melbourne, 1999.

5   In particular: Findlay, Odgers and Yeo 1999; D. Brown, D. Farrier, S. Egger and L. McNamara, *Criminal Laws*, Federation Press, Sydney, 2001; B. Fisse, *Howard's Criminal Law*, Law Book Company, Sydney, 1990; L. Waller and C. R. Williams, *Criminal Law: Text and Cases*, Butterworths, Sydney, 2001; A. Norrie, *Crime, Reason and History*, Weidenfeld & Nicolson, London, 1993; P. Rush, *Criminal Law*, Butterworths, Sydney, 1997; R. Murgason and L. McNamara, *Outline of Criminal Law*, Butterworths, Sydney, 1997; P. Rush and S. Yeo, *Criminal Law Sourcebook*, Butterworths, Sydney, 2000; S. Bronitt and B. McSherry, *Principles of Criminal Law*, Law Book Company, Sydney, 2001.

should be transferable to any context of criminal law. I have chosen substantive and process examples that stimulate the consideration of how criminal law applies in either similar or different jurisdictional settings. The instructor will identify the nature of this similarity or difference as and when it is appropriate. Naturally, as New South Wales is the jurisdiction in which I currently teach, its substantive law predominates, while not representing an exclusive jurisdictional setting for the selected problems.

There is no pre-existing work on which this book is modelled. It is not prepared in a contrived question and answer conversational style such as that adopted by Glanville Williams in *Textbook on Criminal Law*.[6] It draws from the themes and format of Lacey and Wells,[7] and recognises the current developments in legal research and writing as evidenced in Keyzer[8] and Davies.[9] Some problem-based notions similar to those touched on by Clough and Mulhern[10] are here developed.

Problems and their content

Part 3 appears as a selection of topics that reveal the problematic development and application of the criminal law. Reference is made to interesting and controversial features of the law in various Australian settings.

Within each topic, problems are identified. Essential to an appreciation of the problem is a brief identification of its context. The problems take the form of either general issues statements, which focus the discussion to follow, or of brief fact scenarios, which are materials and settings for exercises in analysis.

The problems rely on the discussion in the topic preceding them, and the techniques for analysis discussed earlier in the book. Certain further issues and readings follow each problem. Students should be able to extract enough from the general discussion of the topic and the nominated references to discuss the central issues in each problem that they identify. This book does not supply all the answers, even if there 'all the answers' to such problems are ever available. It is an introduction to techniques of research and analysis, and a guide to other helpful primary and secondary sources. More than anything, however, the book is a celebration of the significance of social context when engaging legal problems.

The problem dimension of the book gives it a function beyond a commentary with reference to further teaching materials. It becomes an

---

6   G. Williams, *Textbook on Criminal Law*, Stevens, London, 1983.
7   N. Lacey and C. Wells, *Reconstructing Criminal Law*, Butterworths, London, 1998.
8   P. Keyzer, *Legal Problem Solving*, Butterworths, Sydney, 1994.
9   M. Davies, *Asking the Law Question*, Law Book Company, Sydney, 1994.
10   J. Clough and C. Mulhern, *Criminal Law*, Butterworths, Sydney, 1999.

instructional device as well as a framework for legal analysis. The problems will be compatible with a student-centred learning approach to the coverage of the course requirements.

Topics around which the problems and substantive analysis are constructed include:

- Crime and society (euthanasia problem)
- Colonisation and the imposition of the criminal law (custom and introduced law problems)
- The phenomenon of crime (criminal sanction as discriminatory regulator problem)
- Criminal justice I: Police powers (youth detention problem)
- Criminal justice II: Court function (pub brawl prosecution problem)
- Criminal justice III: Discretion (drink-driving and sentencing discretion problem)
- Constructing the truth: Bail and verdict (bail application problem)
- Determining criminal responsibility I: Volition and capacity (omission problem)
- Determining criminal responsibility II: Elements of the offence (mistake of fact problem)
- Determining criminal responsibility III: Exceptions to liability, participation and preparation (corporate homicide problem)
- Assault (domestic violence problem)
- Sexual assault and law reform (sexual assault problem)
- Homicide I: Murder (causation problem)
- Homicide II: Non-intentional manslaughter (neglect problem)
- Homicide III: Intentional manslaughter (provocation problem)
- Factors affecting liability I: Self-defence and duress (battered woman syndrome problem)
- Factors affecting liability II: Insanity and automatism (irresistible impulse problem)
- Factors affecting liability III: Intoxication and diminished responsibility (child abuse problem)
- Factors affecting liability IV: Mistake and consent (sport, sex and consent problems)
- Property offences: Dishonest acquisition I (larceny problem)
- Property offences: Dishonest acquisition II (fraud problem)
- Sentencing and punishment I: Sentencing principles (parole problem)
- Sentencing and punishment II: Prison and alternatives (sentencing exercise)

These topics have been chosen, ordered, and classroom tested as an undergraduate course of study in criminal law. The course is not proposed as the definitive structure for such teaching. In its original form this course depended on a small-group teaching environment over a semester.[11] These constraints may not suit other teaching situations. The topics are prepared in such a way that they may be applied or developed in other structural contexts.

While the book does not contain a separate section on ethics and the delivery of the criminal law, ethical concerns are explicit throughout. The approach to considering the criminal law in context is governed by the belief that criminal justice is inextricably bound up with the challenges of ethical professionalism. The problems are designed to expose ethical dilemmas for the intervention of criminal law and process. This approach is rooted in the conviction that ethics is more effectively presented to students in context rather than as abstraction.

---

11 I would like to acknowledge the critical comments of colleagues and students who participated in the undergraduate criminal law program delivered at the University of Sydney, Faculty of Law, in 1999 and 2000, in which a draft of this text and the teaching approach were successfully trialled. Earlier versions of the course structure and some of the problems were the work of Julia Tolmie and Miranda Kaye.

Part 1

The Context of Problems for the Criminal Law

This part is designed as a brief overview of the issues one confronts in a consideration of crime and justice. These issues are presented in a form inviting further debate and analysis, particularly when crime and justice are located within the cultures of modern Australia.

Chapter 1 offers a range of themes about crime, criminal law, and criminal justice that should be addressed before any consideration of substance or process in these areas is approached critically. The themes are presented in a fashion intended to provoke rather than provide answers to concerns about crime, criminal law, and criminal justice. Readers might feel better prepared to engage with these issues after having had the benefit of understanding this text as a whole. While an intelligent response to the issues in this chapter should not rely on pre-existing knowledge, the reader can return to this chapter as the course progresses, and develop ideas on any challenge it proposes. This chapter will set the agenda for the contextual consideration of law and justice. It may also represent a résumé of the central themes for the text. In this respect the chapter forms both an introduction and a conclusion.

The second chapter explores the institutions and operations of the criminal justice process. Discretion is used as a central critical theme, helping to explain the contradictions between ideologies of justice and criminal justice practice.

Chapter 1
Locating Crime and Justice

Introduction

Criminal law is a framework of rules and procedures designed to control social behaviours through the prevention and punishment of criminal activity. The institutions of the criminal law, and the processes they perform, are expected to ensure criminal justice.

It is essential before any discussion of substantive and procedural criminal law to attempt to appreciate crime and justice as significant features of modern and transitional social environments. The interests behind popular representations of crime and justice also require recognition.[1]

Crime and justice are not static social facts. They are constituted by significant state and community relationships. Further, the connections between crime and justice are themselves crucial keys to understanding the status and operation of the criminal law.

At the outset, certain propositions concerning the social position of crime and justice should be considered.

1 Criminal justice may be conceived of as:
    • a social mechanism for the restitution of order and balance;
    • a process for exacting retribution against the moral outrage of crime;
    • an attempt at the protection of the community against harm;
    • a deterrent against the commission of further crime; or
    • various essential connections between each of the above intentions.

---

1   See M. Findlay, *The Globalisation of Crime*, Cambridge University Press, Cambridge, 1999.

Although justice is seen as the product of the criminal law and process, criminal justice is also a wider social concept.

2 Notions of justice depend on:
   • community attitudes to crime;
   • degrees of tolerance of crime throughout the community;
   • popular interpretations of the context of crime;
   • general beliefs in the necessity of the criminal sanction; or
   • the relationships between indigenous and imported value systems.

It is important to realise that law and justice are social constructs. In this respect the community context within which the criminal law has force and the criminal justice process operates is crucial to any appreciation of law and justice.

3 Both crime and justice are relative to the communities in which they are a feature, and rely for their representation on:
   • the prevailing structures of law that govern the community;
   • the nature of society, and levels of social inequality that prevail;
   • the political view and status of the individual; and
   • the position of the state in law enforcement and crime control.

Both criminal law and criminal justice take much of their meaning from the sanction process for their authority. While compliance with the law may be largely a matter of community consensus, when criminal laws are breached, criminal justice is reasserted through the sanction process.

4 The social significance of crime is largely dependent on the criminal sanction (in terms of both institutions and process):
   • sanctions are expected to be applied without discrimination;
   • the sanction must be certain;
   • the sanction process should have immediate effect;
   • sanctions require universal application. (Obviously whether this can be achieved will depend on the context in which such laws are applied.)

One of the most significant contexts for crime is culture. Within indigenous societies, for example, behaviours that might constitute crimes in a bureaucratised context are addressed through a range of customary practices, and more recently through introduced and modified legal traditions, such as the common law.

5   Positioning crime and responses to it within the context of specific cultures requires:
    • a historical appreciation of the recent sociopolitical development of these cultures;
    • an understanding of the behaviours deemed to be or not to be criminal within these cultures, and how they have become so labelled;
    • a working knowledge of the institutions and processes of the law that govern the establishment of criminal liability, with particular reference to areas of distinction; and
    • an examination of penalty and punishment, their forms and institutions.

When looking at the relationship between law and custom it is important not to stop at a conventional or legally focused discussion of *customary law*. To some extent the idea of customary law is created by those who wish to distinguish introduced legal systems from custom, or to legitimise custom in these terms. It is wrong simply to assume that the custom-based systems of social control, sanction and penalty rely on or reflect the same legal frameworks that establish colonial and post-colonial legal systems. Equally, it is misleading to view the socialising effect of custom as law, or customary laws, only as the introduced courts and legislatures do.

Questions regarding the context of crime and justice, therefore, relate to history, culture, social development, the state, and the law. And not only is the existence of justice so dependent, but the need for justice to be seen-to-be done emphasises the fact that justice is a demonstrative notion.

Context of the criminal sanction

The concept of sanction as used here incorporates the structures, institutions, and processes of law exercised through the state, against individuals and behaviours labelled criminal, and which require institutional action as a consequence.

With sanctions directed against individuals and often applied differentially, one must consider the criminal sanction in the context of selective enforcement. Not all laws are enforced all the time. Police do not charge every offender. Prosecutors do not prosecute every offence. Judges do not convict everyone against whom the facts of the case may be proved. In this respect, discretion is an essential feature of the operation of criminal justice.

Selective enforcement through the exercise of discretion may be seen in the following examples:

- The disproportionate investment of law enforcement resources in responses to murder as compared with car theft, even though the incidence of vehicle theft may far outweigh that of murder, and a greater proportion of the community may be affected by it. To some extent, this might be explained by the disparity in police 'clear-up' rates for murder when compared with theft, and the greater community tolerance of theft due to other factors such as insurance. Also, the community recognises the social harm and threat posed by murder as far more significant than that of theft.
- The differential nature of law enforcement activity and investment when directed towards offences against individual persons rather than offences against the community or society. Such disparity can be seen in the application and direction of the criminal sanction against assault as compared with responses to environmental crime. This might be explained by differing relative notions of victimisation, the identification of fault, and the nature of sanction systems applied to the individual rather than the corporate personality.
- The relative apportioning and allocation of law enforcement resources towards offences against individual private property rather than community property. For instance, the disparity in the application and direction of the criminal sanction against theft versus tax evasion or corporate fraud is evidence of this. Again, explanations may lie in varied notions of victimisation, as well as different concepts of what is a crime, who is a criminal, and who is harmed.

Selective law enforcement and the differential application of criminal justice has been a feature of the historical development of the common law. For example:

- policing private property offences at the beginning of the industrial revolution in Britain, which reflected the political significance of the newly emergent propertied classes;
- arrest, conviction and detainment of Aboriginal people in order to advance the colonial interests of European settlement in Australia.

The phenomenon of selective law enforcement suggests that an important context within which to appreciate the development of criminal justice in the recent Australian experience is that of history. Here we are interested not only in legal history, but also in the history of politics, economics, social organisation and culture.

Significance of history

At the outset of any historical analysis of crime and justice it is useful to ask: what do we mean by history? Is it simply a longitudinal progression and plotting of significant events, or more usefully, are we interested in examining the place of law and justice in the context of a *slice of time*? In the relatively short period of European settlement in Australia and the prevalence of common law, an approach to history that simply looks at political and social events over time is limited. A more revealing endeavour is to examine significant situations in the emergence of criminal law and justice, and to analyse these in their social, political, and human detail.

The recent history of laws, sanctions, and punishments across Australia is inextricably bound up with the history of state formation. In turn, the processes of colonisation and independence provide an important backdrop against which the reception and development of the criminal law are to be understood. The following points are crucial to such a historical analysis:

- The place of indigenous law within colonial transition: in particular the denial of the property rights of original inhabitants; the delegitimisation of pre-existing laws, customs, and institutions; the creation of new commercial relationships and reliance; the redefinition of individual and communal rights, and the isolation of the processes and institutions of law from the community.
- Structures of the colonial state claiming their authority and legitimacy from introduced law.
- The transmutation of the law as the institutions of the state adapt to new contexts. On this point note the variety of forms adopted by the colonies of Australia, the varied and conditional recognition of customary land use, and the modification of penalty structures as the necessities of a penal colony were replaced by the requirements of free settlement.

The present position of the criminal law in each jurisdiction—state, territory, and federal—cannot be understood fully without considering its historical context. Why have common law traditions remained so strong in modern, independent legislative states?

In summary:

1   The historical analysis of crime and justice should be conducted:
    - in terms of law; and
    - in terms of the context of the law.
2   The history of the criminal law should be conceived, in terms of its common law origins and regional adaptations, as:
    - a process of rational reconstruction in which principles and logic are often said to underlie decisions motivated by policy and precedent. Crucial to this is the role of judicial pronouncement in 'selling' the law, and its interpretation of the law. Judicial decision-making becomes an enterprise of rationalising rather than rational enterprise.

With principle and policy in conflict the law seems to operate in a climate of contradiction (see Norrie 1993);

- a gradual shift away from the resolution and reintegration of custom to an emphasis on the *certainty* and *impartiality* of the law, as imposed rather than negotiated;
- a move away from viewing crime as a community outrage to regarding it as a violation of legal proscription; and
- a reliance on legal principle rather than community conscience to distinguish criminality.

At the time of the colonisation of Australia, due to the growing centralisation of state institutions in England, the diminution of religious control, and the replacement of feudal patronage with commercial and mercantile interests, the certainty and predictability inherent in legal codes became the aspiration of English common law for the criminal sanction.

3 History in the Australian context of criminal law[2]

This history is one of relationships between political and commercial interests (individual and social) and the exercise of the criminal sanction. To appreciate these relationships and their specific dimensions and consequences one should recall:

- the specifics of colonisation across Australia;
- political and legal adaptations through independence;
- modification of the law and legal process through federation, emancipation and multiculturalism, as well as through international obligations;
- pressures resulting from socioeconomic development;
- the demands of multiculturalism and modernisation, such as
  - the differences between code and common law offence structures
  - the status of certain defence options relative to moral and customary proscriptions (e.g. intoxication).

Rationality and legality

Along with the underpinnings of 'rule of law' criminal jurisprudence and a reliance on the independence of the judiciary comes the expectation that the law is rational and that legality will always equate with rationality.

---

2   A significant collection of works on Australian history contain useful material on the relationship between criminal law and the institutions of criminal justice, and the development of the Australian colonies. See, for instance, R. Hughes, *The Fatal Shore: A history of the transportation of convicts to Australia 1787–1868,* Pan Books, London, 1988.

Ideology and practice

Legal principle depends on judicial interpretation for its existence. For example, to say that guilt must be proved beyond reasonable doubt requires a judicial instruction as to what the term 'reasonable doubt' means. Such interpretation is supposed to be apparent and constant, even though judicial interpretation arises out of adversarial argument focusing on the independent and subjective.

The contradiction between ideology and practice in certain situations of the criminal law allows judges to proclaim the rationality and reason of the law while at the same time propagating its contradictions within their decisions and reasoning. For example, there is the necessity of proving the accused's criminal mental state (through presumptions) on the one hand, and the opportunity to use negligence and strict liability as bases for liability, particularly in regulatory offences, on the other.

Examples of where ideology is confronted with the contradictions of practice in the criminal law include:

- equality before the law, and presumptions as to volition, knowledge and possession;
- equality in treatment before the law, and the limited availability of qualified defences (e.g. diminished responsibility);
- equality in the assessment of liability before the law, and objective bases for liability such as some forms of recklessness and negligence (where the views of the ordinary person rather than the actual beliefs of the accused are used to establish the apparent risk of injury);
- reluctance to individualise penalty (such as the situation where an offence relies on a 'common purpose' rather than the criminal intention of one accused).

Cultural factors

The law's concern for objectivity (rationality and uniformity) and its reflection of material interest explain:

- the emphasis on private property rights, and
- the property focus of penalty, such as through the widespread use of the monetary fine as a penalty.

Factors in the development of formal structures of legal sanction include the construction of pyramids of penalty, and the cultural inversion of issues of seriousness (where the law rather than the community sets the measure). In this respect the most 'socially' dangerous crimes may not seem to carry the highest penalty or even rely on the harm posed by the individual. Other factors may govern penalty and seriousness. For example:

- the common law emphasis on the protection of private property;
- the rejection of notions of individual vengeance, instead placing that responsibility in the hands of the state;
- the rejection of restitution in favour of retribution.

Crime and punishment

Some commentators on the criminal law argue that there are close structural connections between crime and punishment. While the criminal justice process represents punishment as the natural balance to crime, there are certain situations where the prohibited conduct and the penalty may be so similar, and where there is a commonality of interests promoting crime and those promoting punishment, that to view these processes as natural opposites may be an oversimplification.

What are these essential connections? Can punishment ever be viewed as crime, and what distinguishes these behaviours?

Traditional common law principles of punishment involve:

- retributive justice (where the state is represented as the victim, and the state is the initiator of penalty);
- proportionality and just deserts;
- deterrence through the certainty of punishment as it affects the free-willed rationality of offenders and potential offenders;
- the utilitarian (reformist) purpose of punishment, replacing terror.

In order to activate these principles, criminal justice recognised the need to move punishment away from the realm of individual vengeance and community compensation, and into structures and institutions of legality. This meant that the interests that punishment was intended to serve moved into the state sphere.

Interests behind punishment are often revealed through:

- understanding who gets punished (for example, the over-representation of certain ages, classes, and races is evident when one examines imprisonment rates);
- appreciating the structures of penalty which reflect the significance of private property;
- examining the character of the law relying on ideal types, such as the reasonable person;
- realising the predominance of policy over logic in sentencing practice.

In many custom-based cultures, the transition from compensation, restitution, and reconciliation to punishment under the criminal law has led to new interpretations of concepts such as 'victims', 'loss', and 'interest', and even the symbolic significance of punishment.

Criminal justice now operates with a general confidence in the *science* of sentencing and proportionality whereby the measures of guilt are supposedly balanced against state response. Recently, in many Australian jurisdictions, the concern has been for consistency and against leniency in sentencing.

Both individual and general deterrence, which are common justifications for sentencing and punishment, are reliant on notions of rational, individual choice and community consensus. As with other rationales for punishment, the assumed logic behind most penalties is intended to work towards the certainty of the law.

Sources of criminal law in Australia[3]

There is some disagreement about whether an indigenous criminal law existed prior to European settlement (see Yeo 1994). The High Court in *Mabo*[4] left open the possibility, and courts in the states and territories have recently recognised the significance and applicability of native punishment. However, Australian legislative and judicial thinking has a long way to go before harmony is achieved between Aboriginal control, sanction, and punishment traditions, and the mechanisms of introduced law.

The British government transferred jurisdiction over criminal law to the various colonial administrations. Following Federation, the Commonwealth Constitution did not cede exclusive powers over criminal law to the federal government. The newly formed states (and later the territories)[5] retained power to enact criminal legislation. The Commonwealth also could achieve this where it chose to regulate crimes within its region of power and authority (such as customs and excise).[6] Therefore, the criminal law in Australia is largely the province of the states and territories rather than the Commonwealth.

The sources of criminal law are not uniform throughout Australia. The Australian Capital Territory, New South Wales, South Australia, and Victoria largely rely on the common law as the principal source of criminal law.

---

3   A useful discussion of the issue of jurisdiction and criminal law in Australia is found in P. Rush and S. Yeo, *Criminal Law Sourcebook*, Butterworths, Sydney, 2000, Chapter 1.

4   *Mabo v. The State of Queensland* (1992) 66 ALJR 408

5   The Commonwealth delegated powers to enact criminal legislation to the Australian Capital Territory and to the Northern Territory: *Australian Capital Territory (Self Government) Act 1988* (Cth) s. 22, and *Northern Territory (Self Government) Act 1978* (Cth), s. 6.

6   The Commonwealth recently enacted the *Criminal Code Act 1995*. The act is intended to operate from the year 2000, and apply to Commonwealth offences provided the states and territories enact uniform legislation adopting the Act. It is not intended as a Code in the sense of the Codes in the Northern Territory, Queensland, Tasmania, and Western Australia. Rather, it codifies general principles of criminal responsibility to be applied when interpreting criminal statutes.

These jurisdictions do have a substantial body of criminal legislation such as Crimes Acts,[7] but the law is not contained in a single criminal Code (as it is in the Northern Territory, Queensland, Tasmania, and Western Australia).[8]

In the common law jurisdictions the criminal law derives from English law (common and statute), transferred through the colonial administrations. Since independence, the state legislatures have been the only source of new criminal laws. Australian common law in the criminal area has also developed its own jurisprudence and principles since Federation.

In *He Kaw Teh*,[9] the High Court determined that statutory offences in the common law jurisdictions are to be interpreted in accordance with fundamental common law principles of criminal liability. This also holds for those offences not defined by statute. Despite the essential connection in principle between English and Australian common law in the criminal area, and the continuing persuasive authority of English case decisions, the High Court no longer applies English judicial authority as a matter of course.[10] In the Code states and territory, the criminal Codes intend to provide a comprehensive criminal law, and consequently the common law has been almost entirely abrogated. A range of fundamental common law principles or doctrines (such as *mens rea*) have been replaced by the Codes, and offences and defences are now statutory. The language of the Codes is generally interpreted in accordance with ordinary meaning, whereas principle and doctrine in the non-Code jurisdictions are interpreted according to the common law.

Despite the differences in source, structure, and interpretation between the Code and non-Code jurisdictions, there are striking similarities in some areas of criminal law, particularly procedure.[11] Recently this has been enhanced through similar conclusions and developments in law reform. Having said this, Australian jurisdictions experience all the difficulties of codification. Particularly at the Commonwealth level, the efforts at bringing about greater harmony in the principles of the criminal law (through the generation of the *Criminal Code Act 1995*) reveal more than simply the complexity of codification in a federal system. While the common source of

---

7   *Crimes Act 1900* (ACT), *Crimes Act 1900* (NSW), *Criminal Law Consolidation Act 1935* (SA), *Crimes Act 1956* (Vic).
8   *Criminal Code Act 1983* (NT), *Criminal Code Act 1899* (Qld), *Criminal Code Act 1924* (Tas), *Criminal Code Compilation Act 1913* (WA).
9   (1985) 157 CLR 523.
10 *Cullen v. Trappell* (1980) 146 CLR 1.
11 The High Court has recognised the need, where possible, to interpret criminal law principle in such a way as to enhance consistency of interpretation among the Code states and territory, and then within each jurisdiction for the achievement 'of a desirable uniformity in the basic principles of the criminal law throughout Australia' (Kirby J in *R v. Barlow* (1997) 188 CLR 1 at 32).

criminal law in the development of Australia's penal colonies might suggest a fundamental harmony of criminal law across jurisdictions, the political development of the states, territories and the Commonwealth, as well as influences and fashions in law reform, have produced a bifurcated approach to codification, and often very different legislation on fundamental principles.[12] The codification process, however, is relentless, and as the recent rationalisation of criminal procedure and sentencing provisions in New South Wales reveals, it is essential for the development of consistent and rational criminal law even in the common law jurisdictions. What remains problematic in Australia is the possibility of greater legislative harmony in form and content across the criminal laws of the federation.

What is crime?

Crime is dependent on the institutions and processes essential for its definition. Law is paramount among these. Could it be argued therefore that there is no crime without law?

Crime is defined by institutional and procedural responses (such as prosecution, trial, and penalty) to a particular prohibited behaviour.

Along with individualised notions of liability and justice, criminal liability and criminal sanction focus on offenders and offences. Therefore the language of crime causation and control adopts an imagery of the *body and mind* of the individual to be controlled.[13] Further, there is recognition of the social determinants that give criminal behaviour its form in law.

Theories about crime and its causes can be very broadly classified into those concerned with the mind and the behaviour of the individual, and those focusing on social (or state) reaction to that behaviour.[14] In many respects these categories are not easily divided because social determinism appears in some of the behaviourist theories and vice versa. They do provide, however, a framework for understanding that explanations of crime are not only about what people do, but also relate to a community's response to crime. Under these categories appear below some of the main representations and explanations of crime, and their essential characteristics. Along with an individual consideration of these theories, it is useful to reflect on

---

12 A good example of this is, following on from similar detailed law reform debate, the very different approaches in New South Wales and Victoria to intoxication as a defence.

13 This individualised paradigm of criminal liability has led to considerable artificiality in the fashion in which criminal law responds to corporate deviance: see Norrie 1993, Chapter 5.

14 For overviews of criminology theory see D. Downes and P. Rock, *Understanding Deviance*, Oxford University Press, Oxford, 1998; G. B. Vold, *Theoretical Criminology*, Oxford University Press, New York, 1998.

their development and interconnection through the themes and approaches they share.[15]

Crime and the individual

Crime as illness (moral, psychological, social)

- Since the mid nineteenth century there have been representations of crime as either normal or pathological.
- Certain theories of crime see it (and punishment) as confirming the consensual limits of society.
- Is it possible to have societies 'without crime' if the limits of social consensus are clear? Are societies in which there appears to be too much crime to be deemed pathological?
- Considering crime at certain levels as a normal characteristic of modern societies is to remove the moral element from crime.

Born criminal

- The notion of criminality as an essential and inherited trait of personality was consistent with post-Darwinian evolutionary themes popular in Europe at the end of the nineteenth century.
- Attached to a fascination with the study of criminality as a behavioural science was the view of criminal law and punishment as science.
- Social anthropologists at the end of the nineteenth century believed in notions such as the criminal classes, as well as in social engineering directed towards the defeat of such classes.
- These themes of behavioural determinism as a cause of crime conflicted with rational choice notions of criminal liability and the free will of the offender, on which principles of punishment were based.
- In addition, behaviourist explanations of criminality cause problems for the ideology of equality before the law.
- This led to the development of ideas of qualified capacity within the operation of criminal liability.

Behaviourism as an explanation of crime

- Essentially, behaviourist theories were based on the debate between determinism and free will governing choices of crime.
- A positivist approach to the measurement of crime was a necessary component of a behaviourist scientist's explanation of crime.

---

15 Readers should remember that this is a skeletal framework of sometimes complex theory. A more comprehensive study of these issues can be afforded by the study of criminology.

- From a state perspective, the representation of criminal behaviour in figures (official statistics) became crucial for crime control planning.
- A developing policy within crime control strategies, consistent with behaviourist explanations of crime, was the concept of crime as *treatable*.
- Therefore the criminal sanction became an essential behaviour management tool.
- There was a move from body to mind as the focus for punishment.

Learning crime

- If crime, like any social behaviour, could be learnt, then individual meanings of crime were a feature of the learning process.
- Crime could now be considered as a choice resulting from social strain and the alienation of the individual.
- Differential association[16] became a persuasive theory of crime, in which the offender chooses to associate with other individuals who have similar attitudes to criminal behaviour.
- The capability for crime would therefore be enhanced, as would access to otherwise limited wealth and power, through voluntary association with other like-minded individuals.

Crime and opportunity

- The opportunity approach to crime works from the assumption that the primary motivation for human behaviour is materialism and material advancement.
- A lack of opportunities, both individually and socially, will lead to crime choices in order to avoid marginalisation.
- Crime is to be viewed as a factor of social development and modernisation.
- Crime becomes a preferred choice.

Criminal careers

- According to this paradigm, crime is a natural product of criminal associations.
- Like any other profit-producing activity, crime is business.
- Crime choices may result in the redirection of legitimate or stalled careers.
- Crime control needs to focus on ways in which crime business may be made materially unattractive.

---

16 See Downes and Rock 1998, pp. 79–81.

Crime and community reaction

Here the focus for explaining crime moves from individuals' behaviour towards state reaction to crime and the meaning imposed on a variety of criminal contexts.

Labelling

- Crucial to the definition of crime, and the process of making such definitions stick, is the position of the *significant other* (those who observe and are influenced by the labelling process) and *official discourse* (that is, the manner in which the state participates in crime labelling).
- The process of primary and secondary deviance, where an amplification spiral arises and magnifies (diversifies) deviance, is prominent.
- As a result of the initial crime label, those so labelled often make efforts to neutralise its effects.
- Crime labels may not be permanent, as delinquency is something offenders may drift into and out of.

Marginalisation

- Social anomie and individual isolation may be both causes and consequences of crime.
- To combat the marginalising influences of crime, subcultures grow up around inverted value structures.
- Consistent with general trends in social marginalisation based around power and the lack of it, crime is a factor of youth, while victimisation may be a factor of gender.
- Criminal justice and selective enforcement become part of the process of marginalisation.

Crime and development

- As unemployment is a common consequence of social development (socioeconomic modernisation), it is also connected with crime.
- Family dislocation as a feature of development is a causal factor in crime.
- Urban drift and urbanisation are consequences of social development. Young males, in particular, play a central role in both the context of urbanisation and the context of crime. They are disproportionately represented in urban populations, in crime, and in prisons.
- Crime is more likely to be a consequence of economic disparity than of poverty alone.
- Modernisation and cultural strain exist within development paradigms as well as contributing to crime contexts.

Crime and social conflict
- Conflicts over power and authority, and pressures on social cohesion, tend to lead to breakdowns in the traditional structures of social control.
- Recently *left realist*[17] criminologists have called on governments to *take crime seriously* and in so doing to recognise its links to class structures, as well as the need for accountability in the process of justice.

Crime and class
- The private property focus of the criminal sanction suggests a particular class bias in the criminal law.
- Selective enforcement and the imposition of penalty based on class are all too often apparent in systems of criminal justice.
- In this respect the class interests behind the criminal justice process are revealed.

Crime and reintegration
- Crime control may be more effective through the application of methods based in reintegration, such as shaming.
- This obviously depends on a communitarian approach to the criminal law and to crime.

Implicit in any consideration of what causes crime are the consequences that emerge from criminal behaviour and social reaction. The application of the law and its institutions to produce criminal justice is the outcome with which we are presently concerned.

Crime and criminal justice?

Under the notion of criminal justice that comes from common law traditions, individual behaviour is paramount when examining criminal liability. *Classical* or *liberalist* notions of criminal responsibility deem that individuals are not only equal before the law, but also equal in their ability to exercise free choice not to break the law, which they are all assumed to know. Society is constructed on a consensus model, and violations of the norms (laws) identifying such consensus necessitate punishment, in a classical context.

Penalties must be painful in order to counteract the pleasurable consequences of deciding to commit crime. Punishment is based on *less eligibility* principles, so that the conditions of the poorest honest citizens are not worse than those of criminals enduring punishment.

---

17 Downes and Rock 1998, pp. 295–301.

Individual justice

- The reality of the individuals who appear within the criminal justice system, either as perpetrators or victims, is not that they stand as equals, or that they are considered as individuals.
- The reality of the individual interests protected through the law is that wider policy interests often prevail.
- *Neo-classical* modifications of the assessment of criminal liability were required in the criminal law, on the basis of an individual's capacity to commit crime.
- Equality of rights under the law does not equate with equality of responsibility before the law.

Social justice

- Social justice considers social harm as a measure of the seriousness of crime rather than concerns for the welfare of the individual.
- Recognition of selective or generic victimisation, including victimisation by the system, is a product of this context.
- Social justice advances the requirement for restitution and compensation beyond the individual application of sanctions.
- In addition, social justice implies a balancing of community against individual rights.
- One of the difficult issues to resolve in the realm of social justice is the place of the state within the community in its monopoly over criminal law.

Having considered the dimensions of justice, it is important to reflect on the representation of criminal justice as a *system* or a process.

Justice in the system?

- What conditions of consistency, cohesion and predictability are expected of a system? Are the various agencies of criminal justice, operating under shared objectives and complementary practices, necessary for a system?
- What do the tensions inherent in the operations of criminal justice say about the process?
- Is there sufficient accountability within agencies and across the processes of criminal justice to feature as an indication of a professional *system*?
- Are the crimes sometimes perpetrated within the system, and in the name of the system, a challenge to criminal justice?

Justice within the criminal justice process and its institutions is the focus of the following chapter.

Chapter 2

Processing Problems with the Criminal Law

Introduction: System or no system?

The institutional operation of criminal justice is commonly referred to in terms of a system. The image of criminal justice being applied *systematically* is as suggestive as it can be misleading. With regard to those managing the administration of criminal justice, the representation of their policy directions as systematic is useful. For those at work within the institutions of justice, it is constructive to consider their labour and its impact as systematic. Those who are drawn into the operation of criminal justice find consolation in anticipating that its influence over them will be systematic.

Images of the criminal justice process are often based on false assumptions:

- that consensus exists about the nature of criminal justice and the purpose of punishment;
- that there is cooperation and consensus among the various agencies within the justice process, in order to achieve and attain this common view of justice;
- that the operations of this process are in some way complementary and systematic; and
- that if the agencies of criminal justice were examined independently, certain conclusions would become apparent regarding the nature, purpose and operation of the process.

In fact there is no single or overriding aspiration that unifies the institutions and processes of criminal justice throughout Australia. This realisation is complicated by the operational goals of agencies within the process (such as the police, the courts, and correctional instrumentalities) that may conflict and compete. Further, there exist in the operation of criminal justice fundamental contradictions between principle and occupational imperatives. Such divergence has both institutional and process dimensions. Regarding the latter, different imperatives govern the investigative component, the adjudicative component, and the penal component of the process (see Findlay et al. 1999).

The policy commitments at the heart of the operation of criminal justice reflect the following assumptions:

- we have the criminal law and criminal justice to punish wrong-doing;
- the aim of the enterprise is to control crime by punishing offenders;
- the system should be used to denounce certain behaviours, thereby reinforcing social norms; and
- such denunciation will lead to the reintegration of offenders, the deterrence of possible future offenders, and the protection and compensation of victims.[1]

Beneath these sometimes competing themes of criminal justice policy are the individualised operational concerns of the police, lawyers, the courts, and correctional services. These may be prescribed by:

- community expectations;
- the agency's perception of its function, both individually and collectively;
- the nature of the community in which and for which the agency is operating;
- internal bureaucratic constraints;
- individual and collective interpretations of the law being enforced and the agency's mandate therein;
- professional standards and job satisfaction;
- pressures from other agencies in the process; and
- occupational solidarity.

These are the types of influences that may promote divergence among the agencies of criminal justice, and their aims and goals. The exercise of discretion, both individual and organisational, adds to the widening gap between anticipated common goals and disparate practice. Since discretion is essential to the process of criminal justice[2] throughout Australia, as an explanation of justice practice and the nature of justice institutions, it requires some detailed analysis. It should be remembered, however, that while discre-

---

1   For a discussion of the potential reintegration and control outcomes of policy based around denunciation see J. Braithwaite, *Crime, Shame and Re-integration*, Cambridge University Press, Cambridge, 1989.

2   Discretion as the crucial characteristic of criminal justice decision-making is examined by the contributors to K. Hawkins (ed.), *The Uses of Discretion*, Oxford University Press, New York, 1992.

tion may be viewed as a facilitator of justice in the way it softens the harsh application of legal rules, this may at the same time be represented as evidence of partiality and hence injustice. We are concerned not only with the existence and operation of discretion, but also the manner in which it is represented and appreciated.

Discretion: Criminal justice decision-making

Most decisions in criminal justice occur long before a matter ever gets to trial. In fact, criminal justice is administered as a process comprising stages at which significant (and essential) opportunities arise for diversion from the necessity of progression further through this process. Diversion is not just a feature of our criminal justice administration for reasons of efficiency. A process which depends for its operation on the regular exercise of discretion by its principal players will invariably focus on those points at which the flow-through can be regulated.

For instance, the police have been described as *gatekeepers* of the criminal justice process.[3] This analogy is not simply confined to their role as the initial detectors of crime, since this function largely relies on the cooperation of the community in reporting crime. Instead, it is the control that police exercise over individuals' entry into the early stages of the process which confirms their *filtering* capacity.

The police have an obvious and major filtering role in the selection of those people who will eventually appear in the criminal courts. In addition, they have a powerful influence upon subsequent decision points in the criminal justice process in ways that are less obvious than their responsibilities over arrest, charging and bail. For example, the deployment of particular police resources in certain localities, and specific target strategies, may have ramifications for the *crime rate* and its impact on sentencing principles.

Having recognised the significance of the police at the pre-trial stage, the question arises as to what extent the police are the sole or principal gatekeepers of the process. What is the form and extent of interaction between the police and other criminal justice agencies, both in terms of their aims and objectives and in respect of the operational strain that exists between different players at each major stage?

Before proceeding further, it is worthwhile to remind ourselves of one of the central paradoxes in our criminal justice system. While there is an assumed unity of purpose within the system, the administration of the process of justice is characterised by its piecemeal treatment of decision stages, often in isolation from one another. In practice, this challenges the tenability of any binding and shared objective for justice agencies. To appreciate the

---

3   See J. Skolnick, *Justice Without Trial*, John Wiley & Sons, New York, 1966.

tensions that underlie criminal justice, it is necessary not only to examine the role and function of the major agencies at particular stages, but also to understand the interaction between agencies as they exercise discretion throughout the principal stages of the process.

As with so many contradictions existing within the criminal justice process, the reconciliation of competing individual and occupational aims and interests of the parties involved in the pre-trial stage depends on discretion. Any detailed discussion of pre-trial procedures of the police, defence attorneys, the Office of the Director of Public Prosecutions, and the magistracy[4] will be enhanced by some thoughts on the operation of discretion.

Discretion, as it operates within criminal justice, is the principal focus of decision-making, the style employed to make decisions, and the designation of where the responsibility for decision-making resides:

> Discretion is a tool indispensable for the individualisation of justice (governments of laws and men). Rules alone cannot cope with the complexities of modern government ... Where law ends, discretion begins and the exercise of discretion may mean either beneficence or tyranny, justice or injustice, reasonableness or arbitrariness.[5]

As the grist for criminal justice, discretion exists and operates in a variety of forms such as:

- decisions by individual criminal justice agencies;
- organisational and procedural frameworks within which decision-making is structured;
- ideological imperatives that influence decision-making (for example, independence and impartiality); and
- situations where criminal justice and law enforcement responses rely on discretionary decision-making (for example, decisions by police to arrest, or to grant or oppose bail).

Despite policy initiatives to formalise, regulate and make accountable instances of discretion within criminal justice, discretion remains built into the formal and informal structures of policing, sentencing and punishment. The position of discretion within the criminal justice process is complicated by its exercise beyond the bounds of formal legality.[6] These situations are not limited to the illegal exercise of a lawful power or authority. They may also

---

4   See Findlay et al. 1999, Chapter 4.
5   K. Davis, *Police Discretion*, West Publishing Company, St Paul, 1975, p. 12.
6   For a discussion of the individual and environmental factors which influence the selective invocation of police discretion, see G. Travis, 'Police Discretion in Law Enforcement: A Study of Section 5 of the NSW *Offences in Public Places Act*', in M. Findlay et al. (eds), *Issues in Criminal Justice Administration*, George Allen & Unwin, Sydney, 1983.

include instances where a lawful result is achieved by means arguably outside the limits of the law—for instance, when the methods of investigation employed by the police, in order to produce what they view as the just outcome of a criminal trial, have violated due process or legal restrictions on the accumulation of evidence.

The significance and meaning of particular discretionary decisions within the criminal justice process will be determined by the status of the parties involved, and the points at which the decisions are made. The characteristics and situations of individual parties are taken into account in criminal justice decision-making. Consequently, the exercise of discretion is very likely to be influenced by the individual characteristics and values of the decision-makers themselves. It would not be surprising that the discretion not to arrest or charge might be exercised in the suspect's favour, if a police officer viewed a suspect as respectful.

In addition, the fact that parties in criminal proceedings operate within an adversarial setting means that their discretion is directed towards opposing objectives. The very nature of the adversarial process—with the presentation of opposing versions of the evidence, and the employment of opposing arguments—provides some legitimate basis for competing discretionary decisions. Even at its earliest stages, the criminal justice system proceeds in an atmosphere of contest where win, lose or compromise are motivations for discretion beyond any objective distillation or shared vision of justice. Very often the accused, the victim, or the state is the adversary against which a discretionary decision is directed.

Discretion originates in the notion of independence essential to our conceptualisation of the police, the courts, sentencing and punishment. However, it operates within a framework of laws, rules and definitions. Issues such as the elements of the offence, the demeanour of the offender, the visibility of discretion's exercise and regulation, public expectations, and accountability may determine the outcomes of any discretionary decision-making.

Discretion allows for compromise and expediency in the criminal justice process. For example, some observers of policing suggest that conflict between the law governing police powers and police operations in practice is resolved through the individual and collective exercise of discretion. In settling any such conflict, police may even usurp the roles performed by other agencies of the determiners of guilt, or the executors of penalty.[7]

The major stages of the criminal justice process where discretion is exercised are:

- police pre-trial decision-making (for example, apprehension, caution, arrest, diversion, charge, bail, evidence gathering);

---

7   See Findlay et al. 1999, Chapters 3 and 7.

- prosecution pre-trial decision-making (for example, *nolle prosequi*,[8] alternative charges, plea bargaining, witness selection);
- defence pre-trial decision-making (for example, plea bargaining, bail review, plea, witness selection);
- magisterial pre-trial decision-making (for example, issue of warrants, *case to answer*[9] determinations, committal for trial);
- judicial discretion at trial (for example, acceptance of plea, admission of evidence, jury instruction and direction, sentencing);
- decisions on appeal (for example, granting leave, new evidence, conviction and sentence); and
- discretion during punishment (for example, classification, variation, conditions, parole, executive release).

In order to understand the manner in which decisions on justice are made, and interact, a brief description of how the principal professional institutions of criminal justice contribute to the criminal trial may be useful.

Institutions of criminal justice

By far the majority of crimes committed never end up in trial. It has been estimated by the Australian Institute of Criminology (1987) that:

> ... for every 1000 'crimes' committed only about 400 are actually reported to the police, 320 are officially recorded by the police as offences and only 64 are cleared up (60 of these by arrests); 43 persons will be convicted and only one of these imprisoned. So even if we doubled our imprisonment rate we would only be affecting one fifth of one per cent of criminal offending.[10]

Therefore, an examination of the institutions of justice alone will not present a complete or convincing picture of how crime is handled in Australian communities. The factor of tolerance is more significant and yet less recognised than the workings of justice institutions.

Having said this, the institutional dimension of criminal justice is too apparent and too expensive to overlook.

The police

In conventional writing on criminal justice the police force is an organisation of the state charged with the prevention of crime, the protection of life

---

8 The decision by the Attorney-General or the DPP not to continue with a prosecution after a bill has been found.
9 Where it is determined (or not as the case may be) that the prosecution has established a prime facie case against the accused.
10 D. Brown, D. Farrier and D. Weisbrot, *Criminal Laws*, Federation Press, Sydney, 1996, p. 39.

and property, the maintenance of public order, and the investigation, detection and prosecution of crime. In contemporary Australian society other governmental agencies, as well as private-sector organisations and individuals, also conduct many of these functions. What puts the state-based police service in a unique institutional position is its power over the legitimate use of force.

Most of the formal processes of criminal justice rely on the police for their initiation. In this respect Australian police services are crucial to the form and function of state and federal criminal justice processes.

State-based police are institutionally organised as a disciplined service. Most officers within the police institution do not have formal legal qualifications, relying instead on a hierarchy of internal training. The bureaucratic organisation of most police services is around rank, regions of influence, and occupational specialisation.

The police are said to be independent of political control. While responsible to democratic governments, the chief police officer maintains *original* powers conferred by the head of state, which are transferred to individual police officers. This notion of independence is, in practice, vitiated by the rank structure and by the closed nature of the occupational culture.

The police as an instrument of government policy are becoming the principal public service on which politicians rely to enforce legislation and deliver legislative requirements. This expectation ranges from licensing to welfare and information functions. The police are fast becoming one of the few remaining 24-hour government services.

The lawyers

Throughout each Australian jurisdiction lawyers are now organised to provide pre-trial and trial services. Despite the professional structure of the law, which sees individuals admitted to practice by the court following the successful completion of certain tertiary academic qualifications, criminal lawyers work within specific institutional frameworks.

The state and federal prosecutors usually operate out of a directorate, which is structured in much the same manner as a private legal firm. The major difference is that the Director of Public Prosecutions (DPP) is a statutory office with powers conferred by the Attorney-General (the principal law officer of the state). The lawyers in this service are salaried officers.

At the level of the lower courts, solicitors from the legal aid authorities provide the major legal service for the accused. These lawyers may be supplemented by *pro bono* schemes operated by non-government organisations and the law society. Aid lawyers are notoriously burdened by unrealistic case-loads. Legal aid is not provided to everyone for every aspect of the pre-trial and trial process, and the resources of legal aid are fast diminishing.

For more serious crimes, barristers may be provided to the accused through the public defender's service. This is a government service similar in structure to the office of the DPP. Also, in more serious trials, the DPP might instruct senior barristers in private practice to act as Crown (or state) prosecutors.

Depending on financial means, accused persons may instruct solicitors to represent their pre-trial interests from the stage of arrest and charge through committal to trial. Here the lawyer may act to protect the rights of accused persons and to negotiate on their behalf. When a matter goes to trial an accused may instruct an advocate, usually a barrister, to argue his[11] case.

The judicial officers and the jury

Magistrates and judges in Australia are not specially qualified to perform the judicial function. More often than not magistrates will be legally trained and drawn from the legal profession. Judges usually come from the bar.

The judicial profession is organised under an appellate hierarchy and according to a structure based on seniority of service, division of jurisdiction, and superior judicial office. Judges are said to be independent within the separation of powers but in practice are governed by precedent and the risk of having their decisions overturned on appeal.

Jury trial is not a constitutional right in Australia, beyond a limited right in the federal jurisdiction. The jury's function in criminal trials is increasingly eroded through the expansion of the summary jurisdiction and the introduction of an election for trial by judge alone in the superior courts.[12]

The jury in each Australian jurisdiction is drawn originally from the electoral role. This pool is reduced through a process of exemptions, exclusions, ballot, and challenge. Juries are required to deliberate over the facts presented in a trial, and to determine the guilt or innocence of the person charged. They should not be called upon to deliver their verdict unless and until the accused person has pleaded not guilty to the charges.

The correctional institutions

If an accused person is refused bail, he or she will be placed in the custody of the prison or correctional service. The circumstances under which a remandee[13] is detained may be more limited and austere than those under which sentenced or appellant offenders are confined.

---

11 The masculine gender is generally used when referring in this text to the accused. This is meant to emphasise the disproportionate gender representation of male accused persons in the Australian criminal justice system.

12 For instance, see *Criminal Procedure Act* (NSW), ss. 30–33.

13   A person held in custody after bail has been refused.

Depending on the sentence imposed by a judicial officer, any of a variety of corrective services will come into play. For instance, if a probation order is imposed by the court (requiring supervision of a good behaviour commitment), then the offender will be assigned to an officer of the state probation service.

The most commonly used sentence in Australia is the fine. This requires no oversight by correctional agencies unless the fine is not paid (and is called in by the sheriff's office). Other non-custodial sentences such as community service orders may require the supervision of the police or the probation service.

If a sentence of imprisonment is handed down, then the sentenced person will be given over to the custody of correctional services officers. These officers are usually divided into custodial and vocational, programs, and medical staff. The custodial division of correctional services is a disciplined institution and hierarchy. In most states in Australia the advent of private prisons has necessitated a correctional service which is contracted to the state and responsible through the contract to the company provider and the state.

Just prior to and upon release, many prisoners will be given over to the supervision of the parole service. Like probation officers, parole personnel are more likely to have social welfare training than legal training.

Juvenile offenders are usually kept in separate institutional environments. The occupational categories of custodial, programs, and medical staff apply here as well.

The institutions of justice, while connected, have distinctly different organisational and personnel profiles. The common institutional features are:

- complex bureaucracies
- claims for independence
- hierarchies of discipline
- regimes of coercion
- relationships to the state
- internal procedural hierarchies
- limited control over diversionary dispositions
- private sector counterparts
- community obligations
- vested interests in trial outcomes.

Key stages in decision-making

Ashworth (1998) indicates that while it may be possible to identify sites for decision-making within the criminal justice process, they are not discrete individual decisions taken in laboratory conditions. Rather, they should be viewed as decisions taken ... within a given professional context ... it is important to avoid from the outset the dominance of a rationalist notion of decisions taken by individuals independently and based on objective information.[14]

The significant stages of decision-making within the criminal justice process are:

- the victim's recognition of the crime;
- reporting the crime;
- the exercise of police powers (interrogation, investigation, search, arrest);
- identifying a suspect;
- the existence of sufficient evidence to charge and bail;
- engaging legal representation;
- charge bargaining or plea bargaining;
- entering a plea;
- the selection of a mode of trial;
- the decision to prosecute;
- which witnesses to call;
- what evidence is admissible;
- when and how the judicial officer shall intervene;
- how and in what form the verdict shall be handed down;
- the nature of the sentence;
- whether to appeal;
- the nature of executive intervention.

A range of administrative decisions connect and develop these stages. A decision may be, in Ashworth's terms, either 'processural' or 'dispositive'. Put simply, this means whether the consequence of the decision is that the accused person moves on to the next stage in the process, or is diverted out of the process at that point. In addition, each decision stage is, to varying degrees, influenced by rules within which discretion may have sway.

It is worth emphasising that different considerations will have an impact on a processural or a dispositive decision within criminal justice. For instance, the decision by the police to charge a juvenile may be based on evidential sufficiency while their decision to issue a caution may rely more on concerns of public policy. Having said this, both of these general concerns may intermingle in either decision. The distinction between these two forms of decision-making may be less distinct in practice. In certain respects even decisions to divert an accused person away from the criminal justice

---

14 A. Ashworth, *The Criminal Process: An Evaluative Study*, Oxford University Press, Oxford, 1998, p. 9.

process may initiate another form of process, which may have either a treatment or a restorative focus.

So far we have only considered those stages and sites of decision-making which appear to be authorised or legitimate. In any process so heavily dependent on individual and organisational discretion, the excessive use or abuse of power is possible. This may result in a miscarriage of justice of minor proportions and low visibility, or of major proportions and eventual visibility. Such abuse of power is more likely and more difficult to substantiate in the early stages of the process, where the exercise of discretion is one-to-one, and relatively concealed.[15]

Criminal justice in process

As Ashworth concludes:

> ... it is correctly agreed that it is not a system in the sense of a set of coordinated decision-makers ... nevertheless, the inappropriateness of the term 'system' should not be allowed to obscure the practical interdependence of the various stages. Many depend on other agencies for their case-load or their information, and decisions taken by one can impinge on those taken by others.[16]

In the area of production and dissemination of information about crime and justice in Australia, the interconnection between the agents and institutions of criminal justice is perhaps at its clearest.[17] This should not be interpreted as a commonality of purpose, even at this level, except insofar as it relates to the preservation of an individual agency's interests.

The criminal justice process is self-contained and insulated as a mechanism for the production of knowledge. For instance, the official crime rate figures are inextricably reliant on police arrest and charge figures, and on court prosecutions and convictions. Yet these figures may reveal more about police practice, prosecutorial priorities, and court management than they do about criminality.

Any other empirical representations of criminality, such as victimisation surveys, may suffer from the absence of authorisation. The official account of crime remains with the police and the courts, and is highly and often uncritically regarded by politicians and the media. Punishment is not explained through an examination of (and a comparison with) community tolerance of crime, even though far more offenders are dealt with in the community (such as community service orders) than in custodial settings, and much

---

15 For some examples of abuse of power in criminal justice, and analysis of these, see K. Carrington et al., *Travesty: Miscarriages of Justice*, Pluto Press, Sydney, 1991; C. Walker and K. Starmer, *Miscarriages of Justice: A Review of Justice in Error*, Blackstone Press, London, 1999.

16 A. Ashworth 1998, p. 21.

17 See R. Hogg, 'Perspectives on the Criminal Justice System', in M. Findlay et al. (eds) 1983.

more crime goes undetected than comes to police notice. Perhaps because of sensationalism, justice is measured through extremes in the system such as rates of imprisonment.

References to systems and interdependence in criminal justice are very much in the managerial mode. They do not adequately describe the discretionary fashion in which so much of criminal justice is carried out. This emphasis on the management of the system rather than on the people affected by the process is evidenced by the fascination with crime statistics.[18] Criminal justice statistics are a measure of the manner in which accused persons are managed through the process. Victims and accused persons, who all too often feel that they remain on the periphery of the process until a decision is made and imposed, are keenly aware of this.[19] The professional players and the state seem to manage the process for their convenience and justice consequently has the appearance of an outcome favourable to lawyers and government officials. In this respect, the overriding concern for the process is expressed in management terms: resource efficiency, clear-up, file closure, case management, occupancy levels.

It seems clear that criminal justice within the formalised processes described in this book is now so bureaucratised and dependent on the management priorities of its institutional operatives, that it is difficult to claim purposes and aims common to and accepted by all participants in the process. Further, any claims for integration across the process rest with management expectations rather than the interests of offenders and victims.

The values of justice could be criticised as being subservient to the mechanisms developed to bring them about. In addition, the manner in which justice develops and its mechanisms are reformed has become dependent on the way it is represented in the community.

Fair trial

Particularly since the enactment of the *Human Rights Act 1998* in the UK, the debate about what constitutes a fair trial in common law criminal procedure has taken on a rights perspective.[20] This is more sporadically so in Australia, where the state and federal constitutions are largely silent on human rights. In England this silence is filled by the European Human Rights Con-

---

18 Since the early social statisticians such as Quetelet, Gurrrey and Mayhew, working in the early nineteenth century (see Vold 1998, Chapter 3), crime has been a particular and constant focus topic for empirical social research.

19 For a discussion of marginalisation in the courtroom, see D. McBarnet, *Conviction: Law, the State and the Construction of Justice*, Macmillan, London, 1981.

20 For a discussion of the ramifications of the Act for fair trial see M. Findlay, 'Fair Trial and International Criminal Procedure' (forthcoming) *Criminal Law Review*.

vention, in which Article 6 enumerates detailed protections for the accused as guarantees of fair trial.

The Australian courts and certain legislatures such as that of Queensland[21] have accepted that fair trial is largely predetermined through pretrial practice. As mentioned previously, judicial interpretation of police powers has meant that the rights of the accused in many Australian jurisdictions are reliant on best practice rather than actionable rights. The threat of the rejection of resultant evidence, for example, is assumed to amount to judicial control over police investigation practice, yet even so this is highly discretionary.

There has been recent recognition of the need for Australian legislatures to manage pre-trial procedures more clearly, for the sake of fair trial. An example of this is the spate of legislation governing police detention. In New South Wales, the police are able to detain arrestees for a reasonable time, but this has been stipulated in general as no longer than four hours. This represents a conscious compromise between police powers and defendants' rights while at the same time recognising the state's responsibility to intervene in the area. The specialisation of rights is also evident through the particular provisions to control the detention of Aboriginal people, juveniles, and the mentally disabled.

Concerns with access to justice should be seen as having a direct impact on fair trial. In Australian jurisdictions, access is largely viewed as a pre-trial issue. Other concerns focus on legal representation at all stages of the process. Access to trial justice is best explained by viewing both lay and professional involvement within the trial. From either perspective it needs to be analysed on at least three levels:

- access to trial (and those mechanisms which divert participants from the trial, including accused, witnesses, and victims);
- access by those within the trial (the accused through actual representation; child witnesses in particular through specialised procedural provisions; victims through recognition and compensation);
- access to the trial by the community (usually identified by involvement in verdict delivery).

At each level it is not difficult to identify opportunities for access, and impediments to it.

A useful way to expose the reality of access in trials in any context is to identify points of connection between the professional and lay participants in the trial, at crucial points. Legal representation and the interaction between the advocate and the accused are examples of this.

---

21 For example, see the provisions of the *Police Powers and Responsibilities Act 1997.*

The issue may be communication rather than availability of representation. In trials where defendants are of non-English-speaking backgrounds, defence counsel have come from language, cultural and legal traditions very different from the experience of the accused. This has led to difficulties with instruction, communication, and representation, let alone the most effective preparation and presentation of a defence.

While the right to legal access appears as a cornerstone of fair trial ideology, real access for the accused may have been denied through communication failure. The reality of effective lawyer–client communication will become more keenly appreciated in the international context, and will eventually be recognised as an essential element of fair trial through the right of representation. This recognition should then inform debates about comparable access and filter down to local jurisdictions, which tend to focus on service availability rather than the nature of representation and delivery. A new understanding of the relationship between representation and fair trial would transform debates about legal aid and access to justice.

The nature, quality, and availability of legal representation are crucial to fair trial from the perspective of the accused. However, representation or the lack of it may not be evaluated merely in terms of legal aid mechanisms, or principles of equality of alms.[22] With international tribunals, for instance, legal representation may be guaranteed but the differences of language, culture, and experience between the accused and his counsel may qualify the actuality of representation and hence access. In addition, the nature of indictments from international jurisdictions, the limited available defences, and the acceptance of factual generality in establishing either could create conditions where access to the real 'defence' of a fair trial may be reduced.

Thus legal representation is crucial for the nature and quality of access, and hence fair trial. In all Australian jurisdictions the provision of legal aid has been adversely affected by budget cuts. Specific services such as the Aboriginal Legal Service have become the victims of wider political contest and as such the representation they are able to offer is qualified. Because groups in the community who are least able to obtain and communicate with competent and empathetic legal representation are those disproportionately represented before the courts (the young, Aboriginals, those with language comprehension difficulties, the dispossessed), any reduction in legal aid will exacerbate this discrimination.

Fairness in trial procedure in common law will remain governed by the presumption of innocence. Therefore, except in the special inquisitorial

---

22 This is a principle essential for the European courts' interpretation of Article 6 rights. In brief, it refers to a person being afforded reasonable opportunity of presenting his case to a court under conditions that do not place him at a substantial disadvantage relative to his opponent.

court settings,[23] disclosure of evidence and the presumption against self-incrimination should favour the accused. Procedural changes in some jurisdictions, such as the requirements on defence disclosure in Victoria and the abolition of the unsworn statement in others, might be viewed as contrary to this fundamental recognition.

The creation of uniform evidence legislation in Australia[24] has produced, some would argue, a tighter legislative basis for the evidence presented at trial and the manner in which it is negotiated. Evidentiary issues and the rules that govern them are central to the progress of most major criminal trials in Australia. A greater consistency and sophistication of evidence law should, as a result, produce fairer and more certain trial outcomes.[25]

In an adversarial system such as that applying in Australian courts, it is necessary that the parties should be roughly evenly matched. The presumptions and procedural safeguards for the accused should place him in a position where the resources of the state as prosecutor are not overwhelming. This is not, however, the case in the operation of the lower courts where the concerns for due process retire behind the demand for efficiency and the pressure to plead. It is at this level of the criminal law that the challenges to fair trial are more routine, and more often ignored.

In Australia, while there is no constitutional right to jury trial beyond that afforded for serious Commonwealth offences, jury trial is viewed as evidence of fair trial. Again, recent diminutions in the presence and work of the jury might tend to challenge this. The expansion of summary jurisdiction, of electable offences, and the creation of 'judge-alone' trial options for serious offences have led to fewer jury trials.

Fair trial has been considered recently in Australia not only from the perspective of the accused. Concern for the victim is significant and is demonstrated through legislation such as that which prohibits in certain circumstances the exposure of the prior sexual history of the complainant in cases of sexual assault. Further, the views of the victim are regarded as important in the sentencing process and the proliferation of victim impact statements in the criminal courts attests to this. Victims are also now seen as requiring opportunities for criminal compensation as part of the justice process.

Another instance where the rights of victims are now a feature of fair trial is special consideration for child witnesses in child sex abuse cases when

---

23 Such as Royal Commission hearings, and the hearings by bodies such as the NSW Independent Commission Against Corruption, or the Australian Securities and Investment Commission.

24 Now applying in the Commonwealth, the ACT and New South Wales courts.

25 For a more comprehensive discussion of evidence and fair trial, see Findlay, Odgers and Yeo 1999, Chapter 6.

they are being cross-examined by counsel for the accused. Again reforms in the rules of evidence demonstrate a concern for competing rights and interests so as to produce the fairest outcome possible for all concerned.

Access to justice is more than a matter of procedures and structures. Fundamentally access is a question of trial practice, and procedure may only signpost what is expected for a trial to be considered fair. In practice, access relies on prosecutorial discretion, mode of trial, remand issues, and sentencing process. But to understand the actual access offered, these need to be subdivided for analysis in both local and international trial settings. For instance, considerations of the prosecution, sufficiency of evidence, public interest and accountability, disclosure protocols, delay, principles of diversion, governance of evidence delivery, and so on require analysis, as they affect the identified perspectives of access.

Linked to the evaluation of institutional features of the trial, access should follow a critical review of the principal sites of decision-making which influence the trial and construct its progress. These may most simply focus on important justice professionals such as the prosecutor, the defence advocate, and the judicial officer, who have a crucial role in facilitating and overseeing access. Regarding the sentencer, for instance, it is necessary to examine the influence of the prosecutor, decisions to divert, victim impact, complaint adjudication, minimum standards, plea discounting, the provision of reasons, race and gender issues, and the operation of judicial discretion in general.

Once decision-making is identified as an essential element in access, then the relationships that produce these decisions, as well as the relationships that the decisions cement, should be open for evaluation.

Representations of justice

One of the difficulties associated with an accurate understanding of justice is the diversity of ways in which it is represented. And this is not simply a problem of distortion or misinterpretation. The basic sources of community knowledge of crime and justice are varied. Therefore, the possibility of problematic representations of criminal justice being broadcast and forming the basis of official reaction is almost unavoidable.

Personal descriptions or accounts of experiences with agencies and institutions constitute the most popular representations of justice. The accuracy, representativeness, and comparability of such accounts are problematic. However, what they may lack on these measures, they make up for in entertainment value and political impact. Therefore, their potential audience and significance may differ considerably from the official account, while their authority and longevity may outweigh such representations.

Criminal justice systems' records of crime, while suggesting greater credibility as official accounts of crime, are disparate enough to fuel a variety of crime representations.[26] The media are particularly committed to the use of such data as verification of opinion, and politicians often tend to rely on *systems'* data (that is, data which serve as a measure of how the justice system operates) as representations of real crime activity. Associated with these records are the problems attendant on enumerating a social phenomenon such as crime. Not only does there exist a 'dark figure' of crime beyond official statistics, but there is also the 'dark figure'[27] of recorded crime and justice outcomes which plagues any management system.

Whether representations of crime and justice rely on official records, surveys, memoirs, or common sense as their source, the impact of the representation will be as dependent on the means of broadcast and the motives behind the broadcast, as on its proximity to truth. In this respect, the recent shift in the media interest in crime and justice, away from fictionalised representation and towards the widespread televising of actual policing, current court sittings, and life in prison, has brought crime control into the homes and businesses of large sectors of Australian society otherwise not touched by crime. Members of the public are now the observers of police operations, the participants in trials, and the judge and jury of the offender and the system. Even so, these glimpses of crime situations may not leave the viewer any more deeply aware of the complexity of the entertainment phenomenon.

The media saturation of crime and criminal justice in Australian print and broadcasting has done much more to popular representations of crime and justice than simply move the entertainment focus from the imaginary to the actual. It has generated an expectation among the viewing public that it is their right to observe, participate, and pass judgment. Additionally, there has emerged a requirement in the exercise of criminal justice that it be media-friendly and entertaining, as well as being able to achieve the expectations set out for it in media commentary. An example of this is the manner in which recent endeavours to regulate judicial discretion in Australia have been motivated by a media campaign against the perceived leniency of the judiciary.

In most states of Australia, *law and order* politics have had a crucial bearing on the development of criminal justice policy.[28] In fact, government has

---

26 Here it is worth remembering, as Hogg (1983) observes, that the institutions of justice have a unique monopoly over official justice information. Many of the measures of crime and justice are in fact little more than knowledge generated from the operation of these institutions.

27 See R. Hood and R. Sparks, *Key Issues in Criminology*, Weidenfeld & Nicolson, London, 1972, Chapter 1.

28 See R. Hogg and D. Brown, *Rethinking Law and Order*, Pluto Press, Sydney, 1998.

been won and lost over the public's expectations of such policy. Until recently, however, the judiciary has largely been spared the critical public debate about community safety and crime control. Not so now.

Over the past decade there has been a commonality of concern among political parties across Australia that all criminal justice agencies and institutions need to *get tough on crime*. Differences have focused on the strategies that would ensure the toughest response.[29] A significant dimension in this rhetoric is the explicit call for sentencing reform based on the perceived inadequacy of the existing sentencing regime.

Zdenkowski[30] notes that by the 1980s in Australia, as elsewhere in the world, disillusionment with rehabilitation as a sentencing principle stimulated the onset of the age of retribution, and *just deserts* as the ultimate justification for sentencing discretion. As with rehabilitation, this retributive imperative created expectations in governments and communities that what judges did would somehow have a favourable effect on crime control and the fear of crime. However, sentencing is not such an exact science, and the necessary resources were not invested in the evaluation of new sentencing practice in order to refine and rationalise these expectations. The judiciary itself remained largely silent about whether their decisions were or were not assisting in the reduction of crime.

The public disquiet about what judges do is a factor of unrealistic expectations, and misinformation regarding sentencing practice and its consequences. For instance, in New South Wales there exists a community perception that judges are soft on crime. The figures suggest otherwise. Judges in this state are using imprisonment more regularly and imposing longer prison sentences than they have for many years previously. Whether this is having any impact on official or actual crime statistics is moot.

The criticism of the Australian judiciary for failing to do enough in the fight against crime is hurting the judges because it arises from a coalition of views: those of the public, the politicians, other criminal justice agencies, and influential broadcasters and media personalities. The judiciary is more vulnerable to the effects of such criticism because it is based on untestable assumptions: that tougher sentences reduce crime, and that the exercise of judicial discretion plays a crucial and direct role in crime control.

---

29 'Law and order is one issue on which there is more agreement than disagreement. The issue is not whether tough law and order policies work, but how to claim the political high ground of "toughest of the tough". Although less hardline policies can be found in print, the "let's get tough" mindset frames all other policies' (W. Bacon, 'On law and order: The going gets tough', *Sun Herald* (Sydney), 21 March 1999, p. 46).

30 G. Zdenkowski, 'Limiting Sentencing Discretion: Has There Been a Paradigm Shift?' (2000) 12(1) *Current Issues in Criminal Justice* 58.

An interesting but perhaps largely unrecognised result of this climate of criticism has been the introduction of important measures encouraging pro-fessionalisation of the judicial vocation. Consolidation of sentencing laws, better sentencing information,[31] judicial education, and broad statutory guidance have all contributed to the modernisation of judicial decision-making. In addition, judges seem more aware of their profession and its requirements, more mindful of their place in the community, and more will-ing to comment on their task.

The Chief Justice in New South Wales recently conceded that it was appropriate, even necessary, for judges to listen to public opinion when con-structing their sentencing decisions.[32] The question remains, however, to what extent should public opinion influence sentencing policy? Further, how is legitimate public opinion to be elicited and evaluated? Care needs to be taken to distinguish the views of the community from a populist punitive attitude that is ripe for political manipulation.

When carefully constructed surveys of public opinion are taken, it is commonly found that respondents underestimate the severity levels imposed by courts, and the more information they are given about the nature of the offence and the accused the less punitively they react.[33] This suggests that public opinion is often based on misinformation and misun-derstanding. Unfortunately, it seems that recently in Australia the media are complicit in conveying a distorted image about sentencing discretion. The same can be said for the representation of many other aspects of crim-inal justice in Australia.

Criminal justice is no longer hidden in dark alleys, smoky interrogation rooms, or gloomy prison cells. It is up for sale to the networks, and it is there at the dinner table. It cannot exist without glib commentary from reporters and presenters who are there to provide a link with the crime situation and to represent the opinions of the viewers. Still, the barrier of the television screen and the distance of the moralistic news commentary ensure that the *difference* of crime and the criminal is maintained. While we can view the relationship between crime and the controllers of justice, we are almost always left in no doubt as to whose side we are on.

---

31 See I. Potas et al., 'Informing the Sentencing Discretion: The Sentencing Information System of the Judicial Commission of NSW' (1998) 6(2) *International Journal of Law and Information Technology* 99.

32 'The courts must show that they are responsive to public criticism of the outcome of sentenc-ing processes. Public criticism of particular sentences for leniency is sometimes justified' *Jurisic* [1998] A Crim R 259 at 268.

33 See D. Indermaur, 'Public Perception of Sentencing in Perth, WA' (1987) 20(3) *ANZ Journal of Criminology* 163.

Part 2

Solving Criminal Problems

In order for the problems presented in Part 3 to be addressed as practice for legal analysis, skills and learning, a methodology needs to be advanced. What follows will provide a technique for problem-solving which is predictive rather than pro-scriptive. Teachers and students are invited to examine the elements of a method-ology, and their integration, to enable the reader to try out and adapt the method to suit his or her preferred style for problem-solving.

This section should act as a template for the exercises and analysis required in Part 3. Therefore, it may be useful to return to this part when the first few prob-lems are attempted, both to test the utility of this methodology and to rehearse the primary stages of problem-solving.

Chapter 3

The Importance of the Problem

Introduction

Criminal law makes little sense outside a problem context. The crime situations, against which the criminal law is directed, are essentially dependent on relationships and circumstances that provide the elements by which criminal liability is determined or challenged. Therefore, in studying criminal law, problems and problem-solving provide a useful, indeed essential, framework.

Problems enable issues of theory and practice to intersect. For instance, if a student is asked to establish the criminal liability of a corporation in a situation of homicide, this will go beyond the mere application of legal principles to facts. The whole question of the appropriateness of an individualised liability paradigm when applied to corporations will be highlighted. And issues of relative justice when convicting employees rather than companies, or punishing the individual and the corporation for similar offences, will need consideration.

A problem-based approach to criminal law teaching and learning injects real life into the classroom. Both the student and the teacher can take on the role of the lawyer or accused person, the witness or the judge, and thereby visualise the process and the consequences of any decision about criminal liability.

In talking here of *problems,* we adopt a particular sense of the word. A problem involves a factual scenario, and the requirement to direct legal principles and legal reasoning to issues raised by the facts.[1] The method of

---

1   Concerns for theory and context are implicit in the analysis required, and are present in the problems posed in Part 3 of this book.

analysis employed to address the problem is essentially dependent on the result that the problem requires.[2] The need to discuss the legal and social consequences of the problem will involve a consideration of the ambiguities of the law and the efficacy of legal outcomes.

Questions of criminal liability arise out of factual situations. Indeed, it is what *is* fact which is in contest throughout criminal investigations and trials. Problem-based learning allows the student to appreciate the significance of facts, their negotiability, and the need for the process of criminal justice to elicit sufficient facts for a determination of guilt or innocence. The adversarial nature of the criminal trial is a rational product of the contestable nature of facts. The material[3] value of certain facts is also at issue.

Problems in criminal law are intensely human. They involve the recollections of victims and witnesses and the justifications of suspects and accused persons, and they contain relationships wherein harm is caused and justice required. By appreciating the humanity of the problem the student is alive to the importance of communication as a way in which facts are established. The skills of the interviewer become obvious, as does the need to elicit information even in situations where clients and witnesses are reluctant to divulge any.

Criminal law problems are just that: problematic. They enable sides to be taken, debates to be engaged in, and minds to be influenced. As a framework for teaching and learning, the problem can be addressed as a classroom narrative, through written advice and analysis, or by role-play. Whatever medium is adopted, it will invite the acquisition of skills as well as knowledge.

As a means of assessing skills and knowledge, the problem has an established place in the instruction of criminal law. It not only measures a student's grasp of information, but also his or her ability to argue and analyse. Where problems are employed in a research exercise they have the potential to focus the attention of the student, and to mirror some of the methods of legal reasoning that arise from legal authority. In this sense the student can become the lawyer and the judge.

The other great analytical reality of a criminal law problem is that it has no unequivocal solution. Legal authorities[4] may be interpreted to support either side of an argument. Elements of an offence may require interpretation. Even the facts will never be so sufficient and complete as to require a particular outcome.

---

2   For instance, if the problem asks for a consideration of liability then it is the elements of the possible offences (and their outcomes) that will form the framework for analysis.

3   *Material* implies any fact which matters to (or goes to the heart of) the resolution of the issues posed by the problem.

4   This includes primary sources, such as case reports and statutory materials, and secondary sources, such as legal commentaries.

Problems connect the student to life experience. They present ethical dilemmas that the professional lawyer must address. They throw into stark relief the adequacy of legislation and the fairness of the law. In the problem setting, the discriminatory potential of the criminal justice process is revealed. Students cannot avoid the contextual significance of the problem and the consequences of its potential resolutions. The problem involves the student in the operation of the criminal law.

Problem-based approaches to teaching

One of the great challenges for law teachers is relevance. Particularly for making sense of criminal law and its often contradictory principles,[5] it is essential to contextualise rules and procedures within those situations that they are intended to resolve. Context is as crucial for the teacher as it is for the critical analyst of the criminal law.

The problem becomes the context. Arising as it does from hypothetical or actual case scenarios, the criminal law problem provides a framework within which the potential and failings of criminal justice can be explored. Depending on its complexity, the problem can invite such an exploration (at a variety of levels), to be tackled by students with differing degrees of competence.

As a technique for teaching, the problem is a natural extension of case-centred study. However, the problem allows the teacher and the student to move away from often abstract considerations of appeal courts, to examine the criminal law at each stage of its process. This enables a fuller and more satisfying understanding of the interaction between principle and process, as well as the manner in which individual and organisational decision-making and interpretation translate the law into contests and outcomes.

Critics of the problem-based teaching method suggest that it sacrifices substantive knowledge and the coverage of content in the classroom. Such criticism fails to answer the argument that legal education is as much about the refinement of skills and analysis as it is about the acquisition of information and principles.

Problem-based teaching invites the student to learn and practise skills of analysis and argument, by applying these to a designated range of substantive issues. As well as mastering the essential legal research and writing skills, students whose problem-based learning has focused on one area of law or process should have little trouble addressing another area of substantive law or process once a new problem requires this.

---

5   For a discussion of the place of contradiction in the development of legal principles in criminal law, see Norrie 1993, Chapter 1.

In law more than most disciplines of study, it is essential to direct substantive knowledge to authentic analytical activity in order that knowledge can be refined and the techniques of analysis appreciated. This is a consequence of the application of knowledge in a manner that facilitates a better understanding of the analytical tool employed, and how to use it. Through the analysis of problems, students are able to approximate and manipulate the authentic analytical activity, for the purpose of learning within the limitations of the classroom or the mode of assessment. In addition, they are able to distil and universalise complex experiences in an immediate fashion, for an anticipated learning outcome.

The degree to which the problem is embedded in the physical and social world of criminal justice is governed by the teacher's experience of the process and his or her creativity, along with the commitment and imagination of the students to be transported into the world of the problem and their role within it.

As well as helping students perform certain procedures, the problem environment should enable them to stand back and see why it is that things need to be done in a certain way, or not, as the case may be. Further, the student should discover where certain analytical techniques fit and where they do not, and where certain approaches are necessary and others are not.

With criminal law problem–solving, it is anticipated that students' legal skills will be situated in a wide domain, and not just explored in the abstract or as a learning ritual. The domain should be one where the skill has a purpose, and the student is made responsible for its outcome.

Situational learning such as this holds out the potential, as Laurillard[6] suggests, to 'demonstrate the unity between problem, context and solution where the problem is experienced rather than given'. The distinction needs to be made between teaching abstractions (such as legal principles and their application) and enabling students to learn abstractions from multiple contexts (like those presented in the criminal law problem).

> Our argument is that to the degree that abstractions are not grounded in multiple contexts, they will not transfer well. After all, it is not learning the abstraction, but learning the appropriate circumstances in which to ground the abstraction which is difficult.[7]

This should have been written about criminal law problem–solving.

---

6   D. Laurillard, *Rethinking University Teaching: A Framework for Effective Educational Technology*, Routledge, London, 1993, p. 18.

7   J. Brown, A. Collins and P. Duguid, 'Debating the Situation: A Rejoinder to Robinson and Weinberg' (1989) 18(4) *Educational Researcher* 10 at 12.

Problem-based approaches to assessment

Perhaps more than in any other area of substantive legal study, criminal law is assessed through the use of problems. These forms of assessment may range from the complex fact scenario requiring detailed written analysis, to single-issue questions in which a solution is expected.

Reasons for the popularity of problem-based assessment in criminal law include:

- their skills orientation;
- their potential to juxtapose legal principle with real life, and thereby put in critical relief criminal law and criminal justice;
- their expectation for didactic and analytical treatment;
- their potential to represent the challenges for the criminal law, and the process of criminal justice from the perspective of the victim and the offender, the lawyer and the police, the community and the courts;
- their potential to suggest ambiguity and incompleteness in legal outcomes.

Solving a criminal law problem is (or should be) much more than a task of applying the law to a set of facts in order to ascertain their legal consequences. Problems are often constructed so that the legal consequences of their facts are not immediately clear. The issues for the problem and its solution are the essence of this lack of clarity, or its complexity.

A skill to be tested in problem-solving is the resolution of ambiguity. To do this students will have recourse to legal principle, legal authority, rules and conventions of process, matters of public policy, and contextual identifiers. In employing any form of authority, it is necessary that it be directed towards one side of the adversary argument, and balanced against the competing position to test its cogency.

The steps to answering a criminal law problem are discussed below. When the problem is used as a form of student assessment it is essential to be clear, concise, and convincing. The material facts need identification, followed by the issues. The likely offences must be stipulated and their essential elements compared with the facts to see whether and to what extent proofs are present. Essential in this process of analysis is the discussion of definitions and the authorities, which establish the extent and the meaning of the elements of the offences selected.

In order to answer the allegations and proof of criminal liability, defence issues require identification. These can take the form of justifications and excuses (governed by legal principle and authority) or of challenges to the facts presented by the prosecution. The latter is a common but under-recognised defence approach. It is carried out through either the presentation of a different version (or interpretation) of the facts, or through highlighting crucial weaknesses in the prosecution's story.

It might seem trite to emphasise that the determination of criminal liability is a selective and discretionary exercise. It works from rather artificial distinctions and sometimes contradictory principles. Whenever the problem allows you to reflect on this, it affords the opportunity for a critical appreciation of the exercise and its wider ramifications.

Simple tips for answering problem assignments include the following:

- Try to predict and argue for the interpretation (of facts or law) that the relevant court would choose.
- Answer the question asked of you. A question might restrict the discussion to particular offences, or defence responses. It might require you to advocate one side or the other. In particular, be mindful of the task set for the answer. Is it to analyse, discuss, advise, or predict outcomes?
- Don't waste time writing about other issues that are beyond the parameters of the question, or outside the issues that are most relevant to the facts.[8] The determination of relevance and of significance in ordering the elements of your argument are skills that the problem sets out to test.
- Don't provide all you know about any issue which seems to arise from the facts at the risk of sacrificing relevance, significance, and the balance of your answer.
- Remember, it is important to identify where there are insufficient facts to produce a particular outcome. If you have time, it is appropriate to mention whose responsibility it might be to lead that evidence, and the possible consequences for your answer if those facts were present. Don't, however, speculate as if facts were present when they are not incorporated in the problem.
- In any reading time provided, always prepare an outline or a plan for your answer which lists and orders the issues, attaches principles, authorities and definitions, identifies limitations and alternative positions, and links each point to that which follows it.
- Don't waste time repeating or reinterpreting the question.
- Don't write out legislation in full or quote slabs from case authorities. A simple reference may be sufficient.
- Identify case authorities as best you can. Constant reference to citations may not be necessary.
- Be mindful of the precedent value of the case authorities you use.
- Use headings and subheadings.

---

8 A distinction should be made here between reflection on important areas of theory and context, and their necessary or specific inclusion in the written opinion or answer. Where time and word length are limited, you need to guard against distraction from the analytical priorities of the problem.

Advice for problem-solving

Each teacher has his or her own view about the most effective methods for problem-solving. Each of these will rely, however, on common components.

Material facts

Criminal law problems are essentially fact scenarios. But not every fact in the problem is crucial either to the issues raised or to the solution required. For instance, the name of a person may only be important if identity needs to be established. The facts that are essential to the issues, or on which the solution rests, are known as material facts. These should be identified early and then compared with the matters at issue. This is important when assessing what needs to be proved and what facts have not been disclosed, which might be important.

Issues

Each problem will raise issues for solution. These are at the heart of the problem. The issues initially arise as problems of fact that in turn will require the application of legal principles and processes to reach a solution. There will usually be more than one issue raised by the material facts and these may be interrelated or consequentially reliant. Once the issues have been identified they should be prioritised, and the associated material facts located. The manner in which issues are identified and ordered will crucially determine the solution or solutions to be offered.

Legal principles

Criminal law problems are all about establishing or challenging criminal liability. In order to do this one needs to identify likely or significant offences that might be supported by the facts, and then any justifications or excuses that would answer such allegations. Legal principles underlie the definition and proof of an offence. Statutory prescription or case authority comprises and determines the elements of the offence. Legal authority also designates the manner in which defences may be established. The interrelationship between offences and defences may be regulated by legal principle.

Authority

Support for the position one takes in resolving a legal problem needs to be grounded in authority. Common law traditions and their precedent base require that legal authority is hierarchical. Not only is it necessary to call upon the best legal authority in terms of its legislative status or its court standing, but legal authorities also need to be primary and relevant. The views of commentators and texts, while informative and not to be ignored, are not law. Cases and statutory provisions will only form convincing authority for an argument in a problem if they are on the point, and in tune with the material facts and the issues.

Coincidence

Often disregarded as an important component in legal problem-solving is the need for coincidence. Once the elements of an offence have been established, they must then coincide with the necessary proofs for the prosecution's case to be made. At a more procedural level the failure of one side's argument needs to coincide with the success of the other if the adversarial dimension of a legal problem is to be achieved.

Causation

Causation is usually considered in a legal problem as crucial for the proof of who committed the criminal conduct. Causation may be a series of acts and consequences, intersected by intervening acts or the actions of others, which may be represented as the natural or predictable results of previous conduct or omissions. Wherever a problem suggests an interconnection of conduct, causation will emerge as an important issue of proof. With certain offences such as homicide, causation stands as a consistent and central concern.

Justifications and excuse

There are always at least two sides to the dispute or analysis provoked by a criminal law problem. These problems will be constructed to reflect adversarial treatment. Therefore, allegations will need to be met. The most common way in which one side of the problem will be countered is through a questioning or a denial of the interpretation of the material facts. Another is, when these facts are largely accepted, to offer a justification or excuse. It will be rare for these to rest purely on a treatment of the facts. Defences in law must be established in order to claim their legal consequences for one side of the argument.

Once the primary components of legal problem-solving are recognised, the student's task is then to devise a system through which these can be integrated, in order consistently to produce the most convincing outcome or solution available.

In summary, therefore, the method to adopt should be to:

- Read through the fact scenario, bearing in mind what the question requires you to do (for example, advise on liability; construct a defence; brief the prosecution).
- Consider each of the facts for the purpose of identifying what is material.

- Speculate on what important facts or details of facts are missing from the problem, or what requires further elaboration. You may be able to comment in your answer on the absence of facts and the consequences that any such absence may produce. Do not invent or substitute facts that are not provided in the problem.
- Remembering the requirements of the question, identify the issues that are raised by the facts. These issues will usually take the form of what needs to be proved (to what extent), and the best way to respond to any proofs. These issues might include possible offences, likely defences, crucial questions of context, issues of mistake or consent, coincidence, etc.
- Follow the normal process of the trial in resolving the issues identified:
  1. Identify possible offences—ignore or dismiss those offences that are unlikely or overly problematic. Do not simply rely on the most serious offence available. Make certain, when dealing with aggravated offences, that the features of aggravation are present on the facts. Be careful in the presentation of alternative charges, especially when their proof might be mutually exclusive.
  2. List the offences in their order of seriousness. Recognise those offences that are interconnected.
  3. Identify possible offenders. Here, note issues of participation and complicity. Begin your discussion of the liability of the suspect with a consideration of any special features of capacity.
  4. Detail the elements of the offence(s) that require proof; these elements may come from statute or case-law. Refer to the authorities from which you draw these elements. Remember that the elements of each offence may differ. Keep in mind the common difficulties that arise with the establishment of certain offences (e.g. consent in sexual assault).
  5. Relate the material facts to the elements of the offence in order to evaluate proof—take care with composite offences that may have several aspects. Don't forget circumstances and consequences where these are at issue. Look for problems with the coincidence between the conduct and the mental elements of the offence. Determine whether the cause of the crime can be sufficiently and substantially related to the suspect. Refer to legal authorities that are either on the point or in support of your argument, or which you may wish to distinguish.
  6. Identify relevant justifications or excuses. Refer to the authorities that identify tests for proof, and be careful in applying these to the facts (e.g. the balance between objective and subjective tests). Also be aware of the difficulties involved in the presentation of inconsistent or contradictory defence issues.

- Evaluate the prosecution case relative to each offence and each offender. In certain situations it will be possible to draw together particular offence or defence themes.
- Evaluate the defence case relative to what the prosecution is required to prove, what they have proved, what other explanations might be available, and what defence issues have been specifically raised. How do the latter interconnect, and depend on the prosecution proofs?

Part 3

Problems and the Criminal Law

This part of the book recognises the need to introduce some general themes and principles on which the process of establishing criminal liability rests. In addition, it suggests some useful analytical techniques for dealing with the contradictions that surround the application of these principles. The most significant factors affecting liability will be put against these principles and themes so as to present common points of argument and analysis. These introduce the specific topics out of which problems are posed and situated.

The initial two chapters in this part present some of the major issues on which criminal liability is established and challenged. The case-law and legislative authorities relied upon to develop these principles are general and are set out in a simple, often uncontroversial form.[1] This simplicity can be deceptive. The discussion is not intended to act as a substantive text[2] and is here to highlight the legal issues requiring consideration when the topics and problems in Chapter 6 are confronted. Many of the matters raised in the first two chapters (and Parts 1 and 2 of the book) are returned to in the discussion of each topic introducing the problems in Chapter 6.

The novelty of the presentation of legal principles in what follows is the emphasis on what needs to be proved in order to anticipate challenges to criminal liability. The initial emphasis on establishing volition invites considerations conventionally understood as the province of the defence in answering the prosecution case. In the present approach they become instead the crucial foundation of the prosecution case.

---

1   Readers will recognise that these authorities are not comprehensive of all common law and code jurisdictions in Australia. Examples from particular jurisdictions are presented, and in many situations the original authority on which the principle is based will be discussed. This means that when, for instance, the discussion is centred on *mens rea*, a number of English authorities arise for consideration. It is the principle rather than its jurisdiction-specific manifestation that is important here.

2   For a more specific and comprehensive understanding of substantive criminal law these chapters should be read in conjunction with a recognised criminal law secondary source, such as Bronitt and McSherry, 2001; Brown (et al.), 2001.

Part 2

Problems and the Criminal Law

Chapter 4

Establishing Criminal Liability

Introduction

General principles of criminal liability provide the foundations upon which crime and criminality are established in the courts of Australia. Through a complex system of principles and rules to evaluate behaviour, the criminal law endeavours to define, distinguish, and regulate crime.

The establishment of criminal liability on a case-by-case basis requires that the prosecution prove the charges laid; the defence then challenges the prosecution case or denies that it has been established, and where appropriate, the accused person presents factors affecting liability, such as justifications or excuse. In this way the principles of the criminal law translate into the practice and process of criminal justice.

The general principles of criminal liability, and the criminal law that gives them substance, take several forms. More often than not principles of criminal liability have developed through judicial pronouncement, interpretation, and application. Norrie[1] refers to this as justiciable law, or law based on a philosophy of judicial individualism and rational reconstruction. In this way the sometimes contradictory principles of the criminal law appear to reach reconciliation through judicial interpretation and reasoning.

Case reports of appeal court decisions remain a significant source of substantive criminal law, as well as principle, in Australia. The judgments in these reports are written in a language that lays claim to the rationality of the law (at least as it is enunciated through judicial decision-making). Legislation, on the other hand, has been employed to specify particular aspects of

---

1   Norrie 1993, Chapter 1.

criminal capacity, define certain degrees of participation and involvement in crime, codify classes of offence behaviour, and create new offence types. While respecting and obviously reflecting general principles of criminal liability within common law traditions, the crime legislation of Australian jurisdictions generally restates or restructures principles of criminal liability.[2]

Violations of the criminal law are countered through:

- the institutions of criminal justice: by the accumulation of evidence on crimes;
- the negotiation of guilt through bargaining for a plea;
- the calculation of guilt through adversarial trial; and
- the apportioning of punishment by the courts on the basis of the blameworthiness of the offender.

Essential to this process, where guilt is contested, is that the state:

- identify a suspect, establish his or her capacity to commit the offence, prove liability in terms of the specific elements of the offence charged, and
- determine whether there exists any evidence from the accused which would defend or excuse the alleged liability.

Criminal liability relies on admissions or proof that the accused committed the requisite criminal act or prohibited conduct (*actus reus*), accompanied by the necessary mental state. The *mens rea* (guilty mind, or the criminal mental state) is a vital element in a criminal offence and as such must normally be established if a criminal prosecution is to succeed.[3]

Mens rea represents an indicator of blameworthiness, but is by no means the only such indicator. Particularly with regulatory offences created by statute, the prohibited act is punished even when there may be no individual evidence of a guilty mind. Vicarious and corporate liability are also situations where blame is not always the direct consequence of an individual's behaviour, or at least not in terms of who or what might be blamed.

When determining criminal liability, one should appreciate that sets of facts are open to more than one interpretation, resulting in more than one conclusion on liability. This process requires that the court must, therefore, address its attention to the specific ingredients of the offence charged.

Once a prohibited act has been identified and an individual is accused of committing the offence, the next step in any assessment of criminal liability

---

2   In the Crimes Acts of the common law jurisdictions, and the Codes, there is little in the way of declarations of principle. However, this is the substance of the Commonwealth *Criminal Code Act 1995*.

3   It should be remembered that some offences are established through omission on the part of the offender or on status.

is to ask whether the accused had the capacity to commit the offence. Capacity is evaluated in terms of general principles applied to the nature of the offence and the characteristics of the accused, and is governed by certain presumptions of practice.

Volition

Criminal liability generally relies on a prohibited act being committed voluntarily.[4] It would be difficult to establish the volition of every alleged offence if it were challenged by the accused at the commencement of most trials. To avoid such initial probative difficulties, a presumption exists in criminal law (from a common law tradition) that an act committed by the accused was done voluntarily. As a presumption of fact it may be rebutted by the accused through evidence placing volition in doubt.[5]

Volition has bearing on the prohibited act, and the mental state of the agent at that time. To say that an act is voluntary implies that the accused has chosen so to act, and therefore has exerted some conscious control over the action. In *R v. Falconer* (1990) 171 CLR 545 at 550 the High Court held:[6]

> The requirement of a willed act imports no intention or desire to effect a result by the doing of the act, but merely a choice, consciously made, to do an act of the kind done.

With dangerous driving cases, for instance, if the volition focus is on the *actus reus* and not on general notions of fault, then a sleeping driver may not be held liable if he could not clearly be seen to be responsible.[7] In this assessment, liability requires that the voluntariness of the act and the prevailing mental state correspond at the moment the offence is alleged to have been committed.

In *Jiminez* (1992) 173 CLR 572, it was held that even if the court could find a voluntary act in the period of time prior to his falling asleep, and at that point his driving was objectively dangerous, this might only indicate that the *actus reus* (criminal conduct) was committed. It would also be necessary that his voluntary conduct coincide with the required *mens rea* at the time of the commission of the offence.

---

4   See *Burns v. Bidder* [1966] 3 All ER 29.
5   Concerning proof, initially the onus (burden of proof) rests with the prosecution to establish the essential elements of their case beyond reasonable doubt, to the satisfaction of the judge or magistrate. The onus then shifts to the defence to raise a doubt regarding the prosecution case, or to present a justification or excuse. Following this the onus shifts back to the prosecution.
6   In relation to the requirement for volition under s. 23(1) of the *Criminal Code Act 1899* (Qld).
7   See *Jiminez* (1992) 173 CLR 572.

Therefore, one of the essential elements in considering capacity is whether the act or omission of the accused was voluntary.

Presumptions affecting volition and capacity

Presumption as to voluntariness

The issue of the voluntariness of the accused's conduct, and the evidentiary necessities required to challenge it, were discussed in *R v. Falconer* (*supra*). The High Court considered the following facts: Mrs Falconer had been convicted of the wilful murder of her husband, who died as the result of a shotgun blast fired by her. The deceased was violent to the accused and had sexually interfered with her daughters. They were separated. On the day of the death Falconer's estranged husband had entered her house, sexually assaulted her and grabbed her hair. She said that from then on she remembered nothing until she found herself on the floor with the shotgun and the husband dead beside her. The trial judge rejected non-insane automatism (which denies a person's control over his or her actions) as a possible defence. The Court of Appeal reversed the rejection of evidence on whether the shooting had occurred independently of the exercise of her will. The state applied for special leave to appeal to the High Court. There it was held that it is the act that must be willed even though the consequences are unintended.[8] The act is either a bodily action, alone or in company with some quality of the action or consequence caused by it, or an accompanying state of mind which entails criminal responsibility. In this case the court determined that the act is the discharge of the loaded gun and is neither limited to the contraction of the finger on the trigger, nor extended to the injury. The willed act denotes consciousness and choice. A distinction may be drawn between the absence of required intent and the absence of the willed act. The requirement of a willed act imports no intention or desire to effect a result by doing the act, but merely a choice consciously made to do an act of the kind done.

Here the choice was to discharge the gun. In the absence of any contrary evidence it is assumed that the act of an apparently conscious person is willed and done voluntarily. This presumption is an inference of fact. Generally, grounds for refusing to draw the inference only arise when there is reason to believe the agent is unable to control his actions. The prosecution can rely on that presumption to discharge its onus of proof, unless there are grounds for believing the accused suffered an absence of control. The appeal court imposed an onus on the defence to raise sufficient evidence of a loss of volition in order that the prosecution should be put to its proof.

---

8 For instance, the act causing death is willed or foreseen, if not the death itself.

Some commentators have criticised the High Court's position in *Falconer* that the presumption as to mental capacity is an inference of fact from which the accused is required to raise evidence to 'displace ordinary human experience'. The suggestion that the accused carries an evidentiary burden in this respect does not imply any particular standard of proof, and in fact the party carrying that burden may not be required to prove anything. It is illogical to require that the accused prove a particular matter of fact before discharging an evidentiary burden. In the case of insane and non-insane automatism, the jury should consider the factors compatible with soundness of mind (or the alleged mental illness), and if such factors raise a reasonable doubt with respect to intent and voluntariness, then the jury should acquit outright. This provides for the consideration of mental soundness as part of a determination of volition, even where mental illness is not alleged. The difficulty with the proof requirements for challenges to mental soundness has meant that the admission of mental illness as an issue for volition, or even as a *defence*, can be problematic.

The conduct of the accused may be considered involuntary where it was a reflex action, or the result of a muscular spasm. In **Ryan v. R** (1967) 121 CLR 205, the accused was charged with the murder of a garage attendant who had been shot by Ryan during a struggle that occurred as part of an attempted robbery. The prosecution alleged that Ryan had his finger on a loaded, cocked shotgun pointed at the back of the victim, while the accused searched for some rope with his other hand. The victim made a sudden movement, Ryan stepped back and the gun went off. Ryan argued that the firing of the gun was not voluntary, but rather an unwilled reflex action resulting from his surprise at the movement of the victim. The High Court accepted this submission and held that the accused was not responsible for his action. Even so the court upheld his conviction because it was not the pulling of the trigger, but the pointing of the loaded gun that was essential to a consideration of a voluntary *actus reus* in this offence. The High Court held that it was open to the jury to find that the act of pointing the loaded gun at the victim was clearly voluntary and was the operating and substantial cause of death.[9]

Mistake of law and of fact

Essential to the question of whether someone could be criminally liable is the question of knowledge: what the accused actually knew or what he chose in some cases not to know.[10] The other side of such a consideration is allegations of mistake: knowledge of mistaken facts, or facts which generated

---

9   This interpretation was recently followed in *R v. Butcher* [1986] VR 43.
10   Sometimes referred to as wilful blindness.

a mistaken belief. The principal distinction for mistake in criminal law is between a mistake of law and a mistake of fact. The latter can have a vital influence over the issue of liability, particularly if associated with mistaken consent or situations of factual delusion.[11]

The distinction between law and fact is by no means an easy one, nor is it absolute. Many situations of mistake involve issues of both fact and law.

In **R v. Tolson** (1889) 23 QBD 168,[12] the principle was developed that an honest and reasonable mistake of fact will be a ground of exculpation in cases in which actual knowledge is not required as an element of the offence. In common law it has always been a good defence to possess an honest and reasonable belief in facts which, if they were true, would not make the conduct a crime. Honest and reasonable mistake of fact stands on the same footing as an absence of the reasoning faculty and hence capacity. To some extent it also may be seen as an absence of the required mental state.

In **DPP v. Morgan** [1976] AC 182, the husband of the victim invited three men to have sex with his wife. He advised the accused that she might appear to struggle because she was *kinky* and this was the only way that she could become aroused. The court had to decide whether the facts constituted rape despite the alleged honestly held mistake.[13] Because of the nature of the *mens rea* required by the offence (where a refusal of consent and an appreciation of that refusal were crucial), the question was whether the accused could establish an honest belief in the mistaken fact so as to deny the essential element of the charge. Such was not established on the evidence here.

Therefore, unless the elements of the offence require otherwise, if mistake is used to negative an essential fault element of the offence, it need only be honest, and not necessarily reasonable.[14] Reasonableness, or its absence, may be an evidentiary indicator of honesty or otherwise.

The reaction to the *Morgan* decision generally, and among legislators in particular, was to see the reintroduction of the requirement for reasonableness in a variety of different offence situations.[15] This was particularly so

---

11 See references to insanity and insane automatism, pp. 62–65.

12 The facts of this case were that the accused married a second time believing his first wife, then still living, to be dead. The offence was bigamy: remarriage where the partner of the previous marriage is still living. This does not necessarily require knowledge of the continued existence of the original spouse.

13 This offence required the withholding of consent, and an honest mistake may answer this. The requirement in certain offences that the mistake be both honest and reasonable seems to be determined on both evidence and policy. The obligation on the prosecution is to prove all the necessary elements of guilty mind of the accused. Mistake of fact may deny this.

14 See *Arnol* (1981) 7 A Crim R 291.

15 E.g. *Criminal Code Act 1924* (Tas), s. 14.

when looking at the proofs of sexual assault in Australian jurisdictions.[16] In this respect, mistake was put forward as a defence of honesty and reasonableness rather than as a challenge to *mens rea* and volition.[17]

Where the mistake is such as to negative the criminal mental state, the charge is not warranted. If the mistake is one about the facts, which if true would fail to constitute an *actus reus*, then there is no offence.[18] The accused does not have the capacity to commit the offence, the essential facts of which he does not know.[19]

Ignorance of law

Another essential presumption on which criminal liability relies, and over which mistake of law has little influence, is that we are presumed to know the law, and that ignorance of the law is no excuse.[20]

In **Lim Chin Aik v. R** [1963] AC 160, the appellant was convicted of contravening a section of the immigration ordinance of Singapore by remaining there after he had been prohibited from entering the country by an order made by the minister after he had arrived in Singapore. There was no evidence from which it could be properly inferred that the order had or could reasonably have come to the notice or attention of the appellant. The order was never gazetted or published. There was no means for the citizen to discover the new law. The court held that proof of *mens rea* may not be required for statutory offences. As regards regulatory offences and the displacement of *mens rea*, the purpose of the legislation should be to deal with grave social evil. Would putting the defendant here under a strict liability assist in enforcement of the offence? There was nothing the accused person could have done to ensure that he complied with the regulations. If an accused contravened an order of prohibition such as this, common sense would assume that he was aware of the order before he could be said to contravene it. The decision turned on an interpretation of 'contravention'.

---

16 In certain jurisdictions, such as in NSW, despite the essentially subjective requirement in determining the attitude of the accused to consent, the honesty of the accused's mistake is crucially dependent on the reasonableness of his interpretation. In *Kitchener* (1993) 29 NSWLR 696 at 700, for instance, it was held that recklessness as to consent could be shown 'not only where the accused adverts to the possibility of consent but ignores it, but also where the accused is so bent on gratification and indifferent to the rights of the victim as to ignore completely the requirements of consent'.

17 See *Thomas v. R* (1937) 59 CLR 279.

18 One needs to be careful here, particularly where the mistake is as to the identity of the accused or his status, that it is of a type that vitiates an essential element of the offence (e.g. consent in sexual assault)—see *Papadimitropoulos v. R* (1957) 98 CLR 249.

19 Provided the elements of the offence require consideration of his mental state.

20 See *Lim Chin Aik v. R* [1963] AC 160.

The particular situation here went beyond ignorance or mistake. It involved a scenario where an otherwise lawful act had been made unlawful without notice or a change in behaviour.

Brennan J in *He Kaw Teh* (1985) 157 CLR 523 at 567, when approving *Lim's case*, stated there is a presumption that a statute does not impose criminal liability without *mens rea* unless the purpose of the statute is not merely to deter a person from engaging in prohibited conduct, but to compel him to take preventive measures to avoid the possibility that, without deliberate conduct on his part, the external elements of the offence might occur.

Capacity

Too often the consideration of criminal capacity in common law is submerged within the discussion of factors affecting criminal liability, and more particularly of defences. This sometimes tends to confuse the difference between being able to commit the crime, and once having committed what appears to be a crime, being able to raise a satisfactory explanation, justification or excuse. What distinguishes more fundamental considerations of incapacity (both physical and mental) and those factors present to affect the liability of the offender, is volition.

Following are several important qualifications of the presumption concerning volition (that a person's act is voluntary or willed). They recognise such situations as a reflex action,[21] or a child acting as an innocent agent,[22] where questions of volition are fundamental to the determination (or absence) of criminal liability. Insanity, automatism and intoxication will also be discussed in more detail when factors affecting liability, and more particularly defences, are considered later.

Capacity and age (Volition and the age of reason)

The condition of childhood exempts children and young people up to a nominated age from accountability for their actions under the criminal law.[23] In principle the law holds that children who are below the *age of reason* may not be deemed criminally responsible for their actions. When this state

---

21 See *Hill v. Baxter* [1958] 1 All ER 193.

22 E.g. *Walters v. Lunt* [1951] 2 All ER 645.

23 These age boundaries may differ from jurisdiction to jurisdiction. For instance, at common law all children under seven were considered incapable of committing a criminal act. In NSW this has been raised to 10 (*Children (Criminal Proceedings) Act 1987*, s. 5). Up until the child is 14 it is presumed that she or he is incapable of wrongdoing. The age of criminal responsibility in the ACT was recently lifted from eight to 10 and the presumption runs to 14 (*Children's Services Act 1986*, s. 27). In Tasmania the lower age of criminal responsibility is seven years.

of innocence ends and responsibility begins is, in reality, a gradual process. However, the law sets an arbitrary age of responsibility for the purposes of criminal liability. It might also be said that before this age is reached the law does not presume that the child's act was voluntary in the same manner as it would the similar action of an adult.

The age of criminal responsibility is often considered to be at a point where children move from being unable to commit a criminal offence to where it is presumed that they have not. The initial category creates an irrebuttable presumption of law that children below the designated age cannot commit a criminal offence. The second distinction (between the liability of a child and that of a young person) refers to a state where the young person is presumed to be incapable of distinguishing between right and wrong.[24] If the prosecution can prove that the child committed the prohibited act with a *mischievous discretion* (knowledge that when the criminal act was committed, it was wrong), the presumption may be rebutted and capacity restored.[25] Such proof is through strong and cogent evidence that the young person understood that what he or she did was seriously wrong. It appears that the degree of proof required to rebut the presumption diminishes the closer the child's age is to the upper limit of the second category. To appeal successfully against a finding that the presumption was rebutted, the accused needs to show that there was no evidence on which the presumption could have been rebutted.[26]

In *J.M. (a minor) v. Runeckles* (1984) 79 Cr Ap R 255, it was stated that evidence to rebut the presumption of incapacity for a young child must go beyond knowing that her or his act was naughty and mischievous to the degree that she or he knew it was seriously or gravely wrong. It was not necessary to prove that the child knew that the act was morally wrong, although such proof might help to establish the knowledge of serious wrong. The younger the child, the stronger the evidence required to rebut the presumption. Recently, in English case-law, certain horrific cases of child violence have led to a reconsideration of this presumption, as well as the notion of an *age of innocence*.[27]

---

24 This presumption of fact referred to as *doli incapax* has recently been abolished in England and Wales—see *Crime and Disorder Act 1998*. In light of recent concerns about violent crimes of young people the NSW Law Reform Commission is also reviewing the presumption.

25 See *R v. M* (1977) 16 SASR 589.

26 When examining *doli incapax* (this rebuttable presumption as to age and capacity) it is worthwhile recognising the recent debate for its abolition. For a summary, see NSW Criminal Law Review Division, *A Review of the Law on the Age of Criminal Responsibility of Children*, Attorney General's Department, Sydney, 2000.

27 See *C v. DPP* [1994] Crim LR 523.

A particular situation where the criminal capacity of the child influences the liability of others is where an innocent agent is used to commit a crime. For example, in **Walters v. Lunt** [1951] 2 All ER 645, the respondents were charged with receiving certain goods from a child of the age of seven years, knowing the goods to be stolen. The elements of the offence required that the goods were stolen, and that the accused knew that this was the case. Could the adults be guilty of the charge? The problem here was that if the child could not commit a criminal offence, then the goods would not have been stolen and that essential element of the offence would not be present.

Capacity and insanity (Volition and ability to reason)

Obviously the presumption that the prohibited act was committed voluntarily depends to some extent on a capacity on the part of the actor to make a reasoned choice. Such capacity is denied, if the accused is proved insane at the time the prohibited act was committed.

Traditionally in common law, insanity as an issue of criminal capacity is still primarily based on the M'Naghten Rules.[28] Once raised, the usual course is to leave the question of insanity to be decided as fact by the jury, or the judge sitting alone. The questions to be determined are whether the accused had a sufficient degree of reason to know the nature and quality of the act, or being so cognisant, he did not know that what he was doing was wrong. Criminal responsibility connotes control over one's actions, and a power to choose whether or not to abide by the law. An insane agent lacks both such control and power of choice, and therefore cannot be responsible for his actions, or criminally liable for them.

Under the M'Naghten approach it is required that the capacity to reason, as measured by knowledge of the act, be defective due to a *disease of the mind*. The narrow interpretation of this concept by the courts has reduced the effectiveness of insanity as a means of denying volition.[29]

For example, in **Bratty v. Attorney-General (Northern Ireland)** [1963] AC 306, the facts of the case were that the appellant strangled a girl and later said to the police that when he was with her he 'had a terrible feeling' and a 'sort of blackness came over him'. The evidence suggested that maybe this was psychomotor epilepsy, raising three possible defences: automatism; no intention; or insanity. At the trial the jury rejected insanity. The Court of Appeal discussed the wider connotation of the involuntary act beyond automatism.

---

28 See *M'Naghten* (1843) 10 CL & F 200.

29 Another reason for the relatively rare occurrence of this challenge to capacity in a criminal trial is the consequence that the accused may be ordered to be detained for an indeterminate period in a mental hospital. Therefore, insanity will only arise in criminal law (under the McNaughten regime at least) in situations of the most serious charges.

In **Porter** (1936) 55CLR 182, Dixon J plotted the process of establishing insanity. First it was necessary to consider the mind of the accused at the time he committed the act. Then it needed to be determined that the state of mind was one of 'disease, disorder or disturbance'. Finally the disease should be of such a character that the accused could not appreciate that he was doing wrong.

The High Court in **Hawkins v. R** (1994) 122 ALR 27 seems to have entertained the prospect that proofs of insanity, even if they don't establish legal insanity, are relevant to the issue being considered by the jury in determining the formulation of any element of specific intent required to be proved by the prosecution. This was considered logical in light of the common law position on intoxication, but was not an unqualified right to adduce such evidence.

Hawkins is also interesting for its discussion of the appropriate point at which evidence of insanity should be raised. The High Court accepted that in principle the issue of insanity falls before the issue of intent. This supports our earlier contention that concerns of capacity and volition (in which insanity sits), if challenged, will predetermine any evaluation of criminal responsibility through the establishment of conduct and mental state.

More recently, certain Australian jurisdictions have modified the law relating to capacity and insanity through law reform in the mental health area. In this the definition of insanity has been adjusted by concepts such as 'mental illness',[30] 'unsoundness of mind',[31] 'mental incompetence',[32] and 'mental impairment'.[33]

The common law in relation to insanity continues to apply in New South Wales, and its influence can still be seen in the statutory provisions for Tasmania and the ACT. Even the new defence of mental impairment in Victoria adopts the language of M'Naghten.

Permanent or temporary serious mental impairment, unlike defect of reason or disease of the mind, now calls for proof in terms of symptoms rather than processes.[34]

Capacity and automatism (Volition and ability to control actions)

Despite the assumption that no act is punishable if it is involuntary, the courts have consistently limited the circumstances in which involuntariness might be successfully raised.

---

30 *Crimes Act 1900* (ACT), s.428N; *Mental Health Criminal Procedure Act 1990* (NSW), s. 38.
31 *Criminal Code Act 1899 (Qld)*, s. 647; *Criminal Code Compilation Act 1913* (WA), s. 653.
32 *Criminal Law Consolidation Act 1935* (SA), s. 269C.
33 *Crimes (Mental Impairment and Unfitness to be Tried) Act 1997* (Vic), s. 20(2).
34 See the discussion of diminished responsibility at pp. 267–88, 315–16.

An act is not involuntary simply because the agent could not remember doing it, or could not control himself. If an involuntary act proceeds from a disease of the mind it results in a defence of insanity. A disease of the mind is a question for the judge.

The causes of automatism are broadly designated as internal or external, and such uncontrolled actions may occur either consciously or unconsciously and be induced from outside the body or from within. In this respect insanity may be an internal cause of the automatic state, and where this is alleged the M'Naghten tests for insanity apply.

Regarding external causes of automatism, in **Hill v. Baxter** (*supra*), the question was whether the accused had put forward sufficient evidence on a charge of dangerous driving to justify the court's decision that he was unconscious, even though he was physically driving at the time. He alleged that he had been overcome by an unidentified illness. The court held that for automatism to stand in these circumstances, unconsciousness due to sudden illness must entail the malfunctioning of the mental process of the sufferer, but should not be equated with a disease of the mind. Accidental or temporary loss of consciousness should not be equated with insanity.

In **R v. Falconer** (*supra*), several of the judges held that if the psychological blow suffered by the accused would have produced a dissociative state in the ordinary or normal person then it may be regarded as non-insane automatism. If, however, it would not produce this state in the ordinary person then the issue would fail, or the jury should be directed as to insanity. The ordinary person is of normal temperament or self-control and does not possess any of the particular emotional features of the accused at the time of the commission of the offence.

If automatism is externally induced, then questions regarding the *prior fault* of the offender are relevant. In other words, if the accused person does something the consequences of which might reasonably be foreseen, such as the production of a state of automatism, then the justification may not be available to deny capacity. The question here is the reasonable foreseeability of the state likely to induce the incapacity. The test is an objective one where the offence imposes strict liability, or could be satisfied by objective tests for recklessness or negligence, and is subjective where the *mens rea* of the offence requires intention or subjective recklessness.

In **R v. Quick & Paddison** [1973] 3 All ER 354, the accused was undergoing insulin treatment for diabetes, and a strict food intake regime was prescribed in order to manage the illness. The facts were that the accused was a nurse who allegedly caused grievous bodily harm to a patient as a result of a loss of consciousness from a combination of alcohol and lack of food. Medical evidence was raised which showed that the physical condition of diabetes caused a propensity for aggression and temporary lack of consciousness when the treatment regime was not followed. The court held that prior fault prevents a reliance on the defence of automatism or other involuntary conduct. The defence will not succeed if the outward automatic state was foreseen or, in some situations, was reasonably foreseeable. This depends on the *mens rea* of the offence concerned. Where a malfunctioning of the mind is of a transitory character caused by an external factor, it cannot be said to be a disease of the mind and therefore the accused may not always be excused under legal incapacity through insanity. Why won't self-induced incapacity form an excuse in such situations? The authorities here reflect a matter of policy. Evidence sufficient to require that automatism should be considered by the jury must go beyond the defendant's own words and assertions as to his memory or state of mind at the time of the commission of the offence.

Capacity and intoxication (Volition and induced loss of reason)

The criminal courts have in the past been reluctant to entertain intoxication as a legitimate challenge to criminal liability. Traditionally, intoxication has been seen as an aggravating, rather than mitigating or exculpatory, factor in criminal liability. Recently, in Australian jurisdictions where the common law on intoxication does not apply,[35] intoxication has been considered either as an issue in mitigation or aggravation on sentencing, where the offence is not one requiring specific intent.

In assessing criminal capacity, intoxication might be seen to:

- deprive a person of the ability to form the required *mens rea*;
- deprive the person of the ability consciously to control his bodily movements, rendering his conduct involuntary;
- render the person temporarily insane.

Whether intoxication as a challenge to capacity can be raised is a question of evidence. The courts in the remaining Australian jurisdictions where a common law position on intoxication prevails are generally reluctant to be so persuaded.

The antipathy towards raising intoxication against volition particularly centres on voluntary intoxication, which may, in theory at least, negative any capacity for the mental state required by a designated offence. A reluctance by the English courts, in particular, to contemplate and confront the consequences of this position has led to the creation of rather tortuous

---

35 The Australian Capital Territory, South Australia and Victoria still follow the common law on intoxication as an issue for capacity. Victoria only recently reconfirmed this position after an extensive comparison and review of other jurisdictions.

distinctions with regard to the nature of the offence, the mental state required, the form of intoxicant used, and the intentions of the accused at the time of intoxication. Despite its convolution, recent legislative developments in Australia[36] have relied on the distinction between specific and basic intent.

From a strictly logical interpretation of legal principle one might expect that if intoxication, like any other issue of mental incapacity, were to negative the required mental element of the offence, then no offence could be established. However, as is the case with prior fault, policy considerations have put a brake on such a general approach. The case-law has taken two major directions in limiting this general approach:

- Those decisions which distinguish offences requiring specific intent (where voluntary intoxication may deny the mental state) from those requiring basic intent (where voluntary intoxication cannot be so raised);[37]
- Those decisions which distinguish intoxicants taken as medically prescribed (where voluntary intoxication may deny the mental state) from intoxicants taken illegitimately or in abuse of medical prescription (where voluntary intoxication cannot be so raised).[38]

DPP v. Majewski (*supra*) was said to confirm the distinction between specific and general intention advanced in **DPP v. Beard** [1920] AC 479. However, *Beard* also advanced the more general position that if intoxication rendered the accused unable to form the required *mens rea* then there could be no offence. In *Beard* it was said that it is not enough for the intoxication merely to weaken the defendant's restraint or inhibitions, or that as a result of intoxication the accused more readily gives way to a violent passion. A mere malfunctioning of the mind, short of a disease of the mind caused by intoxication, is also not enough for a defence. Distinctions between drunkenness and temporary insanity are far from clear. The permanent effect of habitual intoxication in a physical sense is a useful evidentiary issue if one is seeking to establish a disease of the mind.

Interestingly in his judgment in *Beard*, Lord Birkenhead did not seem to limit intoxication as a defence to offences requiring specific intent. Previous authorities in his view did not restrict the proposition on drunkenness to offences of specific intent. A person cannot be convicted of a crime unless the '*mens* was *rea*'. This broader position seems to have been ignored in the *Lipman* and *Majewski* cases.

---

36 Such as s. 428A-I of the NSW *Crimes Act.*
37 See *DPP v. Majewski* [1977] AC 443.
38 See Hardie [1984] 3 All ER 848.

In **R v. Lipman** [1970] 1QB 152, the facts of the case were that the accused took LSD and had a dream that he was being attacked by giant snakes. Lipman suffocated his girlfriend, in bed with him, as a result of the drug-induced dream. The defence argued that he had no knowledge of what he was doing and no intent to harm his girlfriend. The trial judge directed the jury that the ingestion of the drug was a dangerous act naturally resulting in manslaughter. Therefore, all that was necessary was the proof of the dangerous act. The defendant argued misdirection in that the prosecution was required to prove that the accused intended or foresaw harm from what he was doing. The court held here that while intoxication may be relevant to a question of specific intent, it does not stand as a general defence. Where intoxication falls short of insanity, it can only have the effect of reducing a crime from murder to manslaughter. Manslaughter is not an offence requiring specific intent and, therefore, where intoxication fails to trigger insanity, under such a charge it is not a defence.

The facts in the *Majewski* case (*supra*) revolved around a pub brawl. The accused was asked to leave and refused, butting the publican in the face and punching a customer. Majewski was then ejected and later returned, swinging a broken glass at the landlord and cutting his arm. A fierce struggle ensued when police tried to arrest Majewski and as a result police were injured. Various charges of assault were laid against the accused. To these the defence was that at all material times the accused was acting under the influence of drink. The offences in question did not require specific intent and therefore the court took the view that intoxication did not deny the accused's capacity to commit the offence.

Again, the House of Lords delivered a public policy judgment. The recklessness in actually taking the intoxicants was deemed to satisfy the *mens rea* for assault. Drunkenness was an intrinsic and integral feature of the offence, the other element being the unlawful use of force against the victim (the publican). Together they added up to criminal recklessness. The court reiterated the view that it was no excuse that intoxication had reduced the accused's capacity for self-control and to realise the possible consequences of what he was doing, or even to be conscious of what he was doing.

The High Court of Australia has emphasised the importance of the evidentiary question: whether the accused in his intoxicated state was not capable, and did not form the required mental state for the offence. Decisions on the point such as **O'Connor** (1980) 54 ALJR 349 have relied more on intoxication as potentially denying the capacity to form the requisite *mens rea* rather than forming a particular defence.

The artificiality of the distinction between specific and basic intent was reiterated in recent legislative rejections of the common law position in certain state jurisdictions in Australia. Reservations about the consequences of the *O'Connor* (*supra*) common law position have motivated some state and territory legislatures to reintroduce the specific intent distinction for the purposes of considering intoxication as a defence.[39]

In **R v. Coleman** (1990) 19 NSWLR 467, the Court of Criminal Appeal emphasised that the issue of self-induced intoxication does not require the jury to determine whether the accused had the required capacity, but whether the prosecution had proved that he had the necessary *mens rea*.

---

39 For instance, in New South Wales, the position on self–induced intoxication is now delivered in s. 428 of the *Crimes Act*, which overturns the common law and takes the defence back to the *Majewski* position.

Chapter 5
Elements of the Offences

Issues for proof or challenge

This chapter examines the issues requiring proof for the prosecution case. The emphasis on any particular issue of proof will depend on the elements of each offence. Some of these issues are consistent across offences while others have particular relevance for a designated crime. For instance, in sexual assault the proof of consent has relevance when establishing the criminal conduct and the mental state. For homicide offences, proof concerns might centre on causation or coincidence.

The defence may respond to the prosecution by denying that proof has in fact been established or by challenging any crucial issue or element on which their case relies. In addition, the accused person may propose a justification or an excuse for the allegations raised. These will be examined in more detail in their crucial contexts,[1] as part of the problem exercises in Chapter 6.

The wrongful act or omission

Criminal liability is constructed around the maxim '*actus non facit reum nisi mens sit rea*': an act does not make a person legally guilty unless the mind is legally blameworthy. Essential for an appreciation of the force of this maxim is the understanding that:

---

1   The teaching methodology on which problem-based learning rests avoids a reliance on the presentation of information as knowledge, divorced from context. This book only resorts to such presentation in an effort to provide the most basic understandings from which the contextual analysis of issues such as defences can develop.

- it is not the *actus* that is *reus* but the person and his mind respectively;
- it should be seen as a general principle of liability against which exceptions will be mounted and discussed;
- when examining the ingredients of criminal liability within a particular context it is necessary to consider each particular element of the offence, and whether these relate to conduct or mental state. The specifics of each element of an offence appear in either their statutory or their common law definitions. One should beware of matters of complex judicial interpretation where legal authorities seem to move a concept away from its literal or common sense meaning. Also, it is important to remember that certain elements may take on different meanings (and different requirements of proof) depending on their context; and
- all elements of the offence must be proved before liability may be established.

Where the prohibited conduct is:

- a combination of acts or omissions,
- certain consequences of these, or
- within particular circumstances

then there can be no criminal liability unless the whole of the *actus reus* is present.

In **R v. White** [1908-1910] All ER 340, the appellant's mother was found dead and beside her was a glass containing cyanide, which the appellant had prepared. Medical evidence indicated that the victim had died of a heart attack. She hadn't drunk from the glass and even if she had, there was not enough poison present to kill her. The appellant was acquitted of murder because the crucial element of the *actus reus* was missing (i.e. that the death was directly caused by the actions of the accused). Was attempted murder a more appropriate charge?

In addition, if the offence requires proof of consequences and circumstances, then liability depends on this as much as proof of the conduct in question.

For example, in **Morgan's** case (*supra*), the elements of the offence requiring proof as to conduct included:

- Conduct—sexual intercourse
- Circumstances—unlawful or non-consensual intercourse; and
- Consequences—conduct of the accused produces a denial of consent, and proceeds from it.

It is important in this offence situation to appreciate the often inseparable connection between the elements that establish and qualify criminal conduct, and the manner in which they demonstrate and depend on the prevailing mental state (in this case, consent).

Omissions

As for wrongful omissions and breach of a duty of care[2] standing instead of criminal conduct:

- the issue which establishes the liability of the *omitter* is the duty of care and his attempt to discharge that duty;
- this form of prohibited conduct (omission being deemed here equivalent to conduct) produces a variation on the normal rules regarding causation.[3]

For omissions to found criminal liability, two questions must be asked:

- Is the commission of the offence possible through omission?
- If so, did the accused have a duty to act?

Omission cases are largely in the realm of manslaughter, where the failure to perform a duty seems to establish either:

- the danger of the circumstances; or
- the objective degree of recklessness required by the mental state for the offence.

In *R v. Russell* [1933] VLR 59, the jury was troubled by the liability of a father who stood by while his wife drowned their children and herself. In the foreman's words: 'Assuming that the woman took the children into the water without the assistance of putting them in the water by the man, but that he stood by, conniving to the act, what is the position from the standpoint of the law?'[4] The jury eventually convicted the accused of manslaughter. The appeal court agreed that there had been a breach of parental duty if the accused had assented to the actions of the mother through omitting to intervene.

In the homicide setting omission gives an extended meaning to the notion of *causing death*. *R v. Stone and Dobinson* [1977] 1QB 354 was a case where the defendants undertook to care for the victim. All parties were to differing degrees mentally disabled. The accused made some meagre

---

2   Liability for omissions in common law may be an exception here. For example, an accused may not be liable for the death of a drowning man unless he took steps to recognise some duty of care. Duties are also identified in the Codes, e.g. s. 155 (NT), s. 285 (Qld), s. 144 (Tas), s. 262 (WA).

3   For example, usually the omission is not the substantial or ongoing cause of the prohibited result although the intervention of the accused may have broken the chain leading to that result.

4   p. 61.

attempts to discharge their duty of care to Stone's sister, but her death eventuated after weeks of requiring further care, which they were unable to provide. Here the key to liability appears to be the fact that the defendants had
taken some limited steps to discharge their duty, albeit negligently. Manslaughter charges were preferred against Stone and Dobinson.

The court held that a jury must consider a defendant's undertaking of
care, gross negligence in the discharge of that duty, and the death as a result.
This case is not like the drowning stranger situation. As a lodger and a blood
relative, the victim may have been owed a duty of care, which was confirmed when the defendants took some ineffectual steps to care for her and
thereby recognised this duty.

In determining the relationship between duty and omission in criminal
liability one should consider:

- whether there is a special relationship that may create a duty;
- whether the duty and responsibility have been assumed;
- whether the duty has been imposed by statute;
- whether the defendant has created a dangerous situation out of which a
  responsibility arises.

The distinction between positive acts and omissions rests on more than
simply a failure to act. Thus in *R v. Taktak* (1988) 34 A Crim R 334 the
court considered the liability of an accused who voluntarily assumed the
care of the victim and as part of this did not take action by calling medical
assistance in time. The accused was said to have 'so secluded the helpless
person as to prevent others from rendering aid'. The question was whether
the assumption of a duty (only partially discharged) and the failure to act
combined to satisfy the necessary objective recklessness for manslaughter.

In *R v. Miller* [1983] 1 All ER 178, the accused was intoxicated, and
went to sleep smoking a cigarette. He later awoke with the mattress on fire,
and he simply went into another room and back to sleep without attempting
to put out the fire or calling for assistance. Eventually Miller was awakened
by the police and fire brigade, and left the premises without ever attempting
to extinguish the fire. He was charged with arson. The *actus reus* of the
offence is lighting the fire and failing to take measures within his power to
counteract the danger that he had created; and the resultant criminal damage. The necessary mental state was intending to damage the property
belonging to another, or being reckless as to whether such property would
be damaged. The court took the view that 'if at the time of any particular
piece of conduct by the accused that is causative of the (prohibited) result,
the state of mind which actuates his conduct falls within the description of
one or other of the states of mind that is a necessary ingredient of the
offence ... no law prevents him from being guilty'. The prohibited conduct

includes failing to take measures that were within the accused's powers to counteract a danger created by the accused. It doesn't matter that at the time of commencing the act that created the danger, he was not aware of the eventual danger. Provided that when he was aware and in a position to do something about it, he took no steps to act, then the accused is liable. The court's analysis on the basis of a duty, or continuous act, preferred the concept of *responsibility*; that being an obligation owed to other people.

Status offences

A crime may be defined as being committed even though there is no act or conduct on the part of the accused in the general sense. There may be no requirement of *willed muscular movement*. Instead, it might be enough if there is a state of affairs, or *status*, or situation leading to a prohibited conduct.

This has led to extraordinary results such as those referred to in ***Larsonneur's*** case (1933) 23 Cr App R 74. Here the accused was convicted under the *Aliens Order* 1920, in that she, an alien to whom leave to land in the UK would have been refused, was found in the UK. She had been brought from Ireland against her will in the custody of the police. It was simply a situation deemed to satisfy the elements of the statutory offence. The mental state or conduct of the accused seemed to be subservient to her status.

Despite the wide condemnation of the case, a similar result was reached in respect of the *Licensing Act* (England), and of a status of being found drunk on a highway. In ***Winzar v. Chief Constable of Kent*** [1983] Times 28/3/83, the defendant was taken to hospital on a stretcher but when discovered to be drunk was told to leave. When he was found by police slumped in the corridor, he was taken to a police car parked on a highway outside the hospital. At his trial and conviction for being found drunk on a public highway, the words *found drunk* were interpreted as *perceived to be drunk* (i.e. the police became aware that he was drunk when they were on the highway, and not in the hospital).

In both these cases, the accused were convicted of offences the commission of which was procured by the police (*being found* offences require some act on the part of the finder rather than by the accused).

Causation

The key issue in any consideration of causation is to establish the link between the defendant's act and the culpable result (the *causal chain*).

Causation involves questions of fact and law:

* as to the facts where, but for the accused person's conduct, the victim would not have suffered;

- regarding the law whether, for the purposes of liability, it can be said that the substantial and operating cause of the crime was the conduct of the accused.

The issue of law is affected by general principles either establishing or imputing liability to the accused in terms of causation because of the connection and proximity of the accused's conduct and the prohibited consequences. In addition, Australian authorities are concerned with whether the accused might have been said to have reasonably foreseen these consequences. The case-law here (summarised in *Royall* (1990) 100 ALR 669) centres on those offences where the accused intends an act and due to the reaction of the accused, a criminal consequence occurs. In this respect the mental state of the accused and the consequences being natural and foreseeable are essential to the determination of causation.

The case-law, therefore, breaks down into three areas of conjecture:

- whether and in what circumstances an intervening act will break the causal chain;
- if the intervening act is that of the victim, to what extent does it need to be the natural consequence of the accused's conduct; and
- to what extent does the response of the victim need to be foreseen by the accused, or foreseeable.

Intervening acts or events

The accused is not responsible for the criminal conduct where the prohibited consequence occurs as a result of some subsequent event or act that would have caused the consequence irrespective of the original act of the accused. However, the accused may remain responsible despite the actions of third parties that contributed significantly to the death.

In *R v. Benge* (1865) 4 F & F 504, the accused misread the train timetable so that the track was up when the train came through. In addition, he positioned a signalman short of the regulation distance and the driver of the train was not keeping a good lookout. In this situation there were elements of causal liability and contributory negligence that went beyond the accused. The accused argued that if the driver had been vigilant and the signalman had gone the required distance, then the accident would not have occurred. The court held that so long as the accused person's actions remained the substantial and ongoing cause of the prohibited conduct, it mattered little that the accident might have been avoided if others had not been so negligent. Therefore, not every intervening act or omission of a casual nature will relieve the defendant of the responsibility or liability for the subsequent crime.

Substantial and operating cause

Where the conduct of the accused remains the substantial and operating (ongoing) cause, the intervening act may be in the form of a further injury to the victim by a third party, but not enough to precede or overtake the conduct of the accused as the cause of the prohibited consequence. In some situations, if the intervening act combines with the conduct of the accused to cause the prohibited consequence, then both the accused and the third party may be liable.

In **R v. Smith** [1959] 2 All ER 193, the test of *substantial and operating cause* was advanced. The accused was charged in a court martial with the murder of a fellow soldier, whom he stabbed in a barracks fight. The victim had been dropped on the way to the medical station following the fight. At the medical station the victim was given artificial respiration, which aggravated the wound to the lung, and death resulted. The court held that:

> if at the time of death the original wound is still an operating cause, and a substantial cause, then the death can properly be said to be the result of the original wound, albeit that some other cause of death was also operating. Only if it could be said that the original wounding is merely a setting in which the other cause operates can it be said that the death does not result from the wound … only if the second cause is so overwhelming as to make the original wound part of the history of the prohibited conduct, can it be said that the death does not flow from the wound.

In **R v. Jordan** (1956) Cr App R 152, the accused stabbed the victim, who was admitted to hospital and died some eight days later. The trial judge said there could be no other cause of death but the original wound. Fresh medical evidence on appeal revealed that the cause of death was not the original wound (which had healed by then), but was a result of the introduction of a drug to prevent infection, to which the deceased was intolerant. Further evidence indicated that this treatment was *palpably wrong*. If the jury had heard this evidence they would not have accepted that causation was established. The appeal court held that death by medical treatment necessitated by a felonious injury should be regarded by the court as caused by that injury, provided normal treatment was not followed. It is sufficient to break the causal chain to establish that the treatment in the case in point was not normal treatment. Here the wound was merely the setting in which the medical treatment operated as the cause of death.

In **R v. Malcherek & Steel** [1981] 1 WLR 690, the court examined the situation where, after wounding, both victims were put on life support systems in the course of normal medical treatment. In both cases the victims had their machines switched off after tests indicated that they were brain-dead. Murder convictions resulted from the trials. Appeals on the causation issues concerned whether all the appropriate tests had been carried out to establish brain death. The appeal courts held that at the time of death the original wound was the continuing, operating, and indeed substantial cause of death. The court said it was the time to establish what is the legal meaning of *death*. Even so, the connection between the original injury and the death at the time of brain death was not affected by the legitimate medical decision to turn off artificial support to maintain vital functions. Medical practitioners cannot be said to cause death by discontinuing bona fide treatment that has failed.

Foreseeable consequence

In *R v. Pagett* (1983) 76 Cr App R 279, it was conceded that the accused's conduct might not be the substantial and ongoing cause of death, but could still be seen as having been a sufficient cause of the death. Provided the prohibited consequence occurred as the result of some act or event that would not have occurred *but for the act of the accused*, and which was a *natural consequence* of that act, then the causal connection is established. In such a situation the prohibited consequence must be foreseeable as likely to occur during the normal course of events (a natural consequence in an objective sense). The facts of this case were that police shot a victim who was being used as a human shield by the defendant. The police action could be said to be involuntary, and in any case actions in self-defence or in the legitimate exercise of arrest powers cannot be said to break the causal chain. Human intervention when it consists of an act instinctively done for the purposes of self-preservation or in the exercise of a legal duty cannot break the causal chain.

Cause of victim's conduct

As an exception to the above principle (i.e. where something is not foreseeable) one must *take the victims as you find them*, both in mind and in body. If the defendant's act causes the victim to react in a particular manner or to make an omission which causes the prohibited consequence, then the defendant may be held liable even though the victim's intervening conduct may not be a natural consequence of the defendant's act.

In *R v. Blau* [1975] 1 WLR 141, the victim of a wounding refused a blood transfusion on religious grounds. Because she did not have the transfusion, the victim died as a result of the bleeding from the original wound. The accused was convicted of manslaughter. On appeal it was argued that the victim's refusal to have a blood transfusion was not a natural consequence of the act; it was unreasonable and as such broke the causal chain. The court held that those who use violence on other people must take their victims as they find them. This includes the whole person and not just the physical person. It does not lie in the mouth of the assailant to say that the victim's religious beliefs, which prevented her from accepting certain types of treatment, were unreasonable. The question for decision is what caused the death. The answer is the stab wound.

What is a natural consequence?

In **R v. Hallett** [1969] SASR 141, the appellant had beaten the victim unconscious, because, as he alleged, the victim had made homosexual advances to him while they had been drinking on a beach at night. The appellant left the victim unconscious by the water's edge and he drowned in shallow water with the rising of the tide. At the trial the accused was convicted of murder even though he argued that he had not drowned the victim. On appeal, the question was asked: if, as the appellant agreed, he had left the victim in a position of apparent safety with his ankles in the water, then how did the jury accept that he had caused the death of the victim? The answer was that the victim would not have drowned but for the actions of the appellant. The drowning was a natural consequence of that action: a consequence that might have been expected to occur in the normal course of events. This was foreseeable. It was not the involuntary actions of the unconscious victim that broke the causal chain.

The only other question was whether the action of the sea on the deceased could be seen as breaking the chain of causation. The appeal court held that, on the contrary, this was the ordinary operation of natural forces. It doesn't matter whether the appellant left the victm in a position of mortal peril or not, or whether the drowning was an event that might have occurred in the normal course of events (this might all go to the accused's favour). The action of the accused here was not just leaving the victim unconscious as a result of the earlier acts of violence. The chain of causation could not be broken by the accused's omission to take further steps for the safety of the deceased, even if such omissions were contrary to the accused's original intention, and were excused by his inadvertently falling asleep.

What is reasonably foreseeable?

In the English case of **R v. Roberts** (1971) Cr App R 95, a young woman who was a passenger in the appellant's car injured herself by jumping out of the vehicle while it was moving. The victim alleged that she had jumped because the appellant had said he would beat her up and make her walk home if she did not take her clothes off. The accused had tried to put his hands on her body earlier during the drive. The Court of Appeal rejected the submission that in order for the accused to have initiated the cause, he must have forced the victim to do the acts that resulted in the grievous bodily harm. It stated the test as follows: Is the victim's act a natural result of the accused's act, in the sense that it could have been foreseen as a consequence of what he was doing or saying? The actions of the victim have to be daft or so unexpected as to break the causal chain.

The Australian authorities on causation recently have tended towards an approach consolidating many of the various tests discussed above. In particular, the High Court in **Royall** (*supra*) combined the issues of natural and foreseeable consequences when causation is said to flow from the actions of the accused to the consequential actions of the victim. In particular, the issue of natural or reasonable consequence is directed to what flows from the fear that the act of the accused induces in the victim:

> It would seem to me that in the context of causation the principle is best formulated as follows: where the conduct of the accused induces in the victim a well-founded apprehension of physical harm such as to make it a natural (or reasonable) consequence that the victim would seek to escape, and the victim is injured in the course of escaping, the injury is caused by the accused's conduct. Whether it is necessary for the prosecution to establish also that the mode of escape adopted is a natural consequence of the victim's apprehension for his or her safety does not arise here, for the deceased had no other means of escape.[5]

The mental state

In addition to the identified concern of the law to examine the liability of each individual offender, in practice the question of *mens rea* or guilty mind is usually dealt with comparatively against two (or perhaps three) broad categories.[6] Once a match has been made, and the mental state has been deemed to coincide with the other elements of the offence charged (the criminal conduct in particular), then criminal liability is said to be established.[7]

> 'It is the beginning of wisdom to see that *mens rea* means a number of quite different things in relation to different crimes.'[8]

The mental elements of particular crimes differ widely, and because the general classifications of *mens rea* are broad and often ill-defined, there may seem to be a degree of unreality attached to the exercise of establishing *mens rea* in terms of an actual mental state.

Mens rea is not to be solely equated with:

* physical control at the time of the act

---

5   Mason CJ in *Royall v. R* (1990) 172 CLR 378.
6   Where the mind of the accused is said to be 'intentional', 'reckless', or in certain circumstances 'negligent'.
7   This is not to discount situations of strict liability where an element of the mental state might not require proof, or where presumptions also reduce proof requirements.
8   Lord Hailsham, in *Morgan* [1976] AC 182, at 213.

- volition
- knowledge of the relevant circumstances, or
- foresight of the consequences

although each and all of these may have considerable bearing on the evidentiary substantiation of a particular mental state. Motive should not be confused with criminal mental state.

In *He Kaw Teh* (*supra*), Brennan J suggested that an offence (in particular, one created by statute) can require different mental states directed towards different external elements of the offence (for example, to the circumstances, or to the results of the act). As the High Court conceded, *mens rea* is inherently hard to define, and beset with problems of terminology. It varies depending on whether it is directed towards conduct, circumstances, or consequences. In certain situations it may be constituted by an absence of thought or a 'blindness' as to the consequences.

Brennan J in *He Kaw Teh* indicated that voluntariness and intent are the mental states ordinarily applicable to an act involved in an offence. Knowledge, or the absence of an honest and reasonable but mistaken belief, is the mental state normally applicable to the circumstances in which a relevant act is done or an omission is made. Where a mental state is applicable to results, it may be either foresight of the possibility of their occurrence (if recklessness is an element) or knowledge of the probability or likelihood of their occurrence or an intention to cause them (if a specific intent is an element).

On the issue of knowledge as a component of *mens rea,* the High Court in *Pereira v. DPP* (1988) 82 ALR 217 considered that the offence of importing drugs did not require *actual knowledge* to be proved, as distinct from the guilty mind requiring relevant intention, foresight, knowledge, or awareness. The possession offence, however, required actual knowledge and no less. But this could be inferred from knowledge of suspicious circumstances coupled with a failure to enquire. As such, however, this seems more like constructive knowledge. The court explained that this situation could be summed up in the notion of *wilful blindness*.

It is also wrong to consider *mens rea* as simply equating to an evil mind. This collapses consideration of motive and mental state in a way that may divert the legal analysis away from an actual and more confined consideration of the elements of the offence.[9] In addition, ignorance of the wrongfulness of one's actions (the other side of knowledge) may not negative *mens rea.* As was stated in *R v. Sharpe* (1857) 7 Cox CC 214, it is irrelevant in terms of determining criminal liability that the accused acted for good or bad motives.

---

9   See Norrie 1993.

In *R v. Tolson* (*supra*), Stephen J considered that guilty mind must depend on the subject of the enactment, and various circumstances that may make the construction of the statute (concerning *mens rea*) reasonable or unreasonable. In criticism of the Latin maxim as misleading he stated:

> It naturally suggests that apart from all particular definitions of crimes, such a thing exists as a *mens rea*, or a *guilty mind* which is always expressly or by implication involved in every definition. This is obviously not the case, for the mental elements of different crimes differ widely … The principle involved appears to me, when fully considered, to amount to no more than this. The full definition of every crime contains expressly, or by implication a proposition as to a state of mind. Therefore, if the mental element of any conduct alleged to be a crime is proved to have been absent in any given case, the crime so defined is not committed.[10]

It is rare that the mental state of the victim will have any impact on the evaluation of the *mens rea* of the perpetrator. However, in cases where consent and the accused's appreciation of it are at issue, the knowledge of the victim may be crucial. For instance, in *R v. Morgan* [1970] VR 337, the charge was the rape of a woman with a defective mental capacity. Here the claim the prosecution had to challenge was that consent was actual and informed. To obtain a conviction, the prosecution had to establish that the victim was without sufficient knowledge and understanding to comprehend: (a) that what was proposed to be done was the physical penetration of her body; or if that was not proved, (b) that the proposed act of penetration was one of sexual connection as distinct from an act of a totally different character.

In some situations of complicity, the mental state of the principal offender and knowledge of his intended actions are crucial to the *mens rea* of the secondary party. One must be influential over the other. In particular, with common purpose, the participants reach an understanding or agreement amounting to an arrangement to commit a crime. They are liable for any act that is within the contemplation of that common purpose, and which might be done in the course of carrying out the primary criminal intention.[11]

Presumptions as to mental state

Stephen J. in *R v. O'Connor* (*supra*) recognised:

> For criminal liability to be incurred (cases of strict liability and culpable negligence apart), civilised penal systems have, in modern times, insisted that the accused should be shown to possess a blameworthy state of mind.[12]

---

10 [1886–1890] All ER Rep 26 at 27.
11 See *Johns* (1980) 143 CLR 180.
12 p. 96.

The principle in **Sherras v. De Rutzen** (1985) 1 QB 918 stated that there is a presumption that *mens rea* is an essential element of every offence. For the determination of criminal liability, the importance of the knowledge of the wrongfulness of one's act needs to be established or presumed without successful challenge. In reality, of course, the ordinary citizen often does not know the law, and therefore does not consciously know the wrongfulness of his act. Nevertheless, since he is presumed to know the law, his knowledge of the wrongfulness of an act that does offend a criminal provision must also be presumed.

Prior to **Woolmington v. DPP** [1935] AC 462, the English common law recognised a broad interpretation of the presumption as to mental state, casting an evidentiary burden on the accused to prove he did not intend the natural consequences of his act. It was held in *Woolmington* that, no matter what the charge, it is the obligation of the prosecutor to prove the guilt of the accused. It is not the law that the accused must show evidence to mitigate the charge. The prosecution must prove all the elements of the offence charged through direct or circumstantial evidence, and any other collateral issue on which the prosecution relies. Following *Woolmington* the only burden on the defence is to cast doubt in the mind of the jury as to whether such was his intent (or his *mens rea* in a more general sense). The same would hold if the accused challenged the presumption as to volition.

In **R v. Smythe** (1957) 98 CLR 163, the High Court expressly rejected the interpretation of the presumption that a person intends the natural consequences of his act as relieving the prosecution of the task of proving *mens rea*. The move away from the English court's position at the time culminated in **Parker** (1963) 111 CLR 610. In that decision the High Court set itself directly against the House of Lords in **Smith** [1961] AC 290, which had held that the presumption was an irrebuttable rule. In so doing the High Court broke with the precedent yoke of English legal authority.

In **Sweet v. Parsley** [1970] AC 132, the accused was charged with the management of premises used for the purposes of smoking cannabis. In actuality the accused had simply rented premises in which the drug was consumed without her knowledge. In this case the court wanted to be satisfied, prior to dispensing with the *mens rea* requirements, that parliament so intended when it created the elements of the offence. This would need more than the absence of words such as *knowing* from the legislation; otherwise *mens rea* is an essential ingredient of every offence unless some reason can be found for holding that it is not.

In the Northern Territory decision of **Pregelji and Warramurra v. Manison** (1988) 31 A Crim R 383, the appeal court examined whether the statutory offence of offensive behaviour required the proof of *mens rea*. In considering **He Kaw Teh** (*supra*), the judge adopted the view of Brennan J that *mens rea* is an essential element in every statutory offence unless, having regard to the language of the statute and of its subject matter, it is excluded expressly or by necessary implication.[13] *Mens rea* could not be excluded from offensive behaviour.

> There is no reason that I can see why the law would put persons in peril of criminal responsibility by reason of failing to take a positive action to see such behaviour does not happen. I can see no reason why offensive behaviour should not be treated as an ordinary criminal offence where the penalty for guilt is intended to operate as a deterrent against the prohibited conduct.

Therefore, it was the court's view that it would be wrong at law (and in terms of public policy) to convict persons of offensive behaviour if they were unaware that their conduct could be viewed by others in a public place.

Intention

In *He Kaw Teh* (*supra*), Brennan J took the view that:

> Intent,[14] in one form, connotes a decision to bring about a situation, so far as it is possible to do so to bring about an act of a particular kind or a particular result. Such a decision implies a desire or wish to do such an act or to bring about such a result.[15]

Some offence definitions refer to mental state considerations such as *knowingly, fraudulently, maliciously*.[16] However, in addition to stated mental requirements such as these, there are at least two major *mental states* which the courts interpret as being necessary to establish the criminal liability of an accused in respect of particular offences. They are intention and recklessness. Brennan J distinguishes between voluntariness and general intent as separate mental states, and between general and specific intent as forms of that separate mental state known as intent. Both specific and general intent can be established by knowledge: the latter by knowledge of the circumstances that give the act its character, the former by knowledge of the probability of the occurrence of the result to which the intent is expected to relate.

Intention is recognised as the highest form of criminal mental state (and as such the most difficult to prove, requiring the most convincing levels of

---

13 In the Code jurisdictions, there is no presumption that every offence contains a subjective element: *McMaster v. R* (1994) 4 NTLR 92.

14 *Intentional* in the code jurisdictions has the same meaning as at common law—see *R v. Vallance* (1961) 108 CLR 56.

15 p. 569.

16 Such concepts may be better viewed as component parts, or evidence that establishes the mental states of intention and recklessness.

evidence). What constitutes intention has been the subject of considerable debate in recent case-law authority. Intent has sometimes been equated with purpose and desire, but it is now generally held that these are not of themselves comprehensive enough to represent its meaning fully. In addition, the case authorities have said that intention may exist where desire in particular is not present.

In the case of motive, it is not an essential element of intention, and even may be contrary to it, but does sometimes represent evidence towards intention.

Object of intention

Another approach to understanding intention has been to say that when examining the results (consequences) of an initial act, these may be intended where, even if not desired, their occurrence is foreseen by the agent as being a probable or likely result of his initial act.

In this sense intention has been considered in at least two ways by the courts:

- in terms of degrees of intention; and
- in terms of intention as to acts or consequences of these acts, and even exposure to risk of these.

Intention is either direct or indirect, depending on its relationship to the prohibited conduct of the offence, and any intervening prohibited conduct of which it is a consequence. For example, direct intention is the intention to kill. Indirect (sometimes referred to as implied or oblique) intent is the intention to kill deemed to follow on from an intention to seriously injure in certain circumstances.

Degrees of intention

In the general discussion of *mens rea*, intention is referred to both as:

- a particular form of *mens rea*; and
- a generic notion of *mens rea* where a distinction is drawn between issues of proof, or the availability of defences, for example specific and basic (general) intent.

Unfortunately, intention often is used simultaneously to mean a specific form of *mens rea* as well as a generic classification of *mens rea* (e.g. intent and recklessness; specific and basic intent), in the careless terminology of case-law authority. One should not assume, therefore, that when intention is referred to it is always the same thing or that it is a distinct designation of *mens rea*.

Nature of intention

Intention can mean many things, depending on who is said to exercise it, and in what circumstances it is exercised. As **Maloney's** case [1985] 1 All ER 1025 shows, it can even be inferred. In this case the House of Lords distinguished between actual intention and foresight of probable outcomes.[17]

The facts involved a discussion between a drunken father and son about the latter leaving the army. In addition there was a vague discussion between the two men about personal prowess with a shotgun. The father claimed that even with his crippled arm he could outshoot, out-draw, and out-load his son. For the purpose of the argument two guns were loaded. The father was claimed to have said, 'I don't think you have the guts but if you do, pull the trigger.' The son later indicated that he didn't aim but fired, and as a consequence his father was killed. The son then immediately rang the police stating, 'I have murdered my father.' It was held on appeal that the trial judge's direction referring to 'desiring something to happen whether it is foreseen or not, or foreseeing something whether it was desired or not, as being intention', was not law. Lord Bridge disagreed with the direction by distinguishing intention from foresight of consequences, the latter being relevant only as evidence of intention. He further distinguished intention from motive or desire, preferring *purpose* as being closer to intention. Here oblique or indirect intention could only be established through proof of foresight where the likelihood of the consequences was *little short of overwhelming* or where the result was a *natural consequence* of the original conduct. If this is a correct interpretation, was the court really talking about oblique intention?

The English authorities have tended to take a narrower view of intention than may be seen in Australian case-law. This is no doubt due to the fact that the mental state required for murder in England is only intention, whereas in most of the Australian common law and code jurisdictions the *intention* needed to satisfy murder may also include a *reckless disregard*. This has had a significant impact on the manner in which intention is said to involve foresight of consequences. In Australian common law, foresight of probability appears to be sufficient as proof of the *mens rea* for murder. In the English authorities the debate focuses more on the level of probability required to satisfy a narrower parameter of intention.

---

17 This line of authority has culminated in *Woolin* [1999] 1 AC 82, where Lord Steyne explicitly rejected the possibility that a person's intention can be inferred from his foresight of risk falling short of virtual certainty. This differentiates intention from recklessness in that the accused must seek deliberately to bring about the consequences, or recognise them as a virtually certain concomitant of some other result sought. Unlike the Australian murder cases, it is not enough that the death was foreseeable, or foreseen as probable.

Intention through inference

Despite the fact that intention requires the most subjective considerations of the mental state of the individual accused, such intention is inferred from examining things such as:

- the degree of the likelihood of certain consequences; and
- whether these were foreseen (this is often inferred from the degree of likelihood, and knowledge, and desire).[18]

Discussions of intention, as of recklessness, seem to be couched in the language of premeditation, and evidence of premeditated purpose goes towards inferences about intention.

Features of intention as mens rea

It might be said that the existence and degree of various factors indicate intention:

1 knowledge $>$ of the fact / of consequences $\Big\}$ *degrees of certainty*

2 desire or aim or purpose $>$ relating to the act / relating to the consequences

3 actions taken in order to bring about a certain act or consequences, and their proximity to the mental state.

As discussed earlier, Brennan J in **He Kaw Teh** (*supra*) connected different components of mental state with the three external elements of the conduct he chose to identify:

- voluntariness and intent are the mental states ordinarily applicable to an act involved in an offence;
- knowledge or the absence of a mistaken belief honestly and reasonably held is the mental state ordinarily applicable to the circumstances in which a relevant act is done or omission is made; and
- where a mental state is applicable to results, it may be either foresight of the possibility of their occurrence (if recklessness is an element) or

---

18 This raises the common proof problem in establishing any subjective mental state. In light of the accuseds' denial that they possessed the mental state required, jurors usually infer the accuseds' mental state from surrounding objective circumstances. A juror sometimes reflects on what he or she would have thought in that situation and then transposes this into the mind of the accused. See, *Pemble v. R* (1971) 124 CLR 107.

knowledge of the probability or likelihood of their occurrence, or an intention to cause them (if a specific intent is an element).[19]

Knowledge, considered by the courts as an individual and subjectively assessed mental quality, may be established from inference. An example is with the *knowledge* of consent referred to in s. 61I of the *Crimes Act* (NSW). This includes recklessness as to whether such consent was present. This knowledge requirement takes the offence into the realm of basic intent or subjective recklessness.

In New South Wales, the *Crimes Act* continues to employ the ancient notion of *maliciously* in the definition of many offences. Section 5 of the *Crimes Act* defines 'maliciously' so as to incorporate intention, recklessness, and the notion of *wantonly.* The court in **Coleman** (*supra*), after inviting the legislature to do away with all reference to 'maliciously', held that to prove this element it was necessary for the prosecution to prove an awareness on the part of the accused of the *possibility* that the prohibited consequence would occur. Neither probability nor the degree of harm actually inflicted was required for proof.

Strict (specific) and ulterior (oblique or indirect) intention

Following the High Court decision in **O'Connor** (*supra*), which rejected the distinction between specific and basic intent as analytically suspect when applied to the determination of voluntary intoxication as a defence, specific intent is now back on the agenda in several state jurisdictions. In New South Wales, for instance, as a result of the recent amendment to the *Crimes Act* s. 428, specific intent returns as a distinction on which the availability of certain defences depends.[20] The section refers to specific intent as being an 'intention to cause a specific result', and then goes on to list about 100 offences where this *mens rea* is required.[21]

Specific intention

In the case of **R v. Mohan** [1975] 2 All ER 193, the facts were that the accused person drove his car directly at a policeman and was charged with attempt, by wanton driving, to cause bodily harm to a police officer. The jury was directed that it was sufficient for the prosecution to prove that he was reckless as to whether bodily harm would be caused by his driving. The court held that specific intent was viewed as being similar to aim: a decision

---

19 As at (1985) 60 ALR 449 at 482.

20 Interestingly, the Victorian Law Reform Committee has rejected the specific intent distinction for the offence of intoxication and recommended the retention of the common law position.

21 Somewhat confusingly, many of these offences could also be established through what seems to be the proof of subjective recklessness.

to bring about, insofar as it lies within the power of the accused (a particular consequence), regardless of whether the accused desired the consequence or not. In this case the trial judge was criticised in that it was not enough that the accused foresaw the bodily harm as *likely* or even *highly probable*. Proof was required of the *decision to bring about certain consequences*.

In Brennan J's analysis of intention in **He Kaw Teh** (*supra*), the distinction between specific and basic intent was considered as important for offences where the criminal conduct involves consequences of the accused's actions. Brennan reiterated that, as with most offences, there is a strong presumption that the prosecution must prove that the accused intended to cause the *actus reus*. This intention is general or basic. It is an additional element of the proof that the accused's act was voluntary. Brennan went on to distinguish the concept of specific intent as relating not to acts, but to consequences of these. For instance, if the offence requires proof that the accused caused grievous bodily harm intending so to do, the intent to cause grievous bodily harm must be specific.

Ulterior intent

Ulterior intent is another way of looking at the intent required to bring about consequences: specific intent. Crimes of ulterior intent are those that are defined so that the *mens rea* includes an intention to produce some further consequence beyond the *actus reus* of the initial crime in question, for example intention to seriously injure (assault) causing death (murder). In some situations that further consequence may constitute the *actus reus*, or rather stand as evidence for the original and necessary *mens rea*. Offences requiring ulterior intent thus incorporate in their definitions a consequential requirement as to the accused's mental state, which is additional to the more straightforward *mens rea* discussed in its immediate sense. This intention must apply to both its original act and its consequences. As stated above, in Brennan's view this might equate with specific intent.

This more oblique interpretation of intention was examined in **Hyam's** case (below), where the question of how certain the knowledge of the consequences must be was debated.[22] The difficulty in *Hyam* arose from the requirement in that jurisdiction that the *mens rea* for murder must be an intention to kill or inflict grievous bodily harm.[23]

---

22 *Hyam's* case is also of special importance for those jurisdictions where the *mens rea* for murder is still referred to as 'malice aforethought'. The scope of this concept and its application are discussed in detail in the judgments of this case.

23 In contrast to the law in Australian common law jurisdictions where foresight of probable death or grievous bodily harm is sufficient—see *Crabbe* (1985) 156 CLR 464; *Knight* (1992) 175 CLR 495, 501.

In the case of *Whitehouse v. Lemon* [1979] AC 617, Lord Diplock interpreted the ratio of *Hyam's* case as stating that now no distinction should be drawn in law between the state of mind of one who did an act because he desired it to produce a particular result, and the state of mind of one who, when he did the act, was aware that it was likely to produce the result, but was prepared to take the risk that it might do so, in order to achieve some other purpose which provided his motive for doing what he did. The issue in contest for the majority of judges in *Hyam's* case was whether the degree of foresight of the consequences was enough to form evidence of an intention to commit the prohibited act, as required by the offence of murder in England.

The appeal questions facing the House of Lords in *Hyam v. DPP* [1974] 2 All ER 41, arising from the nature of the trial judge's direction, were:

- How likely were the likely consequences required to be for intention to be implied, and proved?
- How much foresight of those likely consequences was necessary?
- Foresight of what consequences was required for the *mens rea* for murder?

The court did not decide anything about the actual nature of direct intention beyond the fact that it was not necessarily the same as foresight. While *motive*, and *desire*, and *purpose* may each be an important indicator of intention, they did not equate with it, nor was their correspondence with intention necessary.

Lord Hailsham said:

> I know of no better judicial interpretation of intention ... than that given by Asquith LJ in *Cunliffe v. Goodman* [1950] 2 KB 237 at 253: 'An intention ... connotes a state of affairs in which the party intending does more than merely contemplate. It connotes a state of affairs which, on the contrary, he decides, so far as in him lies, to bring about, which in point of possibility, he has a reasonable prospect of being able to bring about, by his own act of volition.'

Hailsham stated that he saw the point of the case as being intention, and asked two initial questions: Is it sufficient to prove simple intent to kill or cause grievous bodily harm? Or should it be asked whether the accused intends to wilfully expose another to the risk of death or grievous bodily harm? He did not believe that knowledge or any degree of foresight is enough to form intention, while they could help the jury infer intent.

Viscount Dilhorne and Lord Cross, though disposed to think that foresight did amount to intention, decided that it was not a sufficient *mens rea* for murder. The minority differed only as to what it was that must be foreseen (for example, Lord Diplock required foresight of injury the consequence of which was death).

When it came to their discussion of foresight, the majority were satisfied individually by differing degrees of foresight of consequences—for example *highly probable, likely,* etc.

Hancock and Shankland [1986] 2 WLR 357 was the case where striking miners pushed a piece of concrete from a bridge onto a passing taxi carrying strikebreakers. Passengers were killed as a consequence. Lord Scarman referred to Lord Bridge's comment in **Maloney** (supra), that the probability of the consequence taken to have been foreseen must be little short of overwhelming before it will suffice to establish the necessary intent. He noted again that both foresight and probability were, while not the same as intention, important evidentiary concerns when establishing intention. Yet he indicated his dissatisfaction with the *Maloney* guidelines for establishing intention. He felt that the absence of any reference to *probable* in the discussion of natural consequences might lead to confusion. At the same time he endorsed Bridge's distinction between the elements of the mental state required for an offence, and the evidence relied upon to prove it.

In **Nedrick** [1986] 1 WLR 1025, Lord Lane stated that in determining intent it had to be asked:

1 How probable was the prohibited consequence?
2 Did the accused foresee that the consequences must be *virtually certain* for the consequences to satisfy the *mens rea* for murder?[24]

The examination of intention in Australian common law treatment of murder, where death resulted as a consequences of the accused's desired conduct, has necessitated a consideration of a reckless disregard of risk.

In **Royall** (1990) 172 CLR 378, the High Court held that to prove reckless indifference to human life within the definition of murder under the *Crimes Act* (NSW), the prosecution had to show that the accused had foreseen the death as possible. The relationship between the *mens rea* for murder and intention is important when examining the component parts of intention.

General or basic intent would appear also to cover those forms of *mens rea* which incorporate *reckless indifference.* Here it seems that the *mens rea* as to the act and its consequences, such as the taking of human life, can be different.

---

24 In *R v. Walker & Hayles* (1990) 90 Cr App R 226, the accused were convicted at the trial of attempted murder. It was held on appeal that *trying to kill* might not be equated with intending a result the accused is not trying to achieve. Outside murder the defendant's desire may not go hand in hand with the intention required for that offence. In the case of attempt they may not have even desired harm. For attempted murder the relevant intent must be to kill. In *Woollin* [1999] AC 82 at 90, the House of Lords confirmed that intention in murder was proved if death or serious injury was virtually certain as a result of the defendant's actions, and he appreciated such was the case.

It is the latter consequence to which the accused is said to be indifferent. The indifference is to foresight of probable consequences.

The High Court in **Crabbe** (1985) 156 CLR 464, after considering the elements of reckless indifference (or what might be referred to as 'wilful blindness'), went on to discuss ulterior intention in terms of the degree of probability and the nature of the outcome foreseen. These answers would then determine the intention necessary to establish homicide in those states where reckless indifference is sufficient *mens rea*.

> It should be regarded as settled law in Australia, if no statutory provision (as to murder) affects the position, that a person who, without lawful justification or excuse, does an act knowing that it is probable that death or grievous bodily harm will result, is guilty of murder if death in fact results. It is not enough that he does that act knowing that it is possible but not likely that death or grievous bodily harm might result.[25]

Transferred intent (Malice)

Where the accused has the intention to commit one criminal act but, due to the intervention of an additional factor such as lack of skill, commits the prohibited conduct against another unintended victim, then the intent (or malice) is transferred. This will obviously only occur across mental states for the same offence (or offences with the same *mens rea*).

Recklessness

Recklessness is generally seen as the alternative *mens rea* for establishing criminal liability. It is often referred to as coming within those offences which are satisfied by basic intent. Because of the evidentiary reliance on issues such as knowledge and foresight in the proof of both intention and the subjective forms of recklessness, there is some degree of overlap between these mental states, and therefore the distinction between forms of *mens rea* is unclear.

A person who does not intend to cause harm but may take an unjustifiable risk, which brings about such harm, can be said to be reckless. The unjustifiable risk must be established in order to ground recklessness. In addition, the prosecution may need to go further depending on the variety of recklessness alleged. For example, it may be necessary to prove that:

1 the accused knew the risk; or
2 he may not have considered whether there was a risk or not, but the reasonable man (ordinary person) would have so done; and

---

25 p. 449.

3 he may have considered whether there was risk and decided that there was none.

The first situation is manifest in **R v. Cunningham** [1957] 2 All ER 912, where the appellant pulled the gas meter from the wall in the basement of his house, which adjoined that of his mother-in-law. He did this in order to steal coins from the meter. The gas stop tap was very close to the meter but the accused did not turn it off. As a result of breaking the meter from the gas pipe, a large amount of gas escaped into the mother-in-law's house and she was partially asphyxiated. The court held that the act was unlawful, and malicious as regards the consequential assault. Malice, as it is referred to in the offence of malicious damage to property, is no longer the old notion of wickedness. It requires either (1) an actual intention to do the particular harm that was done, or (2) recklessness as to whether such harm should occur (which is the same here as foreseeing the risk of harm and yet going on to bring it about). With such offences recklessness involves a conscious and advertent risk-taking. Recklessness is not established merely by proving that the risk taken by the accused was one which a reasonable person would have foreseen and not taken. Obviously this would be significant evidence for the view that the accused had such foresight. But without proof of subjective *mens rea*, the court in *Cunningham* would not say the accused was reckless. In this case, because the elements of the offence require the proof of malice, the *mens rea* must be subjective.

A radical departure from the subjective understanding of recklessness (the second form of recklessness above) is discussed in the case of **Metropolitan Police Commissioner v. Caldwell** [1983] AC 319. In this case recklessness is said to require the proof of adverting to the risk, or if no such advertence occurred, then the risk must have been obvious to the reasonable person who gave thought to the matter. In effect, recklessness under *Caldwell* embraces both advertent wrongdoing and gross negligence.

In *Caldwell,* the facts related to an arsonist who attacked a hotel in order to get back at the owner. He stated that the thought that the lives of the people in the hotel might be endangered never crossed his mind. The court took the view that it should determine whether an objective test could be readmitted into the determination of recklessness, following the very subjective approach of *Cunningham.* The measure of recklessness in this case had to be placed against the *ordinary prudent individual*. If, after having done so, the ignorance of the risk seemed unreasonable, then the absence of subjective considerations cannot be claimed as an answer to recklessness. This test becomes particularly relevant when intoxication is raised. It is suggested that the intoxication itself should be viewed as evidence of recklessness:

... if the defendant does an act which in fact creates an obvious risk that property would be destroyed or damaged, and when he does the act he has not given thought to the possibility that there could be any such risk, or has recognised the risk and has nonetheless gone on despite it, then there is recklessness.

The issue in *Caldwell* is whether the failure to advert to an otherwise identifiable risk is blameless inadvertence, or recklessness.

In *Caldwell*:

1 the higher notion of recklessness implies the conscious undertaking of a unjustifiable risk of which the accused either had some knowledge or at least adverted to; and
2 the lower form of recklessness covers the unjustifiable taking of a risk of which the accused ought to have been aware.

It is important to remember that the offences charged in *Caldwell*, unlike malicious damage, may not necessarily imply subjective recklessness.

R v. Lawrence [1982] AC 510 established in the English courts the same principles as *Caldwell*, but in relation to causing death by reckless driving cases. Recklessness here was not limited to the actual mind causing the death, but included the *state of mind* of a person who without justification took an *obvious* risk simply because he or she failed to consider the possibility of such a risk existing. The court included *heedlessness* within recklessness, as the latter was to possess an ordinary rather than a legal meaning and as such involved both subjective and objective mental states.

The tests in *Caldwell* and *Lawrence* therefore stipulated that recklessness exists if the accused:

• consciously took an unjustified risk, the consequences of which were foreseen (*Cunningham*);
• consciously took an unjustified risk, the consequences of which should have reasonably been foreseen;
• consciously took an unjustified risk, the consequences of which were consciously ignored.

In **Reid** [1992] 3 All ER 674, another death by reckless driving case, both advertence and inadvertence were deemed to involve subjective states of mind. To this extent *Lawrence* was challenged. The court took the view that absence of something from a person's state of mind is as much a part of that state of mind as presence. Inadvertence is a subjective state of mind as much as the disregard of a recognised risk. Recklessness can be inadvertence to risk, and inadvertence generally satisfies recklessness. Diplock's direction in *Lawrence* no longer needs to be followed verbatim in the English courts. The question is whether the accused acted without thought of the risk, or thought of the risk and took it anyway. The exact state of mind of a person is often impossible to calculate and therefore courts infer *mens rea* from what happened. In this regard the actuality of the risk is essential.

This position is different from that discussed by the Australian authorities on wilful blindness (see pp. 94–5). The reference to inadvertence in *Reid* conceived of a situation where the accused did not put his mind to the existence of a risk or otherwise. This is to be distinguished from the situation where the accused decides not to consider or to recognise the risk.

The effect of the second dimension of objective recklessness as proposed in *Caldwell* presented some difficulties for defendants who were anything but the ordinary person.

In **Elliott v. C** [1983] 1 WLR 939, a fourteen-year-old defendant set fire to a shed by pouring white spirit onto the carpet and setting it alight. She realised the contents of the bottle were possibly flammable but she had not handled it before and did not realise how explosive it could be. She gave no thought at the time to the possibility of the destruction of the shed. The risk would not have been obvious to her or appreciated by her if she gave thought to the matter. It was argued that the findings as to recklessness should have been based on the characteristics of the accused at the time. In addition, the offence charged should be considered against the background of such characteristics. Did she destroy the property and did she do so without lawful excuse? No intent existed, but was she reckless? The court held that the accused was literally reckless because she did an act that carried an obvious risk, and did not advert to the risk. However, the court said it would not find her to be reckless on the ordinary meaning of the word. There was no deliberate disregard of a known risk, nor was it a case of mindless indifference to the damage. Failure to give thought to the risk of damage did not constitute a blameworthy cause. A purely objective test was inappropriate in this case; the situation here did not present the same circumstances as reckless driving (*Lawrence*). Only a test where failure to give thought to a risk that would have been obvious to the accused if she had given any thought to the matter would be appropriate to these facts. However, the court felt bound by the precedents of *Lawrence* and *Caldwell*, and found recklessness present.

The High Court has ignored *Caldwell* almost entirely. Exceptionally, McHugh J's judgment in **Royall** (*supra*) mentions *Caldwell* when considering reckless indifference. Like the rest of the court, he went on to reject the objective interpretation. The court's analysis explicitly echoed the *Crabbe* (*supra*) subjective analysis of malice aforethought and recklessness espoused in *Cunningham*.

Australian authorities are not, however, immune to objective concepts of recklessness. A number of cases have used the term 'recklessness' to refer to gross negligence.[26] Despite this, by the time of *Caldwell* the subjective determination of recklessness predominated in Australian jurisdictions. In *Valance* (1961) 108 CLR 56 the subjective interpretation was endorsed by the High Court. However, particularly in the interpretation of advertence to the withdrawal of consent in sexual assault cases, courts in certain Australian jurisdictions have contemplated an apparently objective interpretation of wilful blindness.

Wilful blindness

When knowledge of the risk or wilful blindness is alleged, this tends towards intention as *mens rea*. As the required knowledge of the risk becomes more actual and certain, the closer it comes to implied intention. However, as with intention, knowledge of a risk is not necessarily sufficient for *mens rea* (intention or recklessness), irrespective of its magnitude. Magnitude is a question of evidence for the proof of *mens rea*. Issues such as probability, justification, and benefit to society in general all must be considered.

In *Giorgianni* (1985) 156 CLR 473, Gibbs CJ held that knowledge extended to wilful blindness; however, 'shutting one's eyes to the facts' was not the same as actual knowledge. It could provide evidence of knowledge. One needs to enquire into the nature of the offence when seeking to determine the extent of knowledge required (for example, whether wilful blindness equates with belief, in charges of receiving stolen goods).

Wilful blindness is not a substitute for intention or knowledge in the Australian authorities. However, wilful blindness may provide evidence from which a jury may infer that the accused did possess the necessary element of subjective fault. In *Pereira v. DPP* (*supra*), the majority held: '... a combination of suspicious circumstances and failure to make enquiry may sustain an inference of knowledge or the actual or likely existence of the relevant matter'.[27]

Whether the accused 'merely shut his eyes' is a fact, among others, to be considered in establishing whether the accused had the requisite mental state (including knowledge, and basic intention where it includes reckless indifference).

Wilful blindness has received a broader interpretation when recklessness as the *mens rea* in sexual assault is determined. In certain jurisdictions, such as in New South Wales, despite the essentially subjective requirement in determining the attitude of the accused to the withdrawal of consent, the honesty of the accused's alleged mistake as to consent is crucially dependent on the reasonableness of his interpretation. Therefore, through the evaluation of mistake

---

26 See *MacPherson v. Brown* (1975) 12 SASR 184.
27 p. 220.

as a defence to a charge of sexual assault, requirements for reasonableness introduce objectivity into the evaluation of *mens rea*. In **Kitchener** (1993) 29 NSWLR 696 at 700, for instance, it was held that recklessness as to consent could be shown 'not only where the accused adverts to the possibility of consent but ignores it, but also where the accused is so bent on gratification and indifferent to the rights of the victim as to ignore completely the requirements of consent'. In **Tolmie** (1995) 37 NSWLR 660, it was argued for the accused that if *Kitchener* incorporated notions of inadvertence or negligence into the *mens rea* for sexual assault, this would be inconsistent with a central tenet of the criminal law: that a person should not be subject to serious criminal sanction for actions that he or she was not proved to have intended. Kirby J, recognising that recklessness was not defined in the statutory offence, accepted inadvertence as part of recklessness. He took the view that lack of the merest advertence to consent in the case of sexual intercourse is so reckless that it is the criminal law's business. In this, the law does no more than reflect the community outrage at the suffering inflicted on victims of sexual violence. While not relying on *Caldwell,* Kirby took it to endorse the view that where the accused has not considered the question of consent, and the risk that the complainant was not consenting would have been obvious to someone with the accused's mental capacity if he turned his mind to it, then the accused is said to have been reckless in terms of the elements of the offence.

Recklessness and different offence types

Following the decision in **Reid's** case (*supra*), the application of recklessness is different depending on the specific offences in which it is the mental element. The test for recklessness can vary depending on whether an accused is charged with a:

- Statutory offence: here the *Caldwell* type of recklessness may apply (e.g. reckless driving, criminal damage), depending on the construction of the legislative provision;
- Common law offences: in which the test of recklessness depends on the offence (e.g. objective recklessness may be sufficient for manslaughter; subjective recklessness is required for assault);
- Offences where malice or knowledge are components (the *Cunningham* type of recklessness may be required).

Recklessness is not used as a fault element in the Code jurisdictions in Australia. Although there is no reference to recklessness, the Codes have been interpreted as incorporating recklessness through the use of the term *wilfully.*[28]

---

28 See *R v. Lockwood: Ex parte AG* [1981] Qd R 209.

Recklessness and negligence

What separates recklessness from negligence is that in the former, irrespective of the risk involved, the accused willingly takes an action that will expose him to the likely consequence of that risk.

There is no doubt that deliberation on the mental element necessary to establish legal responsibility has for too long gone no further than arguing for the existence of certain specific states of mind. The suggestion has been that *mens rea* is synonymous with these states of mind and therefore questions of capacity and volition have been relegated to consideration as indicators of, or presumptions flowing from, these states of mind.

The move away from the simple identification of *mens rea* with legally prescribed states of mind is leading to a reconsideration of the mental elements of an offence. The concept of capacity may contain an essential consideration of volition. As such, capacity is central to the realisation of criminal responsibility. It is the accused's capacity to do what the law requires, rather than the fact that he was in a proscribed state of mind when he broke it, that determines the ascription of criminal responsibility.

Moreover, this is so even if the question of capacity as such is not in issue, since capacity in this sense is presumed unless it is deemed. The fact that the accused has been shown to have been in such a state of mind merely raises the presumption that he had the capacity to avoid causing the legally proscribed harm associated with it. It is his failure to displace this presumption, rather than the fact that he was in a legally proscribed state of mind, that gives rise to the ascription of criminal responsibility.

Negligence

Negligence is the failure of the accused to foresee a consequence that a reasonable person would have foreseen and avoided. This objective criterion, which overlaps with the *Lawrence* approach, does not require foresight on the part of the accused. Consequently it might not be viewed as a state of mind at all. The accused may be careless in conducting himself generally, or alternatively he may be careless as to the consequences of his actions.

In past authorities there has been the attempt to rely on degrees of negligence, such as gross negligence or criminal negligence, to establish criminal liability. However, some courts have suggested that gross negligence might simply now be equated with objective recklessness. The degree of negligence required to establish criminal liability obviously is greater than that required under civil law. The actual degree will vary, depending on the elements of the offence concerned.

In Australia, most offences that might be committed negligently are found in statute. The most significant common law offence that can be committed through negligence is manslaughter.[29] In situations where legislation imposes a duty to act, negligence may be sufficient to establish a criminal mental state. It is not the duty which creates the criminal offence, but rather the negligence which supports the liability.[30]

Negligence is the minimum threshold of criminal responsibility for the Code states and territories.

Strict liability

Crimes which are said not to require one or more elements or features of *mens rea* as to one or more elements of the prohibited conduct are known as offences of strict liability. The availability of honest and reasonable mistake as an excuse distinguishes strict liability from absolute liability.[31] What might be considered to distinguish such mistake from a situation in which the person has no reason to apprehend the contrary is discussed in *State Rail Authority v. Hunter District Water Board* (1992) 65 A Crim R 101. In this case the court distinguished between a positive belief in a mistaken set of facts, and a situation where no thought was given to the matter.

In extreme cases the offences can be established by proving the prohibited conduct or consequence despite the *mens rea*. For example, in *Attorney-General v. Demand Enterprises Ltd* [1987] HKLR 195, the facts related to the employment of children presenting false identity cards. Their employers had taken precautions to ensure that all employees were over the legal age for employment. The purpose of the regulatory offence created in the labour legislation was to prohibit child labour entirely. The employer's efforts to comply could only be taken into account when sentencing.

Some situations exist where the mental state is only abrogated with respect to certain elements of the prohibited conduct but not others. In *Lemon; R v. Gay Newspapers* [1979] AC 617, the facts related to a homosexual newspaper publishing an article and pictures depicting lewd acts on the dead body of Christ. The prosecution was for blasphemous libel. The magazine's editor claimed that while he had knowingly published the article, he had no blasphemous intent in so doing. The court held that it was not a question of the publisher agreeing with the prosecutor on the nature of the publication for the prosecution to stand. The law in question was designed to prohibit such publication and what the accused recognised and intended is immaterial.

29　See *Nydam v. R* [1977] VR 430.
30　See *Callaghan v. R* (1952) 87 CLR 115.
31　See *Proudman v. Dayman* (1941) 67 CLR 536.

In *Gammon (HK) v. Attorney-General of Hong Kong* [1981] 3 WLR 437, the appellants were the building contractors, the project manager, and the site agent for building works in Hong Kong. Part of the building under their supervision collapsed. The company was charged with a material deviation from the approved plan in contravention of the *Building Ordinance*. The charge referred to carrying out works in a manner likely to cause injury or damage. The manager and the agent were charged respectively with carrying out works, and permitting works to be carried out, in a manner likely to cause risk of injury or damage. The court held that each provision of the charge requires *mens rea* but is silent as to whether it is in respect of all the parts of the Act which constitute the offence. The appellant company was liable for deviating in a material way from the approved plan even though there was no evidence that it knew its acts or the acts of its agents constituted a material deviation from the plan. Liability for that element was strict but not absolute. *He Kaw Teh* (*supra*) gave clear support to the first three propositions in *Gammon*, and qualified interest in the remainder.

Even where strict or absolute liability is imposed, the volition with which the prohibited conduct is performed may need to be established by the prosecution.

Statutory regulation

Crimes of strict liability are almost always creatures of statute. They are often referred to as *regulatory offences* in that they have been created by the legislature in order to manage the activities of individuals and organisations in a uniform and non-discretionary fashion.

Interestingly, the validity of strict liability offences was recognised by the House of Lords in *Warner v. Metropolitan Commissioner of Police* [1969] 2 AC 256; a year later in *Sweet v. Parsley* (*supra*), the general presumption as to *mens rea* was reaffirmed. Does this pose a conflict in trends of interpretation?

Trends for and against *mens rea*

The case-law seems to confirm the pre-eminence of *mens rea* while at the same time recognising the reality of strict liability offences. To some extent the contradiction has been reconciled through the use of the notion of *honest and reasonable belief*, and mistake of fact as to an essential element of the *mens rea*.

In *Sweet v. Parsley*, Lord Diplock stated that there is nothing unreasonable in requiring a citizen to take reasonable care to ascertain the facts relevant to avoiding a prohibited act. Diplock was reluctant to take from the accused the potential to raise the defence of reasonable mistake through the general imposition of strict liability.

Also, many of the problems associated with the scope of strict liability can be overcome by a close examination of the detailed provisions through

which the legislature creates the offence in question, and the express purpose in creating such offences.[32]

Strict liability in statutory offences is normally the result of the courts'
refusal to read into a statute a provision which is silent on the point, such as
knowingly, in relation to an element of the prohibited conduct of a particular
offence.

One of the earliest and most important cases on the absence of *mens rea*
in statutory offences was **R v. Prince** [1874–1880] All ER 881. The facts
related to taking a girl under the age of 16 out of the custody of her father.
Consent was present on the part of the girl but not on the part of the parent.
The legislation only referred to an absence of consent on the part of the parent. Prince knew the girl was in the custody of her father but had reasonable
grounds for believing that she was 18. He also knew that the father did not
consent. The court held that knowledge of the girl's age was not required by
statute. Age was only relevant to her status as a child. If mistake was to be
raised as a defence it could only relate to the issue of the parent's consent.
Otherwise it was a strict liability offence. The legislation was concerned
with preventing the inherent wrongness of the act, which was the prohibited
taking of the girl from the custody of the father without his consent (her
consent therefore being irrelevant). It was not necessary to construe the
words of the statute so as to create *mens rea* across the knowledge issue, and
the intention to take the girl from the possession of the father was the only
mens rea requiring proof. Therefore, the only question of mistake was as to
the consent of the father. Questions of fault here if they arise will only have
relevance for sentencing.

In some situations the courts have been reluctant to employ a proviso
concerning a defence of reasonable mistake in offences of otherwise strict
liability.

Offence in a social context

Judicial authorities have regularly asked whether these are real crimes or
rather matters for regulation. Are they general or special prohibitions? Are
they subject to amendment? Do they attack a particularly urgent social
problem?

In **Gammon** (*supra*), the Privy Council laid down certain general principles that should govern the court in deciding whether or not a statutory
provision constitutes strict liability:

---

32 For example, *Warner's* case (*supra*), where it was held that if it was the intention of parliament
to punish the possession of drugs then neither the intent nor the knowledge of the accused is
relevant. The *Misuse of Drugs Act* (England) in fact created a *halfway house* where the burden
to prove lack of suspicion, reason to suspect, or ignorance was placed on the accused.

1   First recognise the presumption of law that *mens rea* is required to establish criminal liability.
2   Such a presumption is particularly strong where offences are *truly criminal* in character.
3   The presumption can only be displaced if it is clearly or by necessary implication the effect of the statute.
4   The only situations where the presumption can be displaced are where the statute relates to an *issue of social concern*. Public safety is such an issue.
5   Even where a statute is concerned with such an issue, the presumption stands, unless it can be shown that the creation of strict liability will be effective to promote the objects of the statute, by encouraging greater vigilance to prevent the commission of the prohibited act.[33] In this case the notion of an issue of social concern was less onerous to prove than the *grave social evil* concept propounded in **Lim Chin Aik** (*supra*). In *Lim's* case it was also asked whether putting the accused under strict liability would assist in the enforcement of the law. There must be something that the accused could do directly or indirectly, by supervision or inspection, by improvement of business methods or by exhorting, in order to be capable of influencing or controlling the promotion of the observance of the obligation. If through strict liability the prosecution of a class of people can be shown not to influence the observance of the law, then strict liability is not likely to be interpreted.

In **He Kaw Teh** (*supra*), Brennan J agreed with the first three propositions in **Gammon,** saying of the fourth that it is too categorical an approach to what is, after all, a matter of statutory interpretation. His view of the fifth proposition was that it reflected the purpose of the criminal law, which is to deter a person from engaging in criminal conduct.

The penalties of the criminal law cannot provide a deterrent to a person who is unable to choose whether to engage in the prohibited conduct or not, who does not know the nature of the conduct he may choose to engage in, or who cannot foresee the results that may follow from that conduct (where those results are part of the mischief at which the statute is aimed). It requires clear language from the legislature to impose liability for unknown conduct or unforeseen consequences.

Relationship between strict liability and negligence

Both strict liability and negligence imply that there is either no mental state required or the question of what mental state prevails is not relevant for the establishment of criminal liability.

---

33   Cf. *Lim Chin Aik (supra).*

The developing opposition to *mens rea* is often based on the notion that the harm done by the conduct is worthy of regulation and punishment irrespective of perceived wickedness in states of mind.

The case for dispensing with subjective *mens rea* is:

- there is no difference in moral terms between intention, recklessness, and negligence;
- it is impossible to prove an actual state of mind at the time of the commission of an offence;
- the idea of *mens rea* is outmoded both psychologically and philosophically; and
- *mens rea* is based on notions of responsibility and free will without addressing the arguments of determinism.

Significance of due diligence

In *Alphacell v. Woodward* [1972] 2 WLR 1320, a case involving water pollution by the defendant company, the defendant alleged that it didn't know the pollution was taking place. Mistakenly and not negligently, the company argued, it thought that the filter for its outflow system was effective. Even so, the company was not exonerated. The court held that there was no due diligence defence available and no mistaken belief defence under these circumstances. The company's knowledge as to the pollution was not an essential element of the offence. In addition, the court took the view that the company could have done more to prevent the pollution and hence avoid liability.

In *AIS Pty Ltd v. EPA* (1992) 29 NSWLR 497, the court required a distinction between arguments based on honest and reasonable belief and those relating to due diligence. Due diligence is never available as an extension of the mistake excuse. Otherwise the prosecution may have the onus of proving that someone was not duly diligent. Defendants therefore may be liable under strict liability even though they have not been negligent.

Relationship between *actus reus* and *mens rea*

Coincidence

For criminal liability to be established, *mens rea* and *actus reus* need to coincide.

This simple principle is made more complex by the court's consideration of conduct and mental states as continuous in a *temporal* sense and as a series (for example, where the criminal conduct is a continuing act or series of events it is sufficient that the *mens rea* be manifest at some point during that series or continuance).

The problem is what constitutes continuing conduct, and how it is different from: (1) steps towards the commission of the offence or (2) the consequences of its completion.

As for the mental state prevailing, the question is whether it has been imposed to make up for the absence of a required mental state at the point of coincidence, even though it still may not satisfy the necessary elements of the offence.

Continuing mens rea *across a series of acts*

Thabo Meli v. R [1954] 1 All ER 373 was a case where the appellants planned to take the victim to a hut, get him drunk and strike him over the head. Having carried out this plan, and believing him dead, they took his body and rolled it over a cliff, making it appear to be an accident. As it transpired, the victim died of exposure. Two principal acts were performed: (1) the attack in the hut, and (2) the placing of the body outside. The court had to decide whether these should be viewed as separate acts and as such could be brought about by separate mental states which changed over time. The first act was accompanied by the required *mens rea* but did not cause the death. Were the accused, therefore, not guilty because the necessary *mens rea* did not accompany the act causing death? The original intention ceased long before the death—or did it?

The Privy Council preferred not to divide up a series of acts in considering the completed conduct. The crime didn't fail just because the appellants were under some misapprehension about the time of the completion of their criminal plot. *Mens rea* existed at the time they commenced a series of acts, and there was no intervening act breaking the causal chain in the series of acts. The appellants did all they thought necessary to achieve their criminal purpose, which was achieved.

Mens rea *superimposed*

In *Fagan v. Metro Police Commissioner* [1969] 1 QB 439, the accused accidentally drove onto the policeman's foot. His vehicle remained there even after he was asked by the policeman to get it off. The question before the court was whether an assault[34] had occurred in these circumstances.

The court held that whether the driving onto the foot was accidental or intentional, the accused still knowingly, unnecessarily, and provocatively allowed his car to remain there after the battery was identified. The crucial question was whether the *actus reus* could be considered spent after the car came to rest on the foot, or whether it was a continuing act operating until

---

34 Assault means putting the victim in fear of immediate and unlawful personal violence, and intent or recklessness as to it.

the wheel was removed. The distinction between a continuing and completed *actus reus* is whether the consequences continued to flow. For the offence to be established, the apprehension of the victim must correspond with the intention or the recklessness of the accused. *Mens rea* doesn't have to be present at the commencement of the act, but can be superimposed on a continuing *actus reus*. It cannot, however, change an *actus reus* which is complete and where *mens rea* was absent.

Extent of 'continuing act' principle

In *R v. Church* [1961] 1 QB 59, the appellant took the victim into his van for sex. As it transpired, he was unable to satisfy her, and for this he was reproached by the victim. A fight between them ensued, in which the appellant punched the victim. The appellant tried to revive her, and when not successful he panicked, thinking she was dead, and threw her in the river. As a consequence the victim drowned. The court was now faced with whether the *Thabo Meli* principle on *actus reus* as a series of acts applied to manslaughter. Manslaughter requires more than simply an unlawful act on the part of the accused for liability to be established. The jury must be able to consider the appellant's actions as a series culminating in the victim's death. The accused could have been convicted of murder if the jury considered that the accused's conduct was a series of acts designed to cause death or grievous bodily harm.

Can the mens rea be withdrawn?

In *R v. Jakeman* (1982) 76 Cr App R 223, the appellant booked a flight from Africa to Rome, and then on to London, for the transport of two suitcases containing marijuana. The flight was diverted to Paris and the appellant did not pick up the cases there. Airline officials sent them on to London where again they remained uncollected by the accused. She was charged with *being knowingly concerned with the fraudulent evasion of the restriction on the importation of cannabis*. The trial judge said that her explanation of an intention to abandon her intention to import the drug, prior to the importation having taken place, was irrelevant. The court held on appeal that the guilty mind of the accused at the time the importation commenced prevailed, and by this she brought about the importation of the drug through innocent agents. Her alleged repentance at the time she boarded the plane couldn't save her from the importation conviction, because she had brought about the *actus reus* (through commencing the series of acts) with the necessary criminal intent. The questions were whether the appellant had caused the fraudulent evasion, and whether she did so with the required *mens rea*. When she put bags on the plane she expected and intended to do other acts in order that the crime would be committed. Yet, after beginning the series of acts, did she have a duty to prevent the achievement of the crime? She did not reclaim her luggage, so as not to allow the offence to continue. The fact that someone else did not do that in Paris did not discharge her duty to prevent the completion of the crime.

R v. Miller (*supra*) involved an omission to act, bringing about the consequence of criminal damage. It was argued that this occurred in the absence of *mens rea*. Was this enough to excuse the appellant? The Court of Appeal upheld the conviction because the whole course of conduct constituted continuous actions into which the *mens rea* might be injected. The court held that continuous conduct is relevant to the establishment of criminal liability, as is the *mens rea* across that continuous conduct. Since arson is a *result* crime, the period of continuity might be considerable. The *actus reus* in this case consisted of physical acts and failures to act in a manner within the accused's power so as to counteract the danger his acts created. As such conduct varies from active to passive throughout the series in question, so might the *mens rea*.

Therefore, the general rule is that *actus reus* and *mens rea* must coincide, bearing in mind that the *actus reus* can consist of an ongoing act or a series of connected acts committed in certain specified circumstances leading to the prohibited consequence, and *mens rea* must exist in relation to each of these necessary elements. But it doesn't necessarily follow that the same degree of *mens rea* must apply to each element of the *actus reus*.

Transferred malice

In *Latimer* (1816) 17 QBD 369, the accused swung a belt at a man, wounding someone else accidentally. It was held by the court that if a person has a malicious intent towards one person and in carrying into effect the malicious intent the accused injures another, he or she is guilty of what the law considers malice against the party injured.

R v. Mitchell (1983) 76 Cr App R 293 was a case involving a fight at a post office. The accused pushed an old man onto a woman who fell and broke her leg, and later died of complications from the injury. The accused was charged with manslaughter. It was held that there was no reason in policy why an act calculated to harm one victim should not satisfy the offence of manslaughter if it consequently harmed another victim. The criminality of the actor is the same whether the harm is done against the first or the second victim. There is no need for contact between the accused and the victim, nor is it necessary that the accused directed his actions against the eventual victim for the transferred malice principle to have effect.

The issue of attacks on a pregnant woman and the injury of the child was reconsidered in *Attorney-General's Reference No. 3 of 1994* (1997) Crim LR 829. The appeal court took the view that if the attack was on the pregnant woman, and the child was delivered and eventually died, transferred malice could not be employed to establish a homicide conviction. It was accepted that while the mother and the foetus were distinct beings, the delivered child was a separate victim against whom the necessary intention to injure or kill must be directed if murder were to be established.

Mistake

The significance of objective determinations of states of mind is well illustrated when mistake of fact is raised. For instance, in Australia after *Proudman v. Dayman* (*supra*), and in particular in those offences where the prosecution claims a strict liability interpretation, the courts have required proof beyond reasonable doubt that the accused was not acting under a genuine and reasonable mistake of fact.

In *Beckford v. R* [1988] AC 130, if the defendant believed reasonably in the existence of the facts that would justify the force used in self-defence, he would not intend to use unlawful force. There is no distinction between mistake as to the definitional elements of the offence and mistake as a defence. The subjective test applies to them both, and therefore the facts as the accused honestly believed them would be what the courts should measure against the prevailing state of mind, in order to determine criminal liability.

R v. Williams (Gladstone) (1984) 78 Cr App R 276 involved an assault charge in circumstances where the accused stated that they had mistaken the identity of the victim as a robber, when in fact he was a police officer in the process of effecting an arrest. Here the reasonableness or unreasonableness of the defendant's belief is material to the question of whether the belief was held by him at all. If the belief was in fact held, the unreasonableness of such a belief so far as guilt or innocence is concerned is irrelevant.

In *He Kaw Teh* (*supra*), Brennan J indicated that once the accused has successfully shown that he had reasonable grounds for believing in the mistaken facts, he is not required to prove his mental state as an excuse. This is up to the prosecution to disprove. Knowledge and mistaken belief cannot coexist in respect of a crucial fact or element of the offence. It is therefore necessary to determine what state of mind applies to a particular element of a statute-defined offence once it appears that some mental state is applicable. The absence of an honest and reasonable but mistaken belief can be the mental state applicable to existing circumstances, but only if the *prima facie* requirement of knowledge is excluded. Mistake is a defence in the circumstances, even if knowledge as to the circumstances of the act does not have to be proved in order to establish the necessary *mens rea* of the offence, and if an exculpatory belief about the circumstances would make the defendant's act innocent (if those facts were so). The required *mens rea* is to be determined by reference to the wording of the statute, and its subject matter.

Inferring criminal liability

Vicarious liability

Both vicarious and corporate liability are species of liability where, due to some delegation of authority, an individual or a corporate body can transfer their criminal liability to their superiors, or in some situations the other way around.

The principal issue for establishing liability here is the nature of the delegation and the representation of certain authority.

Master and servant relationships

In criminal law a master is generally not liable for the criminal actions of his servant.[35] However, the employer may be liable if, when the prohibited conduct occurred, the employee was working within his delegated authority, in the course of employment.[36] It does not necessarily follow that an employer can be made criminally liable for something for which he was only civilly liable. The delegation (from master to servant) must resemble the relationship of secondary parties to a crime if liability is to be passed on (i.e. a master is only criminally liable for the actions of his servant where he is a participant in those actions, in the normal secondary party sense).

Two principles prevail in interpreting statutory and other offences as creating the possibility of making a master liable for the acts of his servant:

* where the performance of certain duties has been cast upon the master by statute, and he delegates these; or
* where the acts physically done by the servant are considered to be the master's acts.

Statutory exemptions to the general 'no liability' principle
Delegation
Allen v. Whitehead [1930] 1 QB 211 deals with a situation where under the *Metropolitan Police Act* it was an offence knowingly to permit or suffer prostitutes or persons of bad character to meet in a place where refreshments were served. The accused was the occupier (tenant) of a café and while he received profits from the business, he did not manage it. The employed manager allowed prostitutes to meet in the café even after the accused, having received a warning from the police on the matter, had instructed him not to allow this, and he had put a notice up on the wall to this effect. The accused

---

35 See *Lloyd v. Grace Smith & Co.* [1912] AC 716.
36 See *Minister for Customs v. Australian Films Ltd* (1921) 29 CLR 195.

even visited the café to see that his instructions were being complied with, but on following days prostitutes congregated in the café, with the knowledge of the manager. It was held that the ignorance of the accused was no defence. The acts of the servant and his *mens rea* were to be imputed to the master not simply because the manager was a servant, but because the management of the house had been delegated to him.

The argument that vicarious responsibility is necessary to make the statute operate has special force where the statute is so phrased so as to be able to be committed only by the delegator. This of course could be achieved in other ways beyond vicarious liability. The statute in question in this case provided for an offence to be committed by persons who have or keep any house. The manager was presumably not such a person, and therefore if the absentee keeper was not liable for the acts of the manager then the statute could be denied with impunity.

Doubt about the degree of delegation necessary to bring the principle into operation was evidenced in the case of *Vane v. Yiannopolos* [1965] AC 486. In this case a restaurateur who was only allowed to sell intoxicants to customers consuming a meal instructed his waitress in that regard, and then withdrew to the basement. Without his knowledge she served liquor to persons who were not dining. The court determined that the manager was not guilty of a violation of the provision of the *Licensing Act* because the Act penalises licensees who knowingly sell intoxicants to non-permitted persons. It must be shown that the licensee is not managing the business himself, but has delegated the management to someone else. It was necessary to demonstrate that the licensee fully delegated all management functions and responsibilities. The restaurateur, however, had retained control of the restaurant and had not delegated it to the waitress. The court doubted the validity of the delegation principle, but it was now established law even if its application was confused and produced anomalies.

In *Hawker v. Robinson* [1973] QB 178, it was stated that if there has been a complete delegation of functions then it is irrelevant that it only related to one part of the licensed premises, or that the delegator was still on the premises at the time of the commission of the offence. Here the court believed that the problem with the interpretation of *knowingly* is then up to the legislature to clarify.

Vicarious liability will normally only apply in situations where the employee is acting within the scope of his or her delegation or employment, such as by doing an authorised act in an unauthorised way.

Look at the wording of the statute. If the licensee, for example, commits the offence, then the delegate can only be convicted as an aider or abetter.

Corporate liability

Corporate liability is to some extent a misnomer because the case-law does not talk of aggregating liability, but rather of looking for the *mind of the company* personified through individual liability. In this respect an individualised paradigm of liability is being rather artificially applied to corporations by the courts, which does not reflect the reality of corporate decision-making. This has led to:

- a reluctance to prosecute or convict large and complex corporations;
- a narrowing of the concept of delegation in order to protect management;
- a preference for the conviction of employees or small corporations;
- an inability to address the concept of collective *mens rea*.

The corporate personality is a legal entity which can create liability and be made liable. It may create relationships in a legal sense even though directors and shareholders may come and go. Incorporation does not protect people within the company from liability entirely. The importance of incorporation means that the company may also be made liable under certain offences as well as individuals.

Companies may become liable in two situations:

- vicariously, or
- through the doctrine of identification.

A corporation is identified with its controlling officers. In civil law the privity of the manager is said to be that of the corporation. Those who are said to control or manage the affairs of the company are regarded as the company themselves. Their acts and states of mind are imputed to it whenever they are acting in their capacity as controlling officers. In this way companies can become liable for offences requiring *mens rea,* even in situations where human employees may not be liable.

R v. ICR Haulage LTD [1944] KB 551 was a case where a company's managing director and others were indicted for conspiracy to defraud. The court held that although the crime indicted required a *mens rea*, and although the corporation had no mind of its own, the state of mind of its managing director was imputed to it so that his fraud is its fraud.

A good example of the extension of criminal liability for corporations is where an individual would not be vicariously liable for a common law conspiracy, but a corporation, as in this case, would be held liable.

For the identification principle to be effective, the controlling officers will almost always need to be co-perpetrators or accessories to the offence. In the case of *Tesco Supermarkets v. Natrass* [1971] 2 All ER 127, a branch manager displayed a sign that soap was offered at reduced price. A pensioner tried to buy the product at that price but was refused and was offered the product at the full price. The mistake had been that of the manager. A complaint was made to the inspectorate of weights and measures and an action was brought against the supermarket under trade practices legislation. Tesco blamed the branch manager for failing to notice the price variation of the product. It was said that the company policy was that managers are tightly controlled by the firm's inspectors. The court said, in upholding the defence, that the branch manager was a mere employee, not a controller with whom the company could be identified. The court took an extremely narrow view of *doctrine of identification*. Is the person to be regarded as the company or simply the company's servant in doing things for which the offence stood? The court did not make clear which issues of identification were sufficient for the imputation of liability. This case seemed to turn on the fact that the position of the officer was not high enough in the organisation to act for the company, and that those who gave limited delegation to the manager could not be held liable, because they retained overall authority. If identified as a controller then the company is liable not simply in a vicarious sense, but as if the company were liable itself.

Thus, in evaluating the responsibility of an employee on behalf of the company, a court will consider the employee's status within the organisation (for example, a director or manager) and the nature of the delegation of managerial responsibilities given to the employee by general management. The principle of identification was endorsed in **Universal Telecasters (Qld) Ltd v. Guthrie** (1977) 18 ALR 531.

R v. P & O European Ferries (Dover) Ltd [1990] 93 Cr App R 72 recognised the potential to charge a corporation with manslaughter. However, in this case, despite evidence of individual negligence at various levels within the corporation, the court would not accept that the mental state of the corporation could be inferred or constructed as an aggregate of multiple occasions of negligence on the part of employees. Was there advertence to a risk that the ferry doors remaining open could lead to the serious injury or death of the passengers? Was the person governing the ferry doors identifiable as the company?

On the second question the company was exonerated. Not so in **R v. OLL Ltd** [1994] NLJ 178, where the company became the first in the history of English common law to be convicted of manslaughter and its managing director was given a custodial sentence. Following the death of some teenagers in a boating accident, the defendant company which ran the leisure centre at which the accident occurred, and its managing director, were charged with manslaughter. In the past the rule against the aggregation of fault has prevented successful prosecutions where several company *minds* have known different elements of the risk. The company in this case was relatively small and therefore it was easier to identify the controlling mind. In addition, the risk to which the students were exposed was serious and obvious. There was in fact a letter to the general manager from other instructors specifically warning of risk of injury, of the same type as that which eventuated.

The problems involved in allocating liability to corporations for offences requiring a subjective mental state[37] were recently recognised in the drafting of the *Commonwealth Criminal Code Act 1995*.[38] The Code talks of the liability of directors and *high managerial agents*, and thus recognises the impact of the identification doctrine. But more than this, it contemplates corporate blameworthiness by creating as a fault element a failure by corporations to create and maintain a corporate culture that requires compliance with the relative provisions.

---

37 These difficulties have not been encountered in regulatory offences where strict liability has enabled conviction of corporations through the devices of delegation and vicarious liability.

38 See Schedule, Part 2.5, s. 12.3—Fault elements other than negligence.

Chapter 6

Solving Problems for the Criminal Law

Introduction

The remainder of this text is an exploration of a range of problems set within selected social contexts. The sequence of the chosen topics might be viewed as:

1 the emergence of crime and the criminal law;
2 the processes of criminal justice;
3 what the prosecution needs to prove;
4 responses by the defence;
5 sentencing and punishment.

Within these broad areas are common themes such as discrimination within the criminal justice process, the significance of discretion, the need for reform, and the distance between community expectations and the role of the lawyer and the judge.

Students will find some similarity in the treatment of the topics. A general identification and discussion of the issues precedes the problem scenario and notes on its analysis and resolution. Further readings are provided. This template is not rigid, nor is it essential for the learning process. It is meant as a framework for consistency around which the study or classroom experience may be unified.

The topics are intended to generate many more problem issues than each problem example contains. In this respect the problem-based learning to emerge from this section might employ the example problems as an incentive for the construction and resolution of further problem exercises, which are for the teacher and student to create and wrestle with.

As stated earlier in this book, students should not expect in the coverage of these topics a comprehensive presentation of criminal law and procedure. As the early topics demonstrate, the treatment is contextual, selective and partial. Where law is discussed, its purpose is to provide principles and procedures to be used in the problem-solving endeavour. Students seeking greater substantive knowledge will have the basis for further research throughout case-law, legislation, issues of procedure, and comparative jurisdictional analysis. There are many useful texts and commentaries with this purpose in mind to assist the enterprise.

TOPIC I

CRIME AND SOCIETY

Crucial to understanding crime problems and the criminal law in context is a close and current appreciation of the relationship between crime and society.[1] Complex as Australian society is, social context considerations need to be both specific and interrelated. They also require recognition of the historical construction of Australian society, and the role that legal systems have played in this process.

Crime is a social concept

Crime is a changing and diverse phenomenon. It is not simply individuals or behaviours. Even institutional reactions don't completely explain crime. The phenomenon of crime is better perceived as relationships in certain contexts which produce particular, often harmful results, and usually disapproving reactions.[2]

In modern, bureaucratised societies crime is defined by institutional and procedural responses to particular prohibited behaviours. These reactions in turn tend to bring about further deviant and control responses that may form a spiral of criminality and criminalisation. This spiral is largely dependent on the manner in which crime is represented, and the responses of the community, the justice process, the victim, and the offender.[3]

Relationship between crime and justice

The cultural and social relativity of crime and control priorities is beyond question. Both crime and justice have little specific meaning beyond the communities within which they are represented. This is essential to appreci-

---

1   See Findlay 1999.
2   See Braithwaite 1989.
3   Findlay 1999, Chapter 1.

ate when attempting to establish a convincing connection between crime and justice. It is not as simple as the assumption that justice is the natural and unavoidable consequence of crime. Issues such as the selective enforcement of the law by police challenge that certainty.

Both crime and justice depend on structures of law and society. Individual interests as well as the community's expectations for sanction and control may motivate them.

Crime and justice are activated through individual and institutional choice in climates where opportunities for choice are constrained.[4] Discretion in making crime or control choices is a feature which binds crime to justice, and empowers and affects those caught up in the criminal justice process.[5] Both the forms and institutions of choice operate through levels of discretion (see Chapter 2).

Aims and functions of the criminal law[6]

A fundamental justification for the criminal law is what can be termed the *moral wrongness* approach. This works from the understanding that crimes are a violation of morality as well as the law. Therefore, it is necessary for the criminal sanction to endorse and re-establish morality. Punishment then becomes as much a moral as a legal question.

The *individual autonomy* approach is linked to morality aims in that it holds the offender to be individually responsible for his crime and in some instances to indicate pathology in personality and behaviour through his criminality. This approach has the criminal law performing retributive and/ or deterrent functions. Unfortunately, in reality these have little universal impact; the assumption of rationality or considered individual choice across offenders is, if not a fiction, at least a highly questionable contention.

Crime as harm is the image by which criminal law as a crucial element in community welfare is promoted. Again, this relies on certain assumptions about the community and the place of the offender and the victim within it, which need critical analysis. Further, if the criminal law and its sanctions are said to be consistently balanced on degrees of fault and of harm, then selective law enforcement by police and differential and individualised sentences based on the subjective nature of each offender and the crime may challenge any such objective notion of criminal justice.

A more critical approach to the relationship between crime and the criminal justice process sees the criminal law, its institutions and processes, as merely part of the authority frameworks of the state. The reliance of the

---

4   Findlay 1999, Chapter 6.
5   See Part I, Chapter 2, pp. 21–4.
6   See Findlay et al. 1999, Chapter 1.

legislature on penal provisions to back up so many statutory obligations seems to support such an interpretation. However, the position that the criminal sanction is simply the tool of state authority ignores the large degree to which the criminal law reflects a community consensus on crime and its control. In addition, this form of analysis tends to suggest that the concept of crime, and the need to punish, cannot exist independently of the state, and this may be overstating the state's role in the control process. Finally, to conceive of criminal justice as repression ignores the many situations in which it protects and ensures the rights of the victim and the accused, as well as those of the state.

Sources, prescriptions and influences on the criminal law

Criminal law in Australia was, following European settlement, an introduced framework of doctrines, principles and processes, which had evolved in and for another place and another time. Punishment through the criminal sanction of transportation was one motivation behind the establishment of European settlement here.

An Australian criminal law is difficult to argue for. The multicultural experience of Australia over the past century has strained a process of criminal justice that is English in its roots, class-based in its operation, distanced from the community in its language, and often discriminatory in its outcomes. The disproportionate involvement of Aboriginal people in the Australian criminal justice system attests to this in a very stark fashion.

The professionalisation of criminal justice further removes it from the society it is intended to serve. Recent restrictions on access to justice exaggerate this selective displacement.[7]

The engagement between statute and judge-made law is more than simply a question of the separation of powers. The various interests and pressures that are brought to bear on parliament and the judiciary[8] have the potential further to marginalise criminal justice. Recent law reform initiatives in Australia have identified the power of the media and special interest groups in reshaping criminal justice. The sensitivity of the judiciary to public and political criticism has led to common law being confronted by the one-dimensional demands of *law and order* politics.[9]

The primary forces for change in the recent history of Australian criminal law have included:

- the Commonwealth's push for the codification of legal principles and doctrines;

---

7 See Findlay et al. 1999, Chapter 3.
8 In reference to the exercise of judicial discretion in particular, see Zdenkowski 2000.
9 See Hogg and Brown 1998, Chapters 1, 2, and 6.

- the influence of law and order politics;[10]
- the contest between the legislature and the judiciary to control judicial discretion;
- moves by the High Court to recognise native law;
- the emergence of international criminal law and criminal justice;
- national efforts to control the drug problem;
- the disempowerment of law reform bodies.

Categories of crime

Crimes are often classified in terms of the behaviour associated with their commission, and the consequential harm. The most serious (at least in terms of police energies applied to their investigation, and the resultant punishment) are offences involving death or serious personal injury. The seriousness of homicide in terms of community harm might be a factor in policy decisions taken in relation to tax evasion, corporate fraud, and environmental crime. The attitude of the public and the prioritisation of resources and effort within criminal justice institutions do not reflect this. Offences against the person are generally deemed to require a substantial investment of criminal justice investigation and control. Recently the distinctions between these offences have been sophisticated, focusing on degrees of aggravation. These are measured in terms of the circumstances surrounding the commission of the offence, and particular consequences arising from it.

Traffic offences occupy the greatest proportion of police and court time. They are the circumstances in which the citizen is most likely to come into contact with the criminal law and with justice agencies. Even so, they are generally not regarded as a serious concern within criminal justice or the community.[11]

Occupational health and safety is an area of growing social harm and along with traffic, the context most likely to involve death or serious personal injury for criminal justice to determine. During the industrial revolution this was a fertile ground for the early development of regulatory offences. In addition, it was an initial area of concern for police in their inspectorial function. Recently, however, there has been some confusion over whether this should be the province of the civil or the criminal jurisdiction.

From their initial involvement in criminal justice, the state police have set out to protect public order. Offences in public places and breaches of the peace have brought about conflict between the police and young people,

---

10 See Findlay et al. 1999, Preface to 2nd edition.
11 Until recently this has been evidenced in the ambiguous manner in which the courts have treated the sentencing of traffic offences where death has ensued. Judicial guidelines from the appeal courts (such as in *Jurisic* (1998) 110 A Crim R 259) are an attempt to rebalance state reaction to these offences in the light of growing public concern.

Aboriginals, the unemployed, and all sorts of marginalised groups. The question of whose order is being policed plagues this category of the criminal law. Much the same criticism could be directed towards what has come to be known as crimes against the state. In whose interests are these offences policed, prosecuted and punished?

Property offences (along with traffic) are a staple concern for the police and the lower courts. Some commentators hold that the criminal law has little effective place in the regulation of private property relations due to the tendency to concentrate on the crimes of the poor and powerless.[12] They argue that many instances which currently are managed by the police and the courts would be more effectively settled as commercial relationships. Further, if criminal justice is to intervene in deception and appropriation situations, then this should extend equally to the business end of town. What this contention does not recognise is the common connection between property crime and other offences such as those involving drugs and violence. This may provide sufficient reason for its inclusion as a province of criminal justice. Any critical analysis of property crime needs reflection on the disproportionate interest of criminal justice in the circumstances surrounding minor property crime.

Environmental offences are a recent focus for regulation through the criminal law. The application of strict liability (see pp. 97–101) in order to ensure the vicarious liability of employers and corporations (see pp. 106–10), has been a feature of this development. As corporate liability is regularly at issue with environmental offences, the issue of effective sanctions beyond the liability of the individual militates against the criminal law as a practical control mechanism.

Paternalistic offences or what are sometimes referred to as victimless crimes have caused debate about the overreach of the criminal law. Particularly with drug law enforcement, the criminalisation of certain forms of drug use has exacerbated the drugs–crime link. This presents a problem for those formulating policy, legislators, and law enforcement institutions in recognising that the criminal law, its enforcement and its penalties have a capacity to produce as well as prevent and control crime.

Perimeters of criminal responsibility

The criminal law and the sanctions it imposes are not limitless in terms of either their impact or their resourcing. As a modern social regulator the criminal law creates boundaries within which certain behaviour is permitted and tolerated, and beyond which selective law enforcement and punishment is available and directed.

---

12 See Brown et al. 2001, Chapter 10.

The *social defence* dimension of the criminal justice is crucial for notions of the community and its governance, which rely on consensus and social contract as the explanations for social cohesion. This might explain the popularity of the criminal law, law enforcement and penalties as devices employed by legislators to maintain social order. Consistent with the philosophy underpinning criminal justice in Australia—a philosophy which rests on the rational choice of crime and the state's consequential right and obligation to punish—is the expectation that even the selective application of criminal justice will prevent or control crime. Therefore, the criminal law and its institutions of justice are justified in utilitarian (social defence) terms, as well as through their essential place within modern bureaucratic government.

The individualisation of criminal liability in our system concentrates on the conduct and fault of the offender. Broader notions of social responsibility may be far less prevalent in the criminal law than in other forms of legal regulation.

Since the nineteenth century the criminal courts have countenanced considerations of qualified capacity, and of justification and excuse, which have enabled the individuality and variety of offenders to find some limited judicial consideration. Even so, the ideology of the rational and responsible accused continues to underlie rationales for punishment. This ideology, and recent political policies of *getting tough on crime*,[13] have seen the legislatures in Australia in particular move away from broad interpretations of defences (see Topics 16–19).

Elements of criminal responsibility

Despite the realisation that each offence may require particular proofs, general elements of liability prevail. The conduct of the accused, the circumstances in which it occurs, and its consequences comprise the external elements of the offence. Fault usually resides in the accused's mental state, and the consequences flowing from it.[14]

In order for liability to be established the external element of the offence must be caused by the accused. This must coincide with his fault. In certain situations conduct and fault may be conceded but liability denied through the establishment of justification or excuse.

Extensions of responsibility

Individual responsibility is extended through the law on complicity and the determination of secondary parties to a crime. In addition, preparatory

---

13 See Hogg and Brown 1998.
14 Exceptions to this exist in absolute and strict liability, negligence, and vicarious and corporate liability.

offences such as attempt and conspiracy remove liability from the commission of a substantive offence (see Topic 10). Identification and delegation are conditions through which corporations and employers may become vicariously liable (see Topic 10).

CONTEXT OF THE PROBLEM

The following problem addresses euthanasia. The point of view of the close relative, the suffering of the patient, the professional conduct of the doctor, and the obligations of the state are inseparable. A range of issues such as withholding or withdrawing treatment, conscious procedures for the termination of life, the rights and wishes of the patient, the sanctity of human life, the morality of suicide (and assisting suicide),[15] and obligations to protect against it, are all raised by the fact scenario.

In the Northern Territory an attempt to open the opportunity for the statutory permissibility of mercy killing[16] has been closed by the extraordinary intervention of Federal Parliament.[17] More recently, the legislative options for euthanasia have been debated inconclusively in Victoria. The medical profession and the community remain divided over the issue, and law enforcement practices reflect this ambivalence.

Euthanasia reveals the struggle between legality and morality over the most appropriate motivation for the criminal sanction. It also suggests the symbolic nature of the sanction, when a significant proportion of the medical and general community withdraw their support from its application, or oppose it through action.

PROBLEM

David's mother is dying of cancer. She has been suffering extreme pain for several years and despite recent radical medical treatment, there seems to be little that the doctors can do to reduce her discomfort. Her advanced years make it risky to carry out further surgery and in any case the cancer is too far advanced to warrant such intervention.

For months now David's mother has begged her son to assist in her suicide. He has resisted her pressure despite his deep distress at seeing her suffer. One afternoon David overheard her making a similar request of her doctor. The doctor replied that despite his sympathy for her position his ethics as a doctor prevent him from taking life. In addition, he stated that

---

15 An example of the legal position is found in *Crimes Act* (NSW), s. 31C—Aiding and abetting suicide.

16 *Rights of the Terminally Ill Act 1995* (NT), s. 7(1)(a), allowing doctors to assist in the termination of an adult's life, and the provision of safeguards thereto.

17 *Euthanasia Laws Act 1997* (Cth).

no law in New South Wales would relieve a doctor of criminal liability if he assisted in a suicide.

The following day David's mother again begged her son to help her die, and again he refused. With this the old woman called her son a coward and a disgrace to the memory of his dead father. David had been having nightmares for weeks about his mother's death and he feared he was losing his mind under the pressure. Distraught, confused, and desperately wanting to silence her nagging, David lashed out with his fist and struck his mother on the face, knocking her to the floor. Fearing that he had killed his mother and in a state of blind panic, David set fire to the room in order to conceal the evidence. In fact the woman was only unconscious but a later coronial inquiry revealed that she died as a result of smoke inhalation.

Consider the following questions:

1   Should David have assisted his mother in her suicide? If not, why not?
2   Should the criminal law be used to discourage suicide or euthanasia? If so, how would it achieve this?
3   Do the moral and legal issues in assisting the old woman's death correspond here?
4   As the facts stand, should David be held criminally liable for the death of his mother? What issues have influenced you in this decision?

ENGAGING THE PROBLEM

The mother is the victim for which a legislative response such as the recent Northern Territory legislation was constructed. Were it in her power she would commit suicide, and neither common law nor legislation in Australia would hold her liable for the act, or even for attempting it.[18]

Realising her need for assistance she encourages, incites, coerces, and some might say even provokes her son to carry out her wishes.

She dies, but as much from the mistake or neglect of the son as from his intended conduct. What causes the woman's death, and whether the son's assault or arson coincides with the mental state necessary for a charge of homicide are at issue.

Further, there is a question of what the son actually knew about the nature and quality of his actions in deciding whether to assist in the taking of his mother's life. What his mental state was at the time he struck his mother will have some influence on the determination of his fault.

---

18   Not so for someone assisting a suicide or its attempt—see, for instance *Crimes Act* (NSW), s. 31C—Aiding and abetting suicide.

The prosecution would seek to establish a charge of homicide (murder[19] or manslaughter[20]). The defence would say that the death was not caused by (or was not a natural and foreseeable consequence of) the son's conduct. Also, he did not possess the required mental state at the time she died. In fact they may challenge his capacity to commit the offence. The prosecution would reply by arguing that the son's conduct was substantially connected to the death, and that he was negligent in not checking to see if she was still alive before he set the fire. The son might want to raise a justification or excuse.[21] Should the accused be convicted, the defence will raise in mitigation a range of pressures and obligations weighing on the son's ability to act reasonably and responsibly.

Irrespective of the legal outcome of this problem, moral issues will influence the judge, and the community, in receiving and evaluating the legal outcome. Some say that the criminal sanction is an essential moral statement here, even if it is not a deterrent. Others say that it is non-enforcement of the law, and the ambivalence of the community regarding the use of the criminal sanction here, which undermine the real significance of the criminal law.

The unresolved moral dimension of euthanasia is perhaps well represented through current selective enforcement practice when it comes to policing doctors and families who assist suicide. This nascent tolerance, however, tends to forestall the conflict between law and morality which the euthanasia challenge to the law as it stands would otherwise demand. It also conceals (or masks) the need to critically evaluate the real impact of the criminal sanction in regulating controversial social behaviours, as well as its appropriateness where the law is paternal.

TOPIC 2

COLONISATION AND THE IMPOSITION OF THE CRIMINAL LAW

The criminal law of Australia, in the sense of constitutional legality,[22] is a recent creation. Even up until the end of the nineteenth century it largely

---

19 … where the son intended to kill the mother, or to seriously injure her when the consequence was death. Murder might also stand where the son acted in a way where he had a reckless disregard as to her death and where he foresaw as probable her death resulting from the serious injury he inflicted upon her.

20 Death caused by the act or omission of the son, which was unlawful and dangerous, and which the son performed recklessly or with a negligent disregard for the life or well-being of the mother.

21 That he was not acting voluntarily, that he was acting under an irresistible impulse, that his responsibility was diminished because his mind was not normal, etc.

22 By this I mean law formulated through the legislatures and courts of a constitutionally authorised system of government. It also suggests formal laws that are written and procedural. .

mirrored the laws and legal thinking of England. As an introduced system of law it was imposed on an indigenous population who have been denied any real influence over its development.

Criminal law and the institutions of the criminal process have been and remain important mechanisms and vehicles for colonisation in Australia. The repression of indigenous peoples and culture has been authorised through the criminal law and effected through white man's justice. The double standards of colonial justice saw the police and the courts penalising Aboriginal people for behaviour that would have been ignored or condoned in white settlers. The policing of Aboriginal people has been one aspect of treatment that amounts to genocide. The criminal justice process continues their alienation through the massive over-representation of indigenous people in our courts and penal institutions.

The relationship between law and custom is profoundly significant for the contextualisation of criminal law in Australia. This not only relates to parallel systems of regulation by the state and within Aboriginal communities. Australia as a multicultural society faces the challenge of recognising important cultural controls and expectations within the framework of criminal law and process, which is said to recognise the rights of the accused, protect the community, and have regard to the victim. The extent to which introduced law and custom can appropriately and even practically intersect is an often unrecognised consideration for universalised legal systems in post-colonial situations such as Australia. This may be more so for the criminal law, growing in its importance as a source of social regulation in modern Australia.

Aboriginal law and custom

As with the distinction between law and custom generally, the declaration that Aboriginal tribal societies possessed (and possess) law has depended on the perspective of introduced law and its authority. Up until the recent High Court decisions on the recognition of native land title, introduced law and its institutions have resisted the notion of Aboriginal law.[23] Beyond racism and colonial power, they have rested this view on the absence of structural similarities in Aboriginal culture that could be equated or identified with legality in English culture. This ethnocentric position makes any sympathetic or informed discourse on Aboriginal law impossible to argue in courts so disposed.

When looking at the law's responsibility to recognise and protect Aboriginal culture, representatives of introduced law have squabbled

---

23 See *Cooper v. Stewart* (1889) 14 App Cas 286; *Wedge* (1976) 1 NSWLR 581; *Walker* (1988) 38 A Crim R 150; *Glass* (1993) 63 Abor. L Bull 18.

over what defines and determines *Aborigine*. Conventional *blood-relation* definitions have been rejected in favour of a constitutional approach that recognises Aboriginality in a person of Aboriginal descent who identifies himself or herself as Aboriginal and is recognised as such by the Aboriginal community.[24]

What separates custom from law? Principally, it is the distinction between oral and written traditions. When conceptualising law for Aboriginal custom it is *law* rather than *laws* which requires understanding and legitimacy. Here law represents the unity and immutability of custom rather than the plurality and change featuring in constitutional legality.

The power of one legal tradition over another is evidenced through the authority of introduced legal institutions to declare what will be accepted as law and custom. It is the power to declare and distinguish which constitutes the cultural authority of one perspective over the other. This power is essentially political and repressive, and may have little to do with relative qualities or legitimacy. The process of recognition, or more likely denial, is inherently colonial.[25] Non-recognition continues to undermine the existence and value of fragile traditions. Additionally, non-recognition may lead to injustice when conflicting obligations and proscriptions are reinterpreted or denied legal significance. Aboriginal people in Australia support recognition of their laws, and have suggested processes for coexistence and reconciliation. The struggle for the recognition of land rights and their anticipated coexistence with competing forms of title is an example of this.

Custom has a control potential within Aboriginal communities which recognition might enhance. Particularly for Aboriginal youth who have little exposure to their traditional customs, recognition of the value of customary penalty, for instance, might add a more potent layer to socialisation even in modern urban societies. In addition, it might represent tradition as having a contemporary relevance.

Recognition of Aboriginal custom as law has the potential to compensate for the past injustice that profited from a denial of the existence and integrity of Aboriginal culture. In keeping with this, recognition is consistent with Australia's international obligations.[26]

---

24 Constitution s. 51 (26); *Commonwealth v. Tasmania* (1983) 158 CLR 1 at 274.
25 That is, there is no existence or legitimacy without recognition from the introduced and imposed institutions of government.
26 In making this observation it is important to reflect on the aberrant position recently taken by the Australian government with respect to the United Nations' oversight of convention compliance. Alienation from the UN committee system has largely arisen from the government's reaction to criticism of Australia's record on human rights for Aboriginal people.

Custom and modern rights and obligations

Essential to the contemporary value of custom is the recognition that custom is dynamic. Custom needs to operate within and not beyond dominant cultures. This may call for adaptation and refinement. For instance, custom may not stand when shown to be fundamentally regressive or discriminatory, where a dominant culture values and protects individualised rights.[27]

When reflecting on the relationship between custom and contemporary rights, the question arises: whose rights and whose version of rights? Are we looking at the international lawyers' distinction between first- versus third-generation rights (individualised versus collective or collaborative rights)? And how does one resolve the conflict between competing positions on rights, against a background of custom?

Criminal law

The chronic over-representation of Aboriginal people within the workings of the criminal law cannot be explained away by the perpetual clash between customs, cultures and traditions. Wider issues which influence the exercise of police discretion, in particular, require sensitive investigation to understand how the criminal law acts as an agent of discrimination.

Even when the offences for which Aboriginal people may be charged involve traditional dimensions or obligations, these may be exacerbated by non-customary influences such as alcohol. Alcohol abuse is a strong causal factor in Aboriginal criminality, and if it is true that Aboriginal alcohol abusers are uniquely susceptible to the antisocial consequences of this drug, then culture clash may have some bearing on this recognised path to the attention of the criminal law.[28]

Custom has particular resonance for matters of justification and excuse. Therefore, Aboriginal women might raise issues of traditional and contemporary custom to explain their unique status as violence victims, and their retaliation. More commonly, matters concerning custom obligation are raised to explain and mitigate behaviour which under introduced law may be criminal, and beyond the justification of its limited range of defences. If a better reconciliation were possible between custom-based obligation and the criminal law, and the law better reflected the sanctioning concerns of indigenous people, then there would be less likelihood of the law being rejected or taken into their own hands.

---

27 It is a constant problem for the introduction of rights protections which grow from individual rights paradigms. An example is the tension between the customs of first nation peoples in Canada, and the recently crafted and introduced *Charter of Rights and Freedoms*.

28 There is ample evidence of the correlation between alcohol abuse and crime, particularly violent crime.

The significance of custom punishment as a mitigating factor in sentence has been recognised by the state and territory courts. A major problem with any further recognition is any challenge to the state's monopoly over justice resolutions and the competing *legalities* this may produce.

Perhaps the most significant advance for the criminal law, away from its application as a discriminatory and repressive mechanism, has been the eventual abolition of special 'protective' regimes. These required police interference with Aboriginal lives and communities and violated a conventional premise of the criminal law: that it was not for preventive interventions. More vicious was the reality that through the intervention of state agencies, indigenous tribal family life was criminalised.

Specialised process

Recently, several Australian jurisdictions have introduced into their legislation governing police practice special protections for the Aboriginal accused.[29] These recognise particular vulnerabilities for Aboriginals in custody.[30]

Further, recognition of the unique safety issues involved in the custodial detention of Aboriginal people throughout Australia has led to the recommendation of special provisions governing bail for Aboriginal people.[31]

History of the common law
Criminal law and industrialisation

The criminal law as a significant jurisdiction in common law is relatively recent. Dependent as the criminal law is on the sources of statute and case-law, the emergence and establishment of this jurisdiction depended on an active legislature, and courts which valued criminal practice and jurisprudence.

The permanent location of the King's courts in England and the empowerment of parliament during and following the English Civil War saw a consolidation and expansion of the criminal jurisdiction. The evolution of private property rights before and during the industrial revolution stimulated the intervention of the criminal sanction, and saw the emergence of new criminal justice agencies, such as the police, to protect the new wealth. The criminal law was well recognised as an important control device for the legislature and the courts by the time Australia was colonised. The criminal sanction accompanied the First Fleet as a stimulus for colonisation and a framework for colonial power.

---

29 For example, *Police Powers and Responsibilities Act 1997* (Qld), s. 96.
30 For example, *Crimes (Detention After Arrest) Regulations 1998* (NSW), Part 4.
31 For example, Council for Aboriginal Reconciliation, *National Report: Aboriginal Disadvantage in Meeting Bail Criteria*, Reconciliation and Social Justice Project.

Colonial criminal law in the Australian jurisdictions was a feature of the centralisation of political and administrative power. Initially the role of the governors was to legislate and the job of the military to punish. The Aboriginal population was subjugated by the guns of the settlers but also by the jurisdiction of the rural magistrates, the terror of the border police, and the *protective* decimation by successive colonial executives and religious orders (as evidenced in the stolen generations).

The criminal law and the agencies of criminal justice were employed by colonial administrators to dispossess the Aboriginal people of their land and claims to it. In any case, as courts up to *Mabo* have held, the communal and transient connection of native title could not be comprehended under English law and therefore was denied. The criminal sanction was a technique for then denying occupancy to Aboriginals across Australia. Without concepts of ownership and commercial use, Aboriginal custodians were constantly prevented from claiming legitimate interests in the land across which they had walked and sung for centuries.

The *rule of law* ideology essential for the legitimacy of introduced government relied on criminal law and its punishments to deny and suppress challenge. This ideology also claimed responsibility for (and over) all inhabitants of Australia. It imposed residual and consequent responsibilities on those who enjoyed its protection (even if such enjoyment was clearly partial and initially not shared by Aboriginal people).

As a consequence of the prerogative of mercy, on which the criminal sanction was originally exercised and moderated under English law, the power of the courts and judges expanded through their dominion over the criminal jurisdiction. Mercy was the face of the criminal law turned to Aboriginal accused rather than (until recently) a legal or procedural recognition of their unique vulnerability before the criminal law.

Supremacy of discretion

Criminal justice relies on the exercise of discretion, at a variety of sites within the process. The motivation behind the exercise of discretion in criminal justice may be analysed at individual and institutional levels. Discrimination against Aboriginal interests evolves within both of these frameworks for discretion. The reason for such discrimination may be broad-based and beyond the responsibilities of criminal justice alone. However, discrimination based on race and culture becomes far more potent within criminal justice in terms of the intrusive powers that it contains and directs.

In addition, the exercise of discretion within criminal justice is conventionally difficult to regulate and make accountable. This is particularly so where the exercise of discretion is not highly visible, occurs on a one-to-one basis, and is directed against marginalised segments of the community.

Terra nullius: Legal fictions and their consequences

Put simply, the doctrine of *terra nullius*, subscribed to until recently in all Australian courts, suggested that at the time of colonisation Australia was devoid of human life and habitation. This enabled the law, and the doctrines and interpretation of the courts, to dispossess Aboriginal people of their lands.

Up until the High Court decision in *Mabo,* judicial opinion was that Australia was a series of settled colonies, rather than a conquered nation which required a treaty to formalise the accession. As a consequence, Aboriginal races were not adequately recognised or protected under state laws or the federal Constitution. Little or no attempt was made to recognise and formulate compensation for the loss of native title. Having been deprived of their most valuable asset by colonial settlers, Aboriginal people were never in a position to claim commercial entitlements or to bargain for rights and recognition as citizens on an equal footing in the new nation. As for their status under the criminal law, Aboriginal people were unable to claim the conventional common law protections for a victim or an accused. They were beyond the law's grace but not its terror.

Terra nullius implied no laws predating colonial settlement, no rights to be claimed by the native occupants, because there were no people worthy of an existence and identity under introduced law. This profound and prevailing denial of Aboriginal existence created an environment in which cultural and physical genocide was not actionable at law. The impact of this for the reinterpretation of settler–Aborigine interaction was profound. Extermination, which produced a destruction of culture through colonisation, and later through what has become known as the 'stolen generations', had no reality in law right up until Australia's international obligations demanded a retreat from this arrogant legal fiction. Even so, some might say that the debate surrounding a new Constitution for an Australian Republic, and the political resistance to claims for a somewhat belated treaty relationship between black and white Australia, suggest that the *terra nullius* doctrine remains a subtle but influential factor in modern conservative Australian politics.

Another consequence of the *terra nullius* doctrine was its potential to deny the existence of a war between the Aboriginal people and the settlers. Even where this took on the dimensions of systematic extermination such as in Tasmania, the settlers and their governments could not be called to account, beyond selective prosecutions, for individual incidents of excessive and too public violence. In the twentieth century the paradox between *terra nullius* and the growing *Aboriginal problem* led to a transition from policies of *pacification* to those of *protection*.

At the same moment that the law was working from assumptions of *terra nullius*, it was declaring Aboriginal custom criminal. This worked at all levels of individual and communal experience and attacked fundamental structures of Aboriginal life such as the family. The Aboriginal settlement policies which ghettoised Aboriginal culture tended to intensify the impact of the white man's criminal justice, and the influences of white society such as alcohol abuse increased the likelihood of Aboriginal people coming into contact with the criminal justice process.

Penal colony criminal justice

Initially the laws and processes of colonial criminal justice in Australia were directed at the pacification and containment of the convict population, and the promotion of the commercial and community interests of the colony and its white settlers. The evolution of policing and the courts in particular reflected these priorities.[32]

The division between military and civil order in the early days of the colonies was at best blurred, and commonly non-existent. There evolved a mutuality of interest between the protection of the state and protection of its citizens—among whom Aboriginal people were not included.

The criminal classes in Australia have shifted from the convict émigrés to the native inhabitants. The criminal inheritance has shifted from the crimes introduced with white settlers to the crimes within Aboriginal society exacerbated by the ravages of white culture, and the discriminatory application of white man's criminal justice. Crimes by Aboriginal people against introduced law and culture are portrayed as the legitimate concern of criminal justice. Crimes against the Aboriginal people and their culture have never been recognised with the same legal certainty and priority.

As noted earlier, one of the indicators and facilitators of the emergence of the independent political state within Australia has been the evolution of law that the state monopolises in its own interests. The criminal law and its process are now a major concern for parliaments, and stand as a reflection of community interest in the outcomes criminal justice is meant to ensure. These can vary, from fundamentals such as street cleaning (where the use of public space by Aboriginal people is constantly challenged) through to a refusal to protect the property rights of certain classes within society in the face of the interests of other more powerful groups (e.g. the claims of traditional land owners against government-sponsored mining interests).[33]

---

32 For a wider discussion of these themes, see D. Neal, *The Rule of Law in a Penal Colony: Law and Power in early NSW*, Cambridge University Press, Melbourne, 1991; M. Finnane, *Punishment in Australian Society*, Oxford University Press, Melbourne, 1997.

33 Note the political compromises in this area when it comes to the settling of state and territory native title legislation, in particular the recent agreement between the Federal Opposition and the Queensland Labor Government.

Application of Anglo-Australian laws to Aboriginal people

A range of structural components of introduced criminal law present an uncomfortable fit with traditional Aboriginal culture. These include the following.

Criminal intent

To establish criminal liability within introduced criminal law, the courts look for a designated individual mental state. The mind of the accused person as a collective entity, arising from community obligation and shared interests, is not well reflected within English criminal law traditions. In addition, the fine distinctions between nominated mental states are difficult enough to translate into complex situations of contemporary society. Where the mind of the accused is effectively determined by cultural conditions which celebrate collective rather than individual decision-making, these distinctions may have less relevance and be less convincing indicators of individualised fault.

Offence distinctions

The problematic nature of offence distinctions is well evidenced by property offences which rely on concepts of personal ownership, and their questionable relevance for cultures where either there is no Western notion of private property, or where communal interests prevail. The criminal law is neither likely to protect Aboriginal people from such a cultural context with regard to property ownership, nor to punish them in any way comparable with offenders from a property-based culture.

Objective tests for defences

The reasonable or 'ordinary' person measures for liability or defences will always discriminate against minorities, even where characteristics of personality and culture are taken into account to a limited degree.[34] Recent attempts to introduce into the *ordinary person* concept personal characteristics of the accused recognise the problem, in part. However, the reluctance to accept issues such as susceptibility to alcohol or excitability in particular situations has meant that this personalisation of the test may still ignore important features of particular cultural groups, and that they may continue to be overrepresented in encounters with the criminal law.[35]

---

34 A recent example of this limited approach can be found in *Green* (1997) 148 ALR 659.

35 Also it is unclear whether the courts would accept Aboriginal customary obligation as the foundation for constructing defences such as duress and necessity—see Rush and Yeo 2000; *Warren, Coombes and Tucker* (1996) 88 A Crim R 78.

Strict liability

Those offences in which component issues of fault are not considered, or where due diligence may not be advanced as an answer to liability, seem to discriminate against those minorities in society who do not necessarily benefit from *ordinary* evaluations of competence or responsibility. In addition, regulatory offences usually are designed to protect the best interests of the majority rather than those of minorities. They are heavily reliant on the need to ensure private property rights, and the control interests of the state.

Public order and street offences

With the marginalisation of urban Aboriginals, and the apartheid-like segregation of blacks from whites in country towns, the public domain is now the location for many of the Aboriginal recreations that white Australians may prefer to pursue in pubs and registered clubs. If drinking alcohol in a public place is deemed to be disorderly, then Aboriginals will be more likely to come in contact with the police on this level because of the laws' designation and segregation of private and public space.

Legal representation

The creation of Aboriginal legal services throughout Australia was a clear recognition of the special needs of Aboriginal people when it comes to legal representation, as well as the impediments facing Aboriginals in seeking access to legal services. Given the reality of Aboriginal offenders as *career criminals*,[36] legal representation is both more essential and more demanding. Without such representation it is difficult for the individual Aboriginal offender to confront and resist the institutionalised racism within all levels of criminal justice.

Custody

As the Royal Commission into Aboriginal Deaths in Custody shockingly revealed, the risks to the health and well-being of Aboriginal detainees, in police custody in particular, are extreme. It is more likely that Aboriginals will die in custody than whites, and remembering that they are more regularly detained for drunkenness, refused bail, and given custodial sentences than whites, this correlation will be compounded. It appears to be the experience of custody itself that is so dangerous to Aboriginal people. Almost half of those who die do so within three months of the commencement of detention.

---

36 This is so in the sense that they are likely to have progressed through juvenile institutions to adult jail for minor crimes, are repeat offenders, and have a history of guilty pleas and bad relations with the police.

Juries

Relative to their over-representation as accused persons before the courts, Aboriginal people are significantly under-represented as jurors.[37] If juries are supposed to be comprised of one's peers, and to be representative of the interests of the whole community as well as those more likely to be criminalised, then they have failed Aboriginal accused on these measures.

A reason for the absence of Aboriginal people on juries is the manner of selection. For instance, selection from those listed on the electoral roll or from those living within a nominated radius of a jury trial court may work against the inclusion of Aboriginal people.

Suspicion of and alienation from the processes of criminal justice, including poor Aboriginal–police relations, is an obvious factor in Aboriginal citizens' disinclination to perform their responsibilities as jurors. For those who do front up to court for the purpose, their Aboriginality may be a trigger for challenge.

Over-representation and deaths in custody

The over-representation of Aboriginal people within the criminal justice system in all Australian jurisdictions and the consequent correlation with deaths in custody can be explained in terms of:

- the history of Aboriginal dispossession, and the institutional racism which has been a feature of poor Aboriginal–police relations;
- racism in the criminal justice system generally, as much as it has been both a historical and recent predisposition for white Australia;
- the current socioeconomic position of Aboriginal people, particularly within the cities, leading to the social marginalisation of Aboriginal youth and the destruction of Aboriginal communities through drug and alcohol abuse;
- the public–private space divide, which has the greatest impact in situations of alcohol and drug consumption, and for Aboriginal youth; and
- Aboriginal–police relations, which have never recovered from the role played by the police in the stolen generations saga.

The over-representation problem becomes more stark and disturbing in the realm of Aboriginal youth. The proportion of Aboriginal youths in custody relative to non-Aboriginal youths is even higher than the disproportion between white and black adults. In terms of ongoing criminality, the fact that offenders are more likely to be given a custodial sentence if they have a

---

37 See Findlay 1994 *Jury Management in NSW*.

history of juvenile confinement means that Aboriginals go to prison more often than whites. And prisons produce crime and criminals.

An analysis of the over-representation cannot stop at the recognition of a simple disproportion in rates of imprisonment. One needs also to consider:

- *Nature of offence:* It is likely that Aboriginals will be arrested, charged, refused bail, convicted and imprisoned for the same offences for which non-Aboriginals will be given the benefit of some favourable discretion.
- *Age of offender:* Aboriginals are detained, convicted and imprisoned at much younger ages than non-Aboriginal offenders.
- *Repetition of offences:* Aboriginal offenders are more likely than whites to be arrested and prosecuted for the same repeated offence.
- *Custodial experience:* Aboriginal suspects and offenders end up in custody more often than non-Aboriginals.
- *Regularity of reception into prison:* The revolving door of the prison is more likely to pick up Aboriginal offenders than other groups in society.

Impact of *Mabo*

While Stanley Yeo[38] argues that there may not be a distinct criminal jurisdiction in Aboriginal customary law, he describes a trend for the recognition and coexistence of custom-based sanctions. This could lead to the emergence of a sympathetic understanding of the mechanisms for social control in traditional Aboriginal society, beyond anything that the Australian criminal courts are currently contemplating. In this respect it is not helpful for the courts to focus, as they have, on what was extinguished at settlement, as well as what was more recently extinguished by the Codes and other criminal legislation. This emphasis tends to conceptualise the relationship between Aboriginal custom and social regulation as only valid or legal if it is endorsed or recognise by introduced law.

The approach taken by the High Court in *Mabo* to the question of Aboriginal law may be viewed as revitalised relevance for custom-based sanctions and social regulations for Aboriginal Australia. That decision proposed a structured approach which the courts could follow when determining whether a particular area of native law or form of native jurisdiction exists. By recognising that Aboriginal laws exist as a complex regulatory system, and by suggesting that the contemporary common law of Australia could recognise and incorporate this system in preference to current notions of justice, rights, and freedoms, the High Court anticipates the emergence of a criminal jurisprudence in Australia wherein Aboriginal people and cultures have a place.

---

38 S. Yeo, 'Native Criminal Justice After *Mabo*' (1994) *Current Issues in Criminal Justice* 26.

CONTEXT OF THE PROBLEM

The following scenarios revolve around tensions between custom and introduced law. In jurisdictions within and beyond Australia,[39] the role of constitutional legality in protecting the rights of native peoples and enabling them to protect their community responsibilities is juxtaposed against possible resolutions in custom. The problems raise wide concerns about how individuals and communities can counter the limitations and discrimination of imposed legal systems. Further, individual expectations about rights and responsibilities are contrasted with the obligations of custom. This not only produces challenges to static visions of custom and its hierarchies of power and authority, but also recognises contemporary issues of age, gender, and the place of the individual within many different communities in daily life. Such consideration of the place of the law and its formal institutions within the social control of custom-based communities should provoke a broad consideration of the purpose of the law and realistic expectations for criminal justice.

PROBLEM

Consider the following scenarios:

1 Mere is an Aboriginal mother living in a rural settlement in north-western New South Wales. Her teenage son is a chronic alcohol abuser and recently has been involved in petty theft from people in his own community. The tribal elders have tolerated the son's behaviour up until his most recent transgression but they have now informed Mere that they will be forced to call in the police to deal with her son. Realising the effect that her son's prior criminal record would have on his case before the courts and fearful of what he might do to himself in prison, she begs the elders to impose a traditional penalty. Reconciliation with the victim is an option, as is spearing.[40] Discuss the appropriateness of traditional or state-based penalties in this regard.

2 First Nation people in northern Canada have recently sought and gained concessions to form their own government within the Canadian federation. There is some debate, however, as to whether the Canadian *Charter of Rights and Freedoms* should apply to this *nation* irrespective of the traditional values which the new government will enshrine. Canadian First Nation custom seems likely to discriminate against women in light of the Charter of Rights. How would you resolve this dilemma?

---

39 It was the intention in going outside Australia that the student should realise the more universal nature of problems between custom and introduced law. The problems do not presuppose any knowledge of the laws that operate in these other jurisdictions.

40 Aboriginal custom-based penalties largely focus on physical punishment of the body or banishment. The community may seek reconciliation, restitution, apology or a demonstration of contrition.

3　In Fiji a magistrate can require that a violent husband should *reconcile* with his abused wife rather than impose another penalty. The woman is required to return to court and confirm that the reconciliation has been accepted for proceedings against the abuser to be suspended. What difficulties do you envisage with using such customary penalties in a modern context?

4　Fale is a Western Samoan who has spent all his school years in Auckland before returning to his village in Western Samoa. His family is the subject of a banishment order handed down by the village council, and confirmed by the Land Titles Court. Fale sees the likelihood of losing his family lands due to this *primitive custom* as outrageous, particularly when the Western Samoan Constitution confirms the rights of freedom of movement and freedom of association. What could he do?

Engaging the problem

1　What is the law for? Here we have (in problem 1) an offender whose situation exemplifies the social and criminal justice disadvantages faced by young Aboriginal males. It presents the blurred distinction between offender and victim. The criminal justice system has institutionalised his status as offender and victim both within and beyond his community. The sanctions on offer to those who wish to see the offender controlled, deterred, and reformed may have a limited effect on his re-offending, and produce unsatisfactory outcomes for the victim and the community. The need to consider the purpose of punishment and the potential for integrating penalties is posed by the problem.

2　What does the law protect and empower? The interface between custom and constitutional legality is implicit in this problem. The challenge to conceive of custom as an ever-changing social context is there, for both the drafters of constitutional instruments and the authorities in custom-based governments. Further, the status of women as emancipated citizens in a society that is at the same time customary and modern underlies the consideration of competing *laws*. How the rights and obligations inherent in these *laws* are negotiated for the individual and her community needs to be touched on.

3　Can laws operate beyond their context? This problem suggests difficulties with the integration of custom-based and more formalised justice outcomes. If introduced legal systems combine with (or extrapolate from) customary resolutions without also recognising the manner of their operation within the setting of custom, injustice may result. It is also necessary to consider what lies behind any such integration, and its potential to dilute the social impact of the custom-based resolution.

4　Which law prevails when cultures collide? If custom and its laws remain strong, this may be so because of their ability to resist the influence of competing legal systems. Where does the individual stand if he wishes to be protected by introduced legality within customary communities? It would not be enough in this problem to rely on limited and formal notions of legal *extinguishment*, or superiority of legal language and institutions. The legitimacy of contested legal traditions within traditional communities should be discussed.

ADDITIONAL RESOURCES

Brown, D., Farrier D., Egger, S. and McNamara, L., *Criminal Laws*, Federation Press, Sydney, 2001, para. 2.2.

Cunneen, C., 'The Report of the Inquiry into the death of David John Gundy; Royal Commission into Aboriginal Deaths in Custody' (1991) 3(1) *Current Issues in Criminal Justice* 143–7.

Cunneen, C., *Aboriginal Perspectives on Criminal Justice*, Institute of Criminology, Sydney, 1992, particularly Chapters 1, 2, 3, 7, 8, 9.

Cunneen, C. and Libesman, T., *Indigenous People and the Law in Australia*, Butterworths, Sydney, 1995.

Eames, G., 'Aboriginal Homicide: Customary Law Defences or Customary Lawyers Defences', in Strang, E. and Gerull, S. A., *No. 17 Homicide: Patterns, Prevention and Control*, Australian Institute of Criminology, Canberra, 1993, p. 149.

Findlay, M., 'The Ambiguity of Accountability: Deaths in Custody and the Regulation of Police Power' (1994) 6(2) *Current Issues in Criminal Justice* 234–51.

Findlay, M., Odgers, S., and Yeo, S., *Australian Criminal Justice*, Oxford University Press, Melbourne, 1999, pp. 305–12.

Lincoln, R. and Wilson, P., 'Aboriginal Offending: Patterns and Causes', in Chappell, D. and Wilson, P., *The Australian Criminal Justice System: The Mid 1990s*, Butterworths, Sydney, 1994, Chapter 3.

McDonald, D. and Cunneen, C., 'Aboriginal Incarceration and Deaths in Custody: Looking backward and looking forward' (1997) 9(1) *Current Issues in Criminal Justice* 5.

Yeo, S., 'Native Criminal Justice After *Mabo*' (1994) 6(1) *Current Issues in Criminal Justice* 9–26.

Yeo S., 'Criminal Cases in the High Court of Australia: Walker v. NSW (1994) 69 ALJR 111' (1995) *Criminal Law Journal* 160.

Tuckiar v. R (1934) 52 CLR 335

Walker v. State of NSW (1994) 182 CLR 45

Neal v. R (1982) 149 CLR 305

ADDITIONAL ISSUES

1   Read the *Tuckiar* decision and come prepared to discuss the inherent injustice associated with aspects of the trial judge's statements, and the participation of defence counsel. To what extent does the divergence between culture and values as demonstrated by the white constables, the Aboriginal defendant, the Aboriginal

witnesses, the interpreters, and the character witnesses make a 'just' trial impossible in this case?

2   Read ***Walker v. State of NSW*** (1994) 182 CLR 45 for discussion of the manner in which introduced law and courts confront a challenge to their right of jurisdiction over Aboriginal people. See also S. Yeo, 'Criminal Cases in the High Court of Australia: Walker v. NSW (1994) 69 ALJR 111' (1995) 19 *Criminal Law Journal* 160.

TOPIC 3

THE PHENOMENON OF CRIME

The environment of crime

Crime is about people, places, and situations. More importantly, however, crime should be understood in terms of relationships—between perpetrators and victims, perpetrators and their social environment, victims and the situation of the crime. Looking at crime in this way, rather than focusing on individuals and their behaviour, allows for an appreciation of the essential connections and influences that bring about crime. In addition, this approach allows for an understanding of why crime occurs where and when it does, and the opportunity better to anticipate such occurrences.

Since the early twentieth century when American researchers documented the relationship between crime and urban decay, the environment (particularly in cities) has become a crucial framework for evaluating and predicting crime.[41] Environment is itself a complex notion. The analysis of criminal justice institutions tends to concentrate on the physical and built environment. More significant, however, for the understanding of criminal behaviour and reactions to it is the social and personal environment of the community and the many groups within it, which is the setting for crime.

How do we connect crime and the environment? Generally, we work from the assumption that certain environments will stimulate, foster or attract crime (and changes in these environments may prevent crime). Further, there is the view that particular environments attract certain offenders (and types of offender), and the same for victims. Finally, there is the realisation that some crimes are more likely to be committed in certain environments.

The distinction between the physical and the built environment is helpful for evaluating the environment of crime. Obviously, the physical environment is less amenable to adjustment in order to minimise or prevent crime. Yet it is not difficult to appreciate ways in which certain policing

---

41   Downes and Rock 1998, Chapters 3 and 4.

techniques, for instance, may shift crime situations from one physical environment to another. The built environment is constantly changing and therefore crime prevention should be a feature of such development as is any other legitimate concern in environmental design and management.[42]

The connection between crime and the environment appears to be a suggestively direct and simple one. It is not. By ignoring the complexity of the relationship between crime and the environment, one can draw inaccurate conclusions about crime settings or have unrealistic expectations for the crime prevention potential of environmental change.

Crime environments are best understood by asking the question: why did this person commit an offence in this setting, and yet in the same environment someone else did not?

Crime and the community

Some communities are more criminal than others, but no community has no crime.

The other important truth to remember about the relationship between the community and crime is that by far the greater proportion of crime is tolerated by the community and never comes to police attention. Understanding what crimes we are talking about here and why this is the case will help us to appreciate community attitudes to crime and the willingness of the community to be involved in crime prevention and control.

Concepts of community are themselves often misleading or likely to confuse.[43] A community is not a homogeneous entity. Communities are comprised of many varied collections of citizens, often declaring opposing views on crime and its control. This makes the task of community policing challenging and problematic.

A product of multicultural Australia is communities divided by language and culture. In addition, the generation gap between immigrant parents and native-born children tends to alienate ethnic groups from within and without.

Understanding the place of crime in communities is further complicated where the community in question is transitional. For instance, rural Australia is suffering a divestment of services, the spread of unemployment, a wave of drug use and youth suicide, and a collapse in economic opportunity, which provides a fertile environment for crime and victimisation. In some outer suburbs of our major cities, ethnic ghettos have replaced earlier migrant settlement, producing social tension. This has been exacerbated by the shift of certain crimes, such as drug trafficking, from the inner suburbs of the city

---

42 Findlay 2001 (b)
43 See Cohen 1987.

out to the margins. Crime control is made all the more difficult as a result of the marginalisation of youth in these suburbs.

When we examine the crime characteristics of a community it is not sufficient to focus on offences alone. There is also the problem of limited law enforcement resources. In addition, patterns of victimisation and their relationship to the fear of crime within any community are significant measures for police when evaluating the appropriateness of community expectations for police action.

In order to use the community as an environment within which criminal influence might be measured, and crimes predicted, it is essential that we identify crucial characteristics that can be linked with crime. Principal among these are social demography, economy, and culture.

Age, sex, and race are the primary demographic indicators. They are essentially connected with crime in that the clearest correlation with criminality is based on age and sex. Young males between the ages of 17 and 25 commit the most crime coming to police attention in any community. If a community has a significant proportion of young males it is likely that crime rates (particularly for property and drug offences and violent crimes) will be high.

Secondary demographic indicators are things such as educational attainment, employment categories, school attendance, property ownership, periods of residency, rates of marriage, and so on. These too have specific connections with crime rates and crime types. It is a recognised fact that citizens with complex and stable social connections such as marriage, home ownership, family obligations, and secure employment are less likely to risk involvement in crime than those with loose social bonds.[44]

Another identifier of a community with a high crime rate is economy. Again, however, the connections between the economic health of a community and its members are not simple and straightforward. There is no unequivocal causal connection between poverty and crime. In particular, it seems unlikely that poverty promotes crime within communities whose members are universally poor. The relationship is more likely to be between crime and socioeconomic disparity.[45]

Culture also acts as an important community indicator. When looking at culture for the purposes of crime analysis it is necessary to employ fairly specific notions of culture. For example, there exists an obvious causal relationship between drug cultures and crime. Within ethnicity, however, there might be more direct correlations with crime. The status of women and children in certain ethnic settings has been shown to produce greater rates of domestic victimisation.

---

44 Braithwaite 1989, Chapter 2.
45 Findlay 1999, Chapters 3, 4 and 5.

Within communities there are personal, organisational, and structural characteristics which, if significantly present, may suggest the likelihood of crime. The marginalisation of individuals and groups within the wider community is one of these. A lack of organisation, whether physical or social, tends towards crime. Communities undergoing development or modernisation will be subject to new pockets of criminal behaviour.[46]

Although we have suggested there are networks of connections between crime and the major characteristics of any community, the importance of individual choice should not be overlooked. More often than not people make a conscious choice to commit crime. It is the characteristics within the community which constrain or promote crime choice that need to be understood for a sophisticated crime analysis.

Crime and choice

The significance of choice for situations of crime, crime behaviours and crime relationships is in:

- the way crime becomes an option in particular social situations;
- the manner in which crime becomes the result of choice; and
- how crime may influence and determine other social choices.

To conceive of crime as choice implies a degree of rationality behind crime as decisions and actions. Crime as choice, or a consequence of choice, confounds representations which have crime emerging from social determinants, beyond the influence and involvement of perpetrators and victims. Choice is not compatible with crime being explained exclusively as a definition or a social reaction.

This conceptualisation of crime highlights those actions, responses and social connections which influence and formulate choice, as well as the opportunity provided for the choice to arise at all. Therefore, in relating crime and choice it is conceded that while choice may be constrained by identifiable social determinants, it is choice nonetheless. As such it relies on human interaction and decision-making. The decisions behind choice might range in their rationality from the passion of the moment through careful calculation, but they remain decisions all the same.

Opportunity needs to connect with motive if crime choice is to eventuate. Motive is a more complex issue than rational choice theory suggests. An understanding of the nature of motive is crucial if the deactivation of crime choice, through a reduction of opportunity, is to occur. Otherwise, tampering with opportunity will only lead to a change of crime choice if the original motive remains strong.

---

46 Downes and Rock 1998, Chapters 5 and 6.

In contemporary crime theory, and too often without critical reflection, crime and choice are viewed in simple rationalist terms which concentrate more on deciding not to commit crime than on choosing crime as an option. As Braithwaite observes:

> If the awareness that an act is criminal fundamentally changes the choices being made, then the key to a general explanation of crime lies in identifying variables that explain the capacity of some individuals or collectivities to resist, ignore or succumb to the institutionalised disapproval that goes with crime.[47]

Analysing crime as choice holds out the potential for a better under-standing of the relationship between crime and control within transitional contexts progressing towards globalisation. The development of the crime and control relationship, and the choices of which it is constituted, indicate many of the interests at work on societies and cultures in transition. At the global level, for instance, the proliferation of international drug trafficking and collectivised control efforts will only be fully understood if the *choice stages* of the trade and the incursions of control within those stages are indi-vidually considered. Equally, the market structures of the trade and the motivations for its control within more localised contexts depend upon the international imperatives behind the selective criminalisation of drug use, and enforcement. These specific structures and institutions then mirror the globalisation of capital and consumption. Crime choices within each of these levels and stages of criminal enterprise and regulation are essentially interconnected, and resemble many other *legitimate* enterprise choice options, often without conscious recognition.

Perhaps surprisingly, the factors influencing choices for and against crime are not distinctly different. It is our recognition of them, and the expecta-tions for their effects, which differ. Deterrence theory would have it (and certain control expectations emphasise) that if perpetrators are aware that apprehension is likely, or a severe penalty certain and imminent after the commission of the crime, then a rational choice not to commit crime will result. The *control choice* becomes a matter of utility. However, crime perpe-trators rarely know or think about the precise penalty that may arise, because they do not believe that they will get caught.[48] Had they harboured such a belief then the rationality of any decisions made by them about crime and control could be impugned. The rational choice may be for crime rather than control. The choice is dependent upon very different interpretations of determining factors, from the perspective of the perpetrator or the regulator.

---

47 Braithwaite 1989, p. 4.
48 Analysis seems to support this view. One study has found that only one per cent of burglaries involve the offender being caught in the act (Felson 1994, p. 11).

Further, crime as choice is not always a matter of simple alternatives: to commit crime or not to commit crime. Crime may be the only available or viable opportunity to achieve a desired social end. Or, on the balance of probabilities it is perceived to be the best choice available for the realisation of that end. Crime might also create a context or a relationship of power and dominance where otherwise legitimate outcomes may be ensured. Using violence to command personal favour or market position is a case in point. For instance, extortion and price fixing for a competitive market edge may initially rely on commercial influence or blackmail, but will ultimately be backed up by the threat of force to ensure compliance. Recognising this, the final choice for crime may be preceded by a series of considerations, comparisons, and decisions which view crime through a process of reduction and exclusion. Crime choices and their consequences are therefore available for analysis in these terms.

When considering the crime/choice paradigm it is also too simplistic to presume a common discourse or common frames of reference for decision-making. Crime as choice will be influenced by variations in the meaning ascribed to particular behaviours and consequences. After all, that is what law enforcement and the adversarial criminal trial are all about. In this respect, the practice of neutralisation is important. A juvenile may choose not to rob a small store where the owner is known to him because he can easily personalise the act, or even empathise with the victim. On the other hand, the perpetrator may be comfortable stealing from a large department store because no one is seen to suffer harm directly, and he justifies his action by saying that the firm will pass on the loss to a vast range of customers by a small price increase. Another method of neutralisation is to say that the large store constantly *robs* its customers by charging high prices, and it is good that they *get some of their own medicine*.

Profiles of crime

It makes good sense to try to identify the characteristics of an offender or a crime environment in order to see whether they are sufficiently common across offences, perpetrators or offence situations, to enable their use as future predictors. However, it must be remembered that profiling is an inexact science, and has the potential, if relied on unduly, to distract an investigator from important and unique material evidence in each new crime. It also builds on assumptions and popular wisdom about the causes of crime that may endorse prejudice and discrimination rather than good sense.

A community profile is only as useful as the detailed knowledge acquired about the community in question. Such knowledge may take many forms. Statistical information from the Australian Bureau of Statistics census is an important starting point. This should be refined and developed through a consideration of municipal council data. Other types of formal community information should be available from various federal and state government departments such as education, health, and housing. Other equally important sources of knowledge about a community will come from the people and organisations of which it is comprised.

When profiling a community, one project is the incidence of crime. Another equally important but often overlooked focus is those aspects of the community most in need of protection. This is where the understanding of crime as a relationship comes in handy. The perpetration of crime—where, when, and by whom—is part of any community profile. The same can be said for victims and victimisation.

Communities are rarely the homes for unique crimes or criminals. However, some communities in Australia have become synonymous with crime. In any such situation, surrounding communities may act as feeders or facilitators to that community and important transport routes across and into various communities require inclusion in any crime–community profile.

Prioritising crime

When identifying those crimes with which the police should be concerned, the following are important considerations:

- crimes that are the conventional focus of police interest;
- crimes that police have most success in addressing;
- crimes that police have little success in addressing;
- community expectations for police involvement;
- community harm caused by the crimes in question;
- crimes identified as problems by the police organisation, the government, and the media;
- crimes that lead to further criminality;
- crimes involving the young and the vulnerable;
- crimes that are not met through other agencies and processes (e.g. insurance); and
- crimes where the pattern is unique or accelerating.

Traditionally, street crimes, public order breaches, minor property offences and violations of regulatory regimes, such as public health, have been the common interest of policing. In fact the original Peel police in England, on which some central themes of Australian policing have been modelled, were established to control the *dangerous classes*.[49] This required an obvious presence of police on the streets, preventing disorder and protecting the safety and property of the middle classes. Some might say that little has

---

49 The unruly, the unemployed, and the disrespectful.

changed when we look at the work of uniformed patrols in Australian policing today.

In recent years policing has become more conscious of issues of efficiency. High among the measures of efficiency is the *clear-up* rate. Since the majority of crimes that come to police attention are reported to the police, the successful conclusion of an investigation and prosecution is heavily dependent on the cooperation of the community. One of the most significant factors in clear-up is an admission or confession. One of the reasons why the clear-up rate for homicide remains relatively high is that many offenders confess their guilt and surrender themselves to the police. The same cannot be said for motor vehicle theft, where the clear-up rate is relatively low.

Police seem to have little success in dealing with crimes where the *victim* is a willing participant (such as drug-related offences), or where the community is ambivalent about the crime (for example, the use of cannabis). Further, if the crime is one where market demand is constant (such as the possession or self-administration of heroin), it is extremely difficult for the police to influence the volume of crime. Any offences that connect with such crimes (like housebreaking), will present similar problems for police in clear-up. Until recently crimes that occurred in domestic settings were difficult to police, and insufficiently well reported. However, a change in community and police understanding of domestic violence in particular has produced a distinct improvement in the management of these offences by police. Therefore, issues such as visibility, victim involvement, public appreciation and police attitudes have an important influence over clear-up.

Expectations for crime control may vary from community to community. Such expectations are governed by local perceptions about the prevalence and seriousness of crime, and the fear of victimisation. Community attitudes to these issues are largely governed by secondhand knowledge (gained from the media and popular wisdom), rather than from immediate or personal experience. In this respect it is essential that police actively present the local crime and control picture in a regular and realistic fashion in order to counteract unbalanced or unreasonable expectations.

Essentially, the police are one of the few remaining 24-hour public services. Consequently the community has come to expect that the police will do something about any problem which seems to require an immediate state response. The community also expects the police to provide a range of information services.

The consideration of harm to the community as a criterion for key offences is more problematic. The evaluation of what is harmful is subjective and can produce different responses across communities. Yet some offences which are universally seen as harmful may not justify the investment of police resources allocated to them relative to their collective effect on communities (for instance, homicide). There is also a range of crimes that have become a greater threat to the heath and well-being of communities in recent years (pollution, corporate fraud, illegal immigration), but the police have either suffered from insufficient training, resourcing, or institutional commitment to deal effectively with these emerging challenges. This is made all the more difficult because the nature of these crimes often spreads the victimisation across communities and therefore pressure for police action is defused.

There can be little doubt that the prioritising of crime is an intensely political process in New South Wales. Following the Wood Royal Commission inquiry into police corruption, for example, the government identified child sexual assault as a priority. Talkback radio and the print media in particular are constantly telling the police what crimes they should tackle, and consequently influencing community expectation. Local criminal justice institutions are never insulated against these concerns. Police management also sets the agenda regarding which crimes should be targeted and for which discretion might be exercised. This is especially so in the areas of traffic and juvenile crime.

A crucial consideration for the establishment of crime control priorities is a consideration of those crimes which tend to progress on to other forms of criminality. Drug abuse and property crimes, underage drinking and violence, and illicit gambling and fraud are just some examples of the progressions that policing needs to sever.

Associated with this issue is a consideration of crime patterns in terms of location, offenders, and victims. It is useful to realise that certain *career criminals* will commit a disproportionate number of crimes. Also, certain types of offences such as domestic violence and child sexual assault are likely to be regularly repeated by particular offenders.

Especially at a community level, prioritising key offences must take into consideration the nature and vulnerability of victims. The aged and juveniles are likely targets for some offenders and their protection is paramount.

Obviously the manner in which criminal justice responds to offences will be influenced by whether victims have taken any self-help measures to minimise the harm caused, such as the engagement of private security services or reliance on insurance. It should be remembered, however, that not everyone in the community can afford these protections and even those who can may still look to the police for a reassurance of their safety and the security of their property.

Finally, the pattern of crime in community is a changing thing. Trends in crime come and go, and the identification of key offences needs to adjust to accord with the variation in patterns and trends.

Fear of crime

One of the most significant effects of crime on the community is fear. Fear makes victims out of even those who are unlikely to suffer any harm from crime. This is because there is no essential connection between the fear of crime and its prevalence.

Community ignorance about the reality of crime is something on which fear feeds. Crime and crime stories have become one of the staples of the news and entertainment media. However, many of these stories about crime and policing are misleading, and add to the distorted community understanding of crime.

The exaggeration of fear is used to sell all sorts of things, from films and magazines to the products and services of the expanding private security trade. These merchants rely heavily on people's perceptions of their own vulnerability and of the extent and seriousness of crime—both of which can be extremely inaccurate. The focus is often on crimes that are relatively rare. The fear of murder in a dark alley is an example of an image that tends to distort where the real dangers lie. For example, it is more likely that a woman or a child will be a victim of violence in a domestic setting by a perpetrator familiar to them, rather than being attacked by a stranger in a strange place. Criminal justice policy makers need to be mindful of real vulnerability issues when constructing crime prevention initiatives, particularly the heightened vulnerability in relationships where the perpetrator has a custodial role or is in a position of power: father and sexually abused child, nursing home staff and elderly patient, husband and battered wife.

Because fear is preoccupied with crimes that are difficult to take preventive action against, individuals overlook crimes they are more likely to experience and may have some possibility of preventing. For example, the likelihood of being a victim of burglary in major Australian cities is high, and the steps to lessen this chance can be simple and inexpensive.

A rampant and growing fear of crime tends to discredit the state agencies of criminal justice. Police, for instance, are criticised for not doing enough, not being tough enough, or not being available when needed. Add to this the community suspicion of corruption within policing, and respect for police will suffer.

It is difficult to disabuse the community of mistaken representations of crime, and of the exaggerated fear they produce. The community is suspicious when those involved in the criminal justice system talk down fear or contradict a prevailing media view that is widely believed. The best that governments can do is to regularly circulate current community information on crime occurrences, and to stimulate realistic community crime prevention initiatives.

ADDITIONAL RESOURCES

CRIME AND CHOICE

Bronitt, S. and McSherry, B., *Principles of Criminal Law*, Law Book Company, Sydney, 2001, Chapters 1 and 2.

Brown, D., Farrier, D., Egger, S, and McNamara, L., *Criminal Laws*, Federation Press, Sydney, 2001, paras 2.1.1, 2.1.3, 2.3.4, 2.3.5.

Garland, D., *Punishment and Modern Society*, Clarendon Press, Oxford, 1990, Chapter 1.

RATIONAL NOTIONS OF LAW-MAKING

Brown, Farrier, Egger and McNamara 2001, paras 2.2.1, 2.2.2.

Norrie, A., *Crime, Reason and History*, Weidenfeld & Nicolson, London, 1993, Chapters 1 and 2.

CRIME AS BEHAVIOUR

Sapsford, R., 'Individual Deviance: the search for the Criminal Personality', in Fitzgerald, McLennan and Pawson, *Crime and Society: Readings in Theory and History*, 1981, Chapter 15.

Young, J., 'Thinking Seriously about Crime: Some Models of Criminology', in Fitzgerald, McLennan, and Pawson, *Crime and Society: Readings in Theory and History*, 1981, Chapter 14.

CRIME AS REACTION

Cunneen, C., Findlay, M., Lynch, R., and Tupper, V., *Dynamics of Collective Conflict: Riots at the Bathurst Bike Races*, Law Book Company, Sydney, 1989, Chapters 4 and 6.

Travis, G., 'Police Discretion in Law Enforcement: A Study of Section 5 of the NSW *Offences in Public Places Act 1979*', in M. Findlay et al. (eds), *Issues in Criminal Justice Administration*, George Allen & Unwin, Sydney, 1983, Chapter 14.

TOPIC 4

CRIMINAL JUSTICE I: POLICE POWERS

Police powers[50]

The principal areas of police powers involve arrest, search and seizure in the areas of:

- investigation;
- deliberations on bail;

---

50 A useful discussion of police powers in the context of reform is provided by the Queensland Criminal Justice Commission's comprehensive review of police powers; see Qld CJC (1993–94) *Report on Review of Police Powers in Queensland*, Nos. I–V.

- the determination as to charges laid; and
- the process of prosecuting criminal offences, when police retain such authority.

Ancillary to these powers is the acquiring, retention and dissemination of information by police in a variety of settings. The legislature has also created a range of specific powers, such as police intervention in situations of domestic violence, and the stop and search provisions affecting young people suspected of carrying weapons.

Police powers have various sources and are usually exercised in an atmosphere of individual or organisational discretion. What has come to be known as *original powers* are those powers provided to police in their capacity as constables. Many of these fundamental powers are also vested in individual citizens. However, they are rarely exercised by anyone other than the police. The common law has accepted a range of police powers, which in many situations have been augmented and refined by statute. This is the case with arrest and detention, search and seizure, and police powers to grant bail.

Recently legislative reforms have led to the codification of police powers in certain Australian jurisdictions.[51] However, this is not a universal development and in other jurisdictions the legislative provisions for police powers are not comprehensive. More commonly they are scattered across Crimes Acts and a range of other statutes and regulations, in which the police are expected to enforce specific powers and responsibilities.[52] The usual mix in Australia for sources of police powers is common law, specific and general statutory provisions, administrative regulations and guidelines,[53] and general occupational delegations.

An example of the way in which police powers arise from a conglomerate of sources can be found in the detention of suspects prior to arrest and charge. The common law provides general principles regarding the exercise of police powers of detention. For instance, the case of *Williams* (1986) 60 ALJR 636 establishes that the police cannot arrest someone merely for the purpose of questioning. In New South Wales, recent reform proposals[54] governing police detention were translated into legislation.[55] This legislation establishes a scheme whereby this power is limited to a reasonable period defined in terms of hours and extending across certain times, and subject to

---

51   For example, the *Police Powers and Responsibilities Act 1979* (Qld).
52   Such legislation might cover the regulation of anything from the care and control of domestic pets to the detention of illegal immigrants.
53   Such as Police Commissioner's instructions.
54   These reform proposals addressed the debate about whether detention periods should be designated as 'a reasonable period', or in terms of specified hourly limits.
55   Crimes (Detention After Arrest) Bill 1998, which now stands as Part 10A of the *Crimes Act 1900*.

reviews depending on the nature of the detainee and the stage of the investigation process. The scheme is elaborated in regulations.[56] Finally, the determination of the investigation regime affecting the detainee relies on provisions in the *Evidence Act* and stipulation in the Police Commissioner's Instructions.[57] Investigation is eventually a matter of the exercise of police discretion within these legislative and administrative boundaries.

Another example is arrest being governed by discretion, common law, administrative instructions, and statute. The power to arrest is given generally to the citizen and to the police through common law. Police instructions suggest when arrest or other forms of initiating the prosecution process (such as summons) should be preferred. In New South Wales, as in other Australian jurisdictions, the powers of arrest are specified in legislation.[58] Provisions in this legislation adopt, specify and enhance the common law police powers, for instance, the power of police to apply reasonable force against a person who might be resisting arrest.[59] They also determine the information that is required to be given to arrested parties and its relationship to certain offence situations.[60]

The laws on police powers are regularly revised by the legislature, relative to particular crime concerns and matters of special interest. For example, the introduction of random breath testing necessitated the creation of police powers to stop, detain, and subject motorists to blood alcohol tests without reasonable suspicion of any offence. Another example of a shift in police powers is the question of how to deal with intoxicated persons. The *Intoxicated Persons Act* in New South Wales, for instance, removes the power to arrest persons drunk in a public place and has converted this to a power for the police to remove such individuals to designated places for their personal safety.

In certain situations conventional police powers have been augmented so as to recognise developments in investigation techniques and technology. The common law, for instance, provides to police powers of entry, search and seizure when pursuing individuals suspected of the commission of particular offences. Legislation has qualified these powers by requiring warrants, as well as the establishment of reasonable suspicion. Both federal and state (territory) legislation has recently created specialist powers for the police to intercept various forms of telecommunications.

The average citizen is often unsure of the extent and implication of police powers. For example, when police ask for personal information from individuals in the street, a suspect is generally not required to answer police

56   *Crimes (Detention After Arrest) Regulations* 1998.
57   See *Evidence Act,* ss. 84–90, 137–139; *Police Commissioner's Instructions* (as at 1/4/95) 29–40.
58   Sections 352 ff. of the *Crimes Act.*
59   Section 58.
60   See *Christie v. Leachinsky* [1947] AC 573.

questions. However, legislation such as that which applies to certain public order and traffic situations, and the recent parental responsibility legislation in New South Wales,[61] gives police additional powers to require the provision of such information. Usually, however, the citizen simply accepts that the police have these powers and the police act on the presumption that the information is given voluntarily.

Certain common law presumptions, such as *right to silence*, impose limitations on police investigation practice.[62] Not only is the citizen not required to give information to the police, but after charges have been laid the police should not question the accused. As with many situations in the police powers area, this right to silence is conditional rather than absolute.[63] In most jurisdictions adverse inferences may not be drawn from situations where an accused refuses to answer police questions.[64] In addition, legislation affecting the investigation of corporate crime and corruption has removed the protection against self-incrimination from accused persons in certain situations of investigation.[65]

Another area where police powers have an impact on the rights of individuals, and their privacy, is the identification of suspect persons. For instance, section 353 A of the *Crimes Act* in New South Wales enables the police to search suspected persons and to take photographs and their fingerprints for the purposes of identification. The police may also require a medical examination if they believe that it will yield additional evidence in relation to a crime.

Police Powers in New South Wales: A case study

Sources

As mentioned earlier in this topic, police powers in New South Wales are a conglomerate, from a variety of sources:

- Common law, for example powers specifying the method of arrest;
- Statute, for example the creation of arrestable offences, and the suspicion of offences as reason for arrest;

---

61 See, for instance, *Summary Offences Act 1988* (NSW), Div. 4; *Children (Protection and Parental Responsibility) Act 1997* (NSW).

62 For a discussion of the right to silence see Findlay 1999, Chapter 2.

63 Recently, law reform bodies have proposed, for several jurisdictions, significant qualifications on the *right to silence*. These have revolved around the potential to compel responses in certain circumstances, and a widening of the range of adverse comments that can be made if the right is claimed where answers might otherwise have been forthcoming. For example, see NSW Law Reform Commission 1998, *The Right to Silence*, Discussion Paper 41.

64 This is so for the judge and the prosecutor but not in some situations for a co-accused. See *Bruce v. R* (1987) 74 ALR 219.

65 The powers conferred on investigative bodies such as the National Crime Authority, the Australian Securities and Investment Commission, and the ICAC include such compulsion, and impose indemnities on any evidence so elicited—see Findlay et al. 1999, Chapter 4.

- Guidelines, for example the manner in which questions may be asked after arrest;
- Discretion, for example from the office of constable and original powers.

Legislative issues

Police powers in their legislative form reside mainly in the statutes which principally create criminal offences. Important in these are:

Summary Offences Act
Section 28F: Reasonable directions in public place—Move on power

This provision creates a 'move on' power, exercised in circumstances where the police have reasonable grounds to believe the behaviour in question will cause obstruction, intimidation, or fear. The direction is given for the purposes of reducing these consequences in a public place. When giving the direction the police must provide evidence that they are police (including their names, identifiers, and places of duty), the reason for the direction, and consequences of non-compliance.

Crimes Act
Section 352 (1): Arrest power

Arrest may be effected without a warrant, during or immediately after commission of a summary or indictable offence. In addition, arrest without warrant can be used to detain a person who has committed a felony, in order to bring him or her (and any property which is the substance of the offence) before a justice at the earliest possible occasion. Subsection (2) provides for arrest without a warrant, and detention of a person where a police officer with reasonable cause suspects the commission of an offence. Such a power covers (in a public place) a person whom the police officer, with reasonable cause, suspects of committing a felony.

To effect the arrest, it is sufficient that through the words or conduct of the arresting officer, the apprehended person is aware that he is no longer a free man. Physical seizure is not necessary. The person arrested is entitled to know that he is being arrested and must be told the reason why unless he makes this impossible.

Regarding invitees (conventionally referred to as those assisting police with their enquiries), their freedom to leave, in theory at least, is what distinguishes them from arrestees. It is necessary for the invitee to be aware that he or she can leave at any time. It is unclear, however, whether the police are obliged to provide such information.

There is a common law obligation on police to avoid unreasonable delay in bringing the person before a justice and having him charged. Such a delay will result in unlawful detention. There is no common law power for police to detain a person in order to obtain evidence or to question him. However,

Part 10A of the *Crimes Act* has overridden this and created a conditional power for these purposes.

Crimes Act Part 10A: Detention after arrest for purposes of investigation

Section 354 and following provisions provide for detention after arrest to enable the police investigation of a person's involvement in an offence. This is despite common law requirements to bring a person before justice without delay following arrest. Section 356 stipulates that these provisions apply to persons (including juveniles) under arrest. They do not, however, apply to persons detained under the *Intoxicated Persons Act*. The legislative detention scheme has modified application to juveniles, Aboriginal people, non-English-speakers, and intellectually and physically disabled suspects. It does not relate to people not lawfully arrested. Section 356C enables detention once a reasonable suspicion of involvement in an offence (or other offences) by the suspect is formulated by the arresting officer.

Section 356D stipulates that the *investigation period* will be determined as a *reasonable time*, which according to section 356E is a maximum period of four hours. Section 356G enables the investigation period to be extended through the issuing of a detention warrant (to increase investigation periods beyond four hours and up to eight hours).

Section 356N creates a right for the detainee to communicate with a friend, independent person or legal practitioner during detention. The police have the obligation to facilitate this.

After arrest and charge (s. 353A), a person may be searched and police may take photographs and fingerprints for the purpose of identification. The police may also require a medical examination if the suspect appears ill or intoxicated.

Section 357: Search powers

As with arrest, the powers of police to search are distinguished on the basis of whether a warrant is required. Section 357E states that the power to search without warrant can be exercised upon persons reasonably believed to be conveying stolen property, and other offence-related circumstances. Section 357F covers the entry of premises without warrant. Circumstances enabling the exercise of this power include situations where there is an invitation to enter, by the occupier, and where the police officer reasonably suspects an offence of domestic violence has been or is being committed.

Section 357G provides for entry *with* a warrant where entry is denied, provided again that a reasonable suspicion prevails. Section 357I allows entry by the police with a warrant to search for firearms in relation to a domestic violence offence.

These provisions do not present the definitive picture for police search powers, which are referred to in a variety of other legislative forms.

Evidence Act
Section 139: Police caution
According to this section, evidence obtained during questioning is improperly obtained if, prior to commencing the questioning of an arrested person, the investigating officer does not caution that 'anything that (the person) does say or do may be used in evidence'. Questioning is also improper if the police officer concerned did not have the power to arrest, and the witness's statement was made after the officer formed the view that there was sufficient evidence to establish that the person(s) had committed the offence, and even so the caution had not been administered. The caution must be administered in a language in which the suspect person can communicate fluently. The need for the caution does not apply where other Australian laws require that a person answer questions. The need to caution applies to invitees if they are not allowed to leave or are given reasonable grounds for believing that they cannot leave.

Section 84: Inadmissible evidence
The Act designates as inadmissible evidence any admissions influenced by violence or oppression, or a threat of either. Inadmissibility will only be determined if the issue is raised by the party claiming inadmissibility during proceedings.

Section 85: Reliability of admissions
Consideration of the reliability of an admission or confession arises only in situations where admissions are made as part of official questioning. Such evidence may be declared reliable, despite the circumstances otherwise leading to a conclusion of unreliability, only if the circumstances were such that the truth of the admissions was not adversely affected. In determining this, the court can take into account characteristics of the person making the admission, the nature of the questions, and the nature of the threat or inducement.

Section 90: Discretion to exclude admissions
The court may refuse to admit evidence of admissions (or evidence proving a particular fact) when the evidence is adduced by the prosecution, and having regard to the circumstances in which it was made it would be 'unfair to the defendant to use the evidence'. Note the degree of the court's discretion which this invites.

Section 137: Exclusion of prejudicial evidence

The court must refuse to admit evidence if its probative value is outweighed by 'the danger of unfair prejudice to the defendant'.

Section 138: Discretion to exclude improperly or illegally obtained evidence

Evidence is not to be admitted unless the desirability of admission outweighs the undesirability of admitting the evidence. Evidence is obtained improperly during questioning when the questioners reasonably knew their questioning would impair the suspect's rationality, or where they made a false statement in order to induce a response. Courts need to take into account international obligations when determining propriety and admissibility issues.

NSW Police Commissioner's Instructions

These administrative guidelines are prepared by the Commissioner as instructions for best practice in policing. They do not have any legislative effect and their violation does not necessarily implicate the admissibility of evidence. In terms of powers of investigation, the instructions govern:

* guidelines for questioning;
* consultation of legal representatives;
* showing suspect's statement;
* verification of statements;
* recording of records of interview.

The abuse of power

As mentioned above, many police powers, particularly those specified in legislative form, qualify or override conventional rights of the accused such as the *right to silence* and the protection against self-incrimination. Due to the significant impact of police powers in such settings it is perhaps inappropriate to assume that these protections for the accused have the status of rights. Certainly the options open to a suspect when such rights are violated are limited, and the ability of the accused person to claim these rights is dependent on the power and authority relationships which exist in the investigation situation.

In certain jurisdictions, such the United Kingdom, the powers of the police have been codified and their discretion constrained.[66] However, in most Australian jurisdictions any such constraint upon police discretion is either sporadic or particular, and usually occurs in the context of legislation regarding the presentation and admission of evidence.

---

66 See *Police and Criminal Evidence Act.*

The conditions which enable the abuse of power by police rely on the police monopoly over the physical and human conditions of encounters between police and citizens. The more coercive a police power, and the less transparent its exercise, the more difficult would be any attempt to make the power accountable or to ensure that it complies with legislative constraints. Recent examples of the miscarriage of justice by police in major criminal investigations in the United Kingdom have identified this problem, and led to significant law reform in the area of police powers.[67] These incidents exemplified the problems with accountability at all stages of the criminal justice process, where initial police evidence was obtained through the abuse of power. The traditional oversight of judicial review has not provided the guarantee of justice that either the courts or the legislature would assume. The abuse of investigative power by police, therefore, has not only the potential to contaminate police evidence, but to produce unjust results at a variety of other pre-trial and trial stages.

The discretionary exercise of police powers makes them difficult to regulate effectively. In certain states and territories of Australia, such as New South Wales, the detailed regulation of police powers has been returned to the police and relies on formal instructions issued by the police commissioner. Penalties for the violation of these instructions take the form either of internal occupational reprimand, or of the ultimate rejection of evidence by the courts. The latter is, however, also discretionary and there is no certainty that such a result will be the consequence of an abuse of police investigation powers.

The Royal Commission into the NSW Police Service recently identified a range of situations where police manufacture confessional evidence, produce admissions through inducement or force, and otherwise falsify evidence. Interference with such evidence and the intimidation of witnesses was a convention among certain specialist police investigation agencies in past decades. Inquiries in Queensland, New South Wales, and Victoria have shown such practices to be endemic throughout policing in various Australian jurisdictions.

A case study in such abuse of powers is the exercise of what is known as the police *verbal*. This is where an unsigned record of interview or an admission without written or oral record provides the basis of a police case. This information may be bolstered by the confessions of others (such as prisoner informants), in an attempt to corroborate the unrecorded evidence. Such evidence at trial will result in a dispute based on the credibility of the accused and of the police. In years past judges and magistrates have simply preferred the credibility of the police. However, the attitude of the judiciary

---

67 See Walker and Starmer 1999.

to such police evidence has changed in recent years. Police culture has embraced this practice of 'verballing' based on the need to support a police notion of *morality*. In light of the predisposition to produce convictions for the greater good, police have argued that they face unscrupulous defence counsel, or incompetent magistrates and judges, and therefore the guilty are acquitted. Without the intervention of police, they argue, such outcomes would be more likely. However, this does not overcome the fact that these practices are a violation of the law and therefore challenge the obligation of the police as law enforcement officers.[68]

The response to police verbals in all states and territories of Australia has been the introduction of oral (and some instances video) recordings of records of interview. In addition, the transcription and authorisation of these records is a requirement for their credible admission in a criminal trial.

Reforming the exercise of police powers

Often the impetus for the introduction of further constraints on the exercise of police powers is recognition of a miscarriage of justice. Unfortunately, however, the reform interventions in these circumstances may be little more that crisis management. In addition, as was the case with the Fitzgerald inquiry in Queensland,[69] the reforms may require much political pressure and argument between the time that the problem is exposed, and legislative intervention attempts its resolution.

Reforming the exercise of police powers will always be difficult in an adversarial trial environment. The prosecution case has the significant benefit of police resources in the investigation and presentation of evidence. This also means that a variety of state agencies are joined together in mutual interest with the prosecution. The position of the defence in identifying and exposing the abusive power, if it occurs, is problematic. There will be many interests besides the police committed to denying or explaining away the abuse for fear of its consequences at trial.

The prevailing *law and order* political environment promoted by the media makes the limitation or even regulation of police powers an unattractive option.[70] The issue becomes one of containing the expansion of police powers rather than their comprehensive reform.

Appropriate sites for the reform of police powers include:

---

68 For a detailed discussion of police verbals see Findlay 1999, pp. 53–5.
69 This inquiry arose out of media allegations that state police (and politicians) at the highest level were involved in malpractice. In particular, it was established that the police had gained benefit from vice, gambling, and narcotics.
70 See Hogg and Brown 1998, Chapters 1 and 7.

- evidence gathering by the police;
- requirements for the disclosure of prosecution evidence;
- the audit of police investigations (both internal and external);
- the provision of uniform access to legal aid services;
- a clearer separation of investigative and prosecutorial functions;
- reforms in pre-trial and trial procedures;
- requirements for responsible media reporting;
- the provision of procedural and financial remedies for individuals subject to the abuse of police powers.

Another way to address the reform of police powers is to investigate generic areas in which the police have strained relations with the community. For instance, police–youth relations are a traditional area of concern.[71] This tension is often exacerbated by issues of ethnicity, as well as gang structure. Another community context where tension is apparent is police–Aboriginal relations.[72] There have been significant attempts, both within state police organisations and as result of public inquiries, to address the individual and institutional racism that characterises such encounters.[73]

CONTEXT OF THE PROBLEM

The encounters between police and young people are often difficult, particularly when they occur, as they often do, in public space. The power relations prevailing and the preconceptions that the police and the young person bring to the encounter make it unlikely that things will be viewed at face value, or that conversations will be simple and straightforward.

In the problem below, certain legal obligations and suspicions will predetermine the manner in which the police officer initiates the encounter, and the way that the youth will react. Such encounters are set against contemporary *moral panics* about the threats posed by young males (in particular) in public places, and who should take responsibility for reducing these threats.

Investigation procedures and issues relating to the obligations of the police and the *rights* of the suspect arise early in the scenario. So too does the real imbalance of understanding between the young suspect and the police. The potential for the police to play on this confusion is significant.

Considerations of appropriate parental responsibility, and the role of the police as mediators in violence, conclude the scenario.

---

71 See R. White and C. Alder (eds), *The Police and Young People in Australia*, Cambridge University Press, Melbourne, 1994.

72 See McDonald and Cunneen 1997, Parts 2 and 3

73 See J. Chan, *Changing Police Culture*, Cambridge University Press, Melbourne, 1997, Chapters 6, 9 and 10.

PROBLEM

Consider the following facts and depending on the role nominated for you (i.e. police or suspect), consider your options.

Danny is sixteen and living in a country town. One evening around midnight he is seen by Detective Constable Smith near a public phone booth that appears to have been recently vandalised. Danny is carrying a canvas sports bag and is drinking a can of beer.

Detective Constable Smith approaches Danny and wants to find out his name, his age, and the address of his parents.

Smith thinks that Danny could have sprayed graffiti over the phone booth and that the spray cans are in his bag. In addition, Smith has been searching young people all evening to see if they have been carrying knives, and Danny is just another one who comes along.

DC Smith is in plain clothes and Danny is not sure who he is.

Smith wants Danny to accompany him to the police station to answer some questions. At this stage he is reluctant to arrest Danny.

Danny has never been to a police station and he would like to have someone with him if he is to be asked questions.

Smith takes Danny's arm and walks him to a police car. Danny asks if he is under arrest but gets no reply.

At the station another police office says that he thinks Danny has information about a rape that occurred the same evening and he asks Smith to hold Danny for 'as long as they can', while they make some further enquiries.

Smith asks Danny to describe what he had been doing that night. Danny says he doesn't want to answer any questions. Smith says that if Danny doesn't admit to the vandalism he might be implicated in the rape charge.

Danny tells Smith that he did try to break open the telephone cash box to get the money from the machine, but denies doing the graffiti. Smith searches Danny's bag.

Smith then decides to take Danny back to his parents. On the way home Danny confides to Smith that his father is a very violent man and that's one of the reasons Danny spends so much time on the streets. He says that earlier that evening his father was drunk and waving a gun at Danny and his mother, threatening to kill them both.

Danny's mother comes to the door and has a black eye. Smith cautions Danny and his mother about the boy's behaviour that evening.

ENGAGING THE PROBLEM

This is a problem about process. Do we have an arrest legally effected or are the police dealing with an invitee? When evidence is obtained from Danny is it legally and properly obtained? What might be the consequences if the

evidence is tainted? Finally, there is the consideration regarding the responsibility of the police concerning Danny and the mother in an apparently
violent domestic situation.

In considering the problem, issues of Danny's criminal liability are less
important here than a critical evaluation of the manner in which the police
discharge their investigation functions, the manner in which the suspect's
rights and obligations are dealt with, speculation on the consequences of
these, and the way the police resolve the situation.

ADDITIONAL RESOURCES

Crimes Act 1900, sections 352, 357F–357I.

Evidence Act 1995 (NSW), sections 84, 85, 90, 137–9.

Antrum, M., 'Frisky Business: Police Search Powers and Young People' (1998) 10(2) *Current Issues in Criminal Justice* 197.

Brereton, D. and Ede, A., 'The Police Code of Silence in Queensland: The Impact of the Fitzgerald Inquiry Reforms' (1996) 8(2) *Current Issues in Criminal Justice* 107.

Brown, D., Farrier, D., Egger, S., and McNamara, L., *Criminal Laws*, Federation Press, Sydney, 2001, paras 3.2.1–3.2.9 and 3.6.1–3.6.8.

Dixon, D., 'Reform of Policing by Legal Regulation: International Experience in Criminal Investigation' (1996) 7(3) *Current Issues in Criminal Justice* 287.

Findlay, M., Odgers, S., and Yeo, S., *Australian Criminal Justice*, Oxford University Press, Melbourne, 1999, Chapters 2, 4, and 6.

Hogg, R., 'Perspectives on the Criminal Justice System', in M. Findlay et al. (eds), *Issues in Criminal Justice Administration*, George Allen & Unwin, Sydney, 1983, Chapter 1.

Hogg, R., 'Identifying and Reforming the Problems of the Justice System', in K. Carrington et al. (eds), *Travesty: Miscarriages of Justice*, Pluto Press, Sydney, 1991, Chapter 12.

Lansdowne, R. and Bacon, W., 'Women Homicide Offenders and Police Interrogation', in Findlay et al. (eds), 1983, Chapter 5.

Odgers, S., 'Regulating Police Interrogation: Back to First Principles', in Selby, H. and Freckelton, H. (eds), *Police in Our Society*, Butterworths, Melbourne, 1988.

TOPIC 5

CRIMINAL JUSTICE II: COURT FUNCTIONS

The irrelevance of criminal justice?

The community tolerates the majority of crimes and this means that only a
small proportion of them are reported to the police. The reasons for this
vary, from reluctance of witnesses to get involved to adverse attitudes to the
police. Therefore, in order to get a full picture of crime in the community,

researchers examine what is known as the *dark figure of crime* through methods such as victim surveys and self-report studies.[74]

The process of reporting this ever-diminishing percentage of crime relies on the intimate knowledge of victims, third-party witnesses, and even in some instances, offenders. However, once a crime occurrence is reported to the police, it may not appear in official crime figures unless it is formally actioned, recorded and processed by them. Official crime figures from police sources include:

- crime incidents;
- crimes cleared up by the police; and
- crimes that are proceeded with, to trial, or disposed of (through diversionary processes such as the police caution).

Other sources of official statistics on crime include prosecution figures, court dispositions such as convictions and acquittals, and sentencing statistics. At the *outcome end* of the criminal justice process the empirical relation of sentencing to total crime incidents is relatively minimal.[75]

Therefore, it is important in analysing the appropriate response to crime to remember the significance of community tolerance. The popular image of the relationship between crime and punishment clouds the reality that most crimes never receive attention from the police or the courts.

This fact is explained by the understanding that the criminal justice process works in a selective fashion. For instance, the likelihood of a crime coming to police attention is far greater if it is committed by a young person or an Aboriginal person than if its perpetrator comes from middle-class white Australia or from the corporate sector.

Two tiers of justice

The conventional analytical framework for many law school courses is the examination of appellate court decisions. This tends to produce in the mind of the student the view that either the appellate court format is common, or that the appellate jurisdiction makes up a large part of court work. Neither of these assumptions is true. The appellate court is where the ideology of criminal justice is most apparently on display, where legal principle is focused and discussed, and therefore where legal scholarship largely is interested. As McBarnet[76] suggests, the lower courts are deliberately structured in defiance of the ideology of justice, concerned as they are with direct control

---

74 See Findlay 1999 Chapter 1; Vold 1998, Chapter 19.
75 For instance, it has been estimated that only one out of every thousand criminal incidents concludes with a sentence of imprisonment.
76 McBarnett, D., *Conviction: Law, the State and the Construction of Justice*, Macmillan, London, 1981.

and the efficiency of the process. The lower courts have become the centres for criminal practice and their jurisdiction is growing.

The more serious a criminal offence, the higher will be the court in which it is contested at first instance.[77] As such there seems to be a correlation between the greater level of criminality and the larger investment in procedural legality at its trial. In the lower courts, argument is more over fact than law, and procedure reflects the pressures involved in administering criminal justice in an atmosphere of limited resources, rather than the expectations of adversarial trial ideology.[78]

The relative simplicity of local court procedure is not merely a consequence of simple facts. The constituent elements of the offences dealt with in that jurisdiction, and the lesser degree of gravity of these offences and their consequences, may be expected to justify the relative procedural economy in the lower courts. In fact, it is more likely that concerns for efficiency and the reality of strained resources are responsible for such economy.[79]

One of the most obvious differences between the process in the lower and higher courts is the role of the lawyer. As a result of recent contraction in legal aid funding throughout Australia and the reduction in duty-lawyer schemes, adequate legal representation in the lower courts is becoming much more difficult to obtain. In fact, with the vast majority of matters coming before the lower courts resulting in guilty pleas, some might suggest that the involvement of lawyers is less relevant, or even unnecessary. This, however, should be placed against the understanding that many of those accused before the lower courts are often most in need of legal counsel and assistance at all stages of the investigation and prosecution process.[80]

McBarnet (1981) observes that the divergence between the lower and higher courts in terms of law and procedure is *logic turned on its head*. In the local courts, where 95 per cent of all criminal cases are dealt with, such cases do not seem to be treated as *real law*, and are processed with the advantage of procedures exceptional to criminal law ideology and notions of due process.[81] On the other hand, in the higher courts, where the cases are exceptional, the

---

77 It should be remembered that where indictable offences may be tried summarily this may allow for quite serious matters to be heard in the local courts.

78 In lower court hearings the role of the legal professional and the place for analytical (legal) argument is severely constrained by issues such as case-load, workload, representation and deliberation time.

79 The rate (and atmosphere of inducement) of guilty pleas in the lower courts celebrates the primacy of economy in justice at that level.

80 The demographic information on accused persons in the local court presents a profile of low levels of education and social advantage.

81 For instance, the accused is largely unrepresented, pleas rather than trials prevail, and facts rather than law are paramount.

process is typified by a careful adherence to criminal justice ideology and an individualised rather than routine procedure for trial.

A difficulty with this dichotomous analysis of the courts and the justice they employ is in the distinction between what happens in the court and what is supposed to happen. The lower courts, for instance, are structured against unrealistic expectations for criminal justice, and therefore do not reflect popular (and often misguided) notions about the process of the criminal trial. In the higher courts, an adherence to due process tends to mask procedural irregularities that may have characterised the case in its investigation and pre-trial stages. In addition, any analysis of the two court levels needs to enquire into the informal rules governing local courts, and to examine their structures and sources. Can these informal rules, for instance, be explained by the real intent of the law itself? McBarnet (1981) argues that the inequalities and compromises clearly evidenced in local court procedures and outcomes are in fact institutionalised within the criminal law, and it is only the ideology of criminal justice that would challenge this.

It is necessary to look at the protections of due process not simply as *abstractions* that are ignored by the law, but as processes of law profoundly influenced by their social, economic, and political contexts. Against this, the compromise of due process in the local courts should be analysed from the perspective of its essential relevance to the daily process of criminal justice institutions, as well as with a recognition of the political and economic pressures on the local courts to produce managerial results rather than justice.

The process of punishment

A critical evaluation of criminal investigation and court procedures indicates that the criminal sanction and even the penalty occur well beyond the conclusion of the trial. The exercise of discretion by the police, prosecutors, and the courts allows for summary justice and sanctions from the earliest point of intervention of criminal justice. Particularly in the case of police actions, these sanctions (such as detention, corporal punishment, and abuse) might form more serious and less accountable penalties than any a court may adjudicate.

The relative invisibility of the pre–trial process allows for summary justice without normal regulation; in some instances sanctions that have not been condoned by law or the courts are concealed so that police have the opportunity to divert offenders away from further stages in the process. Such diversion, while justified in many situations and to be commended when formalised,[82] has the consequence of concealing from further enquiry the

---

82 Such as the juvenile cautioning procedures laid down by the Victorian police when dealing with first-time minor drug offences.

exercise of discretion at the point of diversion, and any sanctions that may attach to it.

Investigation techniques and their consequences may clearly have a punitive dimension. Techniques employed by the police have been identified as inducing the production of evidence, which would not have occurred without the threat of sanction at that point. There is little judicial oversight can do to correct such situations if the exercise of discretion is concealed.

It has been suggested that the investigation, prosecution and trial process may also tend further to victimise certain key witnesses in the prosecution case.[83] In particular, victims of sexual assault and child victims, exposed to extensive questioning and cross-examination, may find that they are required to relive the horror of their experience on several occasions following the commission of the alleged offence. Finally, the challenge to character and honesty which may arise as a natural part of the defence response will add to the feeling of victimisation experienced by these witnesses.

The drive for 'efficiency' in criminal justice

In describing the work of justice institutions, efficiency has become a euphemism for managerial or technocratic dominance. The history of criminal justice reveals the constant and increasing involvement of professionals who stand between the community and the outcomes of the process.[84] While the involvement of professionals in the pre-trial and trial process no doubt improves its effectiveness, and legal representation should be more generally available in order to balance the odds between parties to the adversarial process, the more that criminal justice becomes professionalised the more it will be distanced from victims, offenders, and those in the community with an interest in the trial.

The professionalisation of criminal justice tends to stylise the debate that is the adversarial process, as well as leading to specialised language in the conduct of the trial. This can have the consequence of completely confusing and ignoring those for whom the outcome of the trial has the most significant consequences.

Particularly in relation to the workings of the jury, those who would advocate an increased professionalisation of criminal justice suggest that it will increase the accuracy and certainty of decision-making.[85] However, this stands in contradiction to an ideology of criminal justice essentially reliant on representativeness and lay participation. On the one hand we are invited

---

83 See Findlay et al. 1999, pp. 336–8.
84 R. Cotterrell, *Sociology of Law*, Butterworths, London, 1992, Chapter 6.
85 For a general discussion of arguments in favour of the professionalisation of verdict delivery, see M. Findlay and P. Duff, *The Jury Under Attack*, Butterworths, Sydney, 1988.

to participate in criminal justice as members of the community and on the other we are told that it is only for the professional to influence or even to make certain crucial decisions.

As efficiency drives the investigation, prosecution, and trial of criminal offences, then pressure is brought to bear to reduce the rights of the accused and the presumptions on which he can rely. This has been a particular feature which has justified the proliferation of specialist investigation agencies such as the National Crime Authority and the Australian Securities and Investment Commission.[86] The justification for this reduction of rights has been the need to produce effective prosecutions where access to information would otherwise be difficult or denied. In addition, the rationalisation of defendants' rights is said to reduce opportunities for reasonable doubt to develop in the mind of the jury or the single judge.

Efficiency in justice is equated with simple and uncontested outcomes. At the level of the local courts in particular, lawyers and judges, police prosecutors and professional welfare workers have their own occupational reasons for engaging in plea bargaining, pressures to plead, increased disclosure, emphasis on agreed facts, and support for pre-trial determinations, on the basis of paperwork.

Increase in summary jurisdiction

There is clearly a more direct relationship between the local courts and the state. In New South Wales, for example, the working relationship between police prosecutors and the magistrate has always been close, and particularly so in country situations.[87] Magistrates are employees of state justice bureaucracies and therefore have less claim to judicial independence. The procedures of the local courts favour the presentation of evidence by police, and their method of prosecution. Historically, the lower courts have developed to adjudicate a vast range of municipal regulatory functions which also are now a significant component of the state policing function. In post-colonial days the magistrate and the police worked hand in hand in order to advance the interests of the new settlers. The increase in penalties available to local court judges and magistrates has meant that a larger number of offences come within their jurisdiction. Those offences now classified as either summary or indictable are available for trial in the summary courts.[88]

The hierarchy for criminal hearings is set out in legislation. For instance, in New South Wales the jurisdiction of the local courts is identified in the

---

86 For a discussion of the workings of these agencies see Findlay et al. 1999, Chapter 3; A. Leaver, *Investigating Crime*, Law Book Company, Sydney, 1997.

87 Historically these courts used to be known as police courts.

88 For an example of statutory provisions that cover these situations, see *Criminal Legislation Amendment (Sentencing) Act 1999* (NSW).

Justices Act 1902, the *Local Court Act 1992*, and the *Criminal Procedure Act 1986.* The majority of offences found in the *Crimes Act* and the *Summary Offences Act* will appear at least in their initial stages before the local courts. In addition, most regulatory offences and those involving violation of court process are within the summary jurisdiction. In fact, in New South Wales only four per cent of criminal matters proceed to the higher court.

The social reality of the courtroom

Pat Carlen, in her work on magistrate courts in England,[89] emphasises the *theatre* of the courtroom. She discusses the way in which spatial positioning in the court institutionalises power relations irrespective of the *script* of the trial. Further, Carlen refers to the ritual procedures and languages of courtroom practice as 'presenting sites for inclusion and exclusion'. What she means by this is that particularly for the professionals involved in the court, their familiarity with ritual and language gives them some comfort in the environment, while at the same time and for the same reasons alienating those who have only a transient connection with the court or the trial in question. The defendant and the victim who would be otherwise seen as most interested in the outcome are the least likely to feel any level of participation within the ritual.

The spatial demarcation of the courtroom, the ritual of court practice, the rarity of the language, and the mystery associated with various aspects of the court process mark the difference between the professional and the lay persons. Certain apparent and symbolic identifiers of status are crucial in the criminal trial. Replacement of the function of the judge, the inclusion of the jury, the ability of the lawyers to communicate, and the separation between the public and the professionals are all issues here. Perhaps the greatest level of demarcation is that between the accused person and the rest of the court. His position in the dock and the supervision by the police of his comings and goings from the bowels of the courts, and the fact that he is only able to communicate through or with the permission of the professionals, declare him to be different. While an accused person is supposed to benefit from the presumption of innocence, he quite clearly wears the trappings of guilt during the trial.

Carlen identifies the court as an institutional setting charged with the reproduction of structural dominance. The dominance is physical, symbolic, and procedural. It is a dominance where professionalism is valued over community involvement, and where the state and its interests seem to prevail over those of the accused and the victim.

---

89   P. Carlen, *Magistrates' Justice*, Martin Robertson, Oxford, 1976.

The ritual of the courtroom and of court proceeding seems to deny the possibility of certain relationships developing within the trial. For instance, the jury is unable to participate in any real sense beyond its limited right to question through the judge. Juries are often frustrated at the realisation that much of what goes on in the trial and much of the evidence considered by others is kept from them.[90]

Recent developments in court process, particularly in juvenile jurisdictions, have attempted to overcome the limitations of ritual and symbol. These developments have recognised the importance of real life encounters in order to determine criminal justice outcomes.

Procedures for progression up the tiers of justice: NSW case study

The process of the trial may involve a progression from one level of court to another. To show the detail of this it is worthwhile to consider those more serious trials which would normally be heard initially in one of the higher courts.

Committal hearings in the local courts[91]

In New South Wales, the *Justices Act*, Part 4 and the *Crimes Act*, Part 7 identify a committal hearing as a two-step process. Section 41 [2] (3) of the *Justices Act* indicates that a magistrate must determine whether the prosecution evidence is 'capable of satisfying a jury beyond reasonable doubt that the defendant has committed an indictable offence'. After all the evidence has been considered by the magistrate, the magistrate must discharge the committal if he or she considers that 'a jury would not be likely to convict the offender'.[92]

The function of committals is to eliminate weak cases, to disclose the prosecution case, to identify guilty pleas early in the prosecution process, and to rehearse the case and clarify the issues.

Recent changes in the committal process in most states and territories have meant that the hearings are now focused on written statements rather than the oral presentation of evidence. This restricts the defence examination of prosecution materials and may also limit the defence access to prosecution witnesses prior to the trial.

Frequently committal hearings proceed without legal representation for the accused. This absence of representation might explain why the discharge rate for committals is less than 10 per cent.

---

90 See M. Findlay, *Jury Management in NSW*, Australian Institute of Judicial Administration, Melbourne, 1994.

91 For a more detailed discussion of the committal, see Findlay et al. 1999, pp. 117–22.

92 Section 41(6)a.

Jurisdiction of the higher courts

In New South Wales, the Supreme Court and the District Court have broadly concurrent original jurisdictions. The Court of Criminal Appeal (three judges from the Supreme Court) has appellant jurisdiction.[93]

Usually serious offences are heard before a single judge and jury. In certain circumstances the accused may elect to have the matter heard by a judge alone.[94]

Appeals

The appeal process from the Local to the District Court is set out in section 122 of the *Justices Act*. There is a right of appeal against any conviction or order in the local court to the District Court. Appeals may go directly up to the Supreme Court through a *case stated*[95] or as regards procedural writs. Prosecutors can appeal to the District Court from the local court on issues of sentence severity or leniency. All District Court appeals were previously complete re-hearings but this has been abolished through the passage of the *Justices Amendment (Appeals) Act 1998*. A District Court judge can confirm, quash, set aside, increase, or reduce the conviction order or sentence or adjudication appealed against. The District Court judge cannot impose a greater penalty than that available to the magistrate on appeal from a local court.

Appeals from the District to the Supreme Court and then on to the Court of Criminal Appeal are affected by the *Criminal Appeals Act 1912*. A person convicted on indictment may appeal against a conviction on any ground which involves a matter of law alone, with the leave of the court and with a certificate from the trial judge. The right of appeal is limited to grounds of law alone. Prosecution appeals can be against the quashing or stay of an indictment or against sentence. The Supreme Court or the Court of Criminal Appeal can quash a conviction and substitute an acquittal, quash and vary a sentence, or order a new trial. Rarely will the Supreme Court interfere with the wrongful exercise of judicial discretion. The court can find the grounds of appeal substantiated but still dismiss the appeal.[96]

Appeals from the Court of Criminal Appeal to the High Court come about through the granting of special leave to appeal by the High Court.[97] The High Court almost always requires that the appeal be first heard by the Court of Criminal Appeal, and will rarely grant leave for an appeal against sentence. The High Court can hear appeals on conviction, sentence, conviction and sentence, Crown appeals, and stated cases.

Less than a quarter of all criminal appeals are successful.

---

93   Section 41(6)a.
94   *Criminal Procedure Act 1986* (NSW), ss. 16–17.
95   Where a point of law is agreed upon.
96   *Criminal Appeals Act 1912* (NSW), s. 6(1).
97   *Judiciary Act 1903* (Cth), s. 35(1).

CONTEXT OF THE PROBLEM

This problem should be addressed against the background of a detailed observation of the criminal courts carried out by the student.[98] The observation should be designed to:

- view and describe the workings of the court at its various levels;
- explore the relationship between the various key players in criminal hearings;
- analyse the trial experience (or parts thereof) against the critique of McBarnet and Carlen (referred to above);
- compare the manner in which criminal justice is processed at different court levels.

The methodology for these observations will be influenced by the expectations a student has concerning the criminal trial. These will largely be the product of popular culture rather than personal experience. Therefore, it is useful to be exposed to a variety of court settings and locations in order to challenge these preconceptions. Different courts in different localities will present the possibility of observing various types of cases and a variety of participants. By visiting specialist courts (such as the Children's Court), it is possible to see different styles of justice in action. By comparing the observations of the local courts with the higher courts, the *two tiers of justice* may become apparent. Different magistrates and judges will be seen to interpret the matters before them in different ways. By selecting a variety of forms of proceedings (e.g. bail, trial, sentence, and appeal hearings), the common procedural themes can be identified and qualified.

These observations will provide the student with data to test expectations for justice and to construct some critical themes for analysis. The observations, for instance, may reveal:

- Accused persons are generally confused by the court environment and proceedings. Such confusion can lead to a sense of alienation and dispossession.
- Many accused are unrepresented, and for those with legal representation its quality varies.
- Lawyers and judges (magistrates) do not do enough to include the accused in the proceedings.
- Communication avenues in the court are restricted. Much of the action is outside the courtroom.
- It seems that only professionals know what is going on and they keep it to themselves.

---

98 Obviously the nature, extent, and comparative dimension of these observations will differ for students at non-metropolitan universities.

This could then present a picture of criminal justice where the accused should be an active participant in the process but in fact is alienated, ritually degraded, and selectively counselled, and his interests seem trivialised.

PROBLEM

We are involved in a local court hearing, the facts of which concern an assault in a pub. The victim, a bouncer on duty at the pub, has alleged that the accused came up behind him when he was arguing with a drunk on the premises, and smashed a chair across his back. As a result the bouncer was knocked to the ground and suffered a dislocated vertebra.

The police prosecutor has led evidence from the victim and several other hotel staff who witnessed the attack, so as to substantiate the victim's version of events. The defence has chosen not to put the accused in the witness box but has examined the girlfriend of the accused, who was with him at the time of the attack. She has said in examination in chief[99] that she, the accused, and some friends had been drinking in the hotel for several hours prior to the attack. Minutes before, her boyfriend had acted against the bouncer who had pushed his way into the middle of the group of friends and started to 'push his weight around'. At this stage no one recognised him as a hotel employee and he was not wearing a uniform. She went on to give evidence that the bouncer began to intimidate one of their group, a Chinese male of slight build, calling him a 'skinny slope', poking him in the chest, and threatening to 'throw him out into the street if he didn't piss off fast'. She said the accused then intervened with the chair. The witness finally indicated that after the alleged assault, as the police were taking her boyfriend away, he said to her, 'I didn't know he was the bouncer. I just thought he was a dangerous racist about to assault our friend.'

You will be called upon to act as the police prosecutor, the witness, or the magistrate.

ENGAGING THE PROBLEM

This is a dispute as to the interpretation of certain facts. The liability of the accused depends on which witnesses are more credible and which explanation is believed. Some of the crucial witnesses clearly have an interest in a version of the facts. This needs to be exposed, and the credibility of these witnesses tested. Other versions may or may not be supported or challenged by other crucial pieces of evidence. Inferences which may essentially be drawn from the facts as stated may play an important role in the issue of

---

99 Where questions are asked by the person who leads (presents) the witness's evidence as part of her or his case.

liability. In terms of the drawing of inferences it will be necessary to elicit further information from witnesses than is presented here.

In playing out this problem students should gain experience in examination. Lines of questioning need to be developed and the skill of anticipating possible answers practised, as well as the redirection of further examination that this might produce. Competing lines of questioning, from the perspective of either side of the case, should be anticipated and explored. The dynamics of the argument can be enjoyed.

The resolution of the matter and the appropriate outcome is an issue for the magistrate. As such, considerations of doubt will be confronted, along with how effectively the prosecutor can convince the court of liability. Once this matter is settled, issues in mitigation and questions of appropriate penalty may arise for determination.

ADDITIONAL RESOURCES

Australian Law Reform Commission, *Equality Before the Law: Justice for Women,* Report No. 69, Part 1, 1994, Chapter 4, pp. 91–109.

Bronitt, S. and McSherry, B., *Prinicples of Criminal Law,* Law Book Company, Sydney, 2001, Chapter 2, pp. 94–134.

Brown, D., Farrier, D., Egger, S., and McNamara, L., *Criminal Laws,* Federation Press, Sydney, 2001, paras 2.1.9, 3.1.1–3.1.8, 3.2.2, 3.2.10, 3.3.1, 3.3.2–3.3.13, 3.7.2.

Findlay, M., Odgers, S., and Yeo, S., *Australian Criminal Justice,* Oxford University Press, Melbourne, 1999, Chapter 5.

McBarnett, D., *Conviction: Law, the State and the Construction of Justice,* Macmillan, London, 1981, Chapters 1, 7, and 8.

McConville, M., Sanders, A., and Leng, R., *The Case for the Prosecution,* Routledge, London, 1991, Chapters 9 and 10.

Redfern Legal Centre, *The Law Handbook,* Redfern Legal Centre Publishing, Sydney, 1997, pp. 120–141.

Richardson, M., and Reynolds, S., 'The Shrinking Public Purse: Civil Legal Aid in New South Wales, Australia' (1994) 5(2) *Maryland Journal of Contemporary Legal Issues* 349.

TOPIC 6

CRIMINAL JUSTICE III: DISCRETION

Decisions: Discretion or rule-bound?

Discretion is decisions, decision-making, and the process through which decisions are made. In relation to the criminal justice process, discretion is located at various important sites and is vested in the individuals and organisations of the most prominent justice agencies.

No form of discretion is unfettered. Rather, when dealing with discretion it is essential to appreciate the limitations of its exercise and the constraints on the structures and situations in which it arises.

Discretion occurs at all stages of criminal justice. In most respects major discretionary decisions interconnect and may influence individuals and institutions in the process beyond those immediately concerned with the decision in question.

In certain situations discretion is guided and controlled by legal rules. These may take the form of statutory provisions and in this respect have legal force. More likely, however, is the situation where discretion is subject to guidelines constructed by the organisation in which the decision is made. Obviously, issues of formal accountability will be influenced by the function and structure of such regulations. Accountability has recently been identified as crucial for public confidence at all levels of criminal justice throughout Australia. The courts and the judiciary have not been spared.

Discretion and the functions of criminal justice

From the outset of the criminal justice process, the investigation of identified individuals relies on discretion. For instance, the creation of the suspect population when police establish a reasonable suspicion in a particular offence setting is all about discretion. The decision to include a suspect in the early stages of the justice process may be based on police operational practice such as stereotyping, on organisational rules such as the police cautioning juveniles, or on the individual predisposition of police officers as it is constructed by police culture.[100]

Many of the contradictions at the heart of criminal justice have an influence on the exercise of discretion. The ideology of independence is strong evidence of this. The police are said to exercise original powers and to exert the independence of the constable. However, they are part of a disciplined service, which is ordered on the basis of rank. The line where discipline starts and independence ends always produces confusion in attempting to make police discretion more accountable.

The culture of criminal justice clearly binds the discretionary decision-making of certain agents. For instance, the determination by police of reasonable suspicion will be evaluated by reflecting on police culture rather than broad community sentiment. In addition, the loyalties and obligations generated within the component parts of criminal justice, and the suspicion

---

100   For a discussion of cop culture see Fitzgerald, McLennan and Pawson 1981, p. vii.

of others in the system, tend to breed a *brotherhood* type of mentality, which weighs heavily on discretion and its exercise.

Accountability as the other side of discretion is a key concern when examining the function of criminal justice. Accountability needs to be positioned at various levels: focused on the individual decision-maker; directed towards units or agencies empowered to make decisions in nominated settings; and a more systemic approach to accountability which considers the interconnection between sites for decision-making and those involved in these decisions. It is at the more political and systemic level that the accountability of criminal justice is most underdeveloped.

In the exercise of discretion and resultant accountability, there seems to be some relationship between the autonomy of the individual actor or justice agency, the absence of scrutiny associated with the encounter between the actor/agency or suspect, and the triviality of the offence. In that context, miscarriages of justice are most likely in the early stages of criminal justice and at the lower end of the scale of seriousness. Therefore, the assumption that miscarriages of justice relate to celebrated crimes or serious consequences may not be a fair representation of the way in which abuse of power occurs in the exercise of discretion.

Police discretion: A case study

As mentioned earlier, the most fundamental of police powers may require discretion for their activation. The power of arrest, for instance, will be affected by whether a police officer requires reasonable suspicion before exercising the power. In terms of personal considerations that might influence the police in exercising their arrest powers, factors such as the geography of the offence, the demeanour of the suspect, the characteristics of the offence, the timing of its occurrence, and any challenges to respect for the police associated with the offence will stand as important considerations in the exercise of police discretion.[101]

It is common for the legislature in creating new police powers to expand the range of situations in which discretion is required. Examples of this are the entry, search and seizure provisions in situations of domestic violence presented in the NSW *Crimes Act*.[102] The police officers involved must have reasonable grounds to assume that domestic violence has occurred or will occur, or that in the premises to be entered are objects that might facilitate a violent encounter. The police need to consider both the rights of the offender and the protection of any potential victim in determining whether to exercise entry, search and seizure powers in such situations.

---

101 See Travis 1983.
102 *Crimes Act*, ss. 357F–357I.

Judicial discretion: A case study

Under the governance principle of the separation of powers, the independence of the judiciary is paramount. It is said that this ensures the position of the courts in overseeing the democratic exercise of legislative and executive powers.

Judges have discretion throughout the trial, primarily in decisions about the appropriateness and admissibility of evidence. It remains a key characteristic of judicial discretion that judges may determine to admit evidence even where it has been illegally obtained, provided that the probative effect of the evidence outweighs its prejudicial effect. In order to determine this, judges place their knowledge, generated from precedent cases, against the particular conditions of the case before them.

Recently in Australia there has been considerable political and legal debate about the appropriate way to regulate judicial sentencing discretion. Law reform commissions such as the Australian Law Reform Commission and the NSW Law Reform Commission have produced reports on sentencing which compare and detail various options for regulating judicial discretion.[103] In New South Wales, since the early 1990s, the legislature has taken steps to impose legal limitations on the characteristics to be considered as part of the sentencing processes.[104] Particularly, the legislature remodelled the manner in which sentences of imprisonment were calculated, and standardised the minimum term to be served in prison. In addition, it attempted to regulate the manner in which the courts determined sentencing tariffs. The Chief Justice of New South Wales, in several recent Court of Criminal Appeal decisions,[105] has claimed for the court the power to construct and impose guideline judgments aimed at regulating sentencing practice, and limiting the likelihood of sentencing disparity. In Western Australia, there is legislative provision for guideline judgments.[106] In New South Wales the government has given the Attorney-General the opportunity to seek guideline judgments.[107] This does not impede the court in any way from formulating guideline judgments on its own initiative.

In other jurisdictions such as the Northern Territory,[108] Western Australia,[109] and New South Wales,[110] the legislature has introduced mandatory prison sentences where the judiciary are compelled to impose a prison

---

103 For example NSW Law Reform Commission 1996, Discussion Paper 33.
104 *Sentencing Act 1989.*
105 For instance, *R v. Jurisic* (1998) 101 A Crim R 259; *R v. Henry et Ors* (1999) NSWCCA 111.
106 *Sentencing Act 1995* (WA), s.143.
107 *Criminal Procedure Act 1986*, s. 26, s. 28.
108 Mandatory minimum imprisonment for property offenders—*Sentencing Act 1995* (NT), ss. 78A and B.
109 'Three strikes' legislation—*Crimes (Serious Repeat Offenders) Act 1992* (WA).
110 *Crimes (Life Sentences) Amendment Act 1989* (NSW), s. 19A.

sentence for first offences or where a certain number of repeat offence occasions have occurred, or to require the full sentence to be served. In Western Australia, new law has created a *grid sentencing* model, which provides a complex framework of sentencing protocols designed to ensure consistency in sentencing.[111]

Adams J, in *Jurisic* (*supra*), warned against such *statutory impositions* as minimum sentences or grid sentencing. He commented on the difference between a guideline judgment approach, which allows for flexibility in sentencing, and statutory alternatives which do not. In defence of the place of judicial discretion in ensuring the separation of powers he recognised:

> ... the fundamental difference [is] that the former is developed by the courts, which have under the rule of law the fundamental responsibility for measuring, by reference to well settled principles of criminal justice, the extent to which the liberties of the individual should be removed following the commission of the crime.

At the same time he conceded 'the place of parliament in the setting of the proper boundaries, (and) its ultimate powers over the liberty even of the single citizen ...'[112]

Boundaries of permission: the operation of discretion and accountability

As noted earlier, discretion in criminal justice operates within boundaries established through convention, regulation, or legislation. Once the responsibility of individual justice professionals or the agency with which they are associated is identified, the discretionary powers attached to that responsibility operate within nominated constraints. Discretion therefore should be conceived of in terms of these constraints.

Discretionary decision-making in criminal justice is not inherently an open practice. The reluctance of the judiciary to engage in the substantiated and accountable exercise of discretion imposes a boundary on decision-making at this stage of the process. That boundary may prevent a free flow of information and understanding between criminal justice institutions and the communities in which they function. When justice agencies rely on community consensus or popular participation in order to ensure the success of their responsibilities, then a restriction on openness will tend to work against these preconditions.

All justice agencies rely more on compliance than on the use of force to maintain their authority and respect for their position. Again, compliance

---

111 *Sentencing Amendment and Repeal Act 1999* (WA).
112 At p. 270.

depends on the notion of best practice and the generation of trust and confidence across relationships of crime control. Where discretion is exercised in a largely unaccountable fashion, compliance is endangered.

Recently, complaint mechanisms and discipline codes have presented a limited framework in which communities can require greater accountability, and can measure compliance by the criminal justice institutions with community expectations. However, one great impediment to the reasonable and balanced exercise of criminal justice discretion is the assumption that the result of accountability pressures will mean occupational discipline, and perhaps punishment. This negative inference regarding accountability tends to make those who have discretion reluctant to exercise it in an open and predictable fashion.

Criminal justice institutions (and individuals) value respect perhaps more than any other community reaction. As well as utilising shame as a device to enable the exercise of discretion, such institutions and individuals are extremely susceptible to shame directed against them. Recognition of the distinction between shame which is reintegrative and shame which tends to stigmatise is important in activating the shaming process.

The ideology underpinning many criminal justice institutions is one of independence and autonomy. This tends to run contrary to a reliance on accountability and a promotion of accountability mechanisms. Philosophies of independence also generate in the minds of many criminal justice professionals an unnecessary conflict between discretion and accountability.

When responsibility in the use of discretion in criminal justice is required, the situations where this is not the case should generate claims for compensation, or indemnity. The effect of negative outcomes from the exercise of criminal justice discretion is always uncertain in a climate where the *rights* of the citizen or the suspect only rely on guidelines or occupational regulations.

Situations exist in the operation of criminal justice where secrecy is maintained. Secrecy obviously acts as a boundary for the exercise of discretion and an impediment to community consensus and compliance.[113]

The conflict between anonymity and exposure has particular significance for police investigations. Anonymity, as with jury deliberations, may be considered essential to the customs and practices of criminal justice. However, the consequences of limits to information and understanding may be such as to rarify and distance the operation of the agency concerned from the community.

---

113 Note recent concerns expressed regarding the appropriate operation of criminal juries: Findlay and Duff 1988.

Law enforcement through criminal justice is never total, for a variety of ideological and operational reasons. Selective law enforcement indicates that the exercise of discretion is regulated by individual and organisational preference. When these preferences are unknown or are unexplained to the community they tend to generate mistrust, and respect for criminal justice is undermined.

Discretion and access to justice: the availability of legal counsel

The resources allocated to the operation of criminal justice are limited. In recent years *law and order* politics and 'rationalist' economics have combined to produce an increase in funding for police and prisons while financial support for the operation of the courts, and for legal representation, has deteriorated. In a general management sense it is not difficult to appreciate that this causes tensions at important sites of discretion within the criminal justice process. In addition, certain principles on which criminal justice rests are without guarantee if resources such as legal aid assistance are compromised.

The question of accessibility to legal counsel goes beyond the question of resourcing. In several jurisdictions in Australia, the opportunity to claim legal representation and advice at various stages in the criminal process is either unclear or unprotected.[114] Therefore, it would be wrong to assume that an accused person has a right to legal advice or simply to expect this right should be available. In addition, even if such rights did prevail, they would rest with the knowledge of the accused and his or her ability to claim and access such rights. Juvenile rights to the advice and counsel of an adult are set out in legislation. However, the general suspect population's access to legal representation may rely on the instructions of the police, or the largesse of the courts.[115]

With reduced availability of legal counsel at various stages of the criminal process, the effect on the efficiency of the system at later stages is often ignored. Legal representation is not only a means of benefiting suspects or accused persons; it also enables those in the prosecution's team to benefit from knowledgeable responses to their enquiries.[116]

However, it would appear that arguments against legal aid are based on the popular view that this benefit is exploited by the rich and the guilty; as a result of these images the community will tend to support a reduction of resources for legal aid.

---

114 See Findlay et al. 1999, pp. 56–57, 114–17.
115 See *Driscoll* (1992) 57 NSWLR 731.
116 Recently also the Chief Justice of the High Court has expressed the view that no aspect of justice including the courts is well served by the trend towards more unrepresented accused and appellants.

The High Court's position, which avoids identifying legal representation as a right and leaves the matter in the hands of the judge, does not provide further support for arguments about legal aid funding and constitutional guarantees.[117]

Discretion and the enforcement of institutionalised prejudices

The enforcement of the criminal law has a moral dimension. With the police in particular, questions have been raised regarding the nature of that morality. Is it the morality of the individual, *the job*, the state, the *silent majority*, or the community? The law is not clear except in certain specific areas as to what the link between crime and community morality should be.

Certain criminal justice agencies such as the police and the judiciary find their view of the morality they are charged to protect distorted through isolation. This isolation may be generated by the setting of, and in the course of the duties of, their profession, as well as the separation of their responsibilities from the community at large.

Policies which the police and the judiciary are required to enforce may themselves be duplicitous when it comes to reconciling principle with practice. The close association between certain political imperatives and the operation of criminal justice may mean that discrimination and prejudice appear to be institutionalised in the operations of justice and the criminal law. In certain settings political and organisational goals in criminal justice intermingle and are mutually reliant, at least insofar as crucial issues of resourcing are concerned.

The techniques of stereotyping and profiling offenders, on which the police greatly rely, tend to generate and to reinforce prejudices. The judiciary is also susceptible to stereotyping, particularly when it comes to expectations of consistency and uniformity in sentencing.

The regulation of judicial discretion: Guideline sentencing

The main sites for judicial discretion and its regulation have been the admissibility of evidence, and sentencing. The push for regulation complements a prevailing community view that judges are either inconsistent in their sentencing patterns, or are sentencing too leniently.[118] The impact of such opinion has been recognised at the highest levels of appeal courts (see *Jurisic, supra*). In the opinion of Spiegelman CJ:

---

117 See *Dietrich v. R* (1992) 109 ALR 365.

118 Unfortunately this seems to have influenced the attitude of many appeal courts; that inconsistency is confirmed by evidence of leniency. The consequence of this has been that sentencing regulation is now equated with more severe sentencing practice.

> The courts must show that they are responsive to public criticism of the outcome of sentencing processes. Guideline judgments are a mechanism for structuring discretion rather than restricting discretion.

Adams J warned against allowing public opinion or public perceptions to influence sentencing. While the confidence of the public is vital, misreporting and misinformation from the media may form the basis of adverse community opinion about sentencing. The courts must treat with care assertions of what might be the public perception about the exercise of judicial discretion.

Sentencing legislation such as the *Sentencing Act 1989* (NSW), as previously mentioned, has tended to limit the issues that a judge may take into account when determining a sentence, and also has restricted the manner in which certain sentences are conditional as to actual time served. In other state and territory jurisdictions the emphasis on mandatory sentencing for certain offences or certain repeat offences has reduced judicial discretion to the point where judges may be required to sentence in a manner which their individual conceptions of justice would not support. This trend is built on a recent propensity among all Australian legislatures to create hierarchies of aggravation that designate the manner in which particular circumstances or consequences of an offence will require a sentencing range in comparison to offences above and below it. These developments have indicated the willingness of governments to interfere directly with the exercise of judicial discretion, largely in reaction to the view that sentencing is generally both too lenient and inconsistent. Perhaps a motivation for the courts in New South Wales taking a more formal approach to sentencing guidelines was to forestall further legislative intervention and to confirm the potential of the court to self-regulate judicial discretion.

Guideline sentencing is a feature of certain appeal court regimes in various states, and has been so in England and Wales for many years. Recently in New South Wales, particular judgments from the Court of Criminal Appeal have promoted sentencing limitations for traffic offences and robbery. The guideline approach has taken two specific forms:

- in *Jurisic* (*supra*), the court indicated a starting point for custodial sentences from which trial judges should construct their sentences in like or aggravated cases;
- in *Henry* (*supra*), the court proposed a sentencing range within which sentences would be set, again depending on aggravating circumstances.

The intention behind the New South Wales guideline sentencing approach is not so much to bind the trial judge's sentencing, but to provide a means of reducing the inconsistencies and anomalies in the *inexact art* of sentencing. The Court of Criminal Appeal in *Jurisic* recognised the tension between maintaining maximum flexibility in the exercise of judicial discretion on the one hand, and ensuring consistency in sentencing decisions on the other.

Critics of guideline sentencing indicate that not only does it threaten variety and individuality in sentencing practice, but it has also meant that sentences have been pushed to the upper level of sentencing ranges in New South Wales. In certain situations prosecutors are taking matters before the courts which previously they would have chosen not to prosecute because they view the issue of public interest in prosecution as significantly determined by the status of the offence and its penalty within a guideline judgment. The judges themselves have admitted that it is easier to push sentencing ranges up than to move them down. Why is it that consistency is said to equate with greater severity? Further, portraying exceptional cases as the norm for the purposes of guidelines tends to catch the less serious cases within the higher ranges, as was the case with *Henry* (*supra*).

Supporters of sentencing guidelines argue that 'judge shopping'[119] tends to produce inconsistencies in sentences, depending on whether a matter is brought before a lenient judge. In addition, they would argue that consistency is always to be preferred to sentencing disparity. The problem with this position is the assumption that inconsistent sentencing arises to some extent from unjust or lenient considerations. This does not consider the fact that very few cases are similar enough to justify uniform judgments.

Recently the DPP in New South Wales raised the following issues arising out of the present treatment of sentencing guidelines in New South Wales:

- How should the categories suitable for guideline judgments be identified?[120]
- Should a guideline judgment always be at the behest of the Crown (and therefore by implication be directed towards increasing the general level of sentences)?[121]
- How should the effect of a guideline judgment on the offenders concerned be accommodated?
- What approach should be adopted by the court for determining appropriate means of sentence calculation where guideline models differ?[122]

---

119   Where the accused or his lawyers endeavour to have their case listed before a lenient or sympathetic judge.

120   Guidelines in New South Wales are soon to be set for offences of drug importation, and for breaking, entering and stealing.

121   NSW legislation suggests that this will always be the case.

122   The starting point guideline (*Jurisic*) or the sentencing range guideline (*Henry*)?

- How should the court inform itself? What is the status of additional material considered in formulating guidelines (admissible evidence)?
- What is the status of a guideline judgment?
- How can the conflict between Court of Criminal Appeal judgments and the different positions adopted by individual judges within a guideline decision be addressed?
- How should the effect of guideline judgments be evaluated? How will the public know the benefits?

CONTEXT OF THE PROBLEM

Obviously issues of youth and Aboriginality as contained in the following problem influence the encounter between the accused and the police. It is for the judge to distil the impact of such discrimination when considering the appropriate sentence to hand down. The offences to which the accused has pleaded guilty are serious and in light of recent guideline judgments, may demand a custodial term. What issues can the judge consider in weighing up the sentencing decision? How much discretion is available to the judge, and what issues will be unlikely to be considered or unavailable for consideration?

PROBLEM

Dave is a young Aboriginal living in a rural town. He comes from a middle-class family and has never been in trouble with the police. He has had his driving licence for about six months.

Following an end of year school function, Dave drives his white girl-friend to the pub and they have a couple of beers. Despite her suggestions to the contrary, Dave decides to drive her home. On the way back Dave's car skids on the wet road and he collides with an oncoming car. The driver of that car is injured and taken to the hospital by ambulance.

The police arrive at the accident scene and take Dave and his girlfriend to the station. On the way there one of the constables comments, 'What's a nice girl like you doing with a stupid black bastard like this? We will make sure he never drives any fancy cars again.' At the station Dave is subjected to further abuse and is left in a cell all night before his parents are informed. Dave is charged with negligent driving, driving with a blood alcohol content over the legal limit, and aggravated dangerous driving causing grievous bodily harm.

Against the advice of his lawyers, Dave pleads guilty in the District Court. His girlfriend gives evidence regarding the racial taunts of the police during the plea in mitigation on sentence.

You are the judge in this case. How would you exercise your discretion?

ENGAGING THE PROBLEM

Are any of the issues that might have an impact on the admissibility of crucial evidence relevant for the determination of liability? Does the judge have any discretion in this situation over the determination of liability?

The accused is obviously contrite, fearful and intimidated by the circumstances of the offence, his detention, and the prospects of the trial. How can these issues be accounted for, along with his age, Aboriginality, and prior record?

What effect would sentencing regulation and guidelines have on the parameters of sentencing discretion in such a situation?

ADDITIONAL RESOURCES

Brown, D., 'The Royal Commission into the NSW Police Service: Process Corruption and the Limits of Judicial Reflexivity' (1998) 9(3) *Current Issues in Criminal Justice* 228.

Brown, D., Farrier, D., Egger, S., and McNamara, L., *Criminal Laws*, Federation Press, Sydney, 1996, paras 3.2.4, 3.2.5, 3.2.6–3.2.7, 3.4.2, 3.6.2, 3.6.5, 3.6.6.

Findlay, M., 'Acting on Information Received: Mythmaking and Police Corruption' (1987) *Journal of Studies in Justice* 19.

Hogg, R., 'The Politics of Police Investigation', in Wickham, G. (ed.), *Social Theory and Legal Politics*, Local Consumption Publications, Sydney, 1988, p. 120.

Manning, P., and Redlinger, L., 'Invitational Edges of Corruption: Some Consequences of Narcotic Law Enforcement', in Rock, P. (ed.), *Drugs and Politics*, Transaction Books, London, 1977.

Spiegelman, J., 'Sentencing Guideline Judgments' (1999) 11(1) *Current Issues in Criminal Justice* 5.

Jurisic (1998) 45 NSWLR 209

TOPIC 7

CONSTRUCTING THE TRUTH: BAIL AND VERDICT

Notions of guilt or innocence

In principle at least, the criminal trial is said to be an adversarial process through which truth is determined. However, in an adversarial process, the concept of truth is sometimes relative, and often in dispute.

Difficulties with what constitutes the truth within a criminal trial context have led to the qualification that judges manage the law and juries are responsible for finding the facts. This fact-finding function emerges from the consideration of competing stories and contested information. Facts in this respect are those claims that appear to be the most plausible, the most convincing, or the least fallible.

In determining the facts on which the guilt or innocence of an accused, or the predicability of his future behaviour, is to be evaluated, juries (or judges sitting without juries) are said to test whether a doubt might emerge from the story or the explanation before them. Therefore, fact becomes something about which the least reasonable doubt might be raised.

The importance of expert evidence as a source of fact in crime deliberations cannot be overstated.[123] However, again, through the manner in which this evidence is presented it is likely to be contested. This raises particular difficulties for juries when they are called upon to believe the professional expertise from one side, which is then contested by the other.

The emergence of truth in criminal investigation and the trial is often the result of justification rather than material discoveries. The police and the court are usually faced with secondary source information, such as the witnessed evidence of third parties, which explains or supports a particular conclusion on the facts presented. The police, and even more so the judge, will rarely elicit facts for themselves, or have the benefit of personal knowledge and experience of the information on which the case is constructed. Hard evidence is rarely presented before them. Therefore, explanation and justification become significant in the establishment of facts.

Some facts are harder than others to determine through the criminal investigation and trial process. For instance, the mental state of the accused is a matter on which police, prosecutors, and judicial officers will need to make inferential judgments. Juries, when determining whether a particular mental state was present in the mind of the accused, will commonly come to this conclusion through inferences drawn from other observable facts, or through comparisons with their own morals and experiences, or those of other ordinary persons.

The correspondence between particular facts, and their coincidence, are important when considering criminal liability. The need for criminal conduct to coincide with the presence of a particular mental state is an example of this. Other situations might involve certain behaviours coming together in a series of acts or a process of conduct to which particular mental states may correspond.

The situation in which certain facts exist may give these facts their legal relevance. In this respect, the circumstances of an offence may be crucial to the determination of liability. Further, consequences which flow from certain behaviours or certain mental conditions may also constitute crucial dimensions of criminality, or justification and excuses.

---

123 Recently, however, the legislature has manifested its distrust of the manner in which the language of the expert has been used to challenge or replace legal definitions and factual certainty—see reform to the law of diminished responsibility in NSW *Crimes Act*, s. 23A.

The use of a jury or a judicial officer to certify the truth or the factual basis for an argument from one side of the adversarial process becomes significant when these facts or decisions are used to validate certain outcomes. Therefore, the judge's sentence rests on the determination of the verdict. A bail decision (the other potential custodial determination), on the other hand, may essentially rely on the creation and legitimisation of an impression about the applicant, which comes from a range of agreed facts, regarding the likelihood of her or his reappearance.

Truth in the criminal setting is as dependent on its certification as it may be on its origins.

Where the extreme positions of adversarial arguments make it difficult to distil facts or truth, mediation may be necessary to produce a credible determination. Certainly in processes such as the summing up by the judge, mediation of competing facts and the re-evaluation of doubt may bring about a third version of the truth.

In the criminal justice process, the characteristic of truth is said to apply in recognition of normative expectations. The police investigation and the trial are intended to produce results. These results are said to draw towards a conclusion on criminal liability, and therefore guilt. The demands for punishment would not stand so effectively without the implicit connection between the facts, the guilt or innocence of the accused, and the state's responsibility to punish the guilty.

Above all else, it is essential to understand truth (in the context of the criminal trial) as a social concept. Without attempts at considering and locating relevance many of the facts on which decisions about liability are made would be meaningless. Therefore, not only does social relevance inform the conclusions to be drawn from particular facts, but the components of criminal liability also rely on the context of fact in order to justify outcomes or legal principle.

Stages of guilt or innocence

A crucial presumption on which the criminal justice process is said to build reiterates the innocence of the accused parties until they are proven guilty. This produces a range of interesting consequences in relation to proof, and the existence of any obligation to answer allegations. These consequences are not simply procedural. They should mean that the accused person is not required to commit resources to the investigation and trial process unless a case is proved to the satisfaction of the fact finder.

Recently, however, federal legislative developments have undermined the presumption of innocence. For example, in relation to the investigations by certain agencies such as the National Crime Authority and the Independent Commission Against Corruption, suspects are required to answer questions even if these would lead to self-incrimination. The justification for this focuses on the difficulty in establishing a prosecution case in certain instances without the power to extract information from witnesses.

In reality the presumption of innocence rarely holds for police once they have established a suspect worthy of investigation. It would be both impractical and perhaps inconsistent for police investigators to pursue a suspect and at the same time recognise his innocence. Having said this, the presumption of innocence should govern those *due process* protections which are in place to guard against an abuse of investigative power in the construction of the prosecution case.

The presumption of innocence is also under threat in relation to bail. In New South Wales, for instance, the granting of bail is a legislative right. Therefore, accused persons should be able to claim bail unless other conditions are present that would suggest that the risk of release is too great. Recent amendments to the *Bail Act* have created certain situations where that right is denied, and the accused is required to provide a reason as to why bail should be given. In this respect, the presumption of innocence has been reversed.

One might also argue that if the presumption of innocence were strong and universal, individuals should stand equally before the law. Accused persons should have access to similar legal resources and legal counsel as would be made available to the prosecution case. In addition, each accused should have access to legal representation at the important times in the preparation and delivery of his trial. This is clearly not the case and with the recent decimation of legal aid funding throughout Australia, access to useful and appropriate legal representation has been reduced.

In terms of the prosecution, determination is made well before trial of the likelihood of a guilty verdict. Prosecutors need to evaluate the strength of the police case in order to commit additional resources towards the eventual prosecution of the matter. Also, where prosecutors may be invited by defence counsel to withdraw charges, or to bargain down charges from one level to another, the likely success of the prosecution case (and therefore a guilty verdict) crucially influences these decisions.[124]

The production of evidence through the presentation of witnesses at trial is essential for the determination of the guilt or innocence of the accused. The selection of these witnesses and the delivery of their evidence will usually provide the basis for the establishment of a case or its rebuttal. The reliance on witness evidence by the prosecution is essential in order to establish a case to answer. In many situations the defence needs to do little more than

---

124 Another important concern for the exercise of prosecutorial discretion is whether or not a prosecution in all the circumstances would be in the public interest. See Office of the NSW Director of Public Prosecutions, *Guidelines for Prosecutors*.

either challenge the version of the facts presented through cross-examination, or attack the credibility of these witnesses.

The jury (or a judge sitting alone where a jury is not required) are the arbiters of fact, and are responsible for determining the guilt or innocence of the accused. This determination is based, as we have noted, on a conclusion that the prosecution has (or has not) established its case beyond reasonable doubt. The defence only has an onus to answer the prosecution after its case has been established, and the burden on the defence is to raise no more than a reasonable doubt.

The delivery of the verdict is often seen as the paramount stage in determining guilt or innocence. This is so, and yet the process of verdict determination may, as much jury research indicates, occur through the duration of the trial long before the jury retires to deliberate.[125] In addition, it may not only be issues of guilt or innocence on which the verdict of the jury depends. Historically it has been common for juries to return verdicts based on either a dissatisfaction with the law and its outcomes, or reluctance to see severe penalties as the consequence of their decision.

The determination of victims' compensation, a feature of modern criminal justice, has some of the same elements as the consideration of guilt or innocence. Very simply, victims' compensation will not apply unless a guilty verdict is returned. Further, the *degree* of compensation awarded may be a reflection of the *degree* of guilt that the judge apportions in his or her mind to the actions of the accused.

The same is the case with judicial decision-making regarding sentence. In determining what punishment should follow a guilty verdict, a judge or magistrate may consider matters in mitigation that perhaps could not be raised when criminal liability was being evaluated during the trial. Mitigating factors are designed to explain the wider social situation of the offence and the impact that potential sentences could have on this accused.

In traditional justice settings, the executive has the prerogative of mercy to apply to any sentence that may be imposed on a convicted offender. More recently this has been used to create systems where ministerial discretion enables early release of prisoners. Such discretion may take the form of release on licence, systems of parole, and systems of remission.

The final level where the guilt or innocence of the accused is evaluated on an ongoing basis occurs when the community reacts to the prospect of reintegration. In its most obvious form this occurs when prisoners are released back into the community. There are, however, many situations where the community is the site for punishment, and where community reaction is crucial to the possibility of reintegration.

---

125 See Findlay 1994, *Jury Management in NSW.*

Bail

Again, bail is a context in criminal justice decision-making where preliminary evaluations of guilt or innocence and questions of truth are touched on. It should be remembered that decisions on bail are not decisions on guilt alone. In fact, the primary concern surrounding bail in most Australian jurisdictions is whether the accused person is likely to return to custody when required by the courts. However, recent changes to the bail process throughout Australia, reversing the onus of proof for applicants charged with certain serious offences,[126] will tend to suggest that determinations of likely guilt (and associated danger to the community) are influential at this stage.

The right to bail in most states and territories of Australia is based on the prevailing presumption of innocence. For example, section 8 of the New South Wales *Bail Act* provides a right to police bail for minor offences. In support of this right is the presumption in favour of bail which requires the heavier burden of proof to rest with parties opposing the bail application. In most Australian jurisdictions the presumption in favour of bail has been reversed to reflect concerns for particular offences charged. In New South Wales, it was several cases where accused armed robbers had re-offended on bail which stimulated the development of this legislative change. The reversed presumption now extends to serious drug-related offences, and to domestic violence.[127]

Bail may be granted at various stages of the pre-trial and trial process. The police are given certain powers to grant bail after charges have been laid. If bail is refused, application can then be made to the courts for a bail redetermination. The police can pass bail decisions to the courts or these decisions may go directly there depending on the nature of the charges. If court bail is refused then there is a reapplication or appeal process available.

Police bail may be granted by *an authorised officer*. The accused should be informed of his right to contact a lawyer in order to assist in the granting of the bail, and in addition should be informed of his right to bail in minor offences. The New South Wales *Bail Act*, in other circumstances, lists a range of considerations which the authorised officer must reflect upon while making a bail decision. Police bail may be made with or without condition.

In some respects the process of court bail is similar to that of police bail. The major difference is that with court bail the application is argued before

---

126 Usually drug trafficking, armed robbery, and certain violent assaults come within a category requiring the accused to establish why bail should be granted. The presumption in favour of bail is reversed for these offences.

127 See NSW *Bail Act*, ss. 9 and 9A. The amendment to the presumption in favour of bail in New South Wales occurred in 1998 and covered offences of violence, drug-related offences, offences where bail had previously not been complied with, and certain domestic violence situations where the degree of violence alleged was significant.

the judicial officer and both sides have the opportunity to introduce evidence to substantiate their arguments about the factors to be considered in the granting or refusal of bail.

The factors relevant to determining bail primarily revolve around the issue of predicting the applicant's reliability and likelihood of answering the charges at a later date. Section 32 of the New South Wales *Bail Act*, for instance, covers the factors for consideration, including the probability of the accused attending court, the interest of the defendant, the protection of victims or close relatives, and the protection of their welfare and of the community. Regarding the likelihood of reappearance, the person's background and community ties, the history and details of residence, employment and family situation, and prior criminal history can be taken into account. Any previous failure to appear will obviously influence the determination. The circumstances of the offence such as its nature and seriousness, the strength of evidence against the defendant, and the seriousness of the potential penalty may also be considered. As for the interests of the offender, the period he is likely to be on remand and the conditions under which he will be held are primary concerns. In addition, the need to prepare a defence and to obtain legal advice and the requirement of free and lawful access to other aspects of liberty should also be considered. In particular instances where the offender is intoxicated or needs protection, then bail might be refused. Regarding the interest of the community, any likely interference with witnesses or evidence and the likelihood of re-offending are paramount concerns.

In relation to conditions to be imposed on the granting of bail, section 36 (2) of the *Bail Act* addresses sureties or security. Here the accused may rely on an acceptable person to enter a security against a breach of bail, and the accused may be required to enter into an agreement for specific conduct while at liberty. Regarding domestic violence in particular, section 37 (1) provides conditions against assaulting and molesting victims, against harassment or intimidation of victims, and against entry to the victim's premises or attempted contact.

The appeal process for bail is a mixture of fresh applications, or the review of previous applications. In the case of review, courts may examine their own decisions, or bail refused in the lower court may be reviewed by a superior court. The review of bail may be called for by the accused person, by a police informant, or by the Attorney-General. Section 22 of the *Bail Act* suggests no limit to the number of applications that can be made by an accused, but the Supreme Court can refuse further applications if they believe them to be vexatious.

Breaches of bail are now considered to be offences in themselves. The consequence of a breach may be the forfeit of any security that has been offered as a condition of bail, and re-arrest under a bench warrant for the breach of bail.

Bargaining charges

There is a process in contemporary criminal justice where charges, and the pleas associated with these, may be negotiated between the prosecution and the defence.[128] These negotiations are stimulated on the prosecution side by concerns for the efficient use of resources. Accused persons will be inclined to bargain where they believe that as a result it is likely that they will be convicted of a lesser offence, and feel that the case associated with the offence charged is problematic.

The pressure to bargain has increased in recent years. A reason for this has been a growth in the workload of the prosecutors, and the steady state of their resourcing. Regarding the motivation for accused persons to bargain, the clear indication by judges and magistrates that compensation will be given in sentence for those who make pleas has had a stimulating effect on the process of bargaining. In addition, since the court openly recognises that bargaining occurs, it has become a more legitimate part of the criminal justice process.

Charge bargaining is usually carried out with the police at an early point of contact. Either the police will approach an accused with an alternative charge, or the police and the accused's legal adviser will come to some agreement on a lesser charge when the strengths and weaknesses of the case are better known.

Charge bargaining usually occurs in situations where alternative or multiple offences might be the substance of the charges.

Plea bargaining occurs closer to the commencement of the trial. Prosecutors and defence counsel will engage in discussions in order to identify a level of offence to which the accused would be willing to submit a guilty plea. As mentioned earlier, this is to the advantage of the accused in that he could argue for sentence leniency on the basis of contrition and cooperation. The incentive for the prosecution is obviously one of workload, and certainty of conviction. Again, plea bargaining is more likely to occur in the situation where alternative or multiple charges have been laid or could be laid. It recognises prosecutorial discretion to drop higher charges or to prefer alternative charges in reward for a plea. The premium here is the efficiency of the plea rather than justice from the perspective of the prosecution or the defence. In both situations of bargaining the adversarial system is avoided in preference for an administrative resolution.

---

128 See Findlay et al. 1999, pp. 105–6.

Sentence bargaining was for a short time in New South Wales a feature of the District Court process. A formal sentencing indication scheme operated where judges presented the possible range of sentence likely if the prosecution case succeeded. Once the indication was given, an accused could determine whether he was willing to accept sentence within that nominated range.

Verdict

In discussing the verdict in a criminal trial it is important to remember that by far the majority of all matters dealt with in the criminal courts have resulted in guilty pleas. In this respect a verdict is not delivered, in that the accused admits to the charges, and sentencing follows. When charges are contested, the majority of these matters are heard before a magistrate or a single judge alone. While jury trial is the popular representation of the criminal trial in most common law jurisdictions, it is in fact relatively rare. Once it could be said that all serious criminal offences would go before a jury; however, this is now not so. In certain jurisdictions legislative provision has been made for an accused to elect for his charges, of whatever level of seriousness, to be heard by a judge sitting alone.

The symbolic significance of the jury as confirmation of the ideology of criminal justice should never be underestimated. This significance is both historical and strongly associated with independent and democratic government. In certain constitutions such as that of the USA, jury trial is encapsulated as a fundamental right. This is not the case in the constitutional legality of the states and territories of Australia. While the Constitution of the Commonwealth refers to the right of jury trial, it is ascribed to Commonwealth offences alone.[129]

The principal tenets of the ideology underlying the jury are:

- that community participation and lay involvement ensure the democratic nature of criminal justice;
- that the verdict arises out of a democratic understanding between judge and jury;
- that the democracy of the legislature is reflected through jury decision-making;
- that the wider legitimacy of the court process is ensured through participation;
- that the participatory nature of the jury, and its roots in the community, confirm the anti-professionalisation of criminal justice.

---

129   NB Deane J's verdict in *Kingswell* (1986) 62 ALR 161.

Jury ideology is said to advance:

- *representativeness:* the *communion of peers* (who is the peer of the juror?); the fair-minded persons; an impartial body of decision-makers; an independent body of decision-makers; a representative body which reflects the community. If representativeness is to be inclusive of *minority* defendants, such as Aboriginal people, how should the representation of their interests be ensured?[130]
- *impartiality*: Random selection may attempt to protect this but in all jury systems the process of selection is anything but random.[131]
- *independence*: Despite the province of the jury over decisions on the facts, how independent of the influence of judicial direction are jurors?
- *lay participation*: Juries are said to represent the community conscience rather than the letter of the law. But what community?
- *certainty*: The absolute verdict anonymously delivered is said to guarantee a verdict beyond challenge; how is accuracy in decision-making, and the fear of the wayward verdict[132] to be overcome when jury decisions are settled in secret?
- *comprehension*: The collective decision-making process is anticipated to enhance comprehension and yet this has recently been impugned in the face of concerns for complexity.[133]
- *equality and balance between judge and jury:* the jury as finder of facts and the judge as protector of the independence of the jury.

Even a casual consideration of these ideological principles will suggest several inconsistencies and a general sense of contest between major principles. For example, how can representativeness and impartiality, independence and community conscience sit well together as ideals?[134] And yet this incompatibility of ideology seems to do little to impugn its functional significance.

When it comes to analysing the function of the jury in criminal trials in contemporary Australia, it would seem that its symbolic significance in the

---

130 The Runciman Royal Commission on Criminal Justice in the UK (1991–1993) recommended that in such situations a trial judge should have the discretion to ensure that one juror was from the ethnic and cultural background of the accused. It is also useful to reflect on the jurisprudence in the USA on the representativeness of jurors in terms of constitutional guarantees against racial discrimination.

131 See Findlay 1994, *Jury Management in NSW*, Chapters 3 and 4.

132 Waywardness is discussed critically in Findlay 1994, *Jury Management in NSW*, pp. 8–10.

133 The Runciman Royal Commission on Criminal Justice in the UK (1991–1993).

134 For a discussion of incompatible jury ideology, see P. Duff and M. Findlay, 'The Jury in England: Practice and Ideology' (1982) *International Journal of the Sociology of Law* 253.

eyes of the community outweighs its practical presence. The expansion of the summary jurisdiction and the introduction of election for judge-alone trials in serious criminal cases has seen the gradual diminution of jury trial as a feature of Australian criminal justice. However, public confidence in the jury and its status as an important image of criminal justice would give support to the argument that the function of the jury is ideological. The jury tends to legitimise all other institutions and processes in the criminal trial, whether it is present there or not.

To leave the issue of function here would be to dismiss the important role juries continue to have in certain trials. Juries commonly bring down verdicts more explicable in terms of their *common sense* (or community values) than their reflection of legal principle. In fact, jury decisions are sometimes accused by lawyers and judges of being *wayward,* when they seem to ignore the limits of the law to produce an outcome more in line with community values.

Traditionally it has been said that the jury is the master of the facts. It is for the jurors to determine what *facts* they doubt, and what they consider to be convincing. The verdict they deliver is intended to reflect a decision as to whether the case for the prosecution was established beyond reasonable doubt, or brought down by doubt. In reality, juries also depend on the legal explanation of notions such as reasonable doubt, as the context within which they manage and evaluate facts. The distinction between fact and law is not clear-cut, and the jury's mastery of the facts means little without the application of any such facts to the establishment or denial of legal principle. Guilt or innocence rests on fact and law.

The veil over the jury deliberation room is supposed to make the jury's decision more certain, and inviolable. It has, recently, led to criticisms about the decision-making practices of certain juries, the pressure brought to bear on some jurors, and the ability of certain juries to comprehend complex issues of fact and law. With juries not required to justify or explain their decisions, and in states such as Victoria, with jurors legally prohibited from discussing how the decision in their trial was reached, it is difficult to challenge or confirm such criticisms. Perhaps the closed jury deliberation settles nothing more than the rule that a jury acquittal cannot be appealed.[135]

Since it is the product of a collective (and it is hoped representative and impartial) decision-making process, the jury's verdict has the appearance of

---

135 It would seem that at least from the minority judgment of Murphy J in the High Court appeal of *Chamberlain No. 2* (1984) 153 CLR 521 that a conviction by a jury could be overturned if it was considered to be irreconcilable with the facts and fundamentally unjust.

community consensus. The concept of 12 lay participants listening to the evidence and then agreeing on a final outcome suggests more than democracy, but rather a common and complete consensus. This is what is under challenge when legislatures such as South Australia[136] accept a majority verdict. It is said that majority verdicts avoid the delay and expense of hung juries, and the possibility that a single juror might unfairly influence the outcome of the trial. Both these concerns are problematic if one relies on majority verdicts for their solution.

One of the clearest functional advantages of the jury is in terms of community access to justice. Even with the radically reduced presence of the jury in Australian criminal courts, today there remains the regular and relatively random progress of citizens through the courts who would otherwise have little or no opportunity to be involved in the process, and to experience criminal justice at first hand.

The jury acts as a buffer between the determination of guilt and the delivery of sentence. In this respect the judge is placed outside the contest over the facts. The judge can be represented as a dispassionate and impartial determiner of a just and consistent sentence. The wider principles of punishment can be employed by the judge (in delivering sentence), to some extent removed by the individual concerns of each trial.

The jury is generally supported by the community, but never immune from challenge. Many of the criticisms directed against the jury accept the common ideology discussed above but quibble about whether the jury in its current form is capable of achieving these ends.

The debate surrounding majority verdicts has been couched in the concern for which form of decision-making is most likely to produce just, logical and impartial verdicts. The *nobbling* of jurors within the confines of the unanimous verdict was certainly a strong argument in favour of introducing majority verdicts in England. For many of the Australian jurisdictions with majority verdicts it was the concern about the cost, delay and waste of resources said to result from hung trials that exerted pressure for this reform.

The strongest recent attacks on jury decision-making have focused on suspicions about comprehension. Particularly in relation to complex commercial fraud trials, the ability of the untrained juror to understand complex facts, sophisticated commercial environments, and difficult legal distinctions has been doubted. The critics have preferred the introduction of professional assessors to assist the judge in deliberating on such matters. However, there is little to suggest that in the empirical studies on juror comprehension,

---

136 Where for the first three hours of deliberation a jury is required to strive for unanimity and then after the expiration of that time they can return a majority verdict.

complexity is unequivocal and always associated with difficulties in juror comprehension.[137]

CONTEXT OF THE PROBLEM

In the problem that follows, students are to participate in a bail application. As the applicant's lawyer, the prosecutor opposing bail, or the judge, you will need to appreciate and discharge your responsibilities regarding the application. What is it you are trying to achieve from your professional perspective in this exercise? It is also important to recognise the legislative obligations and opportunities contained in the bail legislation in your jurisdiction.

Questions of what has to be argued (proved), to what extent, and by whom require early consideration. The manner in which arguments are constrained by general legal principle and specific legislative requirements will be revealed as the application proceeds. The need to answer the assertions of your opponent or to weigh these up in order to balance competing expectations for bail will feature in the exercise.

Also, critically review your oral presentation in this exercise. The views of the rest of the class as observers will be helpful here.

PROBLEM

Derek Pringle is 19 years old. He lives in accommodation rented by his girlfriend Sarah. He has lived with her for the last two months, but they have had a relationship for seven months. Prior to living with Sarah, he lived with his parents. Sarah is six months pregnant. Derek is currently unemployed, although he states that he has a job offer from his uncle, who is a foreman on a building site. He has had short-term jobs on and off since he left school. He has a number of previous convictions for theft and fraud. He has never been given a custodial sentence. For his last offence he was sentenced to a probation of 18 months by the local court. He is still serving that sentence. He has not previously breached his probation order. He has no record of breaching bail.

Derek was arrested after Mrs Beasley, an 80-year-old woman, contacted the police. She had been awakened in the night by a man entering her bedroom. She had screamed and the intruder had left. She gave a description to the police that fitted Derek. They arrested him and an identification parade was held. Mrs Beasley identified Derek as the intruder. None of the goods

---

137 For a discussion of this issue see P. Duff et al., *Juries: A Hong Kong Perspective*, University of Hong Kong Press, Hong Kong, 1992; M. Findlay, *Jury Management in NSW*, Australian Institute of Judicial Administration, Melbourne, 1994; M. Findlay, 'Juror Comprehension and Complexity: Strategies to Enhance Understanding' (2001) *British Journal of Criminology* 56.

stolen that night from Mrs Beasley's property have been found in Derek's possession. The police charged Derek with burglary but refused police bail. The trial is likely to be held in three months' time in the District Court. The maximum penalty for breaking and entering, for instance under section 111 of the *Crimes Act 1900* (NSW), where there are no aggravating circumstances, is 10 years penal servitude.

Defence: You have been asked to make an application for bail for Derek Pringle. Consider what arguments and criteria from the bail legislation in your jurisdiction you would use in making such an application. Are there any conditions you could think of attaching to the bail to improve your chances?

Prosecution: You have been asked to oppose this bail application. Consider what arguments and criteria from the bail legislation in your jurisdiction you would use to aid your opposition.

Judiciary: After listening to arguments from both sides you are asked to decide on this bail application. What is your decision? What are your reasons for this decision?

ENGAGING THE PROBLEM

At the outset you must be familiar with the bail legislation that applies in your jurisdiction. In order to construct and prioritise your argument (or deliberations), you will need to return to the detail of the legislation constantly.

It is necessary to extract from the minimum facts in the problem those elements of your argument that best support (or challenge) the legislative requirements for bail. In doing so you will realise that your argument is only as strong as the merits and failings of the other side.

The competing interests of the side that you represent and the intentions for bail will constantly inform your argument and presentation. The policy motivations for contradictions in the way bail law has recently evolved will affect your deliberations.

ADDITIONAL RESOURCES

Jury Act 1977 (NSW)

Bail Act 1978 (NSW), sections 8, 8A, 9, 32, 36.

Brown, D., Farrier, D., Egger, S., and McNamara, L., *Criminal Laws*, Federation Press, Sydney, 2001, paras 3.4.3–3.4.4, 3.5.1–3.5.9, 3.7.1–3.7.2, 3.7.4–3.7.8, 3.8.1–3.8.6.

Findlay, M., *Jury Management in NSW*, Australian Institute of Judicial Administration, Melbourne, 1994, Chapters 1, 3, and 7.

NSW Law Reform Commission, *The Jury in a Criminal Trial*, NSW Law Reform Commission, 1996, pp. 14–16, 99–116, 139–59, 181–96.

O'Gorman, T., 'We Need to Know More' (1992) 27(3) *Australian Law News* 10.

Trembath, O., 'Judgement by Peers: Aborigines and the Jury System' (1993) 31(15) *Law Society Journal* 44.

Chamberlain No. 2 (1984) 153 CLR 521

TOPIC 8

DETERMINING CRIMINAL LIABILITY I: VOLITION AND CAPACITY[138]

General principles for determining criminal responsibility

Presumptions

The principles which underpin the determination of criminal liability rely on a range of prevailing presumptions. These include general presumptions about individual knowledge of the law and its consequences, as well as the presumption that people intend the natural consequences of their actions. The latter is often crucial for the establishment of the guilty mental state required by the elements of an offence.

Presumptions are meant to give some degree of certainty to a process of analysis which is full of contradictions. For instance, the suggestion that people intend the natural consequences of their acts implies that all offenders are equally rational and capable of choices. This is obviously not so in practice. However, to move from a basis where concepts of criminal motivation and the determination of fault were entirely dependent on the circumstances of each offence would make it difficult if not impossible to structure a consistent process for determining criminal liability.

Essential to that process is a mechanism where a case against the accused can be proved by the prosecution in order to put the defence to the task of raising a reasonable doubt. This is what the criminal trial is all about. The courts and the legislature have addressed problems associated with proof for the prosecution by creating presumptions which avoid difficult and constant evidentiary argument where doubt may be comparatively easy to raise, or where proof requires special knowledge perhaps available only to the accused. An example of this is certain drugs offences, where, once possession is established, the accused is presumed to have knowledge of what he possessed. Without such a presumption the prosecution would regularly face the accused's denial of knowledge, which may be impossible to disprove. This presumption, as with most, is a presumption of fact. In this respect it simply

---

138 The topics dealing with determining criminal liability rely on an understanding of matters discussed in Chapters 4 and 5. Therefore, the notes that introduce Topics 8–10 will only highlight the major themes expanded upon in the earlier chapters.

puts the onus of proof on the accused to disprove knowledge. In doing so it comes into conflict with another presumption: that of the accused's innocence. Further, it appears to challenge the conventions of criminal liability regarding the requirement that the prosecution establish the accused's criminal mental state.[139]

Presumptions as to the mental state of the accused person are difficult to apply in practice for two reasons:

- it is often complex and difficult to tell whether parliament, in creating an offence, expected that the prohibited conduct (*actus reus*) should be penalised even in the absence of a blameworthy state of mind; and
- if a criminal mental state (*mens rea*) is an element of the offence (as created either by common law or statute), it is not clear what actual mental state is denoted by an imprecise expression such as *mens rea*.

Volition and the relationship to capacity

Criminal liability generally relies on a prohibited conduct which has been done voluntarily. In theory, at least, the prosecution must establish volition as one of the earliest parts of its case, and yet this is rarely considered unless and until volition is challenged or called into doubt by the defence. To avoid any initial probative difficulties which would face the prosecution with always having to establish volition, a presumption exists in criminal law that if an act was committed by the accused it was done so voluntarily. As a presumption of fact it may be rebutted by the accused through evidence placing volition in doubt.

Both the prohibited act and the mental state must be voluntary in order to establish liability. To say that an act is voluntary implies that the accused has chosen so to act, and therefore has exerted some conscious control over the action.

An initial consideration for the prosecution in determining the strength of its case is whether the accused had the capacity to commit the offence. One of the essential elements in considering capacity is whether the act or omission of the accused was voluntary. Children, the insane, those acting in an automatic state, and some intoxicated accused will not be capable of committing the offence because the law deems that their acts were not voluntary.

Where criminal capacity remains for the discussion of factors affecting criminal liability, and more particularly of defences, this tends to confuse the difference between being able to commit the crime, and once having com-

---

139 It is important to recognise that the fundamental principles of criminal liability may be challenged by presumptions of proof. However, the challenges do not stop there. Certain contexts of liability (such as strict liability) work as if these principles may be abrogated and liability can still be established.

mitted what appears to be a crime, being able to raise a satisfactory explanation. What distinguishes more fundamental considerations of incapacity, both physical and mental, are those facts about the accused and the alleged offence which challenge volition: age, ability to reason, ability to control his actions, and self-induced loss of reason.

It is necessary to view, from either perspective of the adversarial trial, whether the actions of the accused are voluntary, and whether the accused has the capacity to commit the offence. As the High Court considered in **Hawkins** (1994) 122 ALR 27, in the case of insanity it falls for determination before the issue of intent. The basic questions in the criminal trial must be: what did the accused do and is he criminally responsible for doing it? These questions must be resolved before deliberations regarding specific mental states required by an offence, and their proof. Only when those questions are answered adversely to the accused can the issue of intent be addressed. That issue can arise only on the hypothesis that the accused's mental condition at the time that the incriminating act was done fell short of incapacity or involuntariness.

CONTEXT OF THE PROBLEM

The scenario below raises considerations of culpability in a suicide and the destruction of children. But this may not simply be a case of neglect or omission. If we accept that the accused had some duty of care for the safety and well-being of his wife and children, and the agreement between the accused and his lover to further destabilise the wife reveals a desire for her harm, then criminal liability here may be composed of several instances of conduct and mental states.

PROBLEM

Peter has lost interest in his wife. He has commenced a sexual relationship with a woman at work and she is pressuring him to leave home. However, this is Peter's second marriage and he does not want to suffer a considerable loss of property in another messy divorce.

Peter's wife is depressed and on medication. She has a history of mental instability and Peter is aware, from speaking with her doctor, that unless his wife is treated with care she may become suicidal.

In an effort to bring about an end to his troubles Peter suggests to his girlfriend that she ring his wife and tell her what has been going on between them.

The next morning when Peter is at the pool doing his daily laps he sees his wife and two children on the other side of the breakwater. He goes across to where she is entering the water carrying the two children. She is sobbing as she holds the children under the water and then disappears below the surface herself.

When the police interview Peter he says that he was so shocked at what he saw that he remembers nothing after seeing his wife entering the water. He is charged with manslaughter.

ENGAGING THE PROBLEM

While you might want to find someone criminally liable for these tragic consequences, an important initial consideration is whether the accused person caused the deaths. Were they a natural consequence of the things he did?

Beyond causation, the type of charge resulting from the omission to act needs to be determined. If there is a homicide here, what form might it take, and what elements need to be established? If the accused's acts or omissions brought about the deaths, then what mental state must he manifest at that moment? Is a pre-existing desire sufficient? Is motive relevant? Is neglect or negligence ever enough? Was his initial encouragement of his lover's actions so dangerous as to be beyond what the ordinary person would have thought or done?

ADDITIONAL RESOURCES

Crimes Act 1900 (NSW), section 18(1)(a), section 611

Summary Offences Act 1988 (NSW), section 4

Bronitt, S. and McSherry, B., *Principles of Criminal Law*, Law Book Company, Sydney, 2001, pp. 147–54, 161–3.

Brown, D., Farrier, D., Egger, S., and McNamara, L., *Criminal Laws*, Federation Press, Sydney, 2001, paras 4.2, 4.3, 4.5, 4.6, 6.3, 6.4.

Findlay, M., Odgers, S., and Yeo, S., *Australian Criminal Justice*, Oxford University Press, Melbourne, 1999, pp. 13–20.

Fisse, B., *Howard's Criminal Law*, Law Book Company, Sydney, 1992, Chapters 1 (E), 6.

Ryan v. R (1967) 121 CLR 205

R v. Falconer (1990) 171 CLR 30

Jiminez (1992) 121 CLR 205

He Kaw Teh v. R (1985) 59 ALJR 620

Bratty v. Attorney-General for Northern Ireland [1963] AC 306

Russell [1933] VR 59

TOPIC 9

DETERMINING CRIMINAL LIABILITY II: ELEMENTS OF THE OFFENCE

PROHIBITED CONDUCT AND CRIMINAL MENTAL STATE

Brennan CJ in **He Kaw Teh** (*supra*) took the view that the act or omission of the accused is the essential foundation of criminal responsibility. In addition, criminal conduct also depends on the circumstances in which the act is done or the omission made. Criminal liability may further depend on the accused's state of mind at the time of the act or omission, as well as the results (consequences) of these other elements (acts, omissions, and mental state).

The conduct, circumstances and results are, in Brennan's view, the 'external elements necessary to form the crime'. The mental element is usually implied within the definition of these external elements. For instance, with common assault the accused must commit an act which puts the victim in fear of immediate and unlawful personal violence. The offence can obviously be committed intentionally, but the common law also says that an accused may have the necessary mental state if he acts with a reckless disregard of whether the victim is made fearful.

Criminal conduct (*actus reus*) can involve acts, omissions, and in certain situations the status of the offender (such as an illegal immigrant) may be sufficient. Often the circumstances in which the *actus reus* occurs may provide its prohibited character (e.g. where sexual intercourse occurs without the consent of the victim). On other occasions the *actus reus* may involve an initial act (which may or may not itself be criminal), and a consequence which will, with the necessary mental state, be criminal. An example of this would be the offence of dangerous driving causing death.

Mens rea, or a criminal mental state, means a number of quite different things when applied to different offences. It might connote several states of mind directed towards individual external elements of the same crime. For instance, in sexual assault there may be an intention to have sexual intercourse with the victim without her consent, or an intention to have sexual intercourse, with a reckless disregard as to whether she consents or not.[140]

Some general mental states, such as *voluntariness,* can represent or establish many separate or specific mental states depending on the situation within the offence scenario to which it refers. Volition might be the ability to control one's actions, knowledge that an action is occurring, or the conscious adoption of responsibility for a particular form of conduct. Lack of volition might mean lack of knowledge, lack of control, or wilfulness. In these respects the establishment of *mens rea* may depend on the nature of the criminal conduct and its relationship with the accused (for example, did he know of its details? Did he perform the conduct in a controlled or conscious fashion?).

Mens rea, in terms of a legal definition, is very generally divided into the states of intention or recklessness. For certain offences negligence may satisfy

---

140   In this situation it is important to recognise that consent goes to the *mens rea* of the accused
        (e.g. knowledge of an absence of consent, or recklessness as to its withdrawal) and the *actus
        reus* of the offence (e.g. non-consensual sexual intercourse).

the required mental state.[141] As artificial as the legal mental state divisions may appear, they broadly coincide with measures of moral culpability. It might also be said that the further *mens rea* moves away from intention and towards negligence the less significant are questions about what the accused actually thought or foresaw and more relevant are the comparisons with what the ordinary person would have thought or foreseen. Therefore, the conduct deemed criminal becomes less connected with the subjective mental state of the accused as we move through recklessness and towards negligence. This is also the case where certain elements of an offence are deemed to create strict liability.

Reliance on what the ordinary person would have done or thought also has an important place in the operation of certain excuses or justifications. For instance, with provocation and self-defence, the question is asked whether the reactions and interpretations of the accused correspond to what the ordinary person would have thought and done.

The imprecision in the description and the application of *mens rea* categories creates difficulties when establishing criminal liability. For example the relationship between knowledge and levels of intent (specific and general) is problematic. Judges are sometimes heard to confuse knowledge with intention rather than recognising knowledge as a component of intention. With the interpretation of liability in certain situations or for particular offences, it is often not clear whether it should be essential that the accused person be proved to possess knowledge of the circumstances that made the conduct criminal, and knowledge of the probability of criminal (harmful) consequences eventuating. Thus, with murder in the common law jurisdictions in Australia, the courts ask whether the accused desired to kill or seriously injure the victim, or whether he foresaw that the consequences of his action were probable. Some debate exists over whether it should be the consequence of death alone which should be foreseen as probable.

Knowledge is also an important component in participation. A secondary party needs to know certain things about the offence that the principal offender commits, in order to share liability. In certain situations the *mens rea* of the secondary party may need to be higher than that of the principal offender.

Causation

It is not enough to establish that prohibited conduct has occurred, and when it did that there was a criminal mental state present. For liability to stand, the

---

141 Although it could be argued that negligence is actually established through the absence of an individual's mental state.

prohibited conduct must connect with a suspect or an accused person, and it needs to be shown that the act or omission of that person caused the offence.

More than one individual may cause a crime. Through complicity or conspiracy a common purpose or an agreement to bring about the crime may be the essence of the offence. There may be several contributing causes of crime. However, for individual liability to be established it is crucial to find that the *actus reus* of the accused was the substantial and operating cause. This can be so even where the harm results as a natural and foreseeable consequence of the victim's actions.

Coincidence

The *actus reus* and *mens rea* of the offence need to coincide (in a temporal and a spatial sense) if liability is to be established. In its simplest sense the accused must possess the required mental state at the same time he causes the harm through his prohibited conduct.

Prohibited conduct is recognised as sometimes comprising a series of acts. In this circumstance, the necessary mental state must be present at some point throughout the series. Where it is the mental state that is continuing, then the *actus reus* must arise at some point while the *mens rea* is prevailing.

There are certain unusual occasions in the process of establishing criminal liability where evidence of a pre-existing mental state may be sufficient for the *actus reus* occurring later. Recently it has been argued that if an accused takes intoxicants with the aim of removing any inhibitions to crime, this is sufficient *mens rea* for those crimes that are satisfied by recklessness.

CONTEXT OF THE PROBLEM

In certain crime situations it is necessary to analyse how particular individuals participate together. Their participation will depend on a joint enterprise and shared knowledge. Mistake as to what the criminal enterprise involves may have an effect on liability, even where certain consequences of knowledge are presumed.

An accused may change his mind as a criminal enterprise evolves. The significance of this, and whether his criminal liability will be affected by a withdrawal of *mens rea,* depends on the nature of the offence, its elements, and when it is said to be complete through the coincidence of mental state and prohibited conduct.

PROBLEM

Sarah was living in Fujian Province in China and times were tough. She was approached by a businessman, Mr Chen, who asked whether she would be interested in acting as a courier for him. Sarah knew Mr Chen's reputation. He had been involved in drug trafficking to Australia for many years.

Sarah had further discussions with Mr Chen during which she indicated that while she would transport cannabis she would have nothing to do with heroin. Eventually Mr Chen presented Sarah with two suitcases and told her that he recognised her concerns and that she didn't need to worry about what was in the cases.

A week later Sarah booked the luggage onto a China Airways flight to Hong Kong, and then to Sydney with Cathay Pacific. Sarah was to change planes in Hong Kong.

When she arrived in Hong Kong Sarah decided not to go through with the arrangement. She thought that as long as she did not board the flight to Sydney her bags would remain in Hong Kong. She did not attempt to pick them up from the baggage claim in Hong Kong.

However, Sarah did not realise that the bags had been automatically booked through to Sydney from China. They arrived in Sydney and were immediately confiscated by customs, as they actually contained 30 kilograms of fine grade heroin.

On Sarah's return to Sydney some six months later she was arrested and charged with the importation of prescribed drugs.

Discuss Sarah's criminal liability.

ENGAGING THE PROBLEM

What does Sarah know about the criminal enterprise and what might be presumed from the degree of knowledge she possesses? The answers to these questions depend on the offence with which she might be charged and the nature of the participation in which she is said to be engaged.

Is her mistake regarding her role in the enterprise relevant to her liability? Mistake here needs to go to an essential element of the offence, and needs to be established as honest and reasonable.

Where does the necessary coincidence between *actus reus* and *mens rea* occur, if at all? The time at which the offence could be said to have been completed will influence your answer, as will a consideration of Sarah's desire to withdraw from the enterprise.

ADDITIONAL RESOURCES

Brown, D., Farrier, D., Egger, S., and McNamara, L., *Criminal Laws,* Federation Press, Sydney, 2001, paras 4.2, 4.3, 4.4.

Fisse, B., *Howard's Criminal Law,* Law Book Company, Sydney, 1992, Chapter 6 (C).

Norrie, A., *Crime, Reason and History,* Weidenfeld & Nicolson, London, 1993, Chapter 3.

Crabbe (1985) 58 ALR 417

Pereira v. DPP (1988) 82 ALR 217

R v. Miller [1983] 2 AC 161

R v. Callighan (1952) 87 CLR 115

Thabo Meli v. R [1954] 1 WLR 228

Church [1966] 1 QB 59

Fagan v. Metropolitan Police Commissioner [1969] 1 QB 439

R v. Beckford [1988] AC 130

He Kaw Teh v. R (1985) 59 ALJR 620

Royall v. R (1991) 172 CLR 378

Topic 10

Determining criminal liability III: Exceptions to liability, participation and preparatory offences

Introduction

This topic examines those areas of the law where criminal liability is established outside the conventional requirements of proving the criminal conduct and the designated mental state of the accused. Strict liability, vicarious and corporate liability (which have been considered in detail in earlier chapters: see pp. 97–9 and 106–110) are examples of where the individualised liability requirements are either diminished for regulatory reasons, or extended beyond considerations of the thoughts and actions of the accused. With strict liability, the presumption that the accused intends the natural consequences of his act takes hold and avoids the requirement on the prosecution to prove the mental element in respect of some conduct, circumstances, or consequences of the offence.[142] Vicarious and corporate liability allow, through delegation, or through the nature of an employment or corporate relationship, for situations in which liability is shared or made generic.

Other exceptions to the conventional process for establishing individual criminal liability occur when a crime is committed collectively or as part of a common purpose. The relationship between the principal and the accessory is crucial for liability.

Further, when the preparatory stages before the achievement of the substantive offence are punished, this is achieved by emphasising the proof of the mental state directed towards a substantive offence, and proximity of preparatory conduct.

Participation and preparatory offences

In what follows we are examining offences where there is either:

* a distance from the substantive offence through incomplete criminal conduct towards the achievement of that offence, or

---

142 This is to be distinguished from the much rarer situation of absolute liability where no mental state requires proof, and merely the conduct of the accused is the focus for liability and penalty.

- a distance from the principal offender through participation in an offence.

Both require a reconsideration of the conventional methods essential for establishing individual liability.

Participation (Complicity)

There are certain situations where the conduct of parties other than the principal perpetrator of the offence may also satisfy the prohibited conduct of the offence. Questions of the designation and the interpretation of such participation centre on:

- degrees of involvement, and
- distance from the principal offender.

The categorisation of complicity includes:

1 Principal in the first degree—the person who performs the criminal act;
2 Principal in the second degree—someone who is present at the commission of the crime and who aids and assists in its commission but does not take the main role;
3 Accessory before the fact—one who takes part in the preliminary stages of the crime by urging or contributing towards its commission;
4 Accessory after the fact—one who has not contributed to the planning or the execution of the offence but who assists after the offence has been committed.

The general distinction in criminal participation is between primary and secondary offenders. The question at the basis of most issues of participation is whether a certain act with a certain degree of associated knowledge demonstrates participation in the crime.

It might be said that the discussion of complicity in jurisdictions such as New South Wales is largely academic in light of Part 9 of the *Crimes Act*, section 345, which makes principals in the second degree liable to the same punishment as principals in the first degree.[143] Section 346 makes accessories before the fact liable to the same form of charge, trial, and punishment as principals.

Establishing participation, however, is far from a theoretical exercise in that the doctrines employed for proving the liabilities of secondary parties may be distinctly different from those required for the liability of the principal. In addition, the acts and mental states anticipated for secondary par-

---

143 Section 351 does the same for accessories to minor offences.

ties may be different from those of the principal, and require separate levels of proof.

In determining the liability of principals and accessories, one should consider whether the defendant is responsible in any way (or to any degree) for the crime in question, where the main role in the offence is performed by another. While traditional technical distinctions between principals and accessories largely have been abolished through legislation, sentencing may be relative to degrees and levels of participation.

Different from preparatory offences such as attempt and conspiracy (which are offences in their own right despite their connection with a substantive offence), complicity depends on the commission of an offence by another party. Therefore, the liability of the secondary party is derivative from the liability of the principal. A secondary party can withdraw from a criminal enterprise at the last minute and is no longer complicit, but may be liable for a conspiracy with the principal because that offence is complete before the moment of withdrawal.

The most complicated issue in complicity is the necessary mental state of secondary parties and its proof. A further contentious issue is whether a secondary party can be liable for the acts of a principal who for some reason cannot be convicted of the offence.

Innocent agency

In **Demerian** [1989] VR 97, the court looked at *innocent agency* and the *doctrine of common purpose*. It was held that where an act which would be a crime if done by A, is caused by A to be done by B, and B does not commit a crime by doing so, the law may regard A as having acted by an innocent agent, and as being guilty of the crime as a principal offender. The party who commits the crime through an innocent agent is treated as a principal offender (see also: **Matusevich** (1977) 15 ALR 117).

Distinctions and degrees of participation

Principal offender (Principal in the first degree)

Where there are several participants in a crime, the principal is the one whose actions or omissions are the most immediate cause of the prohibited conduct. Such conduct must have been directly brought about by the participation and involvement of the accused, the principal party.

In some cases it may be clear that an offence has been committed and that either A or B committed it, but it is not apparent which of the parties committed the crucial conduct nor is it clear whether the other party was an accessory to the prohibited conduct.

It is possible to have two or more principals in the first degree for the same offence, wherein they commit the same conduct or share the essential elements of the *actus reus*. If this situation arises in the pursuit of a common purpose then the general rules regarding causation may be modified. All principals may be deemed to have caused the prohibited conduct despite an intervening act, or where the act is not the immediate, operating, and sole cause of death but was accompanied by the acts or omissions of others.

The distinction between a joint principal and an abetter will sometimes be difficult to draw. Generally it is immaterial in which capacity the secondary party is said to have participated in the crime. The distinction is whether the second defendant participated through his own act rather than his own advice.

Secondary parties (Principal in the second degree)

The case-law on secondary parties is largely concerned with the interpretation of the terms *aid, abet, counsel* and *procure*. In the ***Attorney-General's Reference (No. 1 of 1975)*** [1975] QB 773, the Court of Appeal commented on the distinction under English law: ' … if four words are employed here "aid", "abet", "counsel" or "procure", the possibility is that there is a distinction between each of those four words and the other three, because, if there was no such difference, then Parliament would be wasting its time with four words when two or three would do'.

Aid and *abet* are often considered to represent a single concept; 'aid' denoting the prohibited conduct, and 'abet' the mental state. 'Aid' implies the giving of help, support, and assistance. To 'abet' is to incite, instigate, or encourage. Either activity is sufficient to ground liability as a secondary party, and therefore seeing one as expressing the act and the other as the mental state may not be entirely accurate.

If all four words are used in the charge the evidence is sufficient to establish that the accused's conduct satisfies one concept.

The mental state to establish aiding and abetting requires actual knowledge of, or wilful blindness towards, the circumstances which constitute the offence. This does not necessarily equate with the mental state required of the principal party in the commission of the substantive offence. Rather, the secondary party must know of the principal's mental state and the facts that would make his or her purpose criminal. In ***Johnson v. Youden*** [1950] 1 KB 554, Lord Goddard stated:

> Before a person can be convicted of aiding and abetting the commission of an offence he must at least know the essential matters which constitute that offence. He need not actually know that an offence has been committed because he may not know that the facts constitute an offence and ignorance of the law is not a defence.

The secondary party must have intended to help and encourage the principal in the commission of the offence (See ***R v. Clarkson*** [1971] 3 All ER

344, where an attempt to counsel did not amount to counselling. Non-accidental presence at a scene of a crime is not aiding and abetting. One needs to give wilful encouragement. There must be an intention to encourage, as well as encouragement itself.)

Counselling means that the accused advised or solicited, or encouraged the commission of the offence through the principal. Causation here is not necessary. The accused must counsel before the commission of the offence.

It is probably not necessary to prove that the defendant was influenced in any way by a secondary party, but he must be aware that he has the authority, the encouragement, or the approval of the second defendant to do the relevant acts. As stated in **R v. Calhaem** [1985] 2 All ER 226:

> For example, if the principal offender happened to be involved in a football riot in the course of which he laid about him with a weapon of some sort and killed someone who, unknown to him was the person he had been counselled to kill, he would not … have been acting in the scope of his authority; he would be acting outside it albeit what he had done was what he had been counselled to do.

To *procure* means 'to produce by endeavour'. There needs to be some causal link here between the conduct of the secondary party and that of the principal. Procuring must occur prior to the commission of the principal's prohibited conduct. The mental state required for procuring is similar to that for aiding and abetting.

The other crucial issue about the *mens rea* for secondary parties is the relationship between their minds and the mental state required for the principal. Will the mental state of the latter be sufficient for complicity? Is it possible to be complicit recklessly? Should you be liable if you know that your assistance and encouragement will possibly or probably encourage someone to commit a crime, or is only your intention to produce that result required?

In **Giorgianni** (1985) 156 CLR 473, the defendant owned a truck which was driven by an employee. The truck was involved in an accident when the brakes failed and passengers in another car were killed. The defendant was a mechanic who serviced the truck. The employee and the owner had done work on the truck some weeks before the accident. Evidence showed that the brakes had been repaired in a faulty fashion and that the defendant had been given notice of a problem.

The defendant was charged under s. 52A of the *Crimes Act* (NSW) with culpable driving causing death. The prosecution argued that the defendant had procured a breach of the section allowing the truck to be driven with brakes in a defective state. He was charged as a principal offender under s. 351 of the Act. On appeal from conviction the High Court saw a difficulty in theory with such an offence. There is a problem in connecting contributing parties with an offence which requires an act and a result (culpable driving causing injury or death) and the mental state consistent with procuring both elements of the conduct. However:

> although a person cannot aid and abet, counsel or procure the commission of an offence, even a statutory offence, involving strict liability, without intent based on knowledge of the essential facts which constitute the offence, the requisite intent and knowledge do not, in the case of culpable driving, extend to the occurrence of death or grievous bodily harm which ensues upon the unlawful act the commission of which was aided, abetted, counselled or procured.[144]

Regarding the intent necessary for the complicit offence, even one where strict liability may apply, intent is necessary to prove aiding, abetting, counselling, or procuring, and knowledge of the essential facts of the principal offence is necessary for intent to be established. The knowledge must be actual, not merely imputed. This is the case even where the accused failed to make enquiries or gain the necessary knowledge of a matter he knew of in order to deny knowledge.

Is recklessness sufficient to establish participation here? Liability as an accessory requires intentional assistance or encouragement in doing those things which go to make up the offence. The knowledge need not extend to the precise crime committed, although some similar crime must be contemplated at the time of the intended encouragement. Preparatory and participatory offences are not intended if the accused merely has foresight of the probability of the consequences. Reckless behaviour will not suffice for the necessary intent here.

The exposure to the obvious may evoke the assumption of knowledge but the shutting of one's eyes to the obvious is not an alternative to the actual knowledge required for a secondary party.

It is not sufficient for the prosecution to establish only that the accessory had knowledge of the physical acts done by the principal accused. It must also establish that the accessory was aware that the principal performed the acts with the requisite *mens rea* (see **Stokes and Difford** (1990) 51 A Crim R 25).

Causation

In relation to causation and secondary parties, it is usually necessary to establish some causal link between the participatory act and the principal offence. In the *Attorney-General's Reference* case (1975) (*supra*) the second defendant added alcohol to the first defendant's drink, without D1's knowledge or consent. D2 was held to have procured D1's offence of driving with a blood alcohol content above the prescribed limit, if it could be proved that D2

---

144 Wilson, Deane and Dawson JJ at 503.

knew that D1 was going to drive, and that the ordinary and natural consequence of the added alcohol would be to bring the blood alcohol over the limit. In that sense D2 had caused the commission of the offence.

One can aid someone to commit an offence more easily, quickly, or safely even though it could have been committed without such assistance. Despite the fact that a causal link may have to be established in some situations of participation, it is immaterial whether the aiding or procuring was actually relied upon. Procuring implies causation but not consensus. Abetting and counselling imply consensus but not causation. Aiding requires actual assistance but not actual consensus or causation.

In summary, the issues for participation relate to:

- timing (before the commission of the substantive offence for counselling and procuring; abetting during the commission of the offence; aiding at any time);
- presence at the crime (the abetter must be present in the pursuance of the agreement that the crime should be committed, or present to give assistance and encouragement in its commission. Voluntary presence might suggest that the necessary *mens rea* to abet exists);
- knowledge (knowledge of the circumstances constituting the offence is necessary for secondary participation: it is not relevant that the aid is not given with the motive or purpose of encouraging the crime).

Knowledge of the type of crime

Three principles are involved when considering the knowledge required of secondary parties:

1 If A aids, abets, counsels, or procures B to commit an offence of a certain type, with neither party specifying any particular victim, time or place, A may be convicted as a secondary party to any crime of that type which B commits.
2 If A aids, abets, counsels, or procures B to commit a crime against a particular person, or in respect of a particular thing, A is not liable if B intentionally commits an offence of the same type against some other person or in respect of some other thing.
3 A is, however, liable with B for any acts done by B in the course of endeavouring to carry out a common purpose.

In *R v. Bainbridge* [1960] 1 QB 129, the distinction was drawn between knowledge of the crime that was actually committed, and knowledge of the generality of the criminal enterprise. The accused purchased oxy welding equipment that was later used in a bank robbery. He knew it was to be used for something that was illegal (breaking up of stolen goods), but he did not know it was going to be used for its eventual purposes in breaking into a bank. The court held that it was essential to prove the defendant knew the type of crime that was going to be committed if he were to be convicted as a secondary party. It was not enough that he knew some type of illegality was contemplated. However, if he knew that breaking, entering, and stealing was intended then it was not necessary to prove that he knew which bank was going to be robbed or at what time.

The House of Lords carried this principle to its logical conclusion in **DPP for Nth Ireland v. Maxwell** (1978) 68 Cr App R 128. In this case the accused drove another man to an inn knowing that the other man either intended to plant a bomb or shoot persons at the inn. In fact he planted a bomb. Was the accused therefore liable as a secondary party for the bombing when his degree of knowledge was general? It might have been that the accused would not have been liable if the other man had committed a crime beyond what was in the accused's contemplation when he did the relevant act. A general criminal intention is also not enough.

In some situations it is possible for the conviction of a secondary party when the principal in acquitted.

The difficulty in the Australian jurisdictions now lies with establishing the limits of 'essential matters' about which the secondary party must have knowledge (see **Annakin** (1988) 37 A Crim R 131).

Accessories after the fact
Section 347 of the *Crimes Act* (NSW), for instance, provides for joint trials between principals and accessories after the fact. An accessory after the fact is someone who receives, comforts, maintains or assists the principal who has committed the crime. He need not give assistance of a personal kind.

Joint enterprise and common purpose
The nature of the conduct necessary for an accessory is largely dependent on whether he is there at the scene of the crime as a consequence of a prior agreement, with a purpose in common with the principal. Mere presence at the scene of the crime pursuant to this prior agreement may be sufficient for liability. However, a person is only a participant as part of a group when the group is acting in the furtherance of the common purpose. If one of the party departs completely from the concerted action of the common design, the other parties in the joint enterprise may no longer be responsible for his actions.

Acts are considered as part of a joint enterprise or purpose when they are contemplated or foreseen by the secondary party as a possible result of the enterprise. Unforeseen consequences might also attach to responsibility if they were a reasonable inference from the agreement or purpose. In *Anderson and Morris* [1962] QB 110 the principle of joint enterprise was stated as:

> where two persons embark on a joint enterprise, each is liable for the acts done in pursuance of the enterprise, and that includes the liability for unusual consequences if they arise from the execution of the agreed joint enterprise, but if one of the co-adventurers goes beyond what has been tacitly agreed as part of the joint enterprise, his co-adventurer is not liable for the consequences of the unauthorised act.

The issue of foresight of the consequences of a common purpose was discussed in *Chan Wing-sui v. R* [1984] 3 All ER 877. In this case three appellants were convicted of murder when they entered the victim's apartment to commit robbery with knives, and the victim's death ensued. The trial judge said that the accused could be convicted if they had contemplated that the knife might be so used by one of them with the intention of inflicting serious injury. On appeal it was held that where someone lends himself to a criminal enterprise knowing that potentially murderous weapons are to be carried, and in the event that they are used by his partner with the intent sufficient for murder, he should not escape the consequences by reliance on a nuance of prior assessment only too likely to be optimistic. On the other hand, if it is not even contemplated by the particular accused that serious bodily harm would be intentionally inflicted, he is not a party to the murder. The test of *mens rea* here is subjective. It is what the individual accused in fact contemplated that matters. This may be inferred from his conduct and any other evidence throwing light on what he foresaw at the material time. The prosecution must prove the necessary contemplation beyond reasonable doubt. Where remoteness arises it is for the jury to decide whether the risk as recognised by the accused was sufficient to make him a party to the crime committed by the principal. If the risk was contemplated by the accused and genuinely dismissed by him as altogether negligible, then he would not be guilty. This is not such a case.

The test for common purpose in New South Wales (as set down in *Johns* (1980) 143 CLR 180) is 'liability for any act which was within the contemplation of both himself and the principal in the first degree as an act which might be done in the course of carrying out the primary criminal intention'. Common purpose can be constructed by an accessory before the fact even if he is not present at the crime. In addition, the mental state extends to possible consequences 'so long as these are within the contemplation of the parties to the understanding or agreement'.

What of the situation where one of the participants commits an additional crime over and above the primary objective of the plan to which the parties have agreed? How does the subjective *mens rea* advocated in *Giorgianni* (*supra*) constrain this?

In *McAuliffe and McAuliffe v. R* (1995) 130 ALR 26, the facts related to the McAuliffe brothers and another accused, Davis (who later pleaded guilty to murder), who had agreed to 'roll and bash' a victim on the cliffs at Bondi beach. Sean McAuliffe armed himself with a hammer and Davis with a baton but there was no evidence that David McAuliffe was aware of this before they arrived at the crime scene. They were all experienced fighters. They collectively attacked the deceased, leaving him badly wounded and lying near the edge of the cliff. He was subsequently found dead at the bottom of the cliff. The death was caused by the fall and drowning.

The prosecution case was that the death arose from the common purpose of the accused to rob and roll the deceased. Essential to the establishment of common purpose was that the group planned to attack and inflict serious injury on the victim. The McAuliffe brothers contended that while there was a common purpose to assault a victim, there was no agreement to commit serious injury. The trial judge directed that to find common purpose the jury should find an intention to share in the criminal enterprise of serious injury, or contemplation that the infliction of serious injury by one of the group was a possible incident in the common criminal enterprise. The appeal was on these directions. The appellants contended that the intentional infliction of serious injury needed to be part of the common purpose—that is, that there had to have been an *express agreement* that at least this should be a possible incident.

The High Court held that common purpose (common design, concert, joint criminal enterprise) is where a person reaches an understanding or arrangement with another, amounting to an agreement between them to commit a crime. The agreement need not be express and can be inferred from the circumstances. If one does all that is necessary for the crime then each is equally guilty no matter what part he played. They are also guilty of a crime falling within the scope of the common purpose which is committed in carrying out that purpose. The test is a subjective one as to what was contemplated within the common purpose.

What happens when a party foresees a further crime other than the one that was agreed to, but continues to participate? The secondary party is as much a party to the crime which is incident to the agreed venture as he is when the incidental crime falls within the common purpose. The prosecution needs to prove that the accused foresaw the possibility, and cannot simply rely on the common purpose.

In common purpose it is necessary that the principal be identified (see *Morgan* (1993) 70 A Crim R 340).

Withdrawal

There is a question whether if the accused withdraws prior to the commission of the offence, he will remain complicit in that offence. In **Rook** [1993] 2 All ER 955, the accused failed to turn up on the day for an agreed killing and argued that this was evidence of sufficient withdrawal. It was necessary to establish an unequivocal communication of withdrawal and the taking of steps to neutralise his assistance.

In **R v. Becerra and Cooper** (1975) 62 Cr App R 212, three defendants broke into a house intending to steal. A gave D a knife to use on anyone who might disturb them. When the victim came down the stairs A said, 'There's a bloke coming; let's go,' and jumped out the window. D stabbed the victim, killing him. The Court of Appeal upheld A's conviction as an accessory to murder because he had not effectively withdrawn from the enterprise. What is enough for withdrawal will vary depending on the circumstances of the case and in certain situations may go as high as physical intervention.

If two people embark on a joint criminal enterprise, each is liable for the acts done in pursuance of that agreement within the scope of the joint enterprise. Liability may be as joint principals or as principals and secondary parties depending on the level of participation.

Preparatory offences

Attempt and impossibility

The preparatory offences of attempt, conspiracy and incitement are sometimes referred to as inchoate or incomplete offences. It is better to see them not so much as unfinished offences, but as offences that, while complete in themselves, occur prior to the execution of the principal or substantive offence towards which they are directed, whether or not the substantive offence actually occurs. This is not to say that such offences are not essentially connected to the potential substantive offence. On the contrary, many of the difficulties associated with inchoate offences relate to whether this connection can be sufficiently established, and whether it is possible for the substantive offence to occur.

Section 427 of the *Crimes Act* (NSW), for instance, states that a person who is charged with a substantive offence may be convicted of an attempt. Attempt is a common law offence and as such the penalty is at the discretion of the judge. Section 344A fixes the maximum penalty as the same as that for the substantive offence.

Mens rea for attempt

In order for a person to be convicted of attempt it must first be shown that he had a specific intention to commit that offence (see **Mohan's** case [1976] QB 1) and that he had done an act sufficient to constitute the designated *actus reus*.

The question as regards *mens rea* for attempt has sometimes been seen as relating to whether the mental state for the preparatory offence should be the same as that required for the substantive offence, or whether it should be different. In **Knight** (1992) 109 ALR 225, the High Court held that the *mens rea* required for attempted murder may be subject to a degree of proof higher than that required for murder in that it must be proved that the accused's actions were done with the intention to kill. In **McGhee** (1995) 130 ALR 142, Brennan J agreed that the *mens rea* for attempted murder should be intention, and this must be so because without the physical element of causing death there must be a sufficient mental element that the death be caused.

It was held in **Mohan's** case (*supra*) that attempt requires intention in the true sense of the word and not mere knowledge of the probability of consequences, no matter how high the likelihood. If someone is to be punished for an act on the way to the commission of the substantive offence, then the connection of the mind of the accused to the substantive offence must be at the most specific level.

In this respect the intention for attempt is specifically '... a decision to bring about, in so far as it lies within the accused's power, the commission of the offence which it is alleged the accused attempted to commit, no matter whether the accused desired that consequence of his act or not'.

It is important, however, to realise that:

1 inchoate offences are not examples of punishing *mens rea* alone;
2 inchoate offences do not necessarily require the same *mens rea* as the substantive offence; and
3 because the *mens rea* of the initial stage of the commission of the offence, and the final *actus reus* of the substantive offence are physically and temporally separated, then it is necessary to prove the highest level of *mens rea* towards the commission of the preparatory stage.

Actus reus of attempt

In **Robinson's** case [1916–1917] All ER Rep 1299 what is generally referred to as the proximity test was propounded. This test recognises that the intention to commit a crime is not criminal in itself. Some act must coincide with the intention. Acts remotely leading towards the commission of the offence are not considered to be attempts to commit it, 'but acts immediately connected with it are'. The 'last act' test was also considered in this case. It required that the accused should have done the final act possible in his power to bring the substantive offence about in order for the *actus reus* of attempt to be established.

In **Davey v. Lee** [1868] 1 QB 366, the classification of the 'series test' was developed. In that case the accused were charged and convicted of attempting to steal copper wire from the premises of the electricity board. They ran away after they were detected endeavouring to break into the electricity board property at a point near to where there was a copper store. There were also other stores and buildings on the site and it was argued on behalf of the accused that the acts proven against them were not sufficiently proximate to the stealing of the copper. It was held on appeal that the *actus reus* of attempt was complete if the prisoner does an act which is a step towards the completion of the substantive crime. The step must be immediately and not simply remotely connected to its commission and its performance must reasonably be regarded as not having any other purpose or explanation than the commission of the substantive offence.

> What amounts to an attempt has been described variously in the authorities, and for my part I prefer to adopt the definition given in *Stephen's Digest of Criminal Law* (5th ed.) article 50: 'An attempt to commit a crime is an act done with intent to commit that crime, and forming part of a series of acts which would constitute its actual commission, if it were not interrupted.' As a general statement, that seems to me to be right, though it does not help to define the point of time at which the series of act begins. That, as Stephen said, depended upon the facts of each case. A helpful definition is given in paragraph 4104 in the current (36th) edition of *Archibold's Criminal Pleading, etc.*, where it is stated: 'It is submitted that the *actus reus* necessary to constitute an attempt is complete if the prisoner does an act which is a step towards the commission of the specific crime, which is immediately and not merely remotely connected with the commission of it, and the doing of which cannot reasonably be regarded as having any other purpose than the commission of the specific crime.

In this quote we can find at least three 'tests' (or indicators) of sufficiency for the *actus reus* of attempt.

1 a series of acts which, if uninterrupted, would constitute the commission of the actual offence;
2 an act, which is immediately rather than remotely connected with the commission of the substantive offence;
3 an act which cannot be reasonably regarded as having any other purpose than the commission of the specific crime.

The second classification of 'tests' from this judgment seems to represent the one preferred by the Court of Appeal in **Davey v. Lee**. They attacked what they saw as an over-reliance on the 'last act test' and felt that the correct interpretation of the principle is that if one considers the last act, it is only as an illustration of the fact that the accused has progressed a sufficient distance towards the substantive offence (the proximity test).

The best way to look at these alternative tests is not so much as alternatives at all. In **DPP v. Stonehouse** [1977] 2 All ER 909, for example, it was suggested that by a combination of those indicators or characteristics, the act might be established as being sufficiently proximate for the attempt in question to stand.

The ultimate question to be determined by any measure of the *actus reus* for attempt is that of proximity: was the act of the accused at the time of apprehension sufficiently, temporally, or physically proximate to the actual commission of the substantive offence, for that proximity to stand as unequivocal evidence of acts that would constitute an attempt?

In respect of a series of acts forming the *actus reus*, the approach is not dissimilar to the way in which we view causation questions. An act is sufficiently proximate if it is the first of a series of similar acts intended to result cumulatively in the crime. Thus one who intends to kill another by slow poisoning is guilty of attempted murder as soon as he administers or attempts to administer the first dose, which by itself may not be fatal.

The problem with establishing proximity is the difficulty of finding some consistent measure when the facts and consequent decisions of various cases are compared. For example, why should the *actus reus* of attempt appear to exist in *White's* case [1908–1910] A11 ER 340, and not exist in other such cases? One explanation seems to rest in the courts' view that the arresting authorities may have intervened too soon. In the case of **Hope v. Brown** [1954] 1 WLR 250, Lord Goddard considered whether proximity was achieved by whether the accused had, in his acts, reached a stage where the chances of repentance were slight. This would obviously be influenced by whether or not the law enforcement officers strike too soon.

In *DPP v. Stonehouse (supra)*, the appellant was a Member of Parliament who was convicted of attempting to enable another to obtain property by deception. His life was insured with five different companies for £125,000. In 1974 he faked his death by drowning in Miami, so that his wife, who was not a party to the plan, could claim under the policies. The news of his 'death' was quickly publicised and transmitted to England but the wife didn't claim the insurance money. Five weeks later the appellant was found in Australia and extradited.

Appellant's counsel, among other grounds, contended that Stonehouse's actions in Miami did not constitute attempt. He accepted that these were his final contribution to the fraudulent scheme calculated to induce persons in Miami to believe that he had drowned and communicate as much to England. Nevertheless he contended that the appellant had merely made preparation to create a situation where his wife in innocence could claim and obtain the insurance money. Lord Edmund Davies did not accept the

Robinson principle that for attempt to stand there must be some communication of the false pretence to the insurers:

> The ruling that there cannot be a connection for an attempt to obtain by false pretences, unless the pretense or deception has come to the attention of the intended victim, should not be followed and the court was wrong in treating all preceding acts as mere preparation.

The court did not accept the insistence in **Davey v. Lee** (*supra*) that it was necessary to have the *actus reus* of attempt 'immediately connected' with the full offence. It was also not accepted that the 'series of acts if not interrupted' approach of **Hope v. Brown** (*supra*) should be read to mean that the accused should have taken all possible steps in his power to bring about the substantive offence.

Edmund Davies approved the approach of Hailsham in **Haughten v. Smith** [1975] AC 476, that for attempt to stand it must be shown that there was (a) an intention to commit the offence, and (b) overt acts as part of a series which would constitute the offence if not interrupted, and of sufficient proximity. It should not always be necessary that to be guilty of attempt, a man must have done the last act which he expected to do, and which it is necessary for him to do in order to achieve the consequences aimed at. Even so, as is the case with the use of the non–innocent agent, the wrongdoer may not have progressed sufficiently along the intended path and his actions may still amount to no more than preparation. What has always to be borne in mind is the nature of the substantive offence that is alleged to have been attempted. In this case (unlike *Robinson's* case) the charge was based on the extended meaning of 'obtain' contained in s. 15(2) of the *Theft Act* (UK), that is, 'enabling another to obtain'. If Stonehouse's intention and plan had not been interrupted, the full offence eventually would have been completed. Towards the commission of that offence, for example, the faking of the death (a) was intended to produce that result, (b) was the final act that Stonehouse could perform, and (c) went a substantial distance towards the attainment of these goals.

In order to confirm the proximity of one in a series of acts, the court in **Jones v. Brooks** (1968) 52 Cr App R 614 considered the question of unequivocality. The accused had been observed trying the doors of cars parked in a public street to see if any of them were unlocked. The acts of the accused at the time of the apprehension may have been steps towards the commission of a number of different crimes. But his expressed intention (to drive home any car into which he could gain entry) is relevant not only in establishing the later issue of *mens rea*, but also for identifying the actual *actus reus* towards which the alleged attempt was directed. The expressed intention alone does not amount to criminal intent. There must also be an *actus reus* which is sufficiently proximate to the substantive offence. The surrounding circumstances should be considered by the court to isolate the specific *actus reus* in question, both of the attempt and the substantive offence. When the act is equivocal, consideration of intention is necessary to establish the goal towards which the act is directed. Following this decision the prosecution must prove the act to be sufficiently proximate to the crime the accused intends to commit.

Attempts to do the impossible

Under common law the issue of impossibility in attempt, as well as in the other inchoate offences, is complex. In **Haughten v. Smith** (*supra*), for instance, the House of Lords recognised that sometimes it is a crime to attempt the impossible. The issue debated in this case was what circumstances were necessary for such to be the situation. In *Haughten v. Smith* the impossibility arose from an inadequacy of means rather than an impossibility of ends, and therefore the 'impossibility' was possible in other circumstances. In respect of the empty pocket example Lord Reid and Viscount Dilhorne preferred the earlier 'no liability' decisions, seeing that the 'end' was impossible. Lord Hailsham, on the other hand, saw the question as open and depending on the specific nature of each set of circumstances. Both Viscount Dilhorne and Lord Hailsham agreed that there could be no attempt to steal if the accused entered a house intending to steal and the goods he expected to find were not there.

The logic in *Haughten v. Smith* can be criticised on the basis that if you look at the instances where the court would hold that an attempt had been committed, often the sequence of actions could as well not result in an attempt as those that were said to have such a potential. The eventual determinations were driven by policy rather than logic. The determination of whether the substantive offence could or couldn't be committed is often far from simple and unequivocal.

In **Mai and Tran** (1992) 60 A Crm R 49, the court was called upon to consider the position in New South Wales. M was arrested carrying a block of plaster of Paris that the police had earlier substituted for heroin. He argued that a conviction for attempted possession was unsound because it was impossible for him to possess the drug in this circumstance. Even where it is physically impossible to achieve the substantive offence, a conviction of attempt is possible where the Crown establishes:

1 that the accused intended to do the acts which with the relevant state of mind would comprise the intended crime (if the facts and circumstances were as he believed them to be); and
2 that with the intention, he did some act towards the commission of the crime which went beyond mere preparation and which cannot

reasonably be regarded as having any other purpose than the commission of that crime.

Conspiracy

In the case of **DPP v. Nock** [1975] 2 All ER 645, Lord Salmon referred to the judgment of Lord Tucker in **Owen's** case [1957] AC 602, and said that by stressing the 'auxiliary nature' of the crime of conspiracy, and by explaining its justification as the prevention of the commission of substantive offences, he had placed the crime firmly in the same category as attempts to commit the crime. Both are criminal as sufficient steps towards the commission of the substantive offence. The distinction between the two is whereas a proximate act may be that which constitutes the crime of attempt, the agreement is a necessary ingredient for conspiracy. The importance of the distinction is that the agreement may and usually will occur well before the first step which is sufficiently proximate for attempt. The law of conspiracy thus makes possible an earlier intervention by the law to prevent the commission of the substantive offence. It is this very potential which gives fuel to the critics of the criminal law as a preventive process.

In addition, the argument that shared or common purpose adds to the significance of the crime of conspiracy may be criticised. By concentrating on the collective nature of conspiracies, is the law proposing a second order of harm, one where there is a greater threat to community safety and social harmony posed by collective activity? Is the blameworthiness of the conspirator enough to modify the rigid requirements for individual criminal liability?

Elements of a conspiracy

A conspiracy is an agreement between two or more people to commit an unlawful act, or a lawful act unlawfully. The term 'unlawful' should be considered in its broadest sense to include certain torts, frauds, the corruption of public morals, and the outrage of public decency. In this respect conspiracy goes beyond inchoate offences, which need to be connected in any proximate sense with an intended substantive offence.

Conspiracies may be located under three heads:

- where the end is a crime in itself;
- where the object itself is lawful but the means to be resorted to for its achievement are unlawful;
- where the object is to do injury to a third party or a class, though if the wrong were effected by single individuals it would be a wrong, but not a crime.

As part of the law of conspiracy there is no necessity of express proof of the agreement, such as proof that the parties actually met and had their heads together and then actually agreed to carry out the common purpose. Proof of conspiracy is generally a matter of influence deduced from certain acts done by several people towards, or in pursuance of, an apparently criminal purpose.

Jurisdiction

The issue of the jurisdiction within which the conspiracy was agreed, and its relation to the place where the defence was to be committed, is discussed in **DPP v. Doot** [1973] 1 All ER 940. The respondents, American citizens, formed a plan abroad to import cannabis into the USA by way of England. In pursuance of the agreement, two vans with the drugs concealed in them were shipped from Morocco to Southampton. The drugs were found and the defendants were charged with conspiracy to import cannabis. It was contended for the defence at the trial that the court had no jurisdiction because the conspiracy had been entered into abroad. The Court of Appeal quashed the conviction, holding that the offence of conspiracy was completed when the agreement was made. The House of Lords reversed this decision, finding that although the conspiracy, as a crime, was complete when the agreement was made, it continued in existence so long as there were two or more parties to it intending to carry out the design. It was, for a jurisdictional issue, only necessary to show that wherever formed, the conspiracy was still in existence when the accused were in England.

In the earlier case of the **Board of Trade v. Owen** [1957] AC 602 it was decided that a conspiracy commenced in England or Wales, to do acts in a foreign country that infringe the laws of that country, is not indictable in England unless the contemplated offence itself, if committed in that foreign country, is one for which the indictment would lie in England.

As to the jurisdictional issue, the **Attorney-General's Reference (No. 1 1982)** [1983] 2 All ER 721 suggests that an agreement to obtain property by deception abroad is not indictable as a conspiracy to defraud merely because it will cause a loss to a person in England. The contemplated crime in Lebanon would not have been indictable in England. Damage to the whisky producer in England caused by the fraud in Lebanon was viewed as a 'side effect, or incidental consequence of the conspiracy and not its object'.

Actus reus of conspiracy
The agreement

For conspiracy, the *actus reus* is the agreement. The agreement is central to the concept of conspiracy, even though its fabric may be fairly loose.

The offence is committed as soon as the parties agree and it is immaterial that they never begin to put the agreement into effect.

Although a conspiracy is completed when the agreement is made, it is clear that conspiracy is a continuous and ongoing offence. Therefore the number of persons who may be held liable as parties to some conspiracy, although they joined at different times, will also accumulate so long as the agreement is in force. These participants may be held liable together even if they were not parties to the agreement at the same time. The question for the jury or assessors to consider is: 'Had they this common purpose, and did they pursue it by these common means, the design being unlawful?' This must be distinguished from a mere accidental concurrence of wills, being rather a concurrence resulting from some degree of agreement.

In *R v. O'Brien* (1974) 59 Cr App R 222, it was held that there must be a concluded agreement to commit a wrong and not just negotiations for such an agreement. Therefore, just because the appellant was found photographing the outside of a prison, and documents and plans were found in his house suggesting that he intended to assist in a prisoner's escape, there may not be sufficient grounds on which to establish conspiracy. The court held:

> The essence of a conspiracy is an agreement, and persons do not commit a criminal offence merely by talking about the possibility of committing some wrongful or unlawful act unless they reach the stage when they have agreed to commit that act if it lies in their power. If the jury considered the background of this case and the inferences to be drawn, they could quite properly, and no doubt would, have drawn the inference that O'Brien had told them a pack of lies … They might very well have drawn the inference that it was most unlikely that O'Brien would have done all this entirely by himself without consulting his friends in Luton because he was clearly well known in the Irish nationalist circles in that town. But the point about which the jury must have been in considerable difficulty, had the matter been explained to them, was in saying that the only possible inference to be drawn here was not merely that O'Brien had discussed a prison break with his friends, but that O'Brien had agreed to undertake a prison break with his friends.

The case of *R v. Scott* (1978) 68 Cr. App R 164 is authority for the principle that it is not necessary that all parties to the agreement should have evidenced their consent at the same time, nor that they should have all been in communication with each other, provided they entertained a common purpose and communicated to at least one other party, expressly or tacitly, the object of the conspiracy.

Regarding the parties to a conspiracy, the two or more persons involved in the agreement may in fact be unknown to each other.

The law has been well settled since the case of *R v. Plummer* (1902) 2 KB 339 that if specified persons are jointly charged with conspiracy and one pleads guilty and the others are acquitted, the conviction of the former cannot stand. The law is, however, equally clear that if the indictment charges with conspiracy persons unknown as well as named persons, a conviction of only one of the accused is at least technically good. In such a case the conviction will, in a proper case, be allowed to stand, particularly where, as in the case of *R v. Higgins* (1801) 2 East 5, there is no room for doubt about the existence of the conspiracy but the question is concerned with the identity of one or more of the conspirators.[145]

In joint trials of two or more named persons for conspiracy where no such saving words as 'and with others unknown' are used in the particulars, either two or more must be convicted; no single one may be.

Where the alleged conspiracy involves a number of co-conspirators and a number of separate unlawful acts over a long period of time, the nature and scope of the conspiracy may be problematic. In *Gerakiteys* (1984) 58 ALJR 182, the High Court examined a central conspiratorial agreement and associated conspiracies, which led to the failure on the part of the prosecutor to prove an all-embracing conspiracy as alleged. Where conspiracy is used it is essential—indeed fundamental—that the precise nature of the conspiracy be analysed prior to the commencement of the proceedings. Where a single conspiracy charged is to effect more than one unlawful purpose, the jury may find a single conspiracy to bring about only some of those purposes. The jury cannot, however, find two conspiracies under a count which charges only one, nor find an accused guilty of a conspiracy which is distinct and different from that charged (particularly a consequential but different conspiracy which flowed from that charged). Section 393 of the *Crimes Act* (NSW) provides that the accused may be charged with a conspiracy with 'divers persons' where only one of these is named. Proof will come by establishing the agreement between the accused and any of these people, but not for a distinct and different conspiracy.

The unlawful object

The general heads for the *actus reus* of conspiracy in terms of unlawful purpose are:

- Conspiracy to commit a criminal offence
- Conspiracy to defraud
- Conspiracy to commit a tort
- Conspiracy to corrupt or outrage moral decency

Context of the problem

What follows will encourage consideration of:

- Individual and corporate liability

---

145   Also see *Darby* (1982) 56 ALJR 688 for the High Court's position on this and in particular the dissenting verdict of Murphy J.

- Nature and degrees of participation
- Prohibited conduct through omission
- Causation
- Common purpose and related knowledge

PROBLEM

David is the managing director of a small private zoo operating in the west of Sydney. The zoo was originally established to house circus animals which were no longer considered by their owners to be financially profitable. As a result the zoo has a sizeable collection of lions and other wild cats, which form the nucleus of a 'safari park' within the zoo.

In recent years an increasing number of the visitors to the zoo have been overseas tourists. Of these the large contingent of Japanese have come to expect the 'free range' experience offered by other animal parks in the surrounding region. David has responded to customer demand by setting apart an enclosed section of the zoo in which tourists can handle koalas, and be near other native creatures such as emus and kangaroos. This development is endorsed, as required, within the safety requirements of his business licence.

The local council has imposed strict safety standards on animal park operators within their municipality. David has been warned on several occasions that the 'safari park' in particular must be strictly supervised and that the ratio of animal handlers to tourists must be maintained. Only in the last week he has received correspondence from the council threatening to revoke his business licence if he again fails to comply with their requirements on staff numbers. In order to satisfy this demand David has reinstated a lion handler whom he had sacked for being intoxicated during working hours. David is aware that this staff member has an alcohol problem, but with short notice David has not been able to engage any other trained handlers in order to satisfy the council's demands.

Attendance at the park has been falling and David has been considering the suggestion of his head keeper that they should open a section of the safari park as a free range area. The idea is that several of the older and 'tamer' lions would be placed in the new facility and visitors could approach the lions and photograph their activities at closer range. The head keeper agrees that there is a 'minor safety risk' involved in this experiment but if they 'put the right staff in charge, the risk would be manageable'. Without seeking clearance from the council safety inspector, David advertises the facility.

One day, when the recently reinstated handler was taking a group of Japanese visitors through the 'free range' section of the safari park, one of the lions became aggressive without warning, and mauled a visitor. The tourist later died in hospital from his wounds.

When interrogated by police the handler said that he hadn't asked for the assignment but had been instructed by the head keeper to perform this duty.

Of the accident in particular he said; 'I don't remember anything after the lion rushed forward. I just froze. It was almost like I couldn't control my actions from sheer panic.'

The head keeper said that he always passed his staff duty roster to David at the beginning of each week for his approval. Although David doesn't remember seeing the roster for the week in question he concedes to police that 'it may have crossed my desk with other paperwork'.

The council has now closed down the zoo as a result of 'several further breaches of safety standards'. As part of their investigations they demanded access to David's personnel records. David refused to give these up for fear 'that they could be used against the staff in any criminal proceedings arising out of the accident'.

ENGAGING THE PROBLEM

Assuming that there is an offence here (once the issues of causation and negligence have been established) it is necessary to determine against whom the charge might be directed. Who is the principal offender? If there are secondary parties, what is the nature and degree of participation? A consideration of knowledge and intention will be crucial here. There may have been some common purpose or agreement, but is it sufficient to rest some form of collaborative liability?

Delegation and identification are important concerns when determining whether liability is individual or whether the company can be considered to bear any criminal responsibility. What would be the purpose of corporate liability here?

ADDITIONAL READING

Bronitt, S. and McSherry, B., *Principles of Criminal Law*, Law Book Company, Sydney, 2001, Chapters 3, 8 and 9.

Brown, D., Farrier, D., Egger, S., and McNamara, L., *Criminal Laws*, Federation Press, Sydney, 2001, paras 4.7, 4.8, 5.9, 11.

Corns, C. 'The Liability of Corporations for Homicide in Australia' (1991) 15 *Criminal Law Journal* 351.

Fisse, B., *Howard's Criminal Law*, Law Book Company, Sydney, 1992, Chapters 5 and 7.

Norrie, A., *Crime, Reason and History*, Weidenfeld & Nicolson, London, 1993, Chapter 5.

R v. Oll Ltd [1994] NLJ 178

King v. R (1986) 60 ALJR 685

White v. Ridley (1978) 140 CLR 342

Giorgianni v. R (1985) 59 ALJR 461

Stokes and Difford (1990) 51 A Crim R 24

Tangye v. R (1997) 92 A Crim R 545

Johns v. R (1980) 143 CLR 108

McAuliffe v. R (1995) 183 CLR 108
Clough v. R (1992) 64 A Crim R 451
Hamilton v. Whitehead (1988) 63 ALJR 80
Alister v. R (1984) 58 ALJR 97
DPP v. Stonehouse [1978] AC 55
Gerakiteys v. R (1984) 58 ALJR 182

Topic 11

Assault: Domestic violence

This topic looks at the law on assault and aggravated assault, using domestic violence as a case study. Why was assault not historically prosecuted in the domestic context? How has that changed? In considering the law in context here, the issues to be addressed in answering these questions include:

- the prevalence of domestic violence in Australian society;
- problems associated with common-sense understandings of domestic violence, particularly as these have influenced policing practice;
- the relationship between the law in theory and practical operation, particularly as it addresses gender stereotyping, issues of enforcement, and the interface between criminal and civil law solutions;
- apprehended violence orders and their limitations.

Assault

The traditional definition of assault is putting the victim in fear of violence. Battery, which now is included within the concept of assault, involves the infliction of minimal injury.

Assaults are determined either as common assault, or within a range of aggravated assaults.

Aggravated assaults are classified on the basis of:

- harm (nature of the injury inflicted, or consequence of the assault);
- purpose of the harm (e.g. to resist arrest);
- mental state with which the assault was carried out (e.g. with intent);
- circumstances of the assault (e.g. sexual assault).

The principal forms of aggravated assault involve:

- assault to further a specific intent in which the offence requires the establishment of elements of assault plus the intent to produce consequential harm (e.g. assault with intent to commit murder);

- assault on victims with special status requiring particular protection, or where the relationship between the offender and the victim involves care;
- assault causing particular injuries, such as actual bodily harm or grievous bodily harm. Such offences do not require proof of an additional mental state as to the harmful consequences unless this is expressly stipulated in the legislation. Degrees of harm here are subjectively measured as 'serious';
- assaults using offensive weapons or dangerous substances. A distinction is made here between lawful and unlawful purposes, and the reasonable belief in self-defence;
- assaults in combination with other offences (e.g. robbery);
- assaults with a sexual component. Australian legislation on sexual assault usually presents a range of offences of different degrees of gravity, replacing rape.

The mental state for assault is intention or recklessness, such as intent to assault or recklessness as to the consequences. In **McPherson v. Brown** (1975) 12 SASR 174, the issue was whether proof of recklessness would suffice, with a narrow reading of the meaning of recklessness. In this case the court reiterated the need (unless statutes provide otherwise) to judge an accused in terms of what he intended, knew, or foresaw, and not by comparison with the reasonable and prudent person. The court in **Coleman** (1990) 19 NSWLR 467 considered recklessness as the mental state required for the charge of maliciously inflicting actual bodily harm with intent to have sexual intercourse. Where the facts alleged that the accused acted maliciously through foreseeing certain criminal consequences, then the degree of foresight must be 'probable' where the crime charged is murder and 'possible' for other statutory offences.

Conditional threats

The common law now concedes that words can constitute an assault and conditional threats may be the manner in which fear is conveyed. A threat of harm if it is sufficiently imminent may satisfy the necessary mental state for common assault. In **Zanker v. Vartzokas** (1988) 34 A Crm R 11, where the threat of future violence made the victim jump from a moving van, it was agreed that false imprisonment encompasses both the external and the fault element of assault. In this case the victim was initially detained within the vehicle against his will. In relation to a conditional threat as the basis for an assault, the court in this case held that the fear must be present but the realisation of the threat could be continuing. It was necessary that there was no reasonable escape from the fear or threat. Therefore, imminence is not simply a measure of the duration between the utterance and the realisation of the threat.

In the case of ***Rozsa v. Samuels*** [1969] SASR 205, the assault was said to have arisen from an argument between taxi drivers and threatened wounding. Here the gist of the offence is the creation of fear, in the mind of the person assailed, that unlawful force is to be used against him or her. Can there be an assault where the threat is conditional on the unlawful action of the person threatened? In this case a threatening gesture was accompanied by conditional words. Was there a justification for the conditional threat because of the behaviour of the other man? If so, there would be no assault. Where a threat is in excess of what self-defence requires, assault may arise.

Social context of assault

The common law has for centuries projected a somewhat ambivalent position on violence. Until recently parental discipline and 'manly diversions' have been endorsed and protected while violence as part of consensual sexual gratification has been denied. In many jurisdictions there are greater potential penalties for basic larceny and malicious damage to property than for common assault.

Assault has become a very significant form of crime requiring police attention. Again, until recently police were reluctant to intervene when violence occurred in a domestic setting. Assault in public places, and where it represented a challenge to police, was more likely to generate their interest.

A disturbing relationship exists in Australia between masculinity, alcohol, and violence. Young males are likely to be both the victims and the perpetrators of assault in the vicinity of licensed premises and when intoxicated.

There is a discrepancy between the risk of violent crime and fear of crime victimisation. For instance, women, children, and elderly persons are more likely to be assaulted in the home rather than in a public space, and by those known to them rather than by strangers.

Women are usually the victims of the most serious forms of violence, and for them violence usually comes from the opposite sex. This is not the case when men are the victims.

The conditions that cast certain groups within the community into positions of extreme economic and social marginality in Australian society also expose them to increased risks of victimisation and criminalisation.

Consent as a defence to crimes of violence

Consent may be a defence to assault if it is valid. However, a person cannot always give valid consent to bodily harm falling short of death. It would seem, following the case of ***Donovan*** [1934] All ER Rep 207, that the ordinary person cannot consent to the infliction upon himself of harm that would constitute or exceed bodily harm. Here the defendant was convicted of indecent assault upon a girl of 17. He caned her, with her consent, for sexual gratification. He appealed to the Court of Appeal on a misdirection and was successful. However, the court stressed that the question the jury should have been asked was whether the blows struck by the accused were intended or likely to cause bodily harm to the victim; if so, her consent to such harm would not represent a defence. The court defined bodily harm as 'any hurt or injury calculated to interfere with the health or comfort of the complainant which need not be permanent but must be more than a transient trifling'.

There are standard exceptions to this rule, as in the case where bodily harm arises as part of lawful sporting activity. These instances of what might otherwise be viewed as assault are seen as essentially different from the sexual violence cases. The principle governing the exceptions relates to questions of rules and public policy.

In **R v. Brown** [1993] 2 WLR 556, the appellants were a group of sado-masochists, willingly and enthusiastically participating in the commission of acts of violence against each other for the sexual pleasure they obtained from giving and receiving pain. They pleaded not guilty to charges of wounding and inflicting actual bodily harm on their victims. At the trial the judge ruled that in certain situations the prosecution did not have to prove lack of consent by the victim when establishing assault, and the resultant appeals were based on misdirection.

It was held on appeal that although absence of consent had to be proved for convictions of simple assault, it was not in the public interest that a person should wound or cause actual bodily harm to another for no good reason. In the absence of such a reason, the victims' consent afforded no defence to charges of serious aggravated assault. Satisfying sexual desire was not such a good reason. Since the appellants had admitted to the infliction of injuries which were neither transient nor trifling, the question of consent was therefore immaterial.

The position with violence and children's play is more ambiguous. In **R v. Jones** (1986) 83 Cr App R 276, certain schoolchildren were charged with assault occasioning actual bodily harm. Collectively they injured some fellow students as a result of what the court found was 'rough and boisterous play'. The victims had not consented to such a degree of roughness or danger. The questions here to be addressed in determining liability were whether the accused intended or foresaw such injury, whether they viewed the victims as consenting, and whether there could be particular exceptions appropriate to such 'play' situations. The courts have traditionally not concerned themselves with such activities provided they have not gone too far. What constitutes 'too far' may be a factor of time.

Whether consent renders lawful what would otherwise be unlawful in the case of non-fatal offences against the person depends upon the following principles:

1 A person cannot always give valid consent to bodily harm falling short of death.

There are 'well established exceptions' to the rule that a valid consent will not be given to an act likely or intended to cause bodily harm. 'Manly diversions' are put in separate categories from sexual deviation such as flagellation. The principle governing this and other exceptions may be contained in Stephen J's judgment in **Coney's** case (1882) 8 QBD 534 (a case where participants in a prize fight with bare fists were held guilty of assault):

> When a person is indicted for inflicting personal injury on another the consent of the person who sustains the injury is no defence to the other person who inflicted the injury if the injury is of such a nature, or inflicted under such circumstances, that its infliction is injurious to the public as well as the person injured.

Applying this test, which is primarily one of public policy, it is important to note that Stephen's criterion for exemptions to the *Donovan* rule does not cover consent to the infliction of harm to any degree; only where it is ordinary or incidental to the approved activity.

In certain cases it is the rules of the game rather than the nature of the harm or the public policy governing the context of the assault which differentiate between situations where consent may be given and where it may not.

2 In most sexual activity involving assault, young people under a certain age can't give valid consent.

Sutton [1977] 1 WLR 1086, was a case where the question about whether someone below the age of 16 can offer valid consent was considered. In this case it was agreed that naked boys could consent to being photographed and that touching the boys was not seen as indecent because it was done to indicate the nature of the pose.

On the issue of 'informed consent', the courts have evidenced a greater leniency toward doctors than toward unqualified people who indulge in doubtful practices against the bodies of others. In **Burrell v. Harmer** [1967] Cr LR 165, a tattooist tattooed two boys aged 12 and 13, causing their arms to become inflamed and painful. The magistrates convicted him of an assault occasioning actual bodily harm, rejecting his defence that the boys consented on the grounds that they did not understand the nature of the act, and the conviction was upheld on appeal.

In **Gillick's** case [1984] 1 All ER 365, it was observed that a girl under the age of 16 can consent to an abortion without the consent of her parents. In addition, Woolf J held, in an action for declaration, that a girl under the age of 16 could give valid consent to medical treatment which included the provision of birth control facilities. Some of the judges in this case seem to have been of the opinion that a doctor, who knew that the provision of contraceptive advice to a girl under 16 could encourage a man to have sexual intercourse with her, would not be guilty of abetting the offence, because his intention was to protect the girl, not to encourage unlawful sexual intercourse with her.

3 Where there is an honest (and reasonable) mistake as to the nature of the act forming the basis of the consent, then the mistaken facts will be accepted as fact for the determination of the consent.

In *Williams* [1923] 1 KB 340, the defendant was a singing master who persuaded a female pupil to submit to intercourse under the pretence that it would improve her breathing. His conviction of rape was affirmed. This accorded with the view that if the woman knew nothing about the nature of the act and thought that her instructor was doing something merely to improve her lungs, then her consent could in no way vitiate the sexual intercourse. In such a situation the mistake of fact on the part of the victim became the actual context within which consent was constructed. If, on the other hand, she knew the facts of life and was willing to be persuaded that one of the benefits of the act of sex was an improvement in breathing, then she did not make a mistake as to the nature of the act.

4 An apparent consent will be treated as unreal and hence no defence when:
   • the victim is very young and unable to comprehend the nature of the act committed;
   • the victim's apparent consent is procured under duress; or
   • a person, apparently consenting, is induced to do so by fraud as to the nature of the act, or the identity of the accused. The victim may know the nature of the act but be mistaken as to a collateral fact.

Patterns of victimisation in assault

Particularly in relation to domestic violence, child abuse, and sexual assault, patterns of victimisation are hard to determine largely because of the hidden nature of much violence. This is a consequence of the relationships between victims and offenders, their dependencies, interactions, and unequal status and power. In addition, a reluctance to report to police, or not seeing the police as effective protection exacerbates this reality.

Violent crime in Australia is predominantly in situations of intra-family or intra-community violence. In this respect victimisation is likely to concentrate on particular family members, and groups within communities.

There are two main types of violence victimisation in Australia: confrontational violence between young males; and violence between family members and other intimates. Violence, despite its popular perception, is in fact a less common occurrence in the course and commission of instrumental crimes.

The first large national survey of women and violence in Australia[146] recently found that 23 per cent of women who had been married or in de facto relationships experienced violence by their partner. International studies have shown that for young women (aged 18–23) the risk of violence by a partner is three to four times greater than for women in general. In 1996 the Australian Bureau of Statistics found that 56 per cent of women assaulted by their boyfriends were injured in the last incident, compared with 31 per cent of women assaulted by their de facto or partner.

Domestic violence and legal change

Traditionally certain justification or excuse issues for the criminal law have revolved around the violent combat of males, or the explicable consequences of males losing self-control. More recently, the concepts of provocation and self-defence have been modified to recognise the reality of domestic violence.[147] The cumulative effect of a history of domestic violence may now satisfy the provocative act and the characteristics of an abused woman may bear consideration in determining why she did what she did and whether it was reasonable. For self-defence or duress the ordinary person may be measured to a limited extent against any prevailing history of domestic violence in the life of the accused. The development of syndrome defences is a recent consequence of the court's interest in the situation and circumstances of domestic and gender-based violence.

In most Australian jurisdictions, apprehended violence orders (AVOs) have been passed by legislatures in order to protect victims of domestic violence. The need for these orders is irrefutable despite recent suggestions that they are sometimes used vexatiously, particularly beyond the setting of domestic violence. In a recent AIC report (March 2000), among young women in violent relationships, 45 per cent had been beaten and choked, or their partner had threatened them with a gun. Twenty-nine per cent of the women in the study had sought legal intervention (either contacted police or applied for an AVO or both). The study found that the severity of violence was reduced after legal protection was sought. However, the benefit was not as marked when women only sought help from the police.

---

146 Australian Institute of Criminology, *Report No. 148* March 2000.
147 For instance, *Crimes (Homicide) Amendment Act 1981* (NSW).

An example of recent law reform in the area is the *Crimes (Domestic Violence) Amendment Acts 1982* and *1983*, and the *Crimes Amendment (Apprehended Violence) Act 1999* (all in NSW).

In the *Crimes (Domestic Violence) Amendment Acts 1982* and *1983*, the legislation:

- defined domestic violence offences;
- clarified police powers of entry where domestic violence is reasonably suspected;
- made spouses compellable witnesses;
- created the procedure for apprehended domestic violence orders;
- created special bail provisions for the protection of victims;
- instructed police, rather than victims, to lay charges.

The *Crimes Amendment (Apprehended Violence) Act:*

- defined domestic relationships so as to include same-sex couples;
- created two distinct categories of AVO, recognising the difference in the nature and level of violence in domestic and non-domestic settings; and
- created a new offence of stalking or intimidating with intent to cause physical or mental harm.

New measures to enhance the effectiveness of AVOs include:

- the ability of the court to extend an AVO on its own motion to situations of guilty pleas;
- an expanded definition of domestic violence taking into account Australia's international obligations to protect women and children;
- an expansion of provisions for granting interim orders by telephone; and
- the requirement of the police to record reasons for not initiating criminal proceedings in cases of breaching an AVO.

CONTEXT OF THE PROBLEM

The complexity of domestic violence is illustrated by the facts of this scenario. It exists in contexts of dominance and repression. It feeds on sexist status roles within the family setting, and on the vulnerability of children. All too often it is a feature of progressive victimisation and aggression.

Domestic violence is consistently the precursor to sexual assault, and instances of violence escalate into savage abuse and homicide. The victim may have become 'serialised' because of a sense of helplessness and dependence. The limited and delayed intervention of law enforcement, and their tendency to oversimplify situations of victimisation and responsibility, exacerbate cycles of chronic vulnerability.

Once violence has become a feature of the relationship, the issue is not only what the law can do to punish the perpetrator, but what can be done to protect the victim. Restraining orders are crucial to establishing boundaries for protection but they also fail to recognise complex relationships of dependence. Further, the imposition of penalties and restrictive domains will be likely further to victimise those within ambiguous relationships of dependence and submission. Again, the criminal sanction and law enforcement intervention are rather blunt tools in the process of protecting against domestic violence. Yet they are essential to identify the criminal character of such violence.

PROBLEM

Neville and Helen met when they were both 17. Some time after, they moved in together and they have since been living together for five years. They have had three children. From the start Neville was quite a jealous and controlling person. It was not until Helen was pregnant with their first child, which occurred six months after they started living together, that he first hit her. What actually happened was that she contracted herpes. During their relationship she had never had sex with anyone except Neville and so she confronted him about it. When she did he accused her of being a 'slut' and went into a jealous rage, punching her in the head. She left immediately after this incident and went to stay with her sister. She returned to Neville a few days later after he came to her sister's place with flowers and an apology for having sex with another woman when he had been drunk, and from whom he had contracted herpes. He also apologised for losing his temper and hitting her. He hoped she could find it in her heart to forgive him and 'make a go of it' in the future.

Helen says that after the first instance of violence he became steadily more aggressive to her and the children. Initially they went through periods where the relationship was reasonably happy, broken only by short periods of violence and verbal abuse on his part. Eventually, however, his violence reached a point where it could be described as a 'reign of terror'. He seemed determined to control every area of her life and eventually she found herself continually trying to appease him. She says that because the relationship with Neville was so long-term she can't remember all the details of his violent behaviour, but she does describe several incidents.

Neville kept a gun in the house. At one point he said to Helen, 'Either you'll shoot me one day or I will kill you.' Several weeks after this statement they had a heated exchange in their bedroom. He called her by some racially and sexually derogatory names. He spat on her and made aggressive gestures with what she thought at the time was his hunting knife. She grabbed one of his guns and pointed it at him, saying, 'If you come one step closer to me

I will blow your brains out.' In fact he was not holding a knife. Later he said that she had completely overreacted, as he never intended to threaten her.

Neville got extremely annoyed with one of the children one day. He began to hit the child with the cord from the electric jug. When Helen attempted to intervene he hit her across the face with the flex, saying: 'You and the children are my property. I can do what I like with you. If anyone tries to stop me I will kill them.' As a consequence of this incident the child had cuts on his arms and legs and Helen had a cut above the eye, which required stitches.

Following this incident she left and took the children to stay with her at a women's refuge for a week. Neville called her at the refuge on several occasions to say that she should not think that she would escape him there, and when he chose to he would 'get her'. Terrified, she stopped taking calls from him. One day she went to the Family Law Court. Talking to a friend outside the court, she was not aware of what was happening behind her. Neville stole up behind Helen carrying one of his shotguns. By the time she noticed him he was being hauled off by a plainclothes police officer. When he was placed under arrest Neville threatened the police officer with the rifle and tried to hit him. At the police station Neville said that at first he didn't realise that the arresting officer was with the police. He also said that he only intended to frighten Helen, he never intended actually to shoot her.

ENGAGING THE PROBLEM

There are a variety of assault situations presented in this problem. They raise considerations of how assaults can be conditional and on what words and actions they rely. The constituent elements of aggravated assault and their proofs are also in question here.

Histories of domestic violence involve complex and interrelated situations of assault. Here it may be necessary to consider the particular creation of fear in the context of these histories. The reaction of the victim to the threat may have a bearing on the continuation of the assault. The initial assault may also have some bearing on whether the reaction itself might be considered to be an assault.

The prevention of further assaults in the form of stalking and harassment is a challenge for the law. How complete this protection can be through the application of apprehended violence orders needs to be considered against prevailing threats.

ADDITIONAL RESOURCES

Crimes Act 1900 (NSW), sections 357F–357I, 562A–562V. The definition of 'domestic violence' in section 4.

Blazejowska, L., 'Sorting the Myths and Reality of Domestic Violence' (1994) 32(11) *Law Society Journal* 41.

Brown, D., Farrier, D., Egger, S., and McNamara, L., *Criminal Laws*, Federation Press, Sydney, 2001, paras 7.1.1–7.1.2, 7.1.3, 7.2.2, 7.2.3, 7.2.4, 7.3, 7.7.

Fisse, B. *Howard's Criminal Law,* Law Book Company, Sydney, 1992, pp. 136–65.

Greer, P., 'Aboriginal Women and Domestic Violence in New South Wales', in Stubbs, J. (ed.), *Women, Male Violence and the Law,* Institute of Criminology, Sydney, 1994, p. 64.

Leal, S., and Robson, S., 'The What, Where, When and How of AVOs: A Step by Step Guide' (1994) 32(11) *Law Society Journal* 30.

Mahoney, M., 'Legal Images of Battered Women: Redefining the Issue of Separation' (1991) 90(1) *Michigan Law Review* 1.

Redfern Legal Centre, *The Law Handbook*, Redfern Legal Centre Publishing, Sydney, 1997, pages 1072–85.

Stubbs, J. and Tolmie, J., 'Defending Battered Women on Trial' (1995) 8(1) *The Canadian Journal of Women and the Law* 122.

Trimboli, L. and Bonney, R., *An Evaluation of the NSW Apprehended Violence Order Scheme,* NSW Bureau of Crime Statistics and Research, 1997, particularly pp. vi–vii.

Rozsa v. Samuels [1969] SASR 205

Brown [1993] 2 All ER 75

Barton v. Armstrong [1969] 2 NSWLR 451

Knight (1988) 35 A CrimR 314

Zanker v. Vartzokas (1988) 34 A Crim R 11

Pemble (1971) 124 CLR 107

Everingham (1949) 66 WN (NSW) 22

Ryan v. Kuhl [1979] VR 315

McPherson v. Brown (1975) 12 SASR 174

Clarence (1888) 22 QBD 23

Papadimitropoulos (1957) 98 CLR 249

Pallente v. Stadiums Pty Ltd (No. 1) [1976] VR 331

Carroll v. Lergesner [1991] 1 Qd R 206

Reynhoudt (962) 107 CLR 381

Coulter (1988) 76 ALR 365

Boughey (1986) 60 ALJR 422

TOPIC 12

SEXUAL ASSAULT AND LAW REFORM

This topic will take the case study approach to assault further by examining a sexual assault scenario. Recent developments and trends in the law on sexual assault will be analysed and pressures for reform considered. In particular, the following issues will be addressed: should the *mens rea* for sexual assault contain an objective fault element? Does a more individualised and personal understanding of the victim affect the outcome of cases involving allegations of sexual assault, and in particular questions of consent? Should this be more so than for cases involving other criminal charges? Do the various procedural and evidential provisions affect your responses to the last two questions? In addressing these questions students should be mindful of the competing interests which stimulate law reform through just this type of enquiry.

Conventions about rape

It is useful to introduce a discussion of sexual assault law reform by reviewing some of the conventional wisdom which informed the law of rape as it was. Many of these assumptions arose from a masculine predisposition of the criminal sanction and of law enforcement at that time.

Perhaps an explanation of the way in which the rules of evidence and trial procedure allowed a rape defence to degenerate into the trial of the victim was the image that rape was an easy allegation by malicious women. In that respect, both in terms of trial procedure and the narrow proofs of rape, the law was taken as needing to create special protections to avoid malicious prosecution.

Contrary to the reality that rape was difficult to prove, the law seemed to work from the assumption that it was difficult to deny. On the issues of the testing of the victim's credit, the legal nature and proof of the incident, two arenas of public scrutiny through the committal hearing and the trial, and peculiar requirements for corroboration, the accused received more than the usual benefits of the presumption of innocence.

Conventional presumptions such as those which denied wives and sex workers general opportunities to prosecute for rape challenged the general law on consent. The law seemed to suggest, for certain classes of women and in certain situational contexts, that 'no' may not mean 'no'.

Many accused persons, and unfortunately some in the community, believed and argued that women provoke rape. Such provocation was assumed from the way women dressed and where they tended to socialise. In addition, any stereotype of 'womanhood' other than the devoted mother/wife/girlfriend was interpreted in a sexually permissive context which tended to enhance challenges to consent, and the consequent attitudes of aggressors.

Finally there was an assumption that because of the seriousness of the offence, rape was always reported. In fact only about 25 per cent of all sexual assaults in Australia are reported.[148] This can be explained as much by vic-

---

148 P. Salmelainen and C. Coumarelos (1993) 'Adult Sexual Assault in NSW' *NSW Bureau of Crime Statistics and Research Crime and Justice Bulletin* 2.

tims' aversion to involvement in the criminal justice process and the belief that they will not be protected or believed.

Law reform

In most Australian jurisdictions there have been recent law reform initiatives which have incorporated and developed the common law on rape. In doing this the legislation recognises that rape is assault and that there is more to sexual assault than penetration of a vagina by a penis. Definitions of sexual assault now put the maximum emphasis on the violence of the offence rather than any sexual or 'moral' overtones it may have been assumed to possess.

Law reform in the area recognises the gradations of aggravation in sexual assault, with a corresponding range of penalties. The structure of seriousness in the offences and their penalties relate to the nature and degree of assault and violence involved, and the relationship between the victim and the abuser (and its consequences).

The reforms recognise that sexual assault is not necessarily male–female. Homosexual violence should have at least a similar status. In addition, there is now in law an appreciation that sexual assault means much more than penis–vagina penetration. A variety of sexual intrusions and the fear and violence associated with their perpetration can constitute sexual assault.

Legislative provisions which redetermine the rules of evidence and procedure governing the investigation, prosecution, and defence of sexual assault recognise the potential for further victimisation of the victim through the investigation, committal, and trial. Therefore the prior sexual history of the victim and the status of children as witnesses are among those features of proof which have received special consideration in these reforms.

Developments in the law on sexual assault maintain the significance of consent as a defence but clarify its connection with mistake. Case-law in particular has suggested that community concern for the protection of the victim, and a need to prevent avoidance of the consideration of whether someone is consenting seem to have modified subjective conceptions of recklessness as *mens rea* for sexual assault. The construction of particular offences (such as the use of weapons to compel sexual compliance) removes the emphasis on the proof of non-consent if there is some objective evidence.

Beyond reform of the law of rape, recent legislative revision in the area clarifies and incorporates the law on indecent assault. Homosexual assault is introduced as a dimension of indecency in certain jurisdictions.

An insight into the process of sexual assault law reform is revealed in the recent legislative changes in New South Wales. The *Crimes (Sexual Assault) Amendment Act 1981* created the structure of aggravated assault in a climate where evidence of the assault itself was argued as sufficient to alleviate the need to prove non-consensual sexual intercourse. The Act introduced a complex definition of sexual assault, which went beyond gender-specific rape. The *Crimes (Amendment) Act 1989* reduced the four-tiered aggravation structure to three, increased the penalties for certain offences, and introduced changes to the structures of proof such as the removal of the need to establish consent in situations where objective evidence of assault was present. Despite this apparent shift towards the protection of subjective *mens rea* in the offence, recent case-law has recognised the significance of the context of the assault in constructing the actual *mens rea* that was present.

What follows is a more detailed summary of the present reforms in the NSW *Crimes Act*.

- Section 61H defines sexual intercourse as more than penis–vagina penetration (including entry of the anus, mouth, or other part of the body, with parts of the body or implements). It contemplates male or female offenders and victims by referring to persons rather than to men or women specifically as perpetrators or victims. The definition avoids the focus on the time of penetration, which was essential for rape. The new definition envisages a continuing offence of sexual intercourse. Incitement towards sexual intercourse is incorporated in the definition.
- Section 61I declares that the offence of sexual assault is sexual intercourse without consent and with knowledge that consent is withheld.
- Section 61J creates the structure of offences of aggravated sexual assault. The conditions of aggravation are envisaged as: the malicious infliction of actual bodily harm; threats to inflict such harm; the commission of the offence in company; where the victim is under 16; where the victim is under the authority of the offender; where the victim has a serious physical or intellectual disability.
- Section 61K creates the offence of assault with intent to have sexual intercourse.
- Section 61L defines indecent assault as a situation where the offender assaults and commits an act of indecency.
- Section 61M creates a hierarchy of aggravated indecent assault employing similar grounds of aggravation as in s. 61J.
- Section 61R examines the nature and impact of consent. It confirms the common law position that mistake as to identity of the violator or as to marriage vitiates consent, as does mistake on the part of the victim regarding the suggestion that the sexual intercourse was a legitimate medical procedure. If the offender knows the victim is acting under mistake when consenting then he is taken to know that consent is absent. Threat vitiates consent and physical resistance by the victim is not necessary to demonstrate absence of consent. Apparent submission does not imply consent.

- Sections 61S and T remove presumptions denying sexual capacity on the basis of age, or inability to deny consent due to marriage.
- In the Act the meaning of carnal knowledge (consensual sexual intercourse with a girl under the age of 16) is widened in terms of the new definition of sexual assault.
- Regarding the offence of incest, knowledge as to relationship but not as to consent is required.
- Sex with the disabled or those requiring protection qualifies the consent requirements.
- Section 78G defines homosexual intercourse, and creates a structure on the basis of the age of the victim (below 10, 10–18), and reflecting whether the perpetrator is in a position of trust (e.g. a teacher).
- The offences of gross indecency, bestiality, and sexual assault by forced manipulation are specifically created under the Act.

Mental element in sexual assault

Perhaps the most contested issue in the case-law on sexual assault relates to the necessary mental element and the impact of consent and mistaken belief. In its simplest form the *mens rea* is an intent to have non-consensual sexual intercourse. Subjective recklessness is introduced where the accused either knows that the victim is not consenting and proceeds anyway, or accepts that there is in the circumstances a risk that the victim is not consenting. The degree to which the accused perceives that risk or is willfully blind to that risk is also at issue. There remains some controversy as to whether the discussion of advertence to the risk now incorporates the suggestion that the accused should have foreseen the risk in light of what the community might expect in the circumstances.

The common law position regarding mistaken belief is influenced by the English decision of **DPP v. Morgan** (*supra*) where the requirement as to mistake was that it should only be based on an honest and not necessarily reasonable belief. The relevance of *Morgan* in Australia might be questioned in light of Brennan J's suggestion in **He Kaw Teh** that for protection of the victim in the circumstances of rape it might be necessary to require that the belief in consent was reasonably held. In any case there will be consideration of reasonableness in relation to satisfying the evidence of honest belief; the question is whether juries should be so directed.

Accepting the law that an honest (and perhaps reasonable) mistaken belief in the consent of the complainant may deny the necessary *mens rea* for the offence, any suggestion of recklessness as to consent therefore should be viewed as subjective. **Kitchener** (1993) 29 NSWLR 696 confirms that a failure to advert to whether consent was present·or not may be sufficient for recklessness here. Again, in **Tolmie** (1995) 37 NSWLR 660, it was argued for the accused that if *Kitchener* incorporated notions of inadvertence or negligence into the *mens rea* for sexual assault, then this would be inconsistent with a central tenet of the criminal law—that a person should not be subject to serious criminal sanction for actions which he or she was not proved to have intended. Kirby J, recognising that recklessness was not defined in the statutory offence, accepted inadvertence as part of recklessness. He took the view that lack of the merest advertence to consent in the case of sexual intercourse is so reckless that it is the criminal law's business. In this, the law does no more than reflect the community outrage at the suffering inflicted on victims of sexual violence. While not relying on *Caldwell* (*supra*), Kirby took it to endorse the view that where the accused has not considered the question of consent, and the risk that the complainant was not consenting would have been obvious to someone with the accused's mental capacity if he turned his mind to it, then the accused is said to have been reckless in terms of the elements of the offence.

Prohibited conduct in sexual assault

Interestingly, consent is a feature of both the conduct and the mental elements of sexual assault. The conduct is defined as non-consensual sexual intercourse. Consent is embedded in the *actus reus* and therefore it is an 'integral rather than an attendant' element of the offence (as observed by Brennan J in *He Kaw Teh*).

The denial of consent is now viewed as a crucial identifier of the nature of coercion. Consent is not seen as assumed through submission. Consent is no longer denied through evidence of resistance. Confusion regarding the determination of consent (or advertence to its refusal) is revealed in the case-law through the way something is evidenced, from the thing itself (that is, the actions or inaction of the victim rather than the appreciation of the accused).

Consent when induced by fraud or mistake is now clearly vitiated as an answer to the criminal conduct and the mental state of the accused. Proof of non-consent is at the heart of the difficulty with prosecuting sexual assault. There have always been problems with the 'fresh complaint' requirement (even as qualified for instance in the *Crimes Act* (NSW), s. 405B(2)) while the warning against uncorroborated evidence has been abolished by the *Evidence Act*, s.164. Cross-examination of the victim on prior sexual history is only allowed now in certain limited circumstances.[149]

---

149 Note the complex drafting of the exceptions and the creation of new situations of judicial discretion in *Crimes Act* (NSW), s. 409B.

In *M* (1994) 126 ALR 325 the accused attempted to introduce evidence that the complainant was given to sexual fantasies (which is outside the exceptions contemplated in s. 409B of the NSW *Crimes Act* and as such could not be admitted by the trial judge). The court held that the section created a blanket prohibition against which certain exceptions could stand to protect the accused. However, even then it was not guaranteed that the raising of such exceptions would lead to their admission. There existed a double protection, in that the judge must also decide that the probative value outweighs the prejudicial value of the admission when exercising a discretion to exclude or not to admit. These chances for admission were limited only to the exceptions as laid down. In *M* the conviction of a father for the sexual assault on his 13-year-old daughter was overturned by the High Court on the consideration of the appropriate behaviour of a reasonable complainant.

Significance of 'assault' component in sexual assault

In indecent assault it is necessary that the accused does something to the victim, or threatens to do something which qualifies as an assault. Indecency alone will not satisfy the offence. In *Fairclough v. Whipp* [1951] 2 All ER 834, the defendant, who invited a nine-year-old girl to touch his exposed penis, was found not guilty of the offence of indecent assault. The court held that an invitation cannot amount to an assault. The objective 'indecency' of the exposure was considered in *Rolfe* (1952) 36 Cr App R 4, where the defendant moved towards the victim with his exposed penis, inviting her to have sex with him. The court reiterated that assault means assault. In this situation there was no infliction of unlawful personal violence sufficient to qualify as battery. In *Johnson* [1968] SASR 132, a child welfare officer caned two boys on their bare buttocks. While doing this he exposed his penis and masturbated. Neither boy was aware of what he was doing while caning them. The court held that there was no indecent assault here because of the victims' absence of knowledge.

CONTEXT OF THE PROBLEM

In the scenario that follows, the violent, threatening, and intimidatory nature of sexual assault is illustrated. Further, the diversity of conduct that can constitute sexual assault is on show.

The power relations existing between the perpetrator and the victim make submission and consent problematic. Also, conditional consent is explored. Where 'no' means 'no' is at issue.

The vulnerability of both victims here, and the difficulties associated with reporting, make law enforcement as the principal option contestable.

What do you see as additional solutions beyond the law when considering victim protection?

PROBLEM

Apply the law on sexual assault to the following facts (assuming that these facts occur in addition to the facts outlined in Topic 11):

1   Helen agreed to have sex with Neville one night. She believed that they were going to have vaginal sexual intercourse. Instead he violently and aggressively forced his penis into her anus. She asked him to stop but he continued. Afterwards he explained that he heard her asking him to stop but he didn't believe she meant it because on other occasions of intercourse she would shout 'no' at a peak of ecstasy. Neville left the bedroom, coming across their young son who had come to the door on hearing his mother's screams. Neville yelled, 'What are you listening to, you little pervert?' and blackened the child's eye with a punch.

2   Helen refused to have sex with Neville one night, so he lay on top of her and masturbated. He later said that he didn't care whether she refused or not because she was his wife and he had legitimate sexual needs.

3   Neville and Helen were in bed one night when he began to fondle her sexually. She said, 'Look, I'm not in the mood for sex, OK? Just don't touch me.' He continued to fondle her and said in an aggressive voice, 'I know you want it. I saw the way you were flirting with the guy in the pub earlier tonight.' Helen became frightened that he would go into a jealous rage so she no longer continued to resist intercourse. All she said was, 'Get it over quickly if you must, and wear a condom.' She lay back passively during the intercourse.

4   Helen had a 15-year-old niece who came to live with the couple. She made some pocket money cleaning the house for Helen. One afternoon she was alone with Neville. He said to her, jokingly, 'How about a quick fuck, Sue?' The girl said nothing in response, but looked shocked and embarrassed. He then said, also in a jovial manner, 'I can tell Helen that we have been doing it anyway. Of course if you were nice to me I might be persuaded to keep quiet.' In fact Neville had no intention of telling Helen that he was having sex with Sue. Sue felt scared and overwhelmed. She didn't want to fall out of favour with her aunt and have to go back to live with her family. Seeing her hesitation, Neville continued, 'You know I am your boss and I could sack you if you don't follow my orders!' At this point Sue let Neville have sex with her. He believed that she was 17. He also believed that he had been flirting with her and was flattered that she was attracted to him in response. A week later he asked her to have sex with him again. He made the same threat and she replied, 'Fuck off, you animal!'

   Neither Sue nor Helen told anyone about these incidents until either months or years later.

ENGAGING THE PROBLEM

As has been suggested earlier in this topic, consent and its withdrawal are crucial in the construction of prosecution and defence responses. What the victims have said and done and the situations in which they find themselves should not make it more difficult to claim that consent was absent. In light of the relationship between the accused and the victims and the history of these relationships, how much can we say that he knew regarding the absence of consent in each situation without compromising the essentially subjective nature of the required *mens rea*? What honest and mistaken belief, if any, can be claimed?

When considering the liability of the accused, it is essential to examine the specific offences and the constituent elements with which he would be charged. How do these elements differ and what specific conditions of proof apply? Remember the exercise of discretion here.

ADDITIONAL RESOURCES

Bargen, J. and Fishwick, E., *Sexual Assault Law Reform: A National Perspective,* Office of the Status of Women, Sydney, 1995.

Bronitt, S. and McSherry, B., *Principles of Criminal Law,* Law Book Company, Sydney, 2001, pp. 591–9, 618–32.

Brown, D., Farrier, D., and Weisbrot, D., *Criminal Laws,* Federation Press, Sydney, 1996, paras 4.6 (for the extract of *DPP v. Morgan* [1976] AC 182), 7.5.1–7.5.2, 7.5.3–7.5.4, 7.5.5, 7.5.6–7.5.7, 7.6.1, 7.6.2, 7.7.4–7.8.1, 7.8.2–7.8.6.

Edwards, A., and Heenan, M., 'Rape Trials in Victoria: Gender, Socio-Cultural Factors and Justice' (1994) 27(3) *The Australian and New Zealand Journal of Criminology* 213.

Fisse, B., *Howard's Criminal Law,* Law Book Company, Sydney, 1992, pp. 168–95.

Latham, M., 'An Unreliable Witness? Legal Views of the Sexual Assault Complainant', in Breckenridge, J. and Carmody, M. (eds), *Crimes of Violence: Australian Responses to Rape and Sexual Assault,* Allen & Unwin, Sydney, 1992.

Naffine, N., 'Windows on the Legal Mind: The Evocation of Rape in Legal Writings' (1992) 18 *Melbourne University Law Review* 741.

Naffine, N., 'Possession: Erotic Love in the Law of Rape' (1994) 57 *The Modern Law Review* 10.

Sharpe, A., 'The Precarious Position of the Transsexual Rape Victim' (1994) 6(2) *Current Issues in Criminal Justice* 303.

Sinclair, K., 'Responding to Abuse: A Matter of Perspective' (1995) 7(2) *Current Issues in Criminal Justice* 153.

Wells, C., 'Swatting the Subjectivist Bug' (1982) *Criminal Law Review* 209.

R v. J (1994) 75 A Crim R 522

M (1994) 126 ALR 325

R v. Linekar [1995] 2 WLR 237

Papadimitropoulos v. R (1957) 98 CLR 249

Williams [1923] 1 KB 340

Gallienne (1963) 81 WN (Pt 1) (NSW) 94
DPP v. Morgan [1976] AC 182
McEwan [1979] 2 NSWLR 926
Hemsley (1988) 36 A Crim R 334
Kitchener (1993) 29 NSWLR 696
Rolfe (1952) 36 Cr App R 4
· *Johnson* [1968] SASR 132
Speck [1977] 2 All ER 859

TOPIC 13

HOMICIDE I

This topic will examine the historical development of the law on homicide and its influence on the expansion of justification and excuse within the criminal law. Problems with concepts such as foresight and foreseeability will be addressed. The notion of degrees of homicide will also be considered. How do empirical data challenge popular understanding and media presentation of homicide? The law relating to causation and its inextricable connection to situations of homicide is reviewed.

Patterns of homicide

An interesting feature of homicide is that while it is an atypical criminal offence, it is the stereotypical crime in light of popular representations of criminality. There is both a public and policing fascination with this offence. In representations there is an overconcentration on the individual murderer and on naïve concerns about causation.

Generally, there is a lack of understanding of the social reality of homicide.[150] Achieving this understanding will involve a tearing away of the popular face of homicide as a stranger–danger crime and its repositioning as a consequence of assault and violence, too often in a domestic setting. In this there is recognition of the close relationship between the victim and the offender; in over 60 per cent of all homicides in Australia the victim is known to and associated with the killer.

Homicide is a crime which is socially, culturally, and historically determined. Interestingly, in Australia the homicide rate has remained largely constant since the turn of the nineteenth century, but the nature of homicides has changed, as has the structure and composition of the Australian community.

---

150 For a unique examination of the issue see A. Wallace, *Homicide: the Social Reality* Bureau of Crime Statistics and Research, Sydney, 1986.

Homicide is largely a personal rather than an instrumental crime and it is not ideological in nature. It forms a crime consequential to complex social relationships of marginalisation. Homicide patterns reflect cultural norms.

Homicide is a spontaneous rather than a premeditated crime. Having said this, homicide offenders exhibit a wide range of moral culpability. This is a feature of the social setting of the crime.

In the Wallace study of homicides since the early 1900s, 76 per cent of all spouse killers were male, and of those 46 per cent were were separated from their partners. Around 20 per cent of all family homicides involved victims under the age of 10 and 13 per cent of all offenders committed suicide afterwards.

Tellingly, in terms of the fear of the crime, there are five times as many chances of being killed in a motor vehicle accident as there are of being a victim of homicide.

The legal framework for homicide

Homicide is the killing of one human being by another human being. It may be deemed either lawful or unlawful. Homicide is excusable if it occurs within certain legal justifications, or arises out of misadventure.

Therefore, legitimate state executions, death caused in the apprehension of a fleeing felon, or death through provocation or self-defence may not be punished by the law as homicide. Misadventure usually occurs either through an accident or as a consequence of the commission of a lawful act, unaccompanied by the necessary mental state required for murder or manslaughter.

For a homicide to be substantiated there must be a killing of a 'life in being'. The concept of a life in being is contentious, raising the following questions:

* When is a child alive so it can be a victim of homicide?
* When does a human being cease to be a life in being?

Despite the fact that there may be 'degrees of death' for clinical purposes, these may not correspond to the points of time at law when death occurs.

Homicide is, generally in Australia, divided into murder and manslaughter. What distinguishes these states is the mental state of the offender.

Murder

In its common law form, murder is the unlawful killing of a human being by a person of sound mind, with 'malice aforethought'. This particular mental state incorporates intention and some degree of subjective recklessness.[151]

---

151 Malice is defined in the *Crimes Act* (NSW), s. 5 and indicates the extent to which the concept is a complex combination of intention, recklessness, indifference and wantonness.

The essential ingredients of the offence of murder are:

1   a voluntary act that was intentional and unprovoked; and
2   malice, express or implied, was present at its commission.

Because it is the presence of 'malice aforethought' in the common law jurisdictions, and versions of basic intent in the Code jurisdictions, which separates murder from manslaughter, the determination of the limits of the *mens rea* for murder is fundamental to an understanding of this offence. This is particularly so where manslaughter is defined as every punishable homicide beyond murder. Manslaughter is not so much concerned with the mind of the accused but rather with what the jury would impute to the mind of the reasonable person in similar circumstances to the accused. Some individuals accused of manslaughter may be aware of the consequences of their actions but not to such an extent as to satisfy reckless indifference (i.e. foreseeing the possibility rather than the probability of death).

Malice aforethought in New South Wales, for instance,[152] is deemed to be established by evidence of *one or more* of the following circumstances:

1   an intention to cause death or grievous bodily harm to someone, coinciding with an act or omission causing death;
2   knowledge that the act or omission causing death *will probably* cause the death of or grievous bodily harm to some person, although such a knowledge is accompanied by indifference as to whether death or grievous harm is caused or not, or by a wish that it may not be caused.

Both arms of the test for malice are directed against the accused's *actual state of mind* at the time of the act or omission causing death. If reckless indifference is to be used as the *mens rea* for the offence of murder, then it must be proved through a subjective assessment and not by reliance on the assessment of the reasonable person.

Malice itself was examined by Byrne J. in **Cunningham's** case (*supra*):

> ... in any statutory definition of a crime 'malice' must be taken not in the old vague sense of 'wickedness' in general, but as requiring either (i) an actual intention to do the particular *kind* of harm that in fact was done, or (ii) recklessness as to whether such harm should occur or not (i.e. the accused has foreseen that the particular kind of harm might be done, and yet has gone on to take the risk). It is neither limited to, nor does it indeed require, any ill-will towards the person injured ... With the utmost respect to the learned judge, we think it is incorrect to say that the word 'malicious' in a statutory offence merely means wicked. We think the learned judge was, in effect, telling the jury

---

152 *Crimes Act* (NSW) s. 18.

that if they were satisfied that the appellant acted wickedly and he had clearly acted wickedly in stealing the gas meter and its contents they ought to find that he had acted maliciously in causing the gas to be taken in by Mrs Wade so as thereby to endanger her life. In our view, it should have been left to the jury to decide whether, even if the appellant did not intend the injury to Mrs Wade, he foresaw that the removal of the gas meter might cause injury to someone but nevertheless removed it. We are unable to say that a reasonable jury, properly directed as to the meaning of the word 'maliciously' in the context of s. 23,[153] would, without doubt, have convicted.

Intention and reckless indifference

Despite the criticisms regarding the continued use of 'malice',[154] it prevails as the *mens rea* for murder in the common law jurisdictions. The debate regarding the limits of malice centres on a consideration of the nature of reckless indifference to human life. In **Coleman** (*supra*), for instance, the court was confronted with the issue of whether it would be sufficient that a realisation of the possibility of risk was established, for the conviction of murder to stand. Following the decision in **Crabbe** (*supra*), a realisation of probability was deemed necessary. It was the view of the court that consideration of malice with respect to murder was 'altogether different' from the interpretation of malice in lesser statutory crimes. Even so, much is still left uncertain about the interpretation of malice for murder. What is the scope of reckless indifference? Where does malice inform constructive murder?[155]

In *Crabbe* (*supra*), a road train driver who was intoxicated was banned by the publican and left the hotel. A short time later he returned to the hotel, driving his prime mover into the bar and killing five customers. In the trial there was a direction that foresight of the possibility of death would satisfy reckless indifference. On appeal the High Court held that if wilful blindness did come within the *mens rea* for murder, then the correct direction should refer to foresight of the *probability* of death or serious injury. It was not enough to know that the prohibited consequence was possible but not likely. The mental state would also be sufficient if accompanied by an indifference that the consequence should occur or even the hope that it would not.

In **Royall** (*supra*) it was held that *Crabbe* should apply to the New South Wales murder provisions, with the qualification that the prosecution must prove that the accused foresaw the probability of death. This requires care in New South Wales in directing juries on the intent to cause grievous bodily harm resulting in death rather than reckless indifference. This is particularly

---

153 See *Offences Against the Person Act 1861* (England).
154 See *Coleman* (1990) 19 NSWLR 467.
155 Constructive murder is found in situations where death occurs in the pursuit of a serious offence.

so when the definition of intent, it might be argued, encompasses reckless indifference. The court further held that provided one of the mental states which satisfy murder, and causation, are proved, then it doesn't matter whether the accused intended the death in another way (not death by striking the victim with the ashtray but from falling out of the window while running away). In **Demiririan** (*supra*), where the charges related to a conspiracy to bomb the Turkish Consulate and one of the co-conspirators died, it was held that the accused's recklessness must relate to the act causing death and not merely to the outcome of a series of acts.

The *mens rea* for murder, where reckless indifference is a component of the offence, requires some degree of actual awareness of death as a consequence of one's actions. In **Solomon** [1980] 1 NSWLR 321, it was held that the effect of the section of the *Crimes Act* creating murder (s. 18) gives recklessness a more limited operation in respect of murder, in that foresight of the probability of 'causing death or grievous bodily harm' was not an acceptable direction.

Issues of causation

The requirement that the accused caused the death of the victim identifies causation as an essential problem for homicide. In **McAuliffe** (*supra*), the court regarded the facts as a 'paradigm case of conduct which is regarded as causing death'. The accused bashed a victim near a cliff leaving him seriously wounded and dazed. As a result he fell over the cliff to his death. Commenting on the deliberations in **Royall** (*supra*) concerning when questions of foreseeability should be raised, the court said that there was no question of overreaction on the part of the victim which might bring about the need to enquire into what the reasonable person in these circumstances would have foreseen.

As for the question of the time of death raised in **Malcherek's** case (*supra*), and whether the intervening act had replaced that of the accused as the substantial and operating cause, s. 33 of the *Human Tissue Act 1983* (NSW) provides that a person has died when there has occurred (a) an irreversible cessation of all functions of the person's brain, or (b) an irreversible cessation of the circulation of the blood in the person's body.

Constructive murder

In **Ryan** (*supra*) the facts concerned the shooting of a petrol station attendant after he surprised the accused during the course of a robbery. The question on appeal was whether the act of discharging the gun was voluntary. Voluntariness had to be proved, as well as whether or not the death occurred during the commission of a serious crime. In this respect it could be considered as a situation of constructive murder. Even with constructive murder it is not sufficient to say that no *mens rea* on the part of the accused was necessary. At least the intention to commit the robbery was required. This is what is transferred during the mechanism of constructive murder. Here there was no requirement for the prosecution to prove either a subjective or an objective appreciation of risk of injury or death. It was necessary to show that the victim was killed either during or immediately after the commission of the serious offence.

CONTEXT OF THE PROBLEM

What follows identifies the crucial place of foresight and forseeability for the proof of homicide.

With causation we need to consider whether the act of the victim was reasonably foreseeable as a consequence of the accused's behaviour.

For the proof of *mens rea*, it must be shown that:

- if the accused is charged with murder, he himself foresaw the probability of the death of the victim as a consequence of his conduct (or omission);
- if the accused is charged with manslaughter, the reasonable person would have forseeen the probability of the death of the victim as a consequence of such conduct or omission.

PROBLEM

Discuss Jim's liability for the death of Molly, the six-month-old foetus and Sam on the following facts.

Jim and Molly have been married for a number of years. Jim has lost his job and stress has manifested itself in family violence. One day Jim lost his temper, knocked Molly against the wall and threw a chair at her. He jerked her to her feet and slammed her into a partition. She became unconscious. She then woke to find him pouring water over her. He continued to punch her face, pouring water over her to revive her when she lost consciousness. Finally she slumped to the floor and he stomped on her head. He heard something snap in her neck. The next day he took her to the hospital and said she had sustained her injuries in a car accident. She had black eyes, concussion, fractured ribs, and contusions.

Imagine the following alternative scenarios:

1   A week later Molly is almost physically healed when Jim comes to collect her. As soon as she sees Jim coming towards the doorway with a big bunch of red roses she panics and runs from the hospital. Thinking that Jim has a weapon concealed in the flowers, which he intends to use on her and finish the job, she leaves the hospital grounds, rushes without looking across a busy road, and is struck by a car and killed.
2   Molly is so severely injured that she is put on a life support system. She has every chance of complete recovery in time, provided that the correct

medical treatment is given to her. Some days later, by accident, her chart and name tag are switched by the night nurse. As a result the machine is turned off the following morning by a staff member who mistakes her for another patient. The ward is short-staffed and nobody notices her rapid decline. Molly is dead by midday. During the post-mortem it is discovered that she was six months pregnant.

3   As a consequence of her treatment in hospital, Molly almost completely recovers. However, she remains subject to blurred vision and dizzy spells. During one of these spells she crashes her car and is killed. During the post-mortem it is discovered that her sight could have easily been rectified with some prescription lenses. The doctor who does the post-mortem says that the defect in vision is due to some congenital deterioration in her vision, which the experience of concussion may have exacerbated. In any case, she says that, in her opinion, the doctors at the hospital were grossly negligent in not referring Molly to an eye specialist during her stay in hospital.

4   While Jim is attacking Molly he accidentally cuts their eight-month-old son, Sam, with the knife he is waving around. The child's cut becomes infected and, while Jim does everything possible to get the child the best medical assistance, Sam dies.

5   While Molly is in hospital it is discovered that she has galloping leukaemia. Within two weeks she is dead.

6   While Molly is in hospital Jim robs a petrol station, carrying a sawn-off shotgun. He flees the scene of the crime. Molly is later told of the event and dies as a result of severe nervous shock.

ENGAGING THE PROBLEM

The preceding scenarios build on a variety of challenges to causation, involving intervening acts and the behaviour of the victims as it relates to the accused. Questions of what constitutes life, and the direction of the accused's mental state, must be addressed.

Consider the appropriate offences of homicide to be preferred. Also examine the crucial coincidence between the killing and the necessary mental state.

Concepts of constructive murder and transferred malice will also need to be recognised.

ADDITIONAL RESOURCES

Brown, D., Farrier, D., Egger, S., and McNamara, L., *Criminal Laws,* Federation Press, Sydney, 2001, paras 5.1–5.2, 5.3, 5.4–5.4.5, 5.4.6, 5.10.1, 5.11–5.12.1, 5.12.1–5.12.3.

Fisse, B., *Howard's Criminal Law,* Law Book Company, Sydney, 1992, pp. 27–43.

Norrie, A., *Crime, Reason and History,* Weidenfeld & Nicolson, London, 1993, Chapters 3 and 4.

Rush, P. and Yeo, S., *Criminal Law Sourcebook*, Butterworths, Sydney, 2000, Chapters 6 and 7.

McAuliffe (1995) 183 CLR 108

R v. Coleman (1990) 19 NSWLR 467

R v. Nedrick [1986] 1 WLR 1025

Demirian (1988) 33 ACrR 441

Rhodes (1984) 14 ACrR 124

R v. Solomon (1980) 1 NSWLR 321

Royall v. R (1991) 65 ALJR 451

R v. Malcherek [1981] 1 WLR 690

R v. Smith [1959] 2 QB 35

Hallet [1969] SASR 141

Blaue [1975] 3 All ER 446

Evans v. Gardner (No 2) [1976] VR 525

R v. Cheshire [1991] 3 All ER 670

Pagett (1983) 76 Cr App R 279

Mraz v. R (1955) 93 CLR 493

Crabbe (1985) 58 ALR 417

Munro (1981) 4 A Crim R 67

Hitchins (1983) 9 A Crim R 238

TOPIC 14

HOMICIDE II

This topic considers the law on homicide outside murder. In particular it will address unlawful act manslaughter, manslaughter by omission, and what somewhat misleadingly is called involuntary manslaughter.

Homicide outside murder

Involuntary (unintentional) manslaughter

Unintentional manslaughter is the most common form of manslaughter and covers any death which occurs as a result of:

- an unlawful act or omission by the accused even though the consequence is not desired;
- objective recklessness or gross negligence in doing the act, and in this regard, not acknowledging a duty of care in the case of an omission.

If the unlawful act is done with the attacker's knowledge that the act would 'probably cause death or do grievous bodily harm', then this would be murder in the common law jurisdictions of Australia. If there exists a reasonable doubt about whether the defendant knew the probability of the consequences, then the conviction would be for manslaughter.

For manslaughter to stand, the unlawful act must be such as all sober and reasonable people would inevitably recognise could subject the victim to at least the risk of some harm resulting therefrom, albeit not serious harm. This was the principle expounded in **Church's** case (*supra*).

Unlawful and dangerous act

In this type of manslaughter, the finding that the appellant knew that his unlawful act would subject the deceased to at least the risk of some harm is supported by the evidence, and the required *mens rea* can be inferred.

Some of the difficulties associated with establishing liability in the residual homicide offences which come under the heading of involuntary manslaughter were identified in Lord Aitkin's judgment in **Andrews v. DPP** [1937] 2 All ER 552.

> Of all crimes, manslaughter appears to afford most difficulties of definition, for it concerns homicide in so many different and varying conditions … the law recognised murder on the one hand based mainly, though not exclusively on the intention to kill, and manslaughter on the other hand, based mainly though not exclusively on the absence of the intent to kill, but with the presence of an element of unlawfulness which is the elusive factor.

The facts of this case related to 'unlawful and dangerous act' manslaughter, which has sometimes been referred to as constructive manslaughter. Andrews was a hit and run driver. Another important issue in the case was the discussion of the dimensions of 'criminal negligence'. The court held that 'for the purposes of the criminal law there are degrees of negligence and a very high degree of negligence is required to be proved in order to establish the felony of manslaughter'. Probably 'recklessness' most nearly covers the case in its objective form. This *mens rea* may not be the same as that required for the offence of dangerous driving. It is not enough to rely on the unlawful act alone when establishing the elements of the offence of manslaughter.

The problematic issues when establishing liability for manslaughter are as follows:

- *Actus reus*: what is meant by 'unlawful'?
- Is it necessary that it is dangerous?
- Should there be different criteria applied to acts and omissions?
- Should constructive manslaughter rest on risk of serious injury resulting from the unlawful act?
- *Mens rea*: is it recklessness or gross negligence and what does each mean?
- How objective is the objective test?
- Is inadvertence enough?
- Should duty always be considered?

'Unlawful or dangerous act' manslaughter, or constructive manslaughter, is committed when a person is killed in the course of, or as a consequence of, another unlawful act on the part of the defendant, and only when the defendant is at least negligent as to causing bodily injury.

In fact, this class of manslaughter is little more than a mechanism for inferring certain levels of forseeability for the purpose of determining the very uncertain *mens rea* for manslaughter.

In ***Wilson v. R*** (1992) 174 CLR 313 the accused hit the victim in the face, causing him to fall to the ground and hit his head. The accused's associate then went through the victim's pockets and smashed his head on the concrete. The victim died as a result of brain damage. The most likely cause of death was the fall. Both accused were charged with felony murder. Wilson was convicted of manslaughter and the co-accused was acquitted of homicide charges. On appeal the question was whether the authorities support the view that the intentional infliction of harm through an unlawful act is sufficient for manslaughter. The court was of the view that the measurement of whether an act is dangerous is objective and equates with serious injury as a consequence. The decision endorsed the unlawful and dangerous act determinant of manslaughter and accepts these two heads, along with criminal negligence, as proofs of the offence. An appreciation by the ordinary and reasonable person of the risk of serious injury is required in order to establish 'unlawful or dangerous' act manslaughter. Also, it is necessary that the jury be directed to consider whether the reasonable person would appreciate the act as dangerous (i.e. risking the consequence of serious injury).

The English authority of ***R v. Rungzabe Khan & Tahue Khan*** [1998] Crim LR 830 discussed the issue of unlawful and dangerous act against the context of a pre-existing duty on the part of the accused. The violation or ignorance of the duty was seen by the court as a species of gross negligence.

Meaning of unlawful

In the cases of ***R v. Lamb*** [1967] 2 All ER 1282, and ***R v. Church*** [1965] 2 All ER 72, the appeal courts critically analysed the notion of unlawful acts. For an act to be unlawful it must at least constitute a technical assault. In *Lamb*, the accused and the victim were involved in a game of Russian roulette. The defence raised was one of accident because the chamber of the gun (prior to rotation) was empty. The court held that *mens rea* is now an essential ingredient in manslaughter. The phrase 'unlawful' is in the 'criminal sense of the word' and not unlawful merely in terms of civil liberties.

> When the gravamen of the charge is criminal negligence (often referred to as recklessness) the jury has to consider the accused's state of mind, and whether what he thought he was doing was safe.

If the view of safety is formed in a criminally negligent way then the charge of manslaughter will succeed. Strong though the evidence of criminal negligence was here, the defendant was entitled to have the defence of accident considered by the jury because of what he allegedly foresaw.

In *Church* it was also agreed that for manslaughter a degree of *mens rea* is now required. To define this *mens rea* is a difficult task. It is the element of unlawfulness which is elusive. 'The unlawful act must be such as all sober and reasonable people would recognise must subject the other person to, at least, the risk of some harm resulting, albeit not serious.'

The significance of the unlawful act or omission is obviously increased as the judicial interpretation of the *mens rea* for manslaughter moves in a more objective direction. The unlawfulness relates, then, to the nature of the risk and the forseeability of its consequences.

In **DPP v. Newbury & Jones** [1976] 2 All ER 365, the accused pushed a piece of paving stone off a parapet just as a train was passing beneath. The stone went through the window of the cabin, killing the guard as a result. The accused appealed, unsuccessfully, against their convictions for manslaughter. The point of general importance, which was certified to the House of Lords, asked: 'Can a defendant be properly convicted of manslaughter when his mind is not affected by drink and drugs, if he did not foresee that his act might cause harm to another?'

Salmon LJ said that the trial judge was correct in not directing the jury on the necessity of foresight. It is plain that the accused is guilty of manslaughter if it is proved that he intentionally did an act which was unlawful and dangerous and that act inadvertently caused death. It is unnecessary to prove that the accused actually knew that the act was unlawful or dangerous.

In these consequential situations manslaughter can range from situations which amount to little more than inadvertence, right up to acts not too far short of murder.

The test for foreseeability is objective; that is, not 'Did the accused foresee the risk?' but 'Would the sober and reasonable person recognise its danger?' Persons can be convicted of 'constructive manslaughter' if it is proved that they intentionally acted in an unlawful and dangerous manner, so as to kill someone.

The test as to

- what risk
- risk of what
- risk to whom

is objective and not based on the accused's knowledge.

The problem with the *Newbury* decision is that the word 'intentionally' is unclear. Since the defendant's knowledge need not extend to the qualities of danger and unlawfulness, and so neither does his intention, the conclusion may be drawn that the court requires for the mental element an intentional act. Proof of the unlawful act *per se* may require the proof of some integral mental element.

In *R v. Goodfellow* (1986) 83 Cr App R 23, Lane CJ said that the *Archbold* direction on manslaughter confuses manslaughter caused by an illegal act of violence, and manslaughter caused by the taking of a risk, the dangerous consequences of which the agent was unaware but which would have been obvious to the reasonable, sober person. The instant case was capable of falling into either or both types of manslaughter. His Lordship rejected the submission that the present was not a case of 'unlawful act' manslaughter because the act was not directed against the victim. The questions for the jury were:

1 Was the act intentional?
2 Was it unlawful?
3 Was it an act that any reasonable person would realise was bound to subject some other human being to the risk of physical harm?
4 Was the act the cause of death?

Acts and omissions: Importance of duty of care

In *R v. Lowe* [1973] 1 All ER 805, the accused and a Miss Marshall had been living together and had four children, only one of which had been taken into care. The woman's intelligence was subnormal and Lowe's was below average. The child who was the subject of the indictment was ill for the two months of its life and until 10 days before its death. A few days before it died, Lowe stated that he advised the mother to take the child to the doctor. She stated falsely that she had done so. The child later was found dead from dehydration and gross emaciation. The mother stated that she had been unwilling to disclose its state of health for fear that it should be removed from her and taken into care. Lowe was convicted of manslaughter and of cruelty to the child through wilful neglect.

Philmore LJ concluded that the trial judge had, in an unclear fashion, left it to the jury to say whether they thought that the appellant's conduct towards the child had been reckless and whether its death had been caused thereby. However, he separately stated that if the accused was found guilty on the count of wilful neglect he should also be found guilty of manslaughter. The jury found wilful neglect rather than recklessness.

The question on appeal was whether, following the rejection of recklessness, there can be sufficient *mens rea* for manslaughter with mere neglect, albeit wilful, that would amount to manslaughter.

> The court feels that there is something inherently unattractive in the theory of constructive manslaughter. It seems strange that an omission which is wilful solely in the sense that it is not inadvertent, the consequences of which are not in fact

foreseen by the person who is neglected should, if death results, automatically give rise to an indeterminate sentence instead of the maximum of two years which would otherwise be imposed for the statutory offence.

In this case the court sought to establish a clear distinction between an act of omission, and an act of commission likely to cause harm. Flowing from this was the view that manslaughter should not be the inevitable offence arising from death by omission, even if the omission was deliberate.

An interesting case dealing with the extent to which a duty is required for manslaughter when that duty is accepted but partially performed is *R v. Taktak* (1988) A Crim R 334. The facts were that a heroin addict provided assistance to a prostitute who had overdosed and was left to die by her client. There was some dispute about the evidence regarding the time that the assistance commenced, relative to when medical care was sought. The question before the court was whether the circumstances and the efforts of the accused placed him under a legally recognised duty of care. The court observed that due to the complexity of modern life, such legally recognised duties could not be limited to specific categories or relationships. The issue of whether the appellant voluntarily assumed care of the deceased 'and so secluded the helpless person as to prevent others from rendering aid' became crucial to the determination of his ongoing duty up until the time of the victim's death. In the opinion of the court, the voluntary assumption of care of a helpless human being was crucial to the attribution of manslaughter. It was also necessary to show that the accused was criminally negligent and not merely negligent in his treatment of the deceased. The proofs of liability were advanced as: (a) that there was a duty of care assumed; (b) that the omission of the accused caused the death; and (c) that the neglect of the duty was a violation of the objective test of reasonableness so as to be criminal, and involved a high risk of death.

In the case of *Stone v. Dobinson* [1977] 2 All ER 341, Stone was of an advanced age, below average intelligence, partially deaf, almost totally blind and with no appreciable sense of smell. He lived with Dobinson, who was somewhat intellectually deficient and who had acted as his housekeeper and mistress for some years. They were joined by Stone's younger sister, who suffered from agoraphobia and anorexia nervosa. Over a period of time the sister physically deteriorated and despite certain ineffectual efforts by Stone and Dobinson regarding her welfare, she died from toxaemia and dehydration. Had she been admitted to hospital some weeks before her death she would have been saved. The prosecution alleged that under the circumstances the appellants had undertaken a duty to care for the deceased, who was incapable of looking after herself. They had with gross negligence failed in that duty; such failure was the cause of death and therefore they were guilty of manslaughter. The jury was directed that in order to find the appellants guilty they must find gross neglect amounting to a reckless disregard for the health and well-being of the deceased. It was contended on behalf of the appellants that recklessness in this context meant foresight of the likelihood or possibility of death and serious injury, and a determination nevertheless to persist in not providing care. It was held, in dismissing the appeal, that there had been a duty of care undertaken by the accused, to care for the health and welfare of the infirm victim. What the prosecution must prove is a breach of that duty in such circumstances so that the jury is convinced that the appellants' conduct can properly be described as reckless (that is, having a reckless disregard for the danger to the health and welfare of the victim). Mere misadventure is not enough. The appellants must be proved to have been indifferent to an obvious injury to health, or to have actually foreseen the risk but nevertheless determined to run it. These (indifference and appreciation) are both forms of recklessness and might be considered to be forerunners to the three-tiered test of Lord Diplock in *Caldwell* (*supra*). The court rejected the claim that the defendants' foresight of the consequences had to be proved for manslaughter to stand, and said that a reckless disregard for health and welfare was sufficient.

Although it might be argued that *Stone and Dobinson* is not in conflict with *Lowe* on the point that mere neglect could constitute manslaughter, the test in *Caldwell* invites the jury to consider that an accused is reckless when he does an act which creates an obvious risk, and he has not given any thought to there being the possibility of any such risk. By this are the courts considering mere neglect (*Lowe*), mere inadvertence (*Stone and Dobinson*), or indifference?

In the case of **Kong Cheuk-kwan** [1986] HKLR 648 the Privy Council discussed the determination of inadvertence for manslaughter:

There is however much to be said for the view, most recently and authoritatively expressed by the Lord Chief Justice in *Cato* (1976) 62 Cr App R 41 at p. 48 and again by Lord Hailsham in *Lawrence* [1981] 1 All ER 974, at p. 978 to the general effect that 'reckless' is not a lawyer's word but is a simple and well-understood word of ancient lineage which has been a popular usage for a very long time and that it can thus be safely left to a jury to decide whether the act or omission complained of conforms with their idea of what is reckless. We have no doubt that a father who, over a long period of time, has first-hand experience of the fact that his wife habitually and violently assaults their child of tender years using both hands and feet in doing so, is showing a reckless disregard for that child's health and welfare by neglecting to take any reasonable step to protect her. He had, by condoning it, joined in a course of conduct which not only did not ensure the child's welfare, but put it at positive risk of severe damage. He could not, upon trial, conceivably have escaped responsibility by pleading that he did not appreciate that her health and welfare were greatly at risk. For these reasons the application for appeal must be refused.

For manslaughter, it is necessary to establish that the 'harm' that is risked must, as the Privy Council agreed in *Kong's* case, be likely to cause physical damage. This seems to have forgotten the requirement stated in **Seymour's** case (1983) 76 Cr App R 18 that there must be a high degree of risk of causing death. In *Seymour* the facts concerned a lorry hitting the wife's car after a domestic argument between the wife and the husband, who was the driver of the lorry. The wheel of the car came off, causing fatal accidents with other cars. The court agreed that the *Lawrence* direction could be given in cases of manslaughter. The only modification necessary in such cases is that the jury must be warned that the risk of death being caused by the accused's driving is very high.

Dawson's case (1985) 81 Cr App R 150 was a case involving someone being frightened to death. It was held that the proper direction in relation to the harm that a reasonable person would expect to result from the unlawful act would have been that the requisite harm was caused if the unlawful act so shocked the victim as to cause him physical injury. Either emotional harm *or* physical injury would be enough.

Criminal negligence

In **R v. Buttsworth** [1983] 1 NSWLR 658, the accused was convicted of culpable driving, which involved driving in a risky manner, at high speed, with poor brakes. The semi-trailer he was driving jackknifed into oncoming traffic, killing two people. The court conceded in this case that the criminal law is designed to ensure that drivers fulfil their duty of care to other road users. There must be degrees of neglect in relation to a violation of any such duty and penalties for the resultant offences should be graded accordingly. The question was whether there should be a distinction between negligent and dangerous driving. 'The differences in the various expressions for negligence used in this field of criminal law lie fundamentally in the degree of risk to the safety of others which they are designed to define.'[156]

Manslaughter appears to be the only common law crime that can arise out of negligence. Negligence does not appear even to satisfy general statutory offences. The majority of negligence-based statutory offences arise in the traffic area.

Negligence in this situation should not be considered in terms of objective or subjective tests, actual or potential risks. Rather, the tests are

---

156   O'Brien CJ at 662.

expressed conventionally as degrees of departure from the standards expected of the reasonable person. Was there a duty and should failure to fulfil it be classified as gross negligence?

CONTEXT OF THE PROBLEM

Many of the manslaughter by omission cases relate to scenarios of neglect. Because with manslaughter we are not asking what the accused foresaw, community standards as evoked in the notion of the reasonable man (ordinary person) are the basis for measuring liability. It might be said, therefore, that it is not the criminal mental state of the accused which is being penalised but rather his failure to meet an acceptable standard of care. In this respect the concept and nature of duty need to be addressed; it is the failure to meet them which introduces the culpability.

In these tragic circumstances will the imposition of criminal liability and a sanction benefit the community or the accused? What is the purpose of punishment here and to what degree (and to what effect) can the community be held liable?

PROBLEM

David is a young single parent of rather low intelligence. His new baby has been sickly from the time of its birth and fails to gain weight or improve in condition as the months progress.

The nurse at the baby health centre establishes that the child is not being fed properly and suggests a dietary program to David to remedy the problem. David doesn't understand the details of the diet but says nothing to the nurse at the time. Some weeks after this the nurse visits David at his small flat and finds that the child's condition has deteriorated further. The nurse warns David that if he doesn't follow the diet then the baby could die. David says that the child's mother has deserted them, he has no money and no support, and can't seem to manage. Even so he wants to keep the baby and 'do the best for her'.

A week later the child is admitted to hospital seriously malnourished. Its condition is diagnosed as critical. The paediatrician puts the child on an emergency glucose drip without testing that would have revealed that the child was a diabetic. It dies an hour after admission to hospital.

ENGAGING THE PROBLEM

Here we have an accused of limited understanding being measured against the ordinary parent, with special knowledge conveyed by the nurse. Further, we have an obvious duty of care partially and perhaps negligently discharged. But to what degree and who is entirely responsible, and for what? How do you approach the causation issue?

ADDITIONAL RESOURCES

Crimes Act 1900 (NSW), section 27

Brown, D., Farrier, D., Egger, S., and McNamara, L., *Criminal Laws*, Federation Press, Sydney, 2001, paras 5.4.2, 5.4.4, 5.7, 5.8, 5.10.

Fisse, B., *Howard's Criminal Law*, Law Book Company, Sydney, 1992, pp. 43–76.

Wilson v. R (1992) 174 CLR 313

Wills [1983] 2 VLR 201

Nydam v. R [1977] VR 430

Lamb [1967] 2 QB 981

DPP v. Newbury [1977] AC 500

R v. Stone and Dobinson [1977] QB 354

R v. Taktak (1988) 34 A Crim R 334

Mamote-Kulang v. R (1964) 111 CLR 62

Mitchell [1983] 1 QB 741

Parker v. R (1963) 111 CLR 610

R v. Buttsworth [1983] 1 NSWLR 658

TOPIC 15

HOMICIDE III

This topic will further develop the law on manslaughter, with particular emphasis on voluntary homicide and the partial excuses of provocation and diminished responsibility. The issues associated with establishing partial excuses, and the tests which have developed in the law, will be generally discussed in the context of contemporary expectations for victims of violence. The development of syndrome defences will be alluded to. In addition, we will discuss some ancillary homicides such as abortion.

Voluntary manslaughter: Partial justifications and excuse

It is now accepted that someone can intend to bring about the serious injury or death of the victim, but due to exculpatory matters such as provocation and diminished responsibility, what would otherwise be deemed murder is reduced to manslaughter.

Essential to the consideration of justifications and excuses which tend to mitigate or defend murder is the use of subjective and objective standards. Through the introduction of objective standards in tests for provocation, for instance, the reasoning seems to be to limit the accused's access to excuses where intention is produced by a loss of self-control on the part of the accused (rather than increasing the necessary proofs for the prosecution). In this context, several discrete issues need to be considered:

- the objective standard often operates as a threshold question;
- there are a variety of ways of formulating the objective standards and it should not be assumed that they are all the same;
- whether a subjective or objective standard is being used (and it is usually both), and what personal and cultural standards are entrenched (or indeed possible) when using each of these standards.

Provocation

Provocation is principally an answer to a charge of murder. The reason is that traditionally, in respect of other charges, it is possible to make allowances for provocation in sentence, but not so with the mandatory sentence for murder.

In New South Wales, Victoria, and the ACT, provocation can be argued in cases of non-fatal assault in which the explicit and essential intention is to murder. (If successfully argued here the outcome should be acquittal.) There is some argument that provocation should also be available to charges including attempted murder. In any case the nature of provocation in offence situations other than murder should be considered within the exercise of the discretion to prosecute or commit, and may be viewed in mitigation.

Provocation is an excuse and as such is different from justifications such as self-defence. It is based on a sudden loss of self-control under circumstances where the accused does not entertain a reasonable belief that his life or the lives of others are in danger.

The central questions influencing the development of this mitigating factor are:

1 to what extent was the accused actually provoked?
2 to what extent was such provocation reasonable?
3 to what extent was the level of retaliation resulting from the provocation reasonable and necessary in the circumstances?

The common law on provocation has not only changed considerably over the past 20 years but it differs substantially across jurisdictions. In England, the postwar view on the matter was put forward in cases such as **Duffy** [1949] 1 QB 63, **Mancini** [1942] AC 1 (the authority on reasonable retaliation), **Holmes** [1946] AC 588 (establishing that words may not amount to provocation), and **Bedder** [1954] 1 WLR 1119 (where a young, black, impotent man could be said to have reasonably been provoked relative to these personal characteristics). This represents the transition from the reasonable person to the ordinary person with some of the personal characteristics of the accused.

The process of provocation was laid down in *Duffy's* case, in that the common law rule was established as (a) provocation must be directed towards the accused and (b) it is necessary to show that the accused himself was actually provoked. Thus the formulation of *Duffy's* case limited provocation to acts done:

- by the dead person
- to the accused.

However, in *R v. Davies* (1975) 60 Cr App R 253, it was agreed that provocation might emanate from third parties and (as in *R v. Pearson* [1992] CLR 193) might even be directed towards a third party.

Regarding the dynamics of provocation, Lord Devlin in *Duffy's* case referred to a sudden and temporary loss of control rendering the accused so subject to passion as to make him, for the moment, not a master of his own mind. In determining whether the accused had lost control by being provoked, the jury should take into account all the relevant facts and circumstances, but particularly relevant was whether a sufficient cooling-off time had elapsed between the provocation and the fatal act.

In *R v. Thorton* [1992] CLR 193, the Court of Appeal approved Devlin's principle in *Duffy* that there must be a 'sudden and temporary loss of self control, rendering the accused so subject to passion as to make him or her for the moment not master of their mind'. Even if there was a history of provocative words between the accused and the victim, what is essential is the effect of the words on the mind of the accused at the time of the killing. In some situations an intervening interval of time and a premeditated act of killing may negative the requirement for the loss of self-control. The protracted course of provocative conduct might need consideration as representing the circumstances in which self-control was actually lost. It is the loss of self-control that must be deemed to be sudden.

In *DPP v. Camplin* [1978] 2 All ER 168, a 15-year-old boy killed the victim with a kitchen utensil. The defendant explained that the deceased had sexually assaulted him against his will and then laughed at him when he was overcome by shame. The defendant then lost his self-control and committed the fatal attack. The trial judge declined the invitation of the defence to instruct the jury about the effect of the provocation on a 15-year-old boy: he chose to refer to the 'reasonable man' and not the 'reasonable boy'.

The Court of Appeal, in distinguishing *Bedder's* case (*supra*), held this to be a misdirection on the grounds that youth and the immaturity which naturally comes with it are not deviations from the norm of reasonableness. Youth is not a personal idiosyncrasy and is certainly not an infirmity such as was the defendant's impotence in *Bedder*.

The House of Lords held that section 3 of the *Homicide Act* (England) overruled authorities of the *Bedder* type:

Where on a charge of murder there is evidence on which the jury can find the person charged was provoked (whether by things done or by things said or by both together) to lose his self-control, the question whether the provocation was enough to make a reasonable man do as he did shall be left to be determined by the jury; and in determining that question the jury shall take into account everything both done and said according to the effect which, in their opinion, it would have on a reasonable man.

The question for the jury in this case was:

whether under this section the provocation was such as to make the reasonable man do as the accused did. In so determining they must take into account everything both done and said according to the effect which ... it would have on the reasonable man.

This section did more than say that words would be enough for provocation, and that the issue should be determined by the jury. *The reasonable man must be endowed with the age, sex, and other personal characteristics of the accused*, whether these were abnormal or not. These characteristics may be considered in the opinion of the jury, both in assessing the gravity of the provocation and in assessing the degree of self-control expected of the accused: 'Would the reasonable man have reacted to the provocation in the way the accused did?'

Lord Simon stated:

the judge may tell the jury that a man may not be entitled to rely on his exceptional excitability (whether idiosyncratic, or by cultural, environmental or ethnic origin) or pugnacity, or ill temper, or his drunkenness.

The court in *Camplin's* case decided that it would be also wrong after the judge had so directed to go on and state a third condition, 'that the retaliation must be proportionate to the provocation'. This should only be considered when determining whether the reasonable man would have so reacted to the provocation. The phrase 'reasonable retaliation' is a misconstruction in that (as Lord Diplock asserted) 'the powers of rationalisation bear no obvious relationship to the powers of self-control'.

The difficulty facing those who wish to operate under a hybrid test for provocation is in determining what we mean by the 'characteristics' which may modify the reasonable person in such a way as to give him some resemblance to the accused. On this point, the English Court of Appeal in **Newell's** case (1980) 71 Cr App R 331 stated:

The characteristic must be something definite and of sufficient significance to make the offender a different person from the ordinary run of mankind, and have a sufficient degree of permanence to warrant its being regarded as something constituting part of the individual's character and personality.

In that case the accused had taken an overdose of drugs and had written a suicide note some days before in his grief about his girlfriend leaving him. It was argued on his behalf that these characteristics should all be taken into account when assessing whether a reasonable man would have been provoked to lose his self-control on hearing disparaging remarks made by the victim about the former girlfriend. The court held that 'the accused could not use his intoxication as a reason for his loss of self-control: he is expected to exercise the self-control of a sober and reasonable man'. Chronic alcoholism was not relevant to the provocation, but the other factors may have been relevant in other circumstances.

Reform in the law of provocation

Provocation has been an area of significant law reform and legislative change in Australian jurisdictions. In New South Wales, for instance, the law on provocation has gone through significant revision indicating the interpretive relationship between statute law and common law, as influenced by changes in public opinion.

The fixed penalty for murder, and the reality of provocation in domestic violence settings in particular, are evidence of this. In 1982 the *Crimes (Homicide) Amendment Act* addressed both these issues. The statutory position now accords with the English common law.

In New South Wales the law on provocation is governed by section 23 of the *Crimes Act*. The legislation, which confirms the limitation of provocation to charges of murder, lists the features of provocation as being:

- that the act or omission of the accused is due to a loss of self-control induced by the act of the deceased towards or affecting the accused (including insulting words and gestures);
- that the conduct of the deceased was such as to lead the ordinary person in the position of the accused to have so far lost self-control and to have formed the intent to kill or cause grievous bodily harm;
- where the conduct of the deceased occurred immediately before the act or omission causing death *or at any previous time*;
- provocation is not negatived by unreasonable retaliation, passion which wasn't sudden, or intention.

Therefore for provocation in common law, there must first be conduct by the victim that criminal law will recognise as sufficiently provocative to cause the accused to kill the other person. The task for the courts is to discriminate between provocative and non-provocative conduct. This is a legal standard that may not be shared by the rest of the community.

Regarding this first element, a number of more specific issues are looked at in the case-law:

- Are words sufficient? (See Barwick J in *Moffa v. R* (1977) 138 CLR 601.)
- What kind of conduct or behaviour does the law recognise as provocative (*Parker*)? What are the trigger incidents? What is the legal recognition of the cumulative effect of the situation (*Chhay*, and the recognition of the abuse of wives by their husbands in *Osland*)?
- What is the manner that would and did provoke the accused? (Self-induced provocation discussed in *Thorpe* [1999] 1 VR 326.)

The second element of provocation, by contrast, also sets up a legal standard but the focus of that standard concerns the degree of provocation, often called the 'gravity' or the seriousness of the conduct.

Finally, the accused must lose his self-control. Self-control and its loss are central concepts of the doctrine and as such give rise to legal dispute. The measure of self-control and its loss is formulated in terms of an objective and a subjective test:

- The threshold standard of self-control is an objective standard. The provocative conduct must have been so seriously provocative that it could have caused the ordinary person to lose his self-control, and to lose it to the extent of forming an intent to kill or cause grievous bodily harm.
- If the ordinary person would have lost his self-control to that extent, then at the time of the killing the accused must actually be suffering from a loss of self-control caused by the provocative conduct (the subjective standard).

The ordinary person test

Section 23(2)(b) of the *Crimes Act* (NSW) requires, as does the common law, that the provocation be measured against the ordinary person in the position of the accused. The question that follows is what *personal elements* should be invested in the ordinary person?

Whether the personal or cultural traits of the accused are relevant in the application of the ordinary person standard and if so, which traits and how they are legally relevant are questions discussed in *Stingel v. R* (1990) 171 CLR 312.

There is considerable judicial debate over the fact that an objective standard is to be applied to the gravity of the provocation and in particular the seriousness of the deceased's conduct towards the accused:

- In *Masciantonio v. R* (1995) 129 ALR 575, McHugh J resiled from his position in *Stingel*, now accepting that ethnicity should be a valid personal trait when applying the three elements of the excuse.

- Kirby J in **Green v. R** (1997) 148 ALR 659 accepts that when using an objective standard, the threshold should not be set too low for the community.

In **Stingel** (*supra*), the accused found his former girlfriend and the deceased having sex in a car. When he opened the door the deceased swore at the accused, following which the accused killed him with a butcher's knife. Stingel alleged that he went wild due to his obsession for the girl and his knowledge of the intentions and actions of the deceased. At the trial provocation was not left to the jury. The High Court discussed the totality of the deceased's conduct in determining his loss of self-control. The court said that the provocative conduct must be assessed from the viewpoint of the particular accused. None of the features of the accused will be necessarily irrelevant to an assessment of the content and extent of conduct involved in provocation (including age, sex, race, physical features, personal attributes, personal relationships, and past history). Even mental instability or weakness could be relevant in this evaluation. This would require that the provocative insult be put into context.

The function of the ordinary person test should not be confused with that of the reasonable person in negligence. To do so would be simply to defeat the defence.

There are different levels of ability to control oneself relative to particular groups within society. Such a consideration of the individual's loss of self-control is only relevant to limits within which loss of self-control can still be deemed ordinary. This evaluation of the actions of the ordinary person should be unaffected by any extraordinary attributes or characteristics when determining the gravity of the insult.

Murphy J's judgment in **Moffa** (*supra*) presents a compelling argument for the abolition of the objective test in provocation.

The subjective test in provocation

Was there an actual loss of self-control? In **Parker** (*supra*) the deceased taunted the accused about having sexual relations with his wife and then left with her on a bicycle. The accused put a gun in his car, ran the couple down, injuring them, and then, blaming the deceased for the injuries to his wife, stabbed him in the throat. The trial judge refused to leave provocation to the jury. On appeal the High Court considered the effect of delay and premeditation on provocation. The court must view the actuality of provocation in terms of the actual circumstances in which it was said to have boiled over. The sequence and nature of the acts which led to the death were considered, as was the issue of whether there was a need for a final provocative act.[157]

---

157 See *Chhay* (*supra*).

Self-induced provocation

A defence that might be termed 'self-induced provocation' is available to an accused in certain limited situations. Thus in ***Edwards v. R*** [1973] 1 All ER 152, where the accused was attacked violently by the person he was trying to blackmail, and killed his attacker as a result of his 'white hot rage', the Privy Council held that provocation should have been put to the jury. The court took the view that while a blackmailer cannot rely on the predictable results of his blackmailing and these predictable results may involve a considerably hostile reaction, where such hostile reaction is so extreme as to constitute provocation even for the blackmailer this is a question of degree to be determined by the jury. There was here evidence of provocation fit to go to the jury. In ***R v. Johnson*** [1989] 1 WLR 740, the court said:

> [w]e find it impossible to accept that the mere fact that the defendant caused a reaction in others which in turn caused him to lose his self-control, should result in the issue of provocation being kept from the jury. (The statute) clearly provides that the question is whether things done or said or both provoked the defendant to lose his self-control. If there is any evidence that it may have done then the issue should be left to the jury. The jury would then have to consider all circumstances of the incident including all the relevant behaviour of the defendant in deciding whether he was in fact provoked, and whether the provocation was enough to make a reasonable man do what the defendant did.

In Australian common law the accused cannot rely on provocation that is self-induced unless the reaction of the deceased is excessive. On the basis of ***Quartly*** (1986) 11 NSWLR 332, the NSW Court of Criminal Appeal rejected the strength of 'hearsay provocation', but the legislation may allow it. In *Quartly* the accused was told by his previous girlfriend that the deceased had got her addicted to heroin, beat her, and raped her. The accused was charged with murder for shooting and killing the deceased. His principal defence was intoxication and as such he did not have the intention to kill, but he also wanted provocation to be left to the jury. The trial judge refused to do so on the strength that the suggested provocation was hearsay. The Court of Appeal looked at the new s. 23 provisions in the *Crimes Act* (NSW) on the hearsay and 'presence' issues. It was said that the legislation altered the common law in terms of degree, proportionality, and suddenness of response. The evidentiary principles essential to the common law defence remain, that is, a loss of self-control, caused by the deceased, creating an intention to kill. The actual provocative act should occur within the sight or hearing of the accused and 'involve' the accused and the deceased even if the affront is not directed against the accused.

The legislative reference to 'affecting the accused' does not broaden the common law requirements. The excuse therefore is limited to the situation where the immediate provocation involves someone else and would affect the accused.

In **Thorpe** (*supra*), hearsay provocation was not put to the jury by the judge or by the accused's counsel (who preferred to advance self-defence and automatism) and this was the ground for appeal. The appeal court accepted the authorities that when provocation is available on the evidence it should be left to the jury no matter what course of action is adopted by counsel for the accused. The test is whether there was evidence by which the jury might fail to be convinced that the attack was unprovoked. The provocative act or words must be directed towards the accused, or there must be evidence from which the jury might draw inferences about the ordinary person.

In this case the accused was the initial aggressor. Could provocation following his initial aggression form the basis of an excuse? The actions of the accused would simply be considered along with the questions as to whether the accused was provoked and whether the ordinary person in these circumstances would have done what the accused did.

Leaving provocation to the jury

It is important to consider the role of judge and jury with regard to the provocation defence. In **R v. Burke** [1987] Cr LR 336, the English Court of Appeal did not feel bound to rehearse the exact words of the direction on provocation laid down by Lord Diplock in *Camplin*.

> The judge should remind the jury of any material characteristics of the defendant which might have affected the conduct of the hypothetical ordinary reasonable person in the circumstances of the particular case. It is, however, for the jury to determine which of those characteristics should be attributed to the ordinary person.

This gives a considerable degree of responsibility to the jury. However, it is for the judge to decide when provocation should in fact be left for the jury. This decision is based on a consideration of the evidence before the judge, and often results in a ground for later appeal.

The Australian position on when provocation should be left to the jury has always been a source of appeal points. In **Van Den Hoek v. R** (1986) 61 ALJR 19, the High Court again expressed the view (following *Parker* and **Pemble**) that the trial judge should leave the issue of provocation to the jury where the evidence is sufficient, even where the issue is not expressly raised by the accused. However, it is for the judge to decide when provocation should in fact be left for the jury. On this point, the difference between provocation and self-defence in terms of the loss of self-control is a significant consideration.

Diminished responsibility

Diminished responsibility is a matter in mitigation which has developed in English and Australian law in recognition of the narrow interpretive limitations inherent in the law on insanity.

In *R v. Byrne* [1960] 3 All ER, the accused did not dispute the facts that he had strangled and horribly mutilated the victim. The only defence was that at the time of the killing the accused was suffering from diminished responsibility as defined in the *Homicide Act 1957* (England), s. 2, and as such he could not be responsible for murder, only manslaughter. Medical evidence that the accused was a sexual psychopath was presented at the trial. It was said that he suffered from abnormality of the mind due to arrested development, and as such was not insane as defined under *M'Naghten*. The court held that an 'abnormality of the mind' has to be contrasted with a 'defect of reason'. It is a definition wide enough to cover the mind's activities in all its aspects, not only in the perception of physical acts and matters and the ability to form a rational judgment about whether these are right or wrong, but also the ability to exercise control over these physical acts in accordance with rational judgment. An abnormality of the mind is a question for the jury. The aetiology of the abnormality is a matter to be determined by experts. The next question is whether the abnormality of the mind is such as to substantially impair the mental responsibility of the accused for his acts. Again a question for the jury relates to whether the abnormality is one that affects the accused's self-control.

As was stated in *Inseal* [1992] CLR 35, while intoxication will not support a verdict of diminished responsibility, alcoholism may give rise to an abnormality of the mind arising from a disease or injury if it is proved that the brain has been injured by intoxicants so that there was a gross impairment of judgment and emotional responses, or such impairment arose from a craving for drink which the accused could not resist.

Up until recent law reform (in response to media criticism of the lenient way in which this excuse was being applied), in New South Wales diminished responsibility (s. 23A of the *Crimes Act*) required that the accused at the time of causing the death was suffering from an abnormality of the mind that substantially impaired his mental responsibility for his act. This could be caused by retarded development or disease and it was for the accused to prove, usually through the presentation of medical evidence.

The case-law debate developed over what constituted abnormality of the mind (e.g. in *Purdy* [1982] 2 NSWLR 964 following *Byrne* (*supra*).

Only New South Wales and the ACT recognise though legislation the availability of this excuse. It now can only be argued when charged with the crime of murder, and the effect of a successful plea is conviction for manslaughter.

Following the report of the NSW Law Reform Commission on Partial Defences to Murder (1997) abnormality of the mind was redefined and its causes specified. Substantial impairment of mental responsibility had to be established and the process for proving this was tightened up. Now under s. 23 A the abnormality of the mind must arise from an underlying condition and lead to fundamental impairment of judgment and cognition similar to that required for establishing insanity. Now evidence of opinion that the impairment was so substantial as to warrant reducing liability for murder to manslaughter is no longer admissible. Intoxication and its effects also cannot be recognised for the purposes of this section. The onus is on the accused to prove the excuse. Underlying condition means pre-existing mental or psychological condition, not of a transitory kind.

In *De Souza* (1997) 95 A Crim R 1, the NSW Court of Criminal Appeal reviewed the impact of the new legislative requirements for establishing diminished responsibility. In particular, the court held that the fact that an expert has advanced the opinion that the abnormality of the mind was due to 'injury' is of no significance unless the condition from which the abnormality is said to have arisen, or by which it was said to have been induced, fell within the meaning of the word 'injury' in the section.

CONTEXT OF THE PROBLEM

The following scenario suggests how different factors affecting liability, such as self-defence, provocation, and diminished responsibility, may be inferred from the same facts. The essential point of distinction is around the explanation for the accused losing self-control.

Be mindful of the statutory limitations on any of these 'defence' issues in your jurisdiction, and the proof responsibilities they cast.

PROBLEM

Don has been physically and emotionally abused by his drunken parents for years. He has suffered from the torment of a mother who takes delight in depriving him of love and then feigning interest in him when others are around. His father, a man twice the size of Don, brutalises him through constant beatings. One evening when the father returns from the pub he laughs at Don and calls him a 'disgusting little poof bastard'. He says he will crush Don's genitals so he 'can't play around with little boys anymore'. As he approaches Don, the father trips over and falls heavily on the floor.

Don is red with embarrassment. He knows his father in these moods and fears for his own safety. He is also seized with a consuming anger at the way he has been treated over the years. He cannot turn to his mother for support as she has remained at the pub and will be very drunk when she returns.

Don goes out to the garage and gets his father's hunting rifle. He returns to the kitchen where his father is stretched out and waits in a chair for several hours, intending to confront his tormentor when he regains consciousness. As he sees his father stir, Don's anger and fear returns and he empties the rifle into his father's head. Don is later charged with murder.

ENGAGING THE PROBLEM
Is there a loss of self-control here, precipitated by what, and why?

Can the emotional scars carried by the accused influence the application of the necessary subjective and objective measures, and if so to what extent?

Will the passing of time, the anger felt by the accused, the suggestion of premeditation, and the opportunity for withdrawal diminish the availability of any of the defences in this context of prolonged domestic violence?

ADDITIONAL RESOURCES
Crimes Act 1900 (NSW), section 23.

Brown, D., Farrier, D., Egger, S., and McNamara, L. *Criminal Laws*, Federation Press, Sydney, 2001, paras 6.1.1, 6.7.

Coss, G., 'Revisiting Lethal Violence by Men' (1998) 22(2) *Criminal Law Journal* 5; Molomby, T., '"Revisiting Lethal Violence by Men": A Reply' (1998) 22(2) *Criminal Law Journal* 116; Coss, G., 'A Reply to Tom Molomby' (1998) 22(2) *Criminal Law Journal* 119.

Eames, G., 'Aboriginal Homicide: Customary law defences or customary lawyers' defences', in Strand, G. and Gerull, S. A., *No. 17 Homicide: Patterns, Prevention and Control,* Australian Institute of Criminology, Canberra, 1993, p. 149.

Fisse, B., *Howard's Criminal Law*, Law Book Company, Sydney, 1992, pp. 83–98.

Leader-Elliot, I., 'Sex, Race and Provocation: In Defence of Stingel' [1996] 20 *Criminal Law Journal* 72.

Model Criminal Code Officers Committee of the Standing Committee of Attorneys-General, *Model Criminal Code Discussion Paper: Chapter 5, Fatal Offences Against the Person,* June 1998.

NSW Law Reform Commission, *Partial Defences to Murder: Provocation and Infanticide,* October 1997.

Yeo, S., 'Sex, Ethnicity, Power of Self-Control and Provocation Revisited' (1996) *Sydney Law Review* 304.

Moffa v. R (1977) 138 CLR 601

Quartly (1986) 22 ACrR 252

Van Den Hoek v. R (1986) 61 ALJR 19

Stingel (1991) 65 ALJR 141

The Queen v. R [1982] 28 SASR 321

Parker v. R (1963) 111 CLR 610

Scriva (No 2) [1951] VR 298

R v. Fricker (1986) 42 SASR 436

Gardner (1989) 42 A Crim R 279

Muy Ky Chhay (1992) 72 A Crim R 1

Camplin [1978] AC 705

Dutton (1979) 21 SASR 356

Dincer [1983] VR 460

Croft [1981] 1 NSWLR 126

Hamdi Baraghith (1991) 54 A Crim R 240

Mungatopi (1991) 57 A Crim R 341

Masciantonio (1995) 183 CLR 58

Green v. The Queen (1997) 148 ALR 659

TOPIC 16

FACTORS AFFECTING LIABILITY I

This is the first of several topics that consider the justifications and excuses in criminal law commonly considered as defences. Self-defence, duress, and necessity are examined together not only because they arise out of recognition of the compatibility between intent and justification, but also because of the way they rely on the lawful use of force. Battered Woman Syndrome is adopted here as a case study for the way in which these defences have recently been adapted to the specifics of particular situations of victimisation. Is Battered Woman Syndrome an answer to the problems in raising self-defence faced by women who have killed in the context of domestic violence, or does the representation of the situation as a syndrome tend to portray the circumstances of their victimisation as out of the ordinary? Does the notion of a syndrome connote some sort of transient abnormality rather than a more general endemic problem? Are there any other possible solutions? Does the fact that the accused is Aboriginal have an impact on her likely success in arguing self-defence, with or without Battered Woman Syndrome?

Lawful use of force

Self-defence has some association with the defences of duress, coercion, and necessity, and perhaps as a result, it requires a degree of threat or pressure on the defendant to allow for its activation. Essential to the justification of self-defence is the acceptance of occasions where there is a lawful use of force.

Self-help defences have two limitations in law:

1 the use of force must be necessary in the circumstances, and
2 the amount of force must not be excessive in the circumstances.

In general, self-defence extends to the protection of other persons, the defence of property, the prevention of serious crime, and effecting lawful arrest. This may involve the lawful killing of another in one's own defence.

In the view of Murphy J in **Viro v. R** (1978) 141 CLR 88, self-defence is not strictly a defence. It should be regarded as an act or omission which is not malicious (for instance in terms of s. 18 2 (b) of the NSW *Crimes Act*). In relation to self-defence, the onus is on the prosecution to prove that the accused did not act in his own defence and factual issues such as excessive force, proportionality, and failure to retreat are no longer conclusive.

Self-defence in crime prevention

One of the principal cases on the issue of the entitlement to use force in self-defence and crime prevention is **Duffy's** case [1966] 1 All ER 62. The appellant and her sister were indicted jointly on charges of wounding with intent. The appellant's case was that she went to the assistance of her sister, who was fighting with the person wounded, and she sought to rely on self-defence, a plea she alleged extended to her action in seeking to rescue her sister. The trial judge directed that the defence was not open to her and the appeal was against misdirection. It was held on appeal that apart from any special relations between the person attacked and the rescuer, there is a general liberty, even as between strangers, to prevent a felony. Since the appellant's basic defence was that in cases of necessity she had intervened with the sole object of restoring the peace by rescuing a person being attacked, it should have been left to the jury to decide whether, in view of her proved conduct, such a defence could succeed. The direction should have included the clarification that the person intervening was permitted to do only what was necessary and reasonable in all the circumstances for the purpose of the rescue.

The overlap between the use of force in self-defence and the use of force in crime prevention is examined in **Cousin's** case [1982] 2 All ER 115. It should be remembered that these may be concurrent defences. The same general test is used for both: the use of force must have been 'reasonable in the circumstances'.

In *Cousin's* case the appellant was convicted of threatening to kill R. His defence was that he had a lawful excuse in that he was acting in self-defence by seeking to forestall what he reasonably believed to be a planned attack, and he was seeking to prevent the commission of a felony under s. 3 of the *Criminal Law Act 1967* (England). By stopping the attack, which would have constituted a crime, he was applying lawful force.

The trial judge directed that there was no question of lawful excuse that could arise because the appellant's life was not in danger ('immediate jeopardy'), and the issue of whether the appellant had any lawful excuse for making the threat should be withdrawn from the jury. The appeal court held that in relation to s. 3 of the *Criminal Law Act*, a lawful excuse could exist if the threat to kill was made for the prevention of crime or in self-defence, provided it was reasonable in the circumstances to make that threat.

For authority on the defence of property, see *Walden* (1986) 19 A Cr R 444.

Self-defence

This 'defence' entitles the accused to use force to defend himself and others with whom he has a special relationship, or in order to defend certain property in certain situations, provided the use of force is reasonable in the circumstances.

When it comes to looking at what is *reasonable*, there are two aspects that merit consideration:

1 The use of force by the defendant must have been necessary to counter the danger facing the defendant or others (i.e. an actual attack), or that threatening the defendant and others.
2 The force used must be proportionate to the danger.

Justification

In *Devlin v. Armstrong* [1971] NIR 13, the issue of justification was examined. On different occasions the appellant had exhorted the crowd, who had been stoning the police, to barricade the 'bogside', to keep the police out and to man the barricades so as to fight the police with stones and petrol bombs. She was convicted of inciting to riot and behaving riotously. The defence raised was justification. It was submitted by the appellant that her acts were motivated by an honest and reasonable belief that the police were about to behave unlawfully in assaulting people and damaging property in the 'bogside'. The magistrate found that she had no reasonable ground for this belief. In the Court of Appeal of Northern Ireland, Lord McDermott said that the factual basis for the defence of justification had not been accepted by the trial judge. The assumption at the trial was that the appellant did not in fact behave as she alleged, and this assumption was held as a consequence of both sides withholding certain vital pieces of evidence from the jury at the trial.

The principal question on appeal was whether such a plea of justification would form a defence to such a charge and the answer was 'no'. The common purpose of the crowd, once formed, removes the excuse of honest belief. Even if her apprehensions supplied the motive for her actions, this would fall far short of neutralising her intentions to disorder as manifested by the manner of her participation.

A plea of self-defence can afford a defence where the party raising it uses force not merely to counter an attack, but to ward off or prevent an attack that he honestly and reasonably anticipated. In the past, the case-law required that the attack must be imminent. Grounds for such a belief may exist though they are founded on a mistake of fact. In **Devlin** the court said:

> However reasonable and convincing the appellant's apprehensions may have been, I find it impossible to hold that the danger which she anticipated was sufficiently imminent or specific to justify the actions she took as measures of self-defence.

As will be discussed later, one of the recent developments in case-law authority has been a reinterpretation of the relevance of imminence, particularly with respect to situations of domestic violence.

Bird's case [1985] 2 All ER 513 looked at the relevance of an opportunity to avoid the danger without using force. The appellant had been convicted of unlawful wounding as a result of a fight over a new girlfriend. The jilted lover returned and pushed a broken glass in the victim's face after she slapped him around. The appeal was based on the ground that the trial judge erred in law by directing the jury that before the appellant could rely on a plea of self-defence it was necessary to demonstrate by her actions that she did not want to fight. The appeal court did not agree with the direction. Failure to demonstrate an unwillingness to fight is merely a factor to be taken into account when considering whether the defendant was acting in self-defence, although evidence that the accused tried to call off a fight is likely to be the best evidence to cast doubt on a suggestion that she was the attacker or was acting for reasons of revenge and thus not acting in self-defence.

The issue of what happens when the attack in self-defence was lawful, such as that arising from a restraint prior to an arrest, is discussed in **Pedro v. Diss** [1981] 2 All ER 59. Here a constable attempted to search the defendant. The constable restrained the accused without arresting him, and he hit out at the constable and was then arrested. The court found that the constable had been holding the accused against his will, without arresting him. The court agreed that the forcible detention was unlawful at the time of the assault. It was said here that although a person who is being lawfully arrested may not rely on the justification of self-defence if he assaults the police officer in order to resist the arrest or detention, a person who is not being lawfully arrested or formally detained, may do so.

Proportionality of response

Proportionality of response should be assessed objectively, but regard should be had to all circumstances of the instant case, including the state of mind of the accused at the time. The nature of the test is partly objective and partly subjective, in that a jury or judge must first decide whether in retaliating in the way the appellant did, he actually believed that he was compelled to do so in order to preserve himself from grave harm; and secondly whether in all circumstances that belief was reasonable.

The development of the Australian position is demonstrated in the case ***R v. Howe*** (1958) 100 CLR 448. This was a Crown appeal against an order quashing the homicide conviction due to self-defence. The questions at issue in the appeal were:

1 whether it is an essential condition of the plea as a matter of law that the defendant in the face of a violent assault should have retreated as far as it was as reasonably possible before meeting the attack by force; and
2 the effect of the excessive use of violence on the part of the accused, who but for that would be able to make out a plea of self-defence as an answer to a charge of murder.

The Crown contested the Supreme Court decision that the issue in question (1) was only an element in the consideration of whether the defendant's conduct was ultimately reasonable, and (2) that manslaughter would be an alternative conviction if the force was unreasonable but no more than the accused honestly believed necessary in the circumstances.

The High Court agreed with the Supreme Court. Often the issue of excessive force is complicated by the introduction of mistake. In ***Williams (Gladstone)*** (*supra*), for example, the use of force in a situation of mistaken facts raised the question of reasonableness. The court held here that the prosecution had the burden of proof regarding the unlawfulness of the defendant's actions. If the defendant might have been labouring under a mistake as to the facts, he was to be judged according to his mistaken view of the facts whether or not that mistake was, on an objective viewing, reasonable or not. The reasonableness or unreasonableness of the defendant's belief was material to the question of whether the belief was held by him at all. If the belief was held, its unreasonableness, so far as guilt or innocence was concerned, was irrelevant. This is not necessarily the case for considerations of mistake in certain Australian jurisdictions (see: ***He Kaw Teh*** (*supra*)).

Excessive force

In ***Palmer v. R*** [1971] AC 814, a group of men including the accused went to buy cannabis. The accused had a gun with him. A dispute arose, resulting in the men leaving with the drug without paying. A chase ensued and the victim was shot dead. The accused was charged with murder and claimed self-defence. It was argued that if the accused felt that the force used was reasonable, but objectively it was viewed as excessive, then a third verdict of guilty of manslaughter was available to an accused charged with murder.[158]

The appeal court in *Palmer* said that the simple question was whether the defendant was acting in self-defence. If the prosecution satisfies the jury that he was not, then any other issues of justification or excuse remain, but not self-defence. An assertion that the use of force was considered subjectively necessary or reasonable would await issues in mitigation.

> It is both good law and good sense that [the accused] may do, but may only do what is reasonably necessary. But everything will depend on the particular facts and circumstances [of the case] ... the defence of self-defence, where the evidence makes its raising possible, will only fail if the prosecution shows beyond reasonable doubt that what the accused did was not by way of self-defence. [If this is shown by the prosecution] then the issue is eliminated from the case ... The defence of self-defence either succeeds so as to result in an acquittal or is disproved in which case the defence is rejected.

Issues of provocation, or whether sufficient intent was present for murder, may remain.

In **Zecevic v. DPP** (1987) 162 CLR 645, there was a dispute between neighbours in which the victim stabbed the accused in the chest and threatened to blow his head off. The accused went back to his apartment, took a gun and killed the victim, stating that he feared the victim 'was going to kill me'. The trial judge withdrew self-defence from the jury on the ground that he did not believe the accused saw that an unlawful and serious attack was imminent. One of the grounds of appeal was that for self-defence to be available the accused should not be required to hold a reasonable belief that he was being threatened with death or serious injury. On appeal the High Court changed the *Howe* (*Viro*) tests on the basis that they imposed an onerous burden on judges and juries.

It is for the prosecution to establish that the accused had no belief in the necessity of self-defence or that he did not hold that belief on reasonable grounds. If they fail to establish either, then the accused is entitled to an acquittal.

Absence of an exculpatory belief is now seen as a form of implied *mens rea*. The simple question is whether the accused believed on reasonable grounds that it was necessary in self-defence to do what he did. If the

---

158 See *Howe* (*supra*) where a qualified defence resulting in manslaughter was recognised in situations of excessive force, in circumstances where some lesser force would have been justified. Despite the favour in which such a reduced defence is held in academic and law reform circles, the High Court in *Zecevic v. DPP* (1987) 61 ALJR 375 resiled from *Howe* and came in line with *Palmer*.

accused had that belief and there were reasonable grounds for it, then he is entitled to an acquittal. In determining whether the belief was held, the whole of the circumstances need to be taken into account and the degree of force used might simply be part of those circumstances.

In *Zecevic* the court took the view that despite the possible injustice in convicting someone who may not be morally culpable, the facts in cases of excessive use of force could support either provocation or an argument that intent was not established.

Self-defence as an excuse is not limited to offences of homicide, and it may not be confined to a response to an unlawful attack.[159]

Self-defence and mistake

Following on from *Zecevic*, the subjective/objective question takes on most importance where the accused's belief is based on a genuine mistake as to the nature of the circumstances. Should the belief be tested against an objective standard of reasonableness?

In **Conlon** (1993) 69 A Crim R 92, the accused, who was suffering from a schizoid personality disorder, attacked and killed intruders on his marijuana farm. The Court of Criminal Appeal held that it is the belief of the accused and not of the hypothetical reasonable person in the position of the accused which must be reasonable for self-defence to be established. What did the accused reasonably believe in all the circumstances in which he found himself?

Account must be taken of those personal characteristics of this particular accused which affect his appreciation of the gravity of the threat and the reasonableness of the response. According to *Conlon*, voluntary intoxication is one such personal characteristic.[160]

As with *Williams (Gladstone)* (*supra*) there is a relationship between mistake of fact and self-defence, or the lawful use of force.

In **R v. Oatridge** [1992] Crim LR 205, the Court of Appeal agreed that an accused, who had been abused by her partner on previous occasions, was entitled to have her mistaken view of the incident of abuse, which led to her fatally stabbing the victim, considered by the jury.

> The possibility of the defendant honestly believing that on this occasion the victim was really going to do what he had previously threatened even if this was in fact what he was not going to do was not so fanciful as to require exclusion.

Self-defence is a justificatory defence. Where 'lawful' force is used by mistake against an otherwise innocent victim, it is not a situation of justifi-

---

159 See *Thomas* (1992) 65 A Crim R 269.
160 This decision has now been specifically legislated against in *Crimes Act* (NSW), s. 428F.

cation but rather excuse. Mistake, as far as the courts are concerned, negates blameworthiness, and excuses the defendant from blame. The application of honest mistakes as an excuse is coincidental in terms of the manner in which the courts have developed other 'defence' positions.

Onus of proving self-defence

Kurtic (1996) 85 A Crim R 57 stated that the Crown has to eliminate any reasonable possibility that the accused acted in self-defence. The prosecution must prove either that the accused did not believe it was necessary to act in self-defence in the manner in which he did, or that there were no reasonable grounds to do so. The second part of that test is entirely objective. It is now no longer possible to follow the *Conlon* position that the Crown also has to eliminate the possibility that the accused's appreciation of the gravity of the threat or the reasonableness of his response was reduced by characteristics personal to him, if these involved intoxication. Other types of personal characteristics (such as ongoing victimisation through violence) may influence the subjective and objective evaluations.

Self-defence and the battered woman

In recent case-law, which recognises the position of persons in violent domestic relationships, the courts have focused on:

- the proportionality of response, and
- the imminence of the threat.

In the Canadian case of **Lavelle** (1990) 55 CCC (3d) 97 the accused killed her partner after repeated periods of physical abuse, and on the occasion in question a threat of further violence to come. The court held that the question was not what an outsider would have perceived as a threat, but what the accused perceived in relation to the nature of the threat she faced. Domestic violence was referred to as 'murder by instalment' if the law required the battered woman to wait until the knife is drawn before retaliating or defending herself. It was wrong to say that she forfeited her right to self-defence simply because she stayed in an abusive relationship. In the domestic setting, in particular, the victim must not be required by law to retreat from her home instead of defending herself.

Lavelle was upheld in **Runjanjic and Kontinnen** (1991) 53 A Crim R 362 by the South Australian Supreme Court. This was the first Australian court to recognise what has now become known as Battered Woman (or Battered Wives') Syndrome (BWS). In this case BWS was applied to duress but the court said it was equally applicable to provocation and self-defence. Expert evidence was required on BWS because severe domestic violence is outside the experience of most jurors. The court recognised the danger in converting women's experience into a technical matter for experts.

The contesting issues of policy in the application of BWS are:

- Should special exceptions be developed where women are said to be mentally disabled by special victimisation?
- Is it not better simply to look at the circumstances which govern the creation of the accused's belief, and keep the reasonable person subjective?

The issue of 'learned helplessness' was discussed in the judgments as a mental condition of the syndrome. The question of approaching the victimisation of women in abusive domestic relationships as a syndrome rather than a general condition of the defence at issue was also commented upon.

The court was concerned to place the conventional obligation on the victim to escape within the reality of a violent domestic setting. What binds the victim to the abused, and the prolonged and constant nature of the abuse, also required reflection in the law.

In **Osland**, Gaudron and Gummow JJs' discussion of BWS and provocation and self-defence presents an informed review of the law. A connection is drawn between the abusive relationship and the characteristics of the ordinary person. This judgment recognised that the test may not be what would provoke the ordinary person (because it would not approach the actions of the victim with the heightened awareness of a battered woman), but what would influence the battered woman. Expert evidence on the abusive relationship might also go to establish the gravity of the provocation.

Expert evidence on the abusive relationship might also go to explain the heightened awareness of the accused of danger as relevant to self-defence, particularly as to the risk of death or serious injury and the necessity of avoiding that risk. The history of that relationship may bear on the reasonableness of that belief. An ordinary person may not have that heightened perception of danger, her thinking affected by fear, and the evaluation of the likelihood and reasonableness of escape. Therefore expert evidence on this is relevant.

Note Kirby J's criticism of the notion of syndrome. Evidence on the abusive relationship may help the jury understand the appreciation of the threat and therefore the reason for the assault (beyond revenge). The significance of the perception of danger is not its imminence. It is that it makes the defensive force really necessary and justifies the person's belief that she had no alternative but to take the victim's life.

If self-defence is to be seen as connected to the general doctrine of necessity, then the law of defences stimulated by necessity is flexible in Australian law, due to the guiding principle of 'reasonable necessity'.

Duress and necessity

A difficulty with any defences such as necessity, coercion, and duress lies in the notion of necessity. The courts have over the past century been reluctant to accept that a defendant is compelled to act in a particular way so as to justify his actions except in situations where certain special relationships imply such compulsion (e.g. marital coercion, superior orders) or where the necessary action is to protect innocent lives. Outside such relationships the courts have retreated from any open defence of necessity, traditionally preferring even the extreme positions that an accused should sacrifice his own life rather than the life of another for his own life (see *R v. Dudley and Stephens* (1884) 14 QBD 273). More recently, courts have not accepted economic necessity, no matter how compelling, as a justification for what would otherwise be a criminal offence (see *Southwark London Borough Council v. Williams* [1971] 2 All ER 175).

While duress, again in very special and limited circumstances, has been accepted by courts as a justification, in so doing judicial authority has struggled to impose technical limitations on the scope of the defence, such as the range of offences against which it might be applied.

This area of defences provides a fine example of the reluctance of the common law to open up new avenues of justification no matter how persuasive or logical. An explanation for such reluctance may lie in the issue of proof. Here, once such a defence is raised it remains for the prosecution to disprove it. With matters such as necessity this can be extremely difficult, as the determination of necessity, particularly in crisis situations, may depend on features to which only the defendant might be said to be truly privy.

So rather than expose the prosecution to sometimes impossible burdens of proof, or open up to the defence attractive areas of justification which might all too often be invoked (the 'floodgates argument'), the courts have chosen to limit the availability of the defence through judicial direction concerning the limited availability of the defence in designated circumstances.[161]

Necessity

Necessity arises when a person is able to choose between two courses of action, one of which involves breaking the criminal law, and the other some evil to himself or others, of such a magnitude that it may be argued to justify an infraction of the criminal law. It is usually raised either:

- as part of the self-defence argument or in relation to the use of force for crime prevention; or

---

161 A recent example of this logic is in the judgment of Ward LJ in *Central Manchester Healthcare Trust v. Mr & Mrs A; A (Children)* (2000) Court of Appeal Case No: B1/2000/2969.

- by an otherwise innocent party, against an innocent party.

To what extent necessity prevails as a separate defence has not been settled but it would seem that the case-law has had little to confine it when interpreting the limits of the issue. Necessity has arisen in the case-law either as:

- an argument in itself where the accused says there was no other course of action open to him beyond self-harm or self-destruction; or
- as the underlying theme of more specific defences such as duress (nature of the threat against the accused or close relation), or coercion (special relationship requiring compliance).

Public policy has been a significant motivation behind the negative attitude towards any suggestion of a general defence of necessity. The problem is posed by those unconvinced by necessity that even if necessity is sound in theory, it is extremely difficult, in an evidentiary sense, to predict, define, and categorise those cases where such grave consequences will justify a breach of the law, before they actually occur.

There has been an express reluctance to accept the interpretation of the accused as to what is necessary, particularly in situations of great stress. In addition, it has been considered unrealistic to assess necessity purely objectively, as such assessments may so often be influenced by wisdom after the fact. The facts about a defence and its persuasiveness must ultimately be determined by juries or other fact-finders, and those facts may be absent from the pressures and motives influencing the accused. For example, there may be necessity in a prisoner escaping from a burning cell, but there seems to be no such defence where the motivation is poverty or homelessness, and the crime is theft or trespass.

In the case of **Southwark (London Borough of) v. Williams** [1971] 2 All ER 175, the defendants, two homeless families, were unable to find housing. With the help of a squatters' association they made an orderly entry into houses owned by the borough. The plaintiffs obtained an order for repossession of the houses on the grounds that the defendants were criminal trespassers. The defendants appealed on the ground of necessity.

Lord Denning took the view that the defence of necessity had to be narrowly circumscribed, lest it become the door to many an unjustifiable excuse. 'If hunger were once admitted as a defence for stealing it would be the door through which all kinds of lawlessness or disorder would pass.'

Lord Edmund Davies said that the law regards with deepest suspicion the remedies of self-help and permits resort to them only in special cases. The defence will only succeed in an urgent situation of imminent physical peril.

On the strength of the English decisions such as *Southwark* there seems to be no general defence of necessity. Provided that the rigidity of the law does not prevent people from acting in the way in which the law would wish them to act, then the defence is rarely entertained. For example, if one were to break a regulatory law designed to protect the community interest in order to advance the community interest, then necessity might stand. However, this might also be interpreted as where one higher duty outweighs a lesser or more limited one.

The *cause célèbre* on this point is **R v. Dudley and Stephens** (*supra*). Here three men and a boy were adrift in an open boat for 18 days after their yacht was shipwrecked. The two accused suggested to the third man that they should kill and eat the boy. This they did when the boy was weak. The men ate parts of the boy's body, only to be rescued four days after the killing. In their defence they raised necessity.

The jury in this case found by special verdict that the men probably would have died over the last four days had they not eaten the boy. The boy would probably have died before them, and at the time of killing there was probably no appreciable way of saving life without taking this course of action.

Lord Simon in **DPP for Northern Ireland v. Lynch** [1975] AC 653 took the ratio of the *Dudley and Stephens* case as a rejection of the defence of necessity. It is arguable that due to the dispute over the facts as put in Lord Coleridge's judgment, the case decided little that was generalisable about necessity (e.g. the question as to whether necessity actually existed). Coleridge LJ examined the authorities and found no justification for extending a defence to such a situation. Killing by the use of force necessary to preserve one's own life in self-defence was well recognised but this was an entirely different defence situation. Apart from authority the court clearly thought that the law ought not afford a defence in this case.

The public policy argument saw any move towards such a defence as a great departure from morality. The principle would be dangerous because of the difficulty of measuring necessity, and of selecting a victim.

The boy's consent, either through the casting of lots or directly, may have been a defence as far as the court was concerned, but this seems a difficult position in light of the decisions which relate to consenting to harm above that which is more than trifling or transient. The court also felt that in the absence of a self-sacrificing volunteer it was the duty of all to die.

The present status of *Dudley and Stephens* is doubtful in the light of *DPP for Northern Ireland v. Lynch* (*supra*). It appears to have been conceded by counsel and the dissenting judges in that case that the majority decision to allow a defence of duress to an alleged principal in the second degree to murder was inconsistent with *Dudley and Stephens* at least as far as the conviction of Dudley (who assented, but did not do the killing) is concerned.

Lord Simon (dissenting in *Lynch*) saw a sustainable distinction between necessity and duress:

The only difference is that in duress, the force constraining the choice is a human threat, whereas in necessity it can be any circumstances constituting a threat to life.

If the argument were seen as valid, necessity, like duress, may be regarded as a defence to a principal in the second but not first degree of murder. Lord Morris in *Lynch* thought the majority in no way disturbed the ruling in *Dudley and Stephens* and that the courts recognised duress much more clearly and narrowly than they did necessity as a general defence.

Recently, the English Court of Appeal had cause to reconsider necessity in a case where a health authority and its doctors wanted clarification of their position in separating Siamese twins where one of the children would not survive the operation. This was in the face of the withdrawal of the parents' consent to any such operation. In terms of necessity the courts needed to put the arguments against a consideration of the best interests of the child. In *Re: A (Children)* (2000) Court of Appeal Case No. B1/2000/2969, Ward LJ said of necessity (duress of circumstances) after reviewing the authorities:

> ... the defence is available only if, from an objective standpoint, the accused can be said to be acting reasonably and proportionately in order to avoid the threat of serious injury ... the issue should be left (where available) to the jury who should be asked these two questions: first, was the accused, or may he have been, impelled to act as he did because as a result of what he believed to be the situation, he had good cause to fear that otherwise death or serious physical injury would result; second, if so would a sober person of reasonable firmness, sharing the characteristics of the accused, have responded to that situation by acting as the accused acted. If the answer to both those questions was Yes then the jury should acquit; the defence of necessity would have been established.

In *Loughnan* [1981] VCR 443, which was a case dealing with the necessity of a prisoner to escape threatened death, the court accepted that in exceptional circumstances there may exist a general defence of necessity. The court discussed the *Stephens* approach to necessity as breaking down into three issues:

1 that the criminal act must be done only in order to avoid certain consequences that would have inflicted irreparable evil on the accused or those he was bound to protect;
2 the peril must be immediate; and
3 the response must be proportionate to the peril.

In relation to necessity in the context of abortion, the issue is what constitutes a termination of pregnancy that is 'lawful in the circumstances'.

In the equity case of **K v. Minister for YACS** [1982] 1 NSWLR 311, the issue arose as to whether a termination of pregnancy was necessary to protect the woman from serious danger to her life or physical or mental health. In so determining the court considered whether the context should be on a social, economic, or medical basis. The earlier definition in *Wald*, that there was no legal wrongdoing where a miscarriage is produced by someone with an honest belief on reasonable grounds that termination of pregnancy was necessary to preserve the health and well-being of the woman, was approved.

Necessity in relation to strict liability was examined in **White** [1987] 9 NSWLR 427. In this case a motorist was charged with speeding when he was endeavouring to get a child to medical treatment. It was held that if in other circumstances an honest mistake of fact is a defence to strict liability, then there was no reason why necessity should not also be so.[162]

As mentioned above, the cases of **Loughnan** (*supra*) and **Rogers** (1996) 86 A Crim R 542, both dealing with prisoners escaping custody on the basis of necessity, the three elements of the legal excuse of necessity were confirmed as:

- the seriousness of the evil sought to be avoided;
- the immediacy or imminence of the peril;
- the proportionality or reasonableness of the response.

The courts commented that the ill-defined concept of necessity required qualification on the basis of the imminence or immediacy of a risk of death or serious injury. If an appellant honestly believed on reasonable grounds that it was necessary to break the law to avoid death or serious injury, then he would have an excuse. Questions of reasonableness and proportionality in light of the necessity were important considerations and not just expediency. Any possible alternative courses of action were relevant for the evaluation of necessity.

Duress and coercion

Duress and coercion are closely related to necessity. Once again the defendant is faced with a choice of evils. Should he break the law, or submit to the infliction of some evil on himself or another? They form special cases of necessity, the difference being that the need arises out of the wrongful threats of another to inflict some harm if the criminal action is not taken.

Duress is a defence because 'threats of immediate death or serious personal violence, so great as to overbear the ordinary powers of human

---

162   See also *Dixon-Jenkins* (1985) 14 A Crim R 372 at 378 where activists were forcing people to help prevent a nuclear disaster.

resistance, should be accepted as justifications for acts which would otherwise be criminal'.[163]

Duress must be such that the defendant's act is not voluntary (however, it is not the same as automatism). It is voluntary in the literal sense, but not voluntary in the sense of being a rational choice. The act may be unwillingly but intentionally done.

In pleading duress the accused admits that he had a choice and that he chose to commit the act with which he was charged, but denies that it is a crime. He claims to be excused from liability for deliberately doing acts which would otherwise be criminal, because of the threat to which he was subjected. In the case of **Hudson v. Taylor** [1971] 2 All ER 244, the defendants were accused of giving false evidence at a criminal trial and they were charged with perjury. Their defence was that a man who was present at the trial had, together with others, threatened that he would cut them to pieces unless they gave false evidence.

The trial judge held there was no defence of duress available because the accused were not subject to threats of immediate physical violence. Therefore they were convicted. The appellants were successful in the Court of Appeal. Lord Widgery indicated that despite the concern that criminals might be able to confer immunity on their confederates by threatening them, it is clear that duress is a defence in all offences (outside possibly treason and murder) including perjury.

> The will of the accused has been overborne by threats of death or serious personal injury so that the commission of the alleged offence was no longer the voluntary act of the accused.

Two issues were raised by the appeal:

1 the necessary nature of the threat and in particular whether it needs to be 'present and immediate';
2 the extent to which the right to plead duress may be lost if the accused has failed to take steps to remove the threat, for example by seeking police protection.

It is essential to the defence of duress that the threat be effective at the moment when the crime is committed. To that extent it must be present (not past or future).

---

163 See *Attorney-General v. Whelan* [1934] IR 518.

When, however, there is no opportunity for delaying tactics, and the person threatened must make up his mind whether he is to commit the criminal act or not, the existence of threats at that moment sufficient to destroy his will, ought to provide him with a defence even though the threatened injury may not follow instantly, but after an interval.

The execution of threats could not take place in a courtroom, but they were no less compelling, because they may be carried out in the street outside. The trial judge was wrong on the issue of immediacy. On the second question regarding the requirement to avoid the threat, there was a need to define the defence narrowly:

The accused must avail themselves of the opportunity reasonably open to them to render the threat ineffective.

In deciding whether such opportunity was open to the accused, one must have regard to his age and reason, and to any risks to him which may be involved in this course of action.

The elements of duress and the person of 'ordinary firmness of mind'

In **Lawrence** [1980] NSWLR 122 the navigator of a ship was not initially aware of the purpose of the voyage, which was the importation of drugs, but continued on after he had been threatened with physical violence. It was held here that there was a reasonable opportunity for the mind to reassert itself. The question of the risk involved in taking the opportunity is a question of fact regarding whether the opportunity was reasonably open to him. In considering whether the reasonable person would have responded to the threat in the way the accused did, one should consider the risk involved if the threat was ignored.

The defence of duress is available provided the average person of ordinary firmness of mind, of like age and sex, and in like circumstances to the accused would have done the acts concerned. If the accused fails to avail himself of an opportunity reasonably open to him for his will to be reasserted, the defence is not available. Where threats are for less than death or serious bodily violence then these may be matters for concern in mitigation.

Objective test

In **Abusafiah** (1991) 24 NSWLR 531 the Court of Criminal Appeal held that the objective tests in provocation and duress were not largely analogous. The Crown in replying to duress must establish that there is no reasonable possibility that the person of ordinary firmness of mind and will would have yielded to the threat in the way the accused did.

Duress as a defence to a charge of murder

In **Lynch's** case (*supra*) duress was held to be a defence to a charge of murder, where the accused was a secondary party (principal in the second degree). In this case a well-known ruthless gunman ordered the accused to drive him and accomplices to a place where they killed a policeman. The accused remained in the car while the shooting took place, and drove the gunman away following the murder. Lynch testified that he believed that if he had disobeyed the gunman's instructions he would have been shot. At the trial he was convicted of murder on a direction that duress could not be a defence to such a charge (the old common law rule). The House of Lords in allowing the appeal ordered a retrial. Lord Morris held that despite the fact that Lynch drove the car intentionally, knowing that the gunman intended to murder the policeman, the defence was still open to him. If the intention of the accused and all that he did only came about because of the compulsion of duress, he would have a defence.

Lord Wilberforce found no convincing reason on the authorities why the defence of duress, if it existed at all, should be absolutely excluded in murder cases whatever the nature of the charge. The majority recognised that some threats might be so grave as to cause even the honest and reasonable person to participate in murder and the law must be based on the standards of the honest and reasonable person. The position regarding duress as a defence for the principal in the first degree was left open, although the judges did foresee evidentiary problems in proving the defence.

Lords Simon and Kilbrandon (dissenting) thought that no valuable distinction could be drawn between principals in the first degree and principals in the second degree in murder, and adhered to the common law view. Duress would go more appropriately to mitigation, and the decision was firmly based on public policy grounds.

Abbott's case [1976] 3 All ER 140 was decided the following year and the court held again, by a majority of three to two, that although the defence of duress was available to a person who aids and abets murder, it is not available to the perpetrator of the murder (principal in the first degree). Abbot was a member of a commune which occupied a house in Trinidad. The commune was presided over by M, whom A had reason to believe was a dangerous man. On the direction of M, A took an active part in the murder of a young woman.

At his trial A said he had acted in the murder because M had threatened to kill him and his mother unless his instructions were obeyed. He was convicted. He appealed on the grounds that the trial judge had failed to direct the jury to consider whether, on the evidence, he was entitled to be acquitted because he acted under duress.

The Privy Council had to determine, initially, Abbott's position in relation to the murder. It seemed that there was an argument that he may have
only aided and abetted the stabbing of the girl by holding her down, but
there was no clear decision on his level of participation in the later burying
of the girl alive.

The dissenting judges asked whether any acceptable distinction can be
drawn between a principal in the first degree to murder, and one in the
second degree, the latter having access to duress as a defence. They felt that
none had been advanced. The contribution by a secondary party to the
death may be no less significant than by that of the principal. The distinction
causes a grave injustice because of its rigidity. This case illustrates the
unhappy results of the distinction between duress applying to secondary parties but not principals to murder.[164]

In **Burke** [1987] 2 WLR 568, Bannister and Howe, the co-accused, were
charged on two counts of murder. Their defence was that they feared that
they would be killed by Murray if they did not carry out his instructions.
On the first count they were principals in the second degree and on the
second count, principals in the first degree. The trial judge left duress to the
jury on the first but not the second count. They were convicted on both. In
a separate trial Burke and Clarkson were charged with murder, Burke as
principal in the first degree. His defences were (1) that despite his earlier
agreement to kill the deceased, the gun actually discharged accidentally, and
(2) that he was acting under threat of his life from Clarkson. Burke and
Clarkson were convicted of murder. Bannister, Howe, and Burke appealed
on the ground that the judges ought to have left their defence of duress to
the jury. Lane LCJ upheld the trial judges' direction as properly reflecting
the present law.

The illogicality associated with the common law position on the availability of duress to offences of murder could be cured either by denying the
defence of duress to the aider and abetter or by giving it to the principal in
first degree. It ultimately comes down to questions of policy, and the balance
of the harm caused against the harm to be avoided.

As mentioned earlier, some of the reluctance to open up the use of the
defence of duress has been evidentiary. With the facts of necessity so often
known only to the accused himself, it is difficult to disprove the defence
once it is raised.

---

164 The New South Wales position, as representative of Australian common law, is that which
holds in common law pre-*Howe* ([1987] 1 All ER 771); see *McConnell* [1977] NSWLR 714
where duress was said only to be denied to the principal in the first degree to murder.

The present limitations on access to the defence and its availability support Lord Simon's position (in *Abbott*) that it is dangerous on public policy grounds to allow a deliberate and intentional killer such a defence because he feared for his own life or that of his family. In a world where terrorism is still a real fear, the timing is not right for a liberalisation of the defence.

If duress was a defence to murder, some argue, it should only present a reduction to manslaughter (by analogy with provocation) and not lead to full acquittal.

The Court of Appeal in **Burke** (*supra*) authorised the appeal and certified the following points of law as being of general public importance:

1 Is duress available as a defence to a person charged with murder as a principal in the first degree?
2 Can one who by duress incites or procures another to kill or to be a party to a killing be convicted of murder if that other is acquitted by reason of duress?
3 Does the defence of duress fail if the prosecution proves that a person of reasonable firmness sharing the characteristics of the defendant would not have given way to those threats as did the defendant?

The House of Lords granted leave to appeal. In dismissing the appeals the court answered (1) No (2) Yes (3) Yes. Their lordships decided to depart from their previous decision in *Lynch* and held that duress would no longer be a defence to murder, whether the person charged was the actual killer or only the aider and abetter.

It was neither good morals, good policy, nor good law to suggest, as the majority did in *Lynch*, that the ordinary person of reasonable fortitude was not supposed to be capable of heroism if asked to take an innocent life rather than sacrifice his own. The law should not be altered by extending the defence to the actual killer and there was no fair or rational basis for distinguishing between the killer and those who took some other part in the murder. In cases of hardship there were administrative remedies such as the Parole Board and the use of the prerogative. If duress was to be made available generally as a defence to murder, legislation was the correct means to bring about such a reform.

The issue about the availability of duress for attempted murder came before the Court of Appeal in **Gotts** [1992] 2 WLR 878, where the accused, 16 years of age, was threatened with death by his father unless he killed his mother who had fled to a women's refuge with two other children, from the abuse of father. The accused stabbed his mother but was restrained and she did not die but was seriously injured. He was charged with attempted murder, and pleaded duress. The Court of Appeal upheld the trial judge's ruling that duress was not available for charges of attempted murder. It did not wish to present another anomaly with the non-availability of the offence of murder, and was also persuaded here by the fact that the sentence for this offence was open to the court (here, the defendant was given three months probation). But what about the situation of a mandatory sentence if the mother had died?

The objective test for duress, as laid down in ***R v. Graham*** [1982] 1 WLR 294, was held to be correct and had been correctly applied by the trial judges in these cases. Duress had been rightly stated to contain an objective element involving a threat of such a degree of violence that 'a person of reasonable firmness' with the characteristics and in the situation of the defendant could not have been expected to resist.

The case of ***Valderamma Vega*** [1985] Crim LR 220 emphasised that for duress to stand, the will of the accused must be overborne by the threat. In this respect the accused's will might be seen as involuntary, but not to the same extent as automatism, as the courts recognise that duress does not negative intention. Presumably it means only that he would not have committed the offence but for the threat, and the threat was one that might cause a person of reasonable fortitude to do as he did, but the threat need not be the only motive for the defendant's actions. In *Vega*, the accused was under financial pressure and he had been threatened with disclosure of his homosexual inclinations. Neither matter on its own might be capable of amounting to duress. It was held to be wrong to direct the jury that the threats of death or serious injury also alleged to have been made must have been the sole reason for his committing the offence. If he would not have committed the offence but for the latter threats, the defence was available even if he acted because of the cumulative pressure.

To reiterate, duress is a defence because:

> ... threats of immediate death or serious personal violence so great as to overbear the ordinary powers of human resistance should be accepted as a justification for acts which would otherwise be criminal.

Duress has been accepted as a defence to manslaughter, criminal damage, arson, theft, handling, perjury and contempt of court, and drug offences; and courts have assumed that it would apply to buggery and conspiracy to defraud. It now seems safe to say that duress may be a defence to any crime, except some forms of treason, murder, and possibly attempted murder.

Proof of duress

In **Graham's** case (*supra*), the House of Lords said that the correct direction on duress was that stated by Lane LCJ:

(1) Was [D], or may he have been, impelled to act as he did because, as a result of what he reasonably believed [E] had said or done, he had good cause to fear that if he did not so act [E] would kill him or … cause him serious physical injury? (2) If so, have the prosecution made the jury sure that a sober person of reasonable firmness, sharing the characteristics of [D], would not have responded to whatever he reasonably believed [E] said or did by taking part in the killing?

The direction contains three objective elements. D must have *reasonably* believed; his belief must have amounted to *good cause* for his fear, and his response must be one which might have been expected of a *sober person of reasonable firmness*.

It has been argued that, in the first two respects, this lays down too strict a rule. D should surely be judged on the basis of what he actually believed and what he actually feared. If his actual fear was such that no person of reasonable firmness could have been expected to resist it, he should be excused. He may have been unduly credulous or stupid, but he is no more blameworthy than a person whose fear is based on reasonable grounds.

Regarding duress by an association voluntarily joined, it was said in **Sharp** [1987] 3 WLR 1 that:

where a person has voluntarily and with knowledge of its nature, joined a criminal organisation or gang which he knew might bring pressure on him to commit an offence and was an active member when he was put under such pressure, he cannot avail himself of the defence of duress.

Here the accused was a party to robberies from which he wished to resile.

Fitzpatrick [1977] NIR 20 was a case in which it was held that duress can be no defence to a charge of robbery committed as a result of threats by the Irish Republican Army (a terrorist organisation), because the accused had voluntarily joined that organisation.

CONTEXT OF THE PROBLEM

This is another violent encounter arising out of a relationship moulded by a history of domestic violence. It is an outcome where the particular fears of the accused may come into sharp contrast with the ordinary person's apprehensions and tends to challenge the relevance of these. But with the development of the common law on justifications and excuses, is a syndrome perspective the best way to address these issues?

PROBLEM

Assume the hypothetical facts as stated in Topics 11 and 12 as holding here. Discuss Helen's liability.

Neville, feeling depressed, goes to the pub. He left home telling Helen that she had better have the dinner on the table when he returned, and it had better be good because he 'was in no mood to muck around'. He also said that he thought he would take Sue for a drive after dinner. Helen was so stressed out by the tone of his voice, and her anticipation of what would happen when he got home, that she took some pills the doctor had given her for her nerves. She reasoned that she probably needed a double dose because she was feeling particularly shaky and wanted the effect of the pills to last into the evening after Neville had returned.

Sue then told Helen that she was too frightened to go driving with Neville as he had forced her to have sex with him on previous occasions and continued to pressure her to do so. Helen replied, 'That does it. I am going to fix that bastard, otherwise we will never be safe from him. I don't see any other way out.'

On his return after several hours of drinking, Neville was shot dead by Helen who had taken up a defensive position in the hallway. Helen is charged with murder.

ENGAGING THE PROBLEM

As with our consideration of problems of provocation and self-defence, the reaction of the accused when compared with that of the ordinary person is of crucial concern in this scenario. Because of the charge, what limitations are presented concerning the availability of a defence here?

If the accused is going to argue the necessity of what she did, what needs to be established about her perception and its reasonableness? Does mistake have any bearing here?

ADDITIONAL RESOURCES

Brown, D., Farrier, D., Egger, S., and McNamara, L., *Criminal Laws*, Federation Press, Sydney, 2001, paras 6.8, 6.10.

Fisse, B., *Howard's Criminal Law*, Law Book Company, Sydney, 1992, pp. 98–110, 540–52.

Hubble, G., 'Feminism and the Battered Woman: The Limits of Self-Defence in the Context of Domestic Violence' (1997) 9(2) *Current Issues in Criminal Justice* 113; Stubbs, J. and Tolmie, J., 'Feminism, Self-defence and Battered Women: A Response to Hubble's "Straw Feminism"' (1998) 10(1) *Current Issues in Criminal Justice* 73.

Leader-Elliot, I., 'Battered but not Beaten: Women Who Kill in Self-defence' (1993) 15 *Sydney Law Review* 1.

Schneider, E., 'Equal Rights to Trial for Women: Sex Bias in the Law of Self-Defence' (1980) 15 *Harvard Civil Rights–Civil Liberties Law Review* 623.

Sheehy, E., Stubbs, J., and Tolmie, J., 'Defending Battered Women on Trial: The Battered Woman Syndrome and its Limitations' (1992) 16(6) *Criminal Law Journal* 369.

Stubbs, J., 'Self-defence and Defence of Others', in Graycar, R. and Morgan, J. (eds), *Work and Violence Themes: Including Gender Issues in the Core Law Curriculum,* materials prepared for DEET, 1990, pp. 8–16.

Stubbs, J., and Tolmie, J., 'Battered Woman Syndrome in Australia: A Challenge to Gender Bias in the Law?', in Stubbs, J. (ed.), *Women, Male Violence and the Law,* Institute of Criminology, Sydney, 1994, p. 192.

Yeo, S., 'The Threat Element in Duress' (1987) 11 *Criminal Law Journal* 165.

Viro v. R (1978) 141 CLR 88

Zecevic v. DPP (1987) 71 ALR 641

Beckford v. R [1988] AC 130

Conlon (1993) 69 A Crim R 92

Lavelle (1990) 55 CCC (3d) 97

Runjanjic and Kontinnen (1991) 53 A Crim R 362

Hickey (1992) 16 Crim LJ 271

R v. Dudley and Stephens (1884) 14 QBD 273

Southwark London BC v. Williams and Anderson [1971] 1 Ch 734

Loughnan [1981] VR 443

Davidson (1969) VR 667

Wald (1971) NSWDCR 25

CES and Anor v. Superclinics (Australia) Pty Ltd & Ors (Unreported, CA NSW, 22 Sept 1995)

Re Appeal of White (1987) 9 NSWLR 427

Rogers (1996) 86 A Crim R 542

Hurley [1967] VR 526

R v. Lawrence (1980) 1 NSWLR 122

Hudson & Taylor [1971] 2 QB 202

Brown [1986] 43 SASR 33

Williamson [1972] 2 NSWLR 381

Palazoff [1986] 43 SASR 99

Abusafiah (1991) 24 NSWLR 531

Haydon (No 2) (1984) 156 CLR 532

Lynch [1975] AC 653

Abbott [1977] AC 755

Howe (1987) 2 WLR 568

TOPIC 17

FACTORS AFFECTING LIABILITY II

In this topic[165] we revisit those defences in which the mental state of the accused is affected, and which may also be seen as relevant to questions of capacity, or voluntary manslaughter. In particular, insanity and automatism will be discussed. The interrelationship between these offences will be of particular interest. In examining these defences we will look at those issues of pathological mental process which have earlier been touched upon as challenging volition and capacity.

The accused who pleads:

1   insanity, either at the time of the offence, or at the time of trial (unfitness to plead);
2   insane automatism; or
3   diminished responsibility because of substantial impairment of cognition, through an abnormality of the mind arising from an underlying mental condition

claims psychological factors which set him fundamentally apart from the presumed rational and intentional person. As such, his responsibility should be treated as fundamentally differently from what would be expected of the rest of the community.

As defences, these can be seen as representations by the accused that he is not normal and therefore needs to be judged accordingly. By contrast, the accused who relies on intoxication, sane automatism, or mistake will often accept that he is like everyone else but due to some temporary or transitory state or situation, needs to be judged in relation to different facts. Beliefs which are induced by mistake, intoxication, or sane automatism rest on aberrations which challenge the frailty of the normal, rather than claims to the abnormal.

This distinction between the abnormal and the normal mental state defences are not always clearly distinguished in the case-law. It is in issue in the themes of:

• internally and externally induced psychological disorder, and
• permanent or temporary psychological indisposition or disorder.

---

165   Some of the text in this topic is a reiteration of discussion in Chapter 4. The purpose is to remind students of essential issues in both contexts.

Interestingly these defences cast, to varying degrees, the onus of establishing their existence onto the accused. The burden imposed varies depending on the nature of the claim. But in almost every case therapeutic disciplines are called upon to assist in establishing these defences. As the recent reforms in the law of diminished responsibility in New South Wales attest (which have negated the reliance on expert evidence alone), the law's view of medical evidence is somewhat sceptical. From the other perspective, the psychiatrist expert is often uncomfortable with the arcane legal language of pathology and its manifestations in this area, or the artificial distinctions between disorders as classes of defences.

Whether these issues are defences depends on:

- their relationship with the elements of the offence and their proof;
- the manner in which they need to be established;
- the time at which they should be argued (see *Hawkins*); and
- whether they have an independent and distinct basis rather than simply challenging whether the elements of the crime have been established.

The historical development of these concessions to the doctrine of classical criminal responsibility will betray to some extent the nature of these issues. The courts have reluctantly accepted consideration of mental incapacity or pathology as defences to responsibility and in so doing have imposed a range of proof and outcome restrictions which have lessened their attractiveness as defences.

There is considerable interaction in the field of the psychological or mental pathology (disorder) offences. This is particularly represented in automatism. These interactions can produce competing claims to the defences in the same factual situations which sometimes seem to indicate inconsistency.

While these defences have evolved through the common law and some, such as automatism, retain their foundations, others have found legislative definition. For example, in New South Wales insanity is covered by the mental illness provisions in s. 38 of the *Mental Health (Criminal Procedure) Act 1980*. The definition of insanity in that jurisdiction is a combination of common law and provisions in the *Mental Health Act 1990*.

Insanity (Volition and ability to reason)

In Australia the classic statement of the defence of insanity comes from the judge's directions in the High Court decision of **Porter**. These are derived from the rules set out in the *M'Naghten* case. The rules cover both situations of delusion and prevailing insanity. The defence is established through proof of:

- pathology (defect of reason from a disease of the mind), or
- cognitive impairment (not knowing the nature and quality of the act or that it was wrong).

In **Stapleton v. R** (1952) 86 CLR 358 the High Court interpreted wrongness as a moral rather than simply a legal determination.

Traditionally in common law, insanity as an issue of criminal capacity is still primarily based on the M'Naghten Rules (see **M'Naghten** (1843) 10 CL & F 200). Once raised, the usual course is to leave the question of insanity to be decided as fact by the jury, or the judge sitting alone. The questions to be determined are whether the accused had a sufficient degree of reason to know the nature and quality of the act, or being so cognisant, he did not know that what he was doing was wrong. Criminal responsibility connotes control over one's actions, and a power to choose whether or not to abide by the law. An insane person lacks both such control and power of choice, and therefore cannot be responsible for his or her actions, or criminally liable for them.

The M'Naghten approach requires the capacity to reason as measured by knowledge of the act to be defective due to a 'disease of the mind'. The narrow interpretation of this concept by the courts has reduced the effectiveness of insanity as a means of denying volition.

For instance, in **Bratty v. Attorney-General for Northern Ireland** [1963] AC 306 the appellant strangled a girl and later said to the police that when he was with her he had a terrible feeling and a sort of blackness came over him. The evidence suggested that maybe this was psychomotor epilepsy, raising three possible defences: automatism; no intention; or insanity. At the trial the jury rejected insanity. The Court of Appeal discussed the wider connotation of the involuntary act beyond automatism.

The questions posed in *M'Naghten's* case which have given rise to the greatest discussion are the second and third questions:

- What are the proper questions to be submitted to the jury, where a person alleged to be afflicted with insane delusion with respect to one or more particular subjects or persons, is charged with the commission of a crime (murder, for example), and insanity is set up as a defence?
- In what terms ought the question to be left to the jury when the act was committed?

The judges answered both questions together, their opinion being:

that the jurors ought to be told in all cases that every man is to be presumed sane, and to possess a sufficient degree of reason to be responsible for his crimes, until the contrary be proved to their satisfaction and that to establish a defence on the ground of insanity, it must be clearly proved that, at the time of the committing of the act, the party accused was labouring under such a defect of reason, from disease of the mind, as not to know the nature and quality of the act he was doing; or, if he did know it that he did not know he was doing what was wrong. The mode of putting the latter part of the question to the jury on these occasions has generally been, whether the accused at the time of doing the act knew the difference between right and wrong: which mode, though rarely, if ever, leading to any mistake with the jury, is not, as we conceive, so accurate when put generally and in the abstract, and when put with reference to the party's knowledge of right and wrong in respect to the very act with which he is charged. If the question were to be put as to the knowledge of the accused solely and exclusively with reference to the law of the land, it might tend to confound the jury by inducing them to believe that an actual knowledge of the law of the land was essential in order to lead to a conviction; whereas the law is administered upon the principle that every one must be taken conclusively to know it, without proof that he does know it. If the accused was conscious that the act was one which he ought not to do, and if that act was at the same time contrary to the law of the land he is punishable; and the usual course therefore has been to leave the question to the jury, whether the party accused had a sufficient degree of reason to know that he was doing an act that was wrong: and this course we think is correct, accompanied with such observations and explanations as the circumstances of each particular case may require.

Where a person suffering under an insane delusion as to existing facts commits an offence in consequence thereof, the judges in *M'Naghten* indicated that the answer to a question of insanity must depend on the nature of the delusion; assuming the accused labours under a partial delusion only, and is not in other respects insane, he must be considered in the same situation as to responsibility as if the facts with respect to which the delusion existed were real.

Sullivan's case [1984] AC 156 saw the House of Lords accept that the M'Naghten Rules have provided a comprehensive legal definition of insanity since 1843 and yet they are rarely invoked in trials. Their importance is in the limits they pose for the legal responsibility of the mentally abnormal. Further, they set referential limits to the defences of automatism and diminished responsibility.

In *Sullivan* the defence to a charge of assault occasioning actual bodily harm was that D attacked the victim while recovering from a minor epileptic seizure and did not know what he was doing. The House of Lords held that the judge had rightly ruled this raised the defence of insanity. The defendant had then, obviously, pleaded guilty to the charge, of which he was manifestly innocent, and his conviction was upheld. This shows the error of considering legal insanity as a full defence. It also shows the dangers inherent for a defendant in putting his state of mind at issue in the trial. Medical experts may attest to the factual nature of his condition, but it is for the judge to say whether this is evidence of a defect of reason from a disease of the mind, for the law sees these as legal rather than medical concepts.

In **Beard's** case [1920] AC 479 the court considered whether drunkenness could amount to insanity. Lord Birkenhead said:

> That insanity, whether produced by drunkenness or otherwise, is a defence to the crime charged. The distinction between the defence of insanity in the true sense caused by excessive drinking, and the defence of drunkenness which produces a condition such that a drunken man's mind becomes incapable of forming a specific intention, has been preserved throughout the cases. The insane person cannot be convicted of a crime … but, upon a verdict of insanity, is ordered to be detained during His Majesty's pleasure. The law takes no notice of the cause of the insanity. If actual insanity in fact supervenes, as the result of alcohol excess, it furnishes as complete an answer to a criminal charge as insanity induced by any other cause …

but in **R v. Davis** (1881) 14 Cox C C 563 Stephen J. said:

> … but drunkenness is one thing and the diseases to which drunkenness leads are different things; and if a man by drunkenness brings on a state of disease which causes such a degree of madness, even for a time, which would have relieved him from responsibility if it had been caused in any other way, then he would not be criminally responsible. In my opinion, in such a case the man is a madman, and is to be treated as such although his madness is only temporary …

In *Davis's* case delirium tremens was accepted as the defect of reason from a disease of the mind.

In **Porter** (1936) 55CLR 182, Dixon J established insanity by first considering the mind of the accused at the time he committed the act. Then it needed to be determined that the state of mind was one of 'disease, disorder or disturbance'. Finally the disease should be of such a character that the accused could not appreciate that he was doing wrong.

In *Porter* Dixon J made this direction regarding defect of reason from a disease of the mind:

> The next thing which I wish to emphasise is that his state of mind must have been one of disease, disorder or disturbance. Mere excitability of a normal man, passion, even stupidity, obtuseness, lack of self-control, and impulsiveness are quite different things from what I have attempted to describe as a state of disease or disorder or mental disturbance arising from some infirmity, temporary or of long standing … that does not mean that there must be some physical

deterioration of the cells of the brain, some actual change in the material physical condition of the mind as disease normally means when you are dealing with other organs of the body where you can see and feel and appreciate the structural changes in fibres, tissues and the like. You are dealing with a very different thing with the understanding. It does mean that the functions of the understanding are through some cause, whether understandable or not, thrown into derangement or disorder.

In **Kemp** [1957] 1 QB 399, the accused was charged with causing grievous bodily harm to his wife with intent to feloniously murder her. The accused was suffering from a physical disease called arteriosclerosis, or hardening of the arteries. There was evidence that this disease induced a mental condition of melancholia. Other evidence was given that the disease did not lead to melancholia but only to a congestion of blood in the brain, which would bring about temporary lapses of consciousness, making the person irrational or irresponsible. On this evidence it was said the condition of arteriosclerosis could lead to a mental disease but only in a later stage of its development. Devlin J said:

> The primary thing that has to be looked for is the defect of reason. 'Disease of the mind' is there for some purpose, obviously, but the prime thing is to determine what is admitted here, namely, whether or not there is a defect of reason. In my judgment, the words 'disease of the mind' are not to be construed as if they were put in for the purpose of distinguishing between diseases which have a mental origin and diseases which have a physical origin, a distinction which in 1843 was probably little considered. They were put in for the purpose of limiting the effect of the words 'defect of reason'. A defect of reason is by itself enough to make the act irrational and therefore normally to exclude responsibility in law. But the rule was not intended to apply to defects of reason caused simply by brutish stupidity without rational power. It was not intended that the defence should plead: 'Although with a healthy mind he nevertheless had been brought up in such a way that he had never learned to exercise his reason, and therefore he is suffering from a defect of reason.' The words ensure that unless the defect is due to a diseased mind and not simply to an untrained one there is no insanity within the meaning of the rule.

The disease of the mind must have given rise to the defect of reason. Reason must be impaired and not simply absent or avoided. Is this the same as used in 'he didn't know what he was doing'? This would limit the defence greatly if so interpreted.

The terms 'nature' and 'quality' were originally held to mean the physical character of the act (**Codere** (1916) 12 Cr App R 91). Is quality the moral rather than physical aspect of the deed? The court did not agree.

On the issue of the extent of the application of the M'Naghten Rules, the case of the **Attorney-General for Northern Ireland v. Gallagher** (*supra*) said that if the accused was suffering from a disease of the mind which was insufficient to bring him under the M'Naghten defence, the fact that the disease was exacerbated by intoxication at the time would not make the defence of insanity available to him. In this case the defendant's psychopathy was quiescent and without drink it could not have brought the condition required for the insanity defence into play. If the psychopathy had, however, been caused by drink, he may then have had a sufficient disease of the mind to come under M'Naghten.

In *R v. Quick & Paddison* (*supra*), which is primarily a case on automatism, the trial judge originally ruled that the defendant Quick had raised the insanity defence and the defendant immediately pleaded guilty. The appeal accepted that the alleged mental condition brought about by an external factor, such as the use of insulin, should have been left to the jury as automatism. If it had been caused by an internal factor such as diabetes, the defence would have been ruled as insanity.

The distinction between external causes, which may give rise to a defence of non-insane automatism, and internal factors, which can only give rise to a defence of insanity (or insane automatism), has been criticised. The recurrence of the disease should not be seen, as *Bratty* suggests, as another determinant of the appropriate use of insanity as a defence, as in *Quick*.

The High Court in *Hawkins v. R* (1994) 122 ALR 27 seems to have entertained the prospect that proofs of insanity, even if they don't establish legal insanity, may, if relevant to the issue, be considered by the jury in determining the formulation of any element of specific intent required to be proved by the prosecution.

More recently, certain Australian states have modified the law relating to capacity and insanity through law reform in the mental health area. In this the definition of insanity has been adjusted by concepts such as 'mental illness' (*Crimes Act 1900* (ACT), s. 428N; *Mental Health Criminal Procedure Act 1990* (NSW), s. 38); 'unsoundness of mind' (*Criminal Code Act 1899* (Qld), s. 647; *Criminal Code Compilation Act 1913* (WA), s. 653); 'mental incompetence' (*Criminal Law Consolidation Act 1935* (SA), s. 269C), and 'mental impairment' (*Crimes (Mental Impairment and Unfitness to be Tried) Act 1997* (Vic), s. 20(2)).

The common law in relation to insanity continues to apply in New South Wales, and its influence can still be seen in the statutory provisions for Tasmania and the ACT. Even the new defence of mental impairment in Victoria adopts the language of *M'Naghten*.

Permanent or temporary serious mental impairment rather than defect of reason or disease of the mind now calls for proof in terms of symptoms rather than processes.

Insanity is a defence to all crimes and it results in a full acquittal. However, this is conditional on some referral to therapeutic incarceration, which is indeterminate. The conditions under which this detention is maintained and the medical discretions on which its termination depends make it an unattractive defence and it now is largely restricted to crimes of murder.

Irresistible impulse

As a development of the relationship between insanity and automatism, the matter of irresistible impulse was discussed in the ***Attorney-General for South Australia v. Brown*** [1968] SASR 467. This case is authority for the English and Australian position that the law does not recognise irresistible impulse as a symptom from which the jury may infer insanity under the M'Naghten Rules. Brown killed his employer for no apparent reason. It was said that the accused was schizoid and couldn't have helped what he was doing, but he would not have done it if a policeman was present. The point of referral to the Privy Council was that the High Court felt that the jury should have been directed to consider whether Brown's ability to control himself or his impulses prevented him from knowing that what he was doing was wrong.

The Privy Council said that cognisance should be given to irresistible impulse when deciding on matters such as diminished responsibility.

> The law recognises that mental disease is manifested in a lack of knowledge or incapacity to have knowledge of the nature and quality of one's actions or if its character is a wrong act.

The court approved of Lathan CJ's statement in ***Sodeman*** (1936) 55 CLR 192, where he said

> ... it should be remembered that ... the law recognises mental disease mani-fested in what is called irresistible impulse, may also be manifested in a lack of knowledge or incapacity to have knowledge, of the nature and quality of the act or of its quality as a wrong act. Such as impulse may be evidence of this very lack or incapacity. Indeed that was the effect of the medical opinions given in the evi-dence of this case and this aspect of the case was definitely put to the jury.

Automatism (Volition and ability to control actions)

Despite the assumption that no act is punishable if it is involuntary, the courts have consistently limited the circumstances in which involuntariness might be successfully raised.

For example, Lord Denning in *Bratty* (*supra*) stated that an involuntary act is an act 'done by the muscles without any control by the mind such as a spasm, a reflex action or a convulsion; or an act done by a person who is not conscious of what he is doing, such as an act done whilst suffering from con-cussion or whilst sleep-walking'.

An act is not involuntary simply because the actor could not remember doing it, or could not control himself. If an involuntary act proceeds from a disease of the mind it results in a defence of insanity. A disease of the mind is a question for the judge.

The causes of automatism are broadly designated as internal or external, and such uncontrolled actions may occur either consciously or unconsciously and be induced from outside the body or from within. In this respect insanity may be an internal cause of the automatic state, and where this is alleged, the M'Naghten tests for insanity apply.

Automatism and insanity are sometimes crucially connected and in some situations the determination of their relationship is crucial to the dispute. One reason that the interaction is crucial is that automatism deals with the relevance of evidence to the substantive law. For example, if the accused leads evidence that his action was unwilled, then this might also be consistent with the conclusion that he was insane. There may be little legal difference between a defect of reason and a defect of will. They both refer to a cognitive incapacity, although there may be differences as to duration and cause. In other situations they might both share proof of unconsciousness.

Automatism is one of the few areas where the law recognises the unconscious.

Where the accused is suffering from non-insane automatism, the proof and verdict advantages are more attractive to the defence than is the case with insanity. The distinction between insane and non-insane automatism was established by the House of Lords in *Bratty v. Attorney-General for Northern Ireland (supra)*. In that case the defence raised either automatism or insanity. The trial judge directed the jury fully on insanity but did not put automatism to them. He felt that automatism could not stand outside insanity.

The principle of *Bratty* was that where the only cause alleged for an involuntary act is a defect of reason due to a disease of the mind, the judge need not direct the jury as to automatism in addition to insanity. The court said that an act cannot be regarded as involuntary simply because the actor can't remember it nor because he couldn't control his impulse to do the act. They interpreted 'involuntary' in a very narrow manner, perhaps because of the influence of diminished responsibility.

The additional point was made that not every involuntary act will lead to an acquittal. Where such an act is provoked, or caused by the prior actions of the accused, it may not be a defence. Involuntary action will be a defence against specific offences such as murder, but not manslaughter, where intention may not be specifically proved. In *Bratty's* case the prosecution relied on the presumption as to volition. It was necessary then for the defence simply to rebut that presumption on the evidence. The onus would then shift to the Crown. But when, as was the case here, the defendant only raises automatism in the context of insanity, the burden remains with the defence to prove same.

Naturally an accused person who wishes to plead automatism will be reluctant to claim that it is of the insane variety and the question arises whether, on the defence of automatism, the judge or the prosecution can raise the issue of insanity when it has not been led by the defence. A negative reply was given to this by the court in *R v. Charleson* [1955] 1 WLR 317, where the accused was charged with unlawfully and maliciously causing grievous bodily harm by striking his young son with a mallet and throwing him out the window. It was said that this behaviour resulted from a cerebral tumour. The defence was that the accused was unconscious at the time.

Barry J directed the jury that the case did not involve insanity since the defence had not been raised by the accused, who alone was competent to do so. The accused was acquitted after the jury was told that he would not be guilty if his acts were purely automatic and his mind had no control over them. The court in *Kemp* (*supra*) disagreed and said that the judge could raise insanity, but distinguished *Charleson* by saying that it was a case where the medical evidence did not indicate insanity. But surely the question of the disease of the mind is a question for the judge? Because of Lord Denning's support (in *Bratty*) of *Kemp*, on the point about rights to raise the defence, *Kemp* would appear now to be the better authority.

Causes of automatism

Regarding external causes of automatism, in *Hill v. Baxter* (*supra*) the question was whether the accused had put forward sufficient evidence on a charge of dangerous driving to justify the court's decision that he was unconscious, even though he was physically driving at the time. He alleged that he had been overcome by an unidentified illness. The court held that for automatism to stand in these circumstances, unconsciousness due to sudden illness must entail the malfunctioning of the mental process of the sufferer, but should not be equated with a disease of the mind. Accidental or temporary loss of consciousness should not be equated with insanity. The driver of the car could not be said to be 'driving' at the material time when he was prevented from exercising directional control over the vehicle due to the loss of consciousness. It is not enough for the defence to say, 'I did not remember anything'. They must present some prima facie evidence of loss of consciousness, beyond assertion.

In *R v. Falconer* (*supra*) several of the judges held that if the psychological blow suffered by the accused (externally caused) would have produced a transient dissociative state in the ordinary or normal person, then it may be regarded as non-insane automatism. If, however, it would not produce this state in the ordinary person then the issue would fail, or the jury should be directed as to insanity. The ordinary person is of normal temperament or self-control and does not possess any of the particular emotional features of the accused at the time of the commission of the offence.

Bailey [1983] 1 WLR 760 and *Hardie* [1984] 3 All ER 848 put forward the principle that intoxicants may be usefully divided on the grounds of the predictability of their effects. Where it is common knowledge that a drug is liable to cause the taker to become aggressive or dangerous or to do unpredictable things, that drug can be classed along with alcohol (and takes on its effects in a legal sense). Where there is no such common knowledge, as in the case of a sedative drug, different rules apply.

In *Bailey*, a diabetic failed to take sufficient food after taking insulin. He caused grievous bodily harm and his defence was that because of this failure he was in a state of automatism. Interestingly the Court of Appeal held that self-induced automatism other than that due to intoxication from alcohol or drugs may provide a defence to crimes of basic intent.

> The question in each case will be whether the prosecution had proved the necessary element of recklessness. In cases of assault, if the accused knows that his action, or inaction are likely to make him aggressive, unpredictable or uncontrolled, with the result that he may cause some injury to others and he persists in that action or takes no remedial action when he knows it is required, it will be open to the jury to find that he was reckless.

The automatism seems to be treated as arising from the failure to take food rather than the taking of insulin. Also the court saw the drug use, or the accused's failure to combine it with food in this case, as being different from intoxication caused by alcohol or dangerous drugs.

In *Hardie* the defence to a charge of damaging property with intent to endanger the life of another or being reckless as to whether another life was endangered was that he had taken Valium, a sedative, to calm his nerves, and that this had resulted in intoxication precluding the *mens rea* for the offence. The judge, following *Majewski* and *Caldwell*, directed that this could be no defence. The Court of Appeal quashed the conviction, saying that *Majewski* could not apply because Valium is:

> wholly different in kind from drugs which are liable to cause unpredictability or aggressiveness … if the effect of a drug is merely soporific or sedative the taking of it, even in some excessive quantity, cannot in the ordinary way raise a conclusive presumption against the admission of proof of intoxication for the purpose of disproving *mens rea* in ordinary crimes, such as would be the case with alcoholic intoxication or incapacity or automatism resulting from the self-administration of dangerous drugs.

These cases, then, appear to apply where intoxication is self-induced by some means other than by alcohol or dangerous drugs. In these cases the test of liability is stated to be one of recklessness:

> If he does appreciate the risk that (failure to take food) may lead to aggressive, unpredictable and uncontrollable conduct and he nevertheless deliberately runs the risk or otherwise disregards it, this will amount to recklessness.

It is clear that the recklessness which must be proved is:

1   subjective, an actual awareness of the risk of becoming aggressive, etc., not recklessness of the *Caldwell* type; but
2   'general', not requiring foresight of the *actus reus* of any particular crime, such as is required in the case of a sober person charged with an offence involving the **Cunningham** type of recklessness. The defendant will be liable for any crime of recklessness the *actus reus* of which he happens to commit under the influence of the self-induced intoxication; and
3   awareness that one may lose consciousness may be sufficient where a failure to exercise control may result in the *actus reus* of a crime, as in the case of careless or reckless driving.

Prior fault

If automatism is externally induced, then questions regarding the 'prior fault' of the offender are relevant (that is, if the accused person does something the consequences of which might reasonably be foreseen as the production of an automaton state, then the justification may not be available to deny capacity). The question here is the reasonable foreseeability of the state likely to induce the incapacity. The test is an objective one where the offence imposes strict liability or could be satisfied by objective tests for recklessness or negligence, and is subjective where the *mens rea* of the offence requires intention or subjective recklessness.

In *R v. Quick & Paddison* (*supra*), the court held that prior fault prevents a reliance on the defence of automatism or other involuntary conduct. The defence will not succeed if the outward automatic state was foreseen, or (in some situations) was reasonably foreseeable. This depends on the *mens rea* of the offence concerned.

Procedure with the defence

As to the procedural aspects of the defence, Lord Denning said, in *Bratty's* case, that

> whilst the ultimate burden rests on the Crown in the crime, nevertheless in order to prove that the act was voluntary, the Crown is entitled to rely on the presumption that every man has sufficient mental capacity to be responsible for his crimes: and if the defence wish to dispute that presumption they must give some evidence from which the contrary may be inferred.

This position was echoed by Barwick CJ in **Ryan's** case (1967) 121 CLR 205. In **Falconer** (*supra*) the defence was required to present evidence sufficient to put the prosecution to proof in establishing that the actions of the accused were voluntary. This would be to the extent at least to challenge the presumption of fact as to volition.

CONTEXT OF THE PROBLEM

The limitations of the defences relating to mental pathology are apparent. For instance, if an accused argues that his actions are not voluntary due to some compulsive commitment or irresistible impulse, why should he be constrained to confine this within the legal rigours of insanity?

In much of the case-law, the limits of these defences are recognised through the attempt to raise insanity, automatism, and absence of volition in the same situation. Why does this occur?

Particularly with insanity, the language of the defence, its reliance on strict proofs of cognition, and its notions of mental disease certainly seem to require modernisation and sophistication. Why have the courts and the legislature been reluctant to move in this direction? Is it recognition of the uncomfortable communication between legal and medical sciences in the courtroom?

PROBLEM

Examine the issues of public policy versus mental state in these three case scenarios, and argue for law reform where appropriate.

1   A young boy who is a passionate and committed anti-vivisectionist burns down an abattoir and claims that he couldn't resist the impulse to protect the cows that were to be slaughtered there.
2   The 'robotic' woman who says that she was acting like a machine at the time of the offence argues for the benefit of the insanity, automatism, and involuntary action defences.
3   A psychiatrist confirms that a young girl who poured lighting fluid on the floor of a shed and lit it did not appreciate the consequences of her action as well as might an adult of developed mental capacity.

ENGAGING THE PROBLEM

Conventionally the proof of criminal liability requires capacity and volition, preceding the coincidence of prohibited conduct and the criminal mental state. Each accused person has an individual mental state, or a unique excuse when it comes to denying volition, cognition, or comprehension. Yet these defences tend to force the debate about mental pathology or the loss of control into narrow categories. It is almost as if the law wants to create a notion of the ordinary insane person or the reasonable automaton.

In each problem the accused will seek recognition of his or her special circumstances and predispositions. To what extent does the law allow for this? How should it change to recognise the real limits of individual liability?

Also consider the logical difficulties in running any of these defences together.

ADDITIONAL RESOURCES

Brown, D., Farrier, D., Egger, S., and McNamara, L., *Criminal Laws*, Federation Press, Sydney, 2001, paras 6.2, 6.3, 6.4.

Chunn, D. and Menzies, R., 'Gender, Madness and Crime: The Reproduction of Patriarchal and Class Relations in a Psychiatric Court Clinic' (1990) 1 *Journal of Human Justice* 33.

Fisse, B., *Howard's Criminal Law*, Law Book Company, Sydney, 1992, pp. 106–112, 422–34, 447–75.

Fraser, D., 'Still Crazy After all These Years: A Critique of Diminished Responsibility', in Yeo, S. (ed.), *Partial Excuses to Murder*, Federation Press, Sydney, 1990, p. 112.

Hunter, J. and Bargen, J., 'Diminished Responsibility: "Abnormal" Minds, Abnormal Murderers and What the Doctor Said', in Yeo, S. (ed.), *Partial Excuses to Murder*, 1990, p. 125.

Ierace, M., 'Acting for the Intellectually Disabled Offender' (May 1987) *Law Society Journal* 42.

Chayna [1993] 66 A Crim R 178

R v. Falconer (1990) 65 ALJR 20

R v. McGarvie (1986) 5 NSWLR 270

M'Naghten (1843) 8 ER 718

Porter (1933) 55 CLR 182

Willgoss (1960) 105 CLR 295

A-G for SA v. Brown [1960] AC 432

Kemp [1957] 1 QB 399

Quick [1973] QB 910

R v. Bailey [1983] 1 WLR 760

Stapleton v. R (1952) 86 CLR 358

Windle [1952] 2 QB 826

Radford [1985] 42 SASR 266

R v. Joyce [1970] SASR 184

Hawkins (1994) 179 CLR 500

Topic 18

Factors affecting liability III

This topic concentrates on intoxication as a defence for the purpose of exploring the ways in which law, morality, and public policy intersect. In addition, the presumptions as to mental state and coincidence will be critically analysed in the context of the development of conditional approaches to intoxication as a defence. Broader issues of harm and the exacerbation of liability will also be considered. A further example of recent pressures to reform defences is in the case of diminished responsibility.

Intoxication

Much of the debate surrounding the status of intoxication as a defence is examined in detail in the Australian High Court decision of ***O'Connor*** (1980) 146 CLR 64. Here the nature of intoxication was discussed and its status as an excuse, or an aggravating factor for criminal liability, was put. The effect of intoxication on *mens rea*, both immediately prior to taking the intoxicant and at the time of the commission of the offence, was examined from the perspective of law and policy. But the most contentious of points is the decision related to voluntary intoxication, and whether any version of this precludes the availability of a negation of *mens rea* through intoxication as a defence.

The issue of intoxication and its effect on *mens rea* has never been treated by common law as a simple matter. From a strictly literal or logical position on determining criminal liability one would expect that if, like any other factor affecting liability (e.g. mistake), it were to negative the required *mens rea* or deny the facts said to constitute an *actus reus*, no offence could be proved by the prosecution. But as is the situation with 'prior fault', policy considerations put a brake on such a general approach.

Further, it seems that, at least from the ***Gallagher*** [1963] AC 49 position, one must consider a combined mental state, that is, the mental state possessed by the accused at the time of the commission of the offence, as influenced by his mental state just prior to taking the intoxicant. This shows how far public policy can override legal rationality, in that the requirement for coincidence is simply ignored when establishing criminal liability and considering the reckless ingestion of intoxicants.

Development of intoxication as a defence

The traditional common law position is that voluntary intoxication is no defence to a criminal charge. Now the courts take the view that if the accused's incapacitating condition is caused by some prior fault, he cannot escape liability on the ground of automatism or perhaps other involuntary conduct. However, where an offence charged requires proof of a subjective *mens rea*, the accused may still escape liability on the basis of a reduced or negatived mental state due to intoxication, voluntary or not. In English law, such negation may only occur where the mental state required is specific intent. Again, the reasoning behind such a distinction is public-policy oriented.

The present position on intoxication as a defence under statute law in jurisdictions such as New South Wales, which rejects the *O'Connor* position, seems to be that voluntary or self-induced intoxication is a defence to a criminal prosecution only if:

1   it causes such a disease of the mind as to bring the M'Naghten Rules into play; or
2   a specific intent is necessary as an essential element of the offence, and because of intoxication the accused lacks such specific intent.

As shown by Lord Denning in ***Attorney-General for Northern Ireland v. Gallagher*** [1963] AC 349 at 382, the defence of intoxication can be broken down into two categories: where the consequence of the intoxication is automatism, or where the intoxication brings about a fundamental mistake of fact. In the latter case the evidence of drunkenness usually leads to circumstantial evidence that the mistake was made. It is necessary to determine what effect the intoxication has on the required mental state, and whether that mental state is directed towards essential facts necessary for the prohibited conduct to be proved. If the accused honestly believed that the facts were such as not to form the *actus reus* of the offence, then the offence may not be proved.[166]

In the historically leading English case of ***Beard*** [1920] AC 479, it was said that intoxication is a defence only if it rendered the defendant incapable of forming the necessary *mens rea*. Proof of incapability was conclusive evidence that the *mens rea* was not present. However, it is arguably not a defence to show that, although he was perfectly capable of forming the *mens rea*, he did not do so on the occasion in question. Drunkenness is therefore highly relevant to refutation of the presumption of intent, reason, or volition which might otherwise arise from the accused's conduct.

If, however, the effect of the intoxication was not sufficient to negative the required mental state and the accused's drunkenness merely weakened the restraints and inhibitions which normally govern persons' conduct, this cannot be raised as a defence (e.g. 'he would not have behaved the way that he did but for the alcohol'). This would be so if the person had the necessary *mens rea* but the alcohol negatived or impaired his ability to judge between right or wrong, or even though in his drunken state, he found the impulse to act as he did to be irresistible.

---

166 This does not stand when considering mistake on which defences such as self-defence are founded, if the mistake is due to intoxication. See *O'Grady* (*supra*).

Intoxication and insanity

In terms of recent case development, the first exception to the original rule that drunkenness is no defence is where the intoxication produces a distinct disease of the mind so that the person is, under M'Naghten, insane. In common law it must be such that because of the disease, he did not know the nature and quality of his act, nor that it was wrong. As was said in **Quick's** case (*supra*), a mere malfunctioning of the mind due to intoxication does not constitute a disease of the mind. However, habitual intoxication can sometimes lead to permanent changes in the brain, leading to a state which could be considered insanity.

There are obvious difficulties in defining a disease of the mind, and distinctions between temporary insanity induced by drink and simple drunkenness are far from clear. The distinction becomes important in the case of someone who does not know that his act was wrong due to drunkenness. Only where this exception to the general rule applies will the accused's appreciation of the legal implications of his conduct become relevant. Ignorance of the wrongfulness of the conduct is irrelevant in the case of those who are sane but drunk.

In the case of *Beard* (*supra*) it was held that there is no defence where through self-induced intoxication the accused more readily gave way to some violent passion, or did not know that what he was doing was wrong. Beard raped his female victim and suffocated her. His defence at the time was that he was drunk. The House of Lords allowed the appeal of the prosecution against an acquittal. Constructive malice existed at the time of this decision and the felony/murder rule substituted a sufficient *mens rea* for rape for the *mens rea* required for murder. On the assertion that the intoxication was an arguable cause of insanity, the court took the view that once the disease of the mind is proved to result in insanity, the court does not distinguish as to how the insanity is caused. If, however, the evidence of intoxication does not imply a disease of the mind, or falls short of incapacity to form the necessary intent, then the question as to whether the defendant knew that his acts were wrong is irrelevant.

Interestingly, Lord Birkenhead did not seem, in his judgment, to limit the defence of intoxication to offences requiring specific intent. After commenting on this type of exception he went on to say that the proposition to be deduced from earlier authorities on drunkenness was not an exceptional rule applicable only to cases in which it is necessary to prove specific intent. Speaking generally, he said that a person cannot be convicted of a crime unless the '*mens* was *rea*'. The fact that Birkenhead was of the opinion that drunkenness could be a defence in some cases other than those requiring proof of specific intent has been ignored in subsequent cases.

These authorities do not see drunkenness merely as an application of the ordinary requirement of *mens rea*.

In *Attorney-General for Northern Ireland v. Gallagher (supra)* the judgments emphasised that if the accused was suffering from a disease of the mind insufficient to bring it within the M'Naghten Rules (for example, because it would never induce anything more than a lack of control) the fact that drunkenness exacerbated the disease at the material time would not make the defence of insanity open to the defendant. In this case the accused drank whisky before killing his wife, in order to give himself the courage to go through with the act. He formed the intent to kill her prior to intoxication.

As a defence Gallagher raised both exceptions to the general presumption of volition: that he was insane, and that drunkenness prohibited him from having the necessary intent. Evidence was presented that the accused was psychopathic and the condition could have been exaggerated by drink so that he would lose control.

The House of Lords held that their decision would have been different (not against the accused) if the psychopathy had been caused by the drink and was of itself sufficient to create a disease of the mind under the M'Naghten Rules. Even a plea of diminished responsibility could not be used when only supported by drunkenness itself.

Intoxication as a defence to offences requiring specific intent

Under English common law, and the provisions which apply in some regions, drunkenness forms a defence where specific intent is an element of the offence in question and the intoxication prevents the forming of that intent (see **Lipman** [1970] 1 QB 152).

In defence, Lipman declared that he had no knowledge of what he had done and that he had no wish to harm the woman, whom he had suffocated under the drug-induced belief that she was a snake. The trial judge directed the jury that it would suffice for manslaughter if the Crown proved that he:

> must have realised before he got himself in that condition that he did by taking the drug, that acts such as those which he subsequently performed and which resulted in death, were dangerous.

The appellant declared this to be a misdirection. He contended that the prosecution had to prove that the accused had intended to do acts likely to result in harm, or that he foresaw that harm would result from what he was doing.

The Court of Appeal said that evidence of the drug-taking was relevant to the question of intention for offences requiring specific intent. This does not mean that intoxication itself represents a defence, but that the state of intoxication may be incompatible with the actual offence charged and therefore negatives commission of the said offence.

In cases where the intoxication falls short of insanity, such a condition of recklessness, at the time of committing the offence causing death, can only have the effect of reducing the crime from murder to manslaughter. Manslaughter is not an offence requiring specific intent; therefore intoxication short of insanity provides no defence. Lipman may have been convicted of murder under the law of this region.

In **DPP v. Majewski** [1977] AC 443, the House of Lords confirmed the rule, obscurely stated in *Beard's* case, that evidence of self-induced intoxication negativing *mens rea* is a defence to a crime requiring specific intent, but not to a charge of any other crime.

In the case of crimes not requiring specific intent, the accused may be convicted if he was voluntarily intoxicated at the time of committing the offence, though he did not have the *mens rea* required in all other circumstances for that offence, and even though he was in a state of automatism at the time of committing the offence.

These authorities rest on definitions of specific and basic intent and the nature of the distinction. Majewski was charged with four counts of assault occasioning actual bodily harm and three counts of assaulting police in the exercise of their duty, resulting from a pub brawl. The defence was that at all material times the accused was acting under the influence of a combination of drink and drugs, and therefore did not know what he was doing.

The trial judge directed the jury that a self-induced state of intoxication was no defence to an alleged offence which didn't require specific intent.

Public policy protection was at the basis of the judgments in the House of Lords. The court relied on *Beard's* case. The recklessness in actually taking the intoxicants was deemed to be sufficient to satisfy the *mens rea* for assault. The drunkenness itself was an intrinsic and integral feature of the offence, the other element being the evidence of the unlawful use of force against the victim. Together they added up to criminal recklessness. The court reiterated that it was no excuse to suggest that self-induced intoxication had deprived the defendant of the ability to exercise self-control and to realise the possible consequences of what he was doing, or even to be conscious of what he was doing. The jury should be directed to ignore intoxication as raising a defence against offences of this character.

Lord Russell qualified Birkenhead's statement in *Beard's* case regarding drunkenness as a defence more generally, on the basis that

> specific intent cases are not restricted to those crimes in which the absence of specific intent leaves available a lesser crime embodying no need for specific intent, but embrace all specific intent offences, even though no alternative criminal charge is available.

Where self-induced intoxication is relied on by a person charged with a non-specific intent offence, the prosecution need not prove any intent or state of mind normally required for the offence, whatever the definition of the crime may say, nor indeed any voluntary act. The court said

> there is an implied qualification on every statute creating an offence, and specifying *mens rea* other than specific intent. The *mens rea* must be proved except, we must infer, where the accused was intoxicated through the voluntary taking of the drink or drugs.

In Australia, the High Court has emphasised the importance of the evidentiary question: whether the accused in his intoxicated state was not capable and did not form the required mental state for the offence. Decisions on the point such as **O'Connor** (1980) 54 ALJR 349 have relied more on intoxication as potentially denying the capacity to form the requisite *mens rea* rather than as forming a particular defence.

The artificiality of the definitions on which the English authorities rely is exaggerated by the difficult and unconvincing distinction between specific and basic intent. This is a distinction justified only in policy terms. Further, it is a distinction reiterated in recent legislative rejections of the common law position in certain jurisdictions in Australia (Western Australia, Queensland, Tasmania, New South Wales, and the Commonwealth). Reservations about the consequences of the *O'Connor* common law position have motivated some state and territory legislatures to reintroduce the specific intent distinction for the purposes of considering intoxication as a defence. For instance, in New South Wales, the position on self–induced intoxication is now delivered in s. 428 of the *Crimes Act*, which overturns the common law and takes the defence back to the *Majewski* position.

It would appear from the line of English common law authority, and the Australian legislative positions which ascribe to it, that in non-specific intent cases the prosecution does not have to prove that the act was voluntary, or that the lower level of *mens rea* was present, provided intoxication is deemed to stand as evidence of criminal recklessness.

Behind this interpretation of the effect intoxication has on capacity is the circuitous definition of specific intent, which relies for its justification on the availability of voluntary intoxication as a defence.

> A crime requiring specific intent means a crime where the evidence of voluntary intoxication negativing *mens rea* is a defence, and the designation of crimes requiring or not requiring specific intent is not based on principle but policy.[167]

---

167   J. Smith and B. Hogan, *Criminal Law*, Butterworths, London, 1992, p. 210.

As mentioned earlier, interestingly, most state legislatures in Australia have moved away from the common law position of *O'Connor*, to reintroduce the principle that voluntary intoxication is no defence except to offences requiring the proof of specific intent. However, recently the Victorian Law Reform Committee took a different view when approaching the options for law reform.[168] They rejected what they referred to as the *Majewski* model on the basis that the distinction between specific and basic intent is unconvincing, unnecessarily complex, and inconsistently applied, and that it would not act as an effective deterrent. In addition, it did not prevent, on policy grounds, juries considering the exculpatory effect of voluntary intoxication. Why should this be strangely restricted to the context of serious offences? The committee endorsed the fundamental legal principles of the proof of guilty intention and its coincidence with the prohibited conduct. It suggested that the model unnecessarily challenged these and warned (as did Hunt J in *Coleman*) that the assumption that self-induced intoxication amounts to criminal intent came dangerously close to the presumption that a person intends the natural consequences of his act.

The committee also criticised the options for:

- creating special offences of committing crimes while voluntarily intoxicated, and
- viewing intoxication only in terms of mental impairment.

It finally endorsed for Victoria the continued application of *O'Connor*, and confirmed its confidence in the jury by recommending that juries should hear all indictable offences if *O'Connor* is raised. They also recommended that the rules of evidence be modified so that evidence of prior criminal offences of the accused where self-induced intoxication was involved might be admitted.

NSW statutory position: The reformed jurisdictions?

The present statutory position in New South Wales is set out in s. 428 of the *Crimes Act*. Essentially this provides:

- a designation of offences of specific intent as those requiring 'an intention to cause a specific result' (s. 428B(1)). Subsection 2 lists a schedule of over 200 offences that are deemed to possess such a mental element.
- Evidence of the accused's intoxication (self-induced or not) at the time of the commission of the prohibited conduct may be taken into account when determining whether the accused had the intent to cause the specific

---

168   See Rush and Yeo 2000, pp. 597–614.

result necessary in offences requiring specific intent (s. 428C(1)). Such evidence may not be taken into account where, prior to becoming intoxicated, the accused had resolved to do the conduct, or became intoxicated to strengthen his or her resolve to do the conduct (subsection 2).

- In relation to basic intent offences, self-induced intoxication may not be taken into account, whereas involuntary intoxication may be relevant to the determination of the offence (s. 428D).
- Where self-induced intoxication is used as part of an acquittal of murder it may not be taken into account during a subsequent determination of the charge of manslaughter (s. 428E).
- When determining the mental state of the accused person as against that of what the reasonable person would have done, the reasonable person is not to be given the personal characteristic of intoxication (cf. *Coleman*) (s. 428F).
- Self-induced intoxication cannot be taken into account when determining that the criminal conduct of the accused was voluntary or otherwise (s. 428G). However, the person is not responsible for the conduct if it resulted from intoxication that was not self-induced.
- The common law on the effect of intoxication on criminal liability is specifically abolished (s. 428H).

Involuntary drunkenness

Where drunkenness is not self-induced or where it results from the taking of a bona fide prescribed drug (see **Hardie** (*supra*)), the *Majewski* test will not apply. If the accused does or omits to do something so that his intoxication is foreseeable, then the results may be seen as voluntary.

Where the accused is involuntarily drunk, he is not limited by the rules applying to the defences associated with voluntary intoxication. Thus he has the defence of non-insane automatism, or if he were not an intoxicated automaton, then his drunkenness prevented him from having the necessary *mens rea* for the offence, whatever category of prohibited conduct is required by it.

Smith and Hogan draw the 'only safe' conclusion that 'crime requiring specific intent' means a crime where the evidence of voluntary intoxication negativing *mens rea* is a defence and the designation of crimes requiring or not requiring specific intent is not based on principle but on policy.

Under NSW law it is now no use for a person charged with a crime not requiring specific intent, who claims that he did not have the required *mens rea*, to support this defence with evidence that he had been drinking or had taken drugs. By doing so he relieves the Crown of the duty of proving beyond reasonable doubt that he had the required mental state. *Mens rea* ceases to be relevant.

Majewski has been held to be inapplicable where a statute expressly provided that a particular belief shall be a defence to a charge. In ***Jaggard v. Dickinson*** [1980] 3 All ER 716, the defendant had a friend who had invited her to treat his house as if it were his own. When drunk, the defendant went to a house she thought was his but in fact belonged to another person, who barred her way. To gain entry the defendant broke windows and damaged curtains. Charged with criminal damage, she relied on a section of the relevant Act which gave her a lawful excuse if she believed that the person entitled to consent to the damage would have done so had he known the circumstances. D said she believed that the owner would have so consented. Even though the offence itself was not one requiring a specific intent (to which her drunkenness would not have formed a defence by negativing the relevant recklessness involved in damaging the property of another), it was held that she could nevertheless rely on it to explain what would otherwise have been inexplicable and to give colour to her evidence on the state of her belief. This was not the same thing as using drunkenness to rebut the inference of intention or recklessness (thought the court), but in fact it was, from the point of view of logic. This case may be viewed as anomalous, in the light of the common law on intoxication, because the court refused to raise any caveat concerning drunken inducement over an honestly held, but perhaps unjustified, belief.

Diminished responsibility

Diminished responsibility is a matter in mitigation (from murder to manslaughter) which has developed in English and Australian law in recognition of the narrow interpretive limitations inherent in the law on insanity. In Australia only New South Wales and the ACT recognise the defence in legislation. Some states, such as Victoria, have preferred to give judges the power to impose sentences other than life for murder rather than countenance a questionable defence of diminished responsibility.

Diminished responsibility in Australia has been moving closer to the proofs of insanity in response to criticisms of its liberal interpretation by the courts.[169] Until recent law reform, in New South Wales for instance, diminished responsibility (s. 23A of the *Crimes Act*) required that the accused at the time of causing the death was suffering from an abnormality of the mind that substantially impaired his mental responsibility for his act. This could be caused by retarded development or disease and it was for the accused to prove, usually through the presentation of medical evidence.[170]

---

169 See *R v. Chayna* (1993) 66 A Crim R 178.
170 The case-law debate developed over what constituted abnormality of the mind. *Purdy* followed *Byrne*.

Following the report of the NSW Law Reform Commission on Partial Defences to Murder (1997), abnormality of the mind was redefined and its causes specified. Substantial impairment of mental responsibility had to be established and the process for proving this was tightened up. Now, under s. 23 A, the abnormality of the mind must arise out of an underlying condition and lead to fundamental impairment of judgment and cognition similar to that required for establishing insanity. Now evidence of opinion that the impairment was so substantial as to warrant liability for murder being reduced to manslaughter is no longer admissible. Nor can intoxication and its effects be recognised for the purposes of this section. The onus is on the accused to prove the excuse. Underlying condition means a pre-existing mental or psychological condition, not of a transitory kind.

CONTEXT OF THE PROBLEM

Much of the pressure for law reform in the area of intoxication as a defence has come out of the fear of the 'drunkards' charter', which was seen by some as the consequence of the *O'Connor* decision. Those who have challenged and rejected *O'Connor* do so either because of a fundamental distrust of the jury in assessing the evidence, or the moral perspective that intoxication should exacerbate rather than exculpate liability.

The logical place of intoxication and its impact on questions of mental states in liability has been sacrificed on the altar of public policy. The distinction between specific and basic intent, crucial to certain 'reform' positions on the defence, is ambiguous and unconvincing; its application inconsistent. However, it remains a persuasive limitation on the availability of intoxication as a challenge to the establishment of a criminal mental state.

For diminished responsibility, the hurdle has been raised in recent reforms so that proof of the defence now approaches the constraints of insanity. The distrust of medical discourse in the setting of the trial is also evidenced in these reforms.

PROBLEM

1 You are a District Court judge writing up your sentences for two cases recently heard by you. The first was a child neglect case where the accused father admitted that, due to depression and regular and severe drinking bouts following the death of his young wife, he had failed to care for his baby son adequately. As a consequence of neglect the baby died. The second case was one where a famous footballer with a serious drinking problem returned home one evening heavily intoxicated and threw his wife down the stairs. She died of injuries sustained in the fall. How will you entertain the issue of intoxication as it is raised in either case?

2   You are the defence lawyer for a police officer who is suffering from post-traumatic stress disorder. He recently witnessed the brutal killing of his partner of 15 years. Following this event he has been seeing a psychiatrist and the police service psychologist. One evening while on a routine street patrol, your client saw a person who looked remarkably like the killer of his partner. Almost without thinking your client drew his service revolver and fired, killing the suspect. Your client has since been charged with murder. If diminished responsibility were available, how would you construct the defence?

ENGAGING THE PROBLEMS

The issue in Problem 1 is whether in your jurisdiction voluntary intoxication is available as a defence to the offences charged. If it is not, then the very admission of intoxication may remove the onus on the prosecution to prove *mens rea*.

In Problem 2, are the conditions for diminished responsibility fulfilled and is the issue of identity such as to deny this defence? What is it that has to be established by the defence in order to shift the onus back to the prosecution regarding the proof of a criminal mental state? Is mistake here an issue?

ADDITIONAL RESOURCES

Brown, D., Farrier, D., Egger, S., and McNamara, L., *Criminal Laws*, Federation Press, Sydney, 2001, paras 6.4, 6.6.

Fisse, B., *Howard's Criminal Law*, Law Book Company, Sydney, 1992, pp. 435–46.

NSW Law Reform Commission, *Partial Defences to Murder: Diminished Responsibility: Report 82*, 1997.

O'Connor, D. and Fairall, D., *Criminal Defences*, Butterworths, Sydney, 1996, Chapter 12.

Rush, P. and Yeo, S., *Criminal Law Sourcebook*, Butterworths, Sydney, 2000, pp. 580–614.

Crimes Act 1900 (NSW), ss. 23A, 428A

DPP v. Beard [1920] AC 479

Attorney-General for Northern Ireland v. Gallagher [1963] AC 349

R v. Lipman [1970] 1 QB 152

DPP v. Majewski [1977] AC 443

R v. O'Connor (1980) 54 ALJR 349

R v. Martin (1984) 58 ALJR 217

Gittens [1984] QB 698

Jones (1986) 22 A Crim R 42

Tandy (1989) 1 WLR 350

Byrne [1960] 2 QB 396

Desouza (unreported, NSWSC, August 1995)

Terry [1961] 2 QB 314

Topic 19

Factors affecting liability IV

Further into the discussion of defences, this topic examines the issues of consent and mistake. Both reveal much about the significance of beliefs on the part of the accused, mistaken or otherwise. Consent can be connected to mistake through an honest and reasonable belief in facts which would deny the necessary mental state and the criminal conduct. Therefore, in dealing with consent and mistake we are considering factors which may challenge the establishment of criminal liability, both as to the prohibited conduct and to the criminal mental state. Rather than acting as defences, claims of consent or mistake either deny essential elements of the offence charged, or challenge the facts on which the offence is based.

Consent and mistake also suggest that the accused's interpretation of the facts may be crucial to the determination of liability. This has opened up considerable debate concerned with whether consent or mistake, to be entertained in law, are to be measured in a purely subjective sense, or whether the 'ordinary person test' has a place in tempering any recourse to the consent or mistake defence by an otherwise culpable accused.

Consent and mistake rely on establishing an honest belief in their existence. The reasonableness of that belief (in common law) is at least a crucial evidentiary factor in determining whether the mistaken belief or belief in consent was honestly held.

Mistake may form the basis for a reliance on other defence issues such as self-defence.[171] Mistake and consent may be answers to liability when they are not at issue and when public policy allows for them. Consent, in particular, depends on mistake in order to claim reliance on a missing element in the offence.

Consent

Uncontested consent as a 'defence'

A claim of consent relies on the victim having agreed to the conduct in question, and also being in a position to agree.

Consent is conditional on:

- the victim having the capacity to consent;
- the victim's consent being actual; and
- the courts allowing consent to have an influence the offence as a matter of public policy.

---

171 Note, however, that in some jurisdictions such as New South Wales mistake induced through intoxication will not allow for self-defence. Here the intoxication is not taken to be a characteristic of the ordinary person.

Capacity to consent

In most sexual offences, young people under a certain age cannot give valid consent. Nor can they give valid consent if they do not understand the nature of an act.[172]

Re D (A minor) [1984] AC 778 was a case in which the court held that parents could not give effective consent on behalf of their mentally abnormal child for an operation which is not for the benefit of the patient. The mother in this case wished to have her daughter sterilised, and even though she was motivated by a concern for the girl, the court was opposed to extending her vicarious right of consent in this case.

Validity of consent

Consent may be a defence to a charge of assault if it is valid. However, a person cannot always give valid consent to bodily harm falling short of death. It would seem, following the case of *Donovan* [1934] All ER Rep 207, that the ordinary person cannot consent to the infliction upon himself of harm which would constitute or exceed bodily harm. There are standard exceptions (well accepted) to this rule (e.g. in lawful sports). These are seen as necessarily different from the sexual assault cases. The principle governing the exceptions relates to questions of rules and public policy.

Public policy

There are 'well established exceptions' to the rule that a valid consent will not be given to an act likely or intended to cause bodily harm, for example in lawful sports such as wrestling

In certain cases it is the rules of the game rather than the nature of the harm or the public policy governing the context of the assault that differentiate between situations where consent may be given and where it may not. *Billinghurst* [1978] Cr LR 558 was a case where the question of acts done outside the rules of the game was addressed. The court here evinced the general opinion that lawful sports are 'socially approved of'; they are 'manly diversions' that require strength and skill, and provide an acceptable recreational outlet. In this case the jury was directed that rugby players consent to such force as can reasonably be expected during the game if the force was used in the course of play (as opposed to, say, a punch after the play had been stopped). Such consent could be a defence even to a serious injury, such as a fracture of the jaw. It all depended on the nature of the game and the facts surrounding the assault.

In certain situations the court will deny the validity of consent on the basis that to do otherwise might be construed as condoning the conduct in question. In *R v. Brown* (*supra*), the House of Lords held that it was not in

---

172 See *Burrell v. Harmer* [1976] Cr LR 165, in relation to tattooing.

the public interest to condone the infliction of bodily harm for no good reason—and sexual satisfaction was not a good reason. Since the appellants had admitted to the infliction of injuries which were neither transient nor trifling, the question of consent was immaterial.

An apparent consent will be treated as unreal and hence no defence when:

- the victim is very young and unable to comprehend the nature of the act committed;
- the victim's apparent consent is procured under duress; or
- a person, apparently consenting, is induced to do so by fraud as to the nature of the act, or the identity of the accused (he may know the nature of the act but be mistaken as to a collateral fact).

Contested consent in terms of sexual assault
As noted earlier, consent may be an issue in both the prohibited conduct and the required criminal mental state, for example in sexual assault.

Mental element in sexual assault
The *mens rea* for sexual assault requires:

- an intent to have non-consensual sexual intercourse, and
- belief or knowledge that the person is not consenting.

The relevance of the **Morgan** decision on honest mistaken belief is now challenged in light of Brennan J's suggestion in **He Kaw Teh** that for protection of the victim in the circumstances of rape it might be necessary to require that the belief in consent was reasonably held. Consideration of reasonableness in relation to satisfying the evidence of honest belief is now preferred, but should juries be so directed?

Recklessness as to consent in sexual assault is subjective. **Kitchener** (1993) 29 NSWLR 696 confirms that a failure to advert to whether consent was present or not may be sufficient for recklessness here.

Prohibited conduct in sexual assault

- The *actus reus* for sexual assault is non-consensual sexual intercourse. The absence of consent on the part of the victim is embedded in the *actus reus*; therefore it is an 'integral rather than an attendant' element.[173]

In recent law reform, consent and the nature of coercion have been restructured. Now (in New South Wales for instance) it is not essential for

---

173 See Brennan J in *He Kaw Teh* (*supra*).

the prosecution to rely on any evidence from the victim as to her or his resistance in order to establish coercion. Consent can still be denied even where the compliance of the victim seems to be submission.

Both the case-law and legislation in certain jurisdictions recognise that consent induced by fraud or mistake may not vitiate the offence. For the proof of non-consent the conventional 'fresh complaint' requirement has now been heavily qualified.[174] Further, the warning against uncorroborated evidence of complaint by the victim has been abolished.[175] The cross-examination of a victim about her or his prior sexual history has also been forbidden, with certain limited qualifications.[176]

In **M**, the accused attempted to introduce evidence that the complainant was given to sexual fantasies, which was outside the exceptions contemplated in s. 409B of the *Crimes Act* (NSW) and as such could not be admitted by the trial judge. The appeal court held that the section created a blanket prohibition against which certain exceptions could stand to protect the accused, but even then it was not guaranteed that the raising of such exceptions would lead to their admission. The double discretion exists that in addition to adjudication on the exceptions and their application, the judge must decide that the probative value of the evidence in question outweighs the prejudicial value of the admission. This creates an additional discretion to exclude such evidence, and its exercise follows the limitation only of the exceptions as laid down. In this case the conviction of a father for the sexual assault on his 13-year-old daughter was overturned by the High Court on the basis of the appropriate behaviour of a reasonable complainant.

Connection between consent and mistake

Where there is an honest (and reasonable) mistake as to the nature of the act forming the basis of the consent, then the mistaken facts will be accepted as fact for the determination of the consent.

In **Williams** [1923] 1 KB 340, the defendant was a singing master who persuaded a female pupil to submit to intercourse under the pretence that it would improve her breathing. His conviction of rape was affirmed. The conviction accorded with the principle that if the woman knew nothing about the nature of the act and thought that her instructor was doing something merely to improve her lungs, then her consent could in no way vitiate the sexual intercourse. If on the other hand she understood what was occurring and was willing to be persuaded that one of the benefits of the act of sex was an improvement in breathing, then she did not make a mistake as to the

---

174 See, for instance, *Crimes Act* (NSW), s. 405B2.
175 See *Evidence Act*, s.164.
176 See, for instance, the *Crimes Act* NSW, s. 409B.

nature of the act even though in her innocence she may not have realised the man's motives had nothing to do with singing. Since the court did not enquire into that question, the decision might be viewed as unsound.[177]

Mistake

In *He Kaw Teh (supra)* Brennan J. referred to the 'defence' of 'honest and reasonable belief in the existence of facts which, if true, would make his act innocent'. Brennan saw this as raising two issues: (1) whether it can apply to circumstances that, on a proper construction of the statute creating the offence, are an integral part of the act involved (e.g. possession of drugs) and (2) whether it is a defence that the prosecution must disprove. This is bearing in mind that it is up to the defence to establish reasonable belief in mistaken facts. Having done this, then the ultimate onus is on the prosecution to prove the relevant *mens rea* of the offence against the allegation of mistaken belief. If the court finds the belief in mistaken facts to be unreasonable then the belief may be inconsistent with knowledge but may provide the required *mens rea* for the offence (as in recklessness for sexual assault, or possession in a drugs offence). Absence of an honest and reasonable mistaken belief can be the mental state applicable to existing circumstances, but only if the requirement of knowledge is excluded.

The significance of objective determinations of states of mind is well illustrated when mistake of fact is raised. In the common law after ***Proudman v. Dayman*** (1941) 67 CLR 526, and particularly in those offences where the prosecution claims a strict liability interpretation, the courts have required proof beyond reasonable doubt that the accused was not acting under a genuine (honest) and reasonable mistake of fact.

Mistake and its effect on strict liability offences

Again in *He Kaw Teh (supra)* Brennan J indicated that once the accused has successfully raised that he had reasonable grounds for believing in the mistaken facts, he is not required to prove his mental state as an excuse. This is up to the prosecution to disprove. Knowledge and mistaken belief cannot coexist in respect of a crucial fact or element of the offence.

> It is therefore necessary to determine what state of mind applies to a particular element of a statutorily defined offence once it appears that some mental state is applicable. The absence of an honest and reasonable but mistaken belief can be the mental state applicable to existing circumstances, but only if the prima facie requirement of knowledge is excluded.[178]

---

177 See *Papadimitropoulos v. R* (1957) 98 CLR 249 (fraud to induce consent based on the identity of the accused).

178 Brennan J at 241.

Even if knowledge as to circumstances does not have to be proved in order to establish the necessary *mens rea* of the offence, if an exculpatory belief about the circumstances would make the defendant's act innocent, then mistake is a defence as to circumstances. The required *mens rea* is to be determined by reference to the wording of the statute, and its subject matter.

Gibbs CJ in the same case recognised that an honest and reasonable mistake of fact will be a ground of exculpation in which actual knowledge is not required as an element of an offence. Even where the statute excludes the necessity for positive knowledge on the part of the accused, honest and reasonable mistake of fact will still provide an excuse. This creates a middle ground between absolute liability and requiring full *mens rea*.[179]

Mistake of fact as to consent in sexual assault

In determining the relevance of mistake here it is necessary to look at the elements of the offence towards which the mistake is directed. If the issue is whether the defendant was mistaken as to the victim's consent, then it is a subjective determination as to the mental state required for the offence (intent to have non-consensual sexual intercourse, or subjective recklessness as to consent). Again, Brennan J in **He Kaw Teh** observed that it needs to be established whether non-consent is an integral part of the offence or an attendant circumstance. If the latter, should the accused be liable to conviction unless he has reasonable grounds for believing and does believe that the victim consented? Or should he be required to *know* that the victim did not consent? Ultimately this is a public policy question.

CONTEXT OF THE PROBLEM

The division on policy between consent in sport and in situations of sexual gratification is highlighted in these two problems. But the limitations on the availability of consent in both situations may go beyond public policy concerns.

Also, the relationship between consent and mistaken fact may challenge the proof of the necessary mental state. But what is the nature of the mistake and is it relevant to the proof of liability?

Students should not feel bound by certain authorities that may demonstrate a policy approach differing from the one that might prevail in your jurisdiction today. How might you construct arguments around unhelpful authorities? What issues of contemporary social significance might you rely on to persuade an appeal court in Australia today?

---

179 NB: Also reasonable excuse provisions such as in the NSW *Summary Offences Act*, s. 4.

PROBLEM

Discuss the issue of criminal liability in the following scenarios.

1 Peter is a professional cricketer. He has been a fast bowler for the state team for the past 18 months. He realises that his present income and his chance of a test appearance rest with his ability to bowl as fast as possible. In an effort to achieve maximum pace for his deliveries he has developed a reckless bowling style where at least one out of every three balls hits the batsman and not the bat. On several occasions this has led to the injury of his opponents.

    Worried about his liability, Peter asked the team manager what his position was if he injured someone. The manager said that Peter was in the clear, no matter what injury he caused, because the players consented to the danger. On the basis of this advice Peter started targeting the occasional ball at delicate parts of the body. As a result he broke the pelvis of an opponent and was charged with assault causing actual bodily harm.

2 Brian and David are members of a sado-masochist sauna club. They engage in acts of physical injury for sexual gratification. Each and every member of the sauna has to sign a release taking full responsibility for his or her injuries and declaring actual consent. All members of the sauna must be over 18 and 'of sound mind and body'.

    Another sauna member was under 18, unknown to the rest of the sauna participants. His parents found out about the activities at the sauna, and as a result Brian and David have been charged with an aggravated assault.

ENGAGING THE PROBLEM

Particular issues to consider are:

- whether consent is actual, informed and available;
- whether the mistake claimed is honest and reasonable;
- whether consent was within or beyond some accepted policy guidelines;
- whether consent is affected by issues such as age;
- who are the parties with a legitimate interest in the consent?;
- whether a defence can be provided by a third party; and
- what is the actual mental state required in respect of the offences to be charged and with whom do proof requirements rest?

ADDITIONAL RESOURCES

Bronitt, S., 'Rape and Lack of Consent' (1992) 16(5) *Criminal Law Journal* 289.

Bronitt, S. and McSherry, B., *Principles of Criminal Law*, Law Book Company, Sydney, 2001, Chapter 6.

Brown, D., Farrier, D., Egger, S., and McNamara, L., *Criminal Laws*, Federation Press, Sydney, 2001, paras 4.7.3–4.7.5, 4.4.1, 7.4, 7.5.

Fisse, B., *Howard's Criminal Law*, Law Book Company, Sydney, 1992, pp. 147–52, 176–80, 499–539.

O'Connor, D. and Fairall, D., *Criminal Defences*, Butterworths, Sydney, 1996, Chapters 3 and 5.

Wayne, V., 'Rape and the Unconscionable Bargain' (1992) 16(5) *Criminal Law Journal* 94.

He Kaw Teh v. R (1985) 59 ALJR 620

R v. Bonnor [1957] VLR 227

Pallante v. Stadiums Pty Ltd [1976] VLR 331

R v. Donovan [1934] 2 KB 498

R v. Brown [1993] 2 WLR 556

R v. Linekar [1995] 2 WLR 237

TOPIC 20

PROPERTY OFFENCES: DISHONEST ACQUISITION I

This topic discusses the law relating to the basic offence of larceny. In this respect, while touching on codification issues in passing, the discussion will have more relevance to the common law jurisdictions.[180] Is possession or ownership the relevant concept underlying this body of law? How do these two concepts differ? How can possession be distinguished from 'appropriation'? What doctrines have the courts developed in order to plug 'gaps' in the original legal definition of larceny? What offences have the legislatures enacted in order further to address these 'gaps'? Why have such 'gaps' emerged? To what extent should borrowing without consent be criminalised?

Introduction

The scope of transactions and relations covered by the property area of criminal law is considerable. Property offences may range from simple transactions such as stealing from the pocket of another to complex and multifaceted frauds where various forms of finance are dishonestly dealt with by various individuals or legal entities at different stages of financial relationships. Unfortunately police and court attention has, until recently, been conventionally focused on single transaction and individual property offences rather than complex commercial fraud. As a result, the public at large has developed a rather unbalanced attitude to what is serious and socially harmful when it comes to property offences. This has been compounded by the fact that in certain property crimes the victims do not become aware of the offence until long after it has been perpetrated, and

---

180 The Victorian and ACT legislative changes in the area have adopted many of the innovations of the English Theft Act codification (see *Crimes (Theft) Act 1973* (Vic) and *Crimes (Amendmant) Act No. 4 1985* (ACT)). For a critical commentary on this see B. Fisse, *Howard's Criminal Law*, Sydney, Law Book Company, 1990, pp. 283–351. The Code states and territories retain many of the features of the common law of larceny, with some significant derivations such as the acceptance that 'taking and carrying away' may be continuing.

therefore the influence of criminal sanctions is diminished. In addition, the scope of the social harm of certain commercial frauds seems less immediate and threatening than housebreaking or robbery, and therefore the pressure for its policing and punishment seems more deflected.

Also, in contemporary commerce in Australia, the concept of property and relationships of ownership now go far beyond the crude dichotomy of real and personal property which informed the law on larceny. For example, electronic funds transfers now see both the nature and possession of property transformed in an instant with little regard for temporal or spatial limitations. The potential for fraud cannot be covered within the laws of larceny or even more modern concepts of theft, and poses a challenge for the law enforcement agencies, the courts, and law reform bodies.

Another interesting characteristic of property offences is their legislative history.[181] Theft has long been a concern of the criminal law and as the nature of commerce has diversified with time, so has the need to create new offences to meet the threat of unlawful financial and commercial activity. This has led to the piecemeal development of traditional larceny offences and the pressure to codify these as their nature and location become more problematic.

The structure of property offence legislation throughout Australia is rather fragmented, outdated, and inconsistent. In New South Wales, representative of an 'unreformed' common law jurisdiction, the police and the courts are required to address a range of specific offences such as types of larceny, deception, misrepresentation, robbery, housebreaking, fraud, and receiving stolen goods, in contrast to the Code states and territories (and in England) where this area of the criminal law is largely influenced by the generic offence of theft, and the law has been codified.

Property offences appear as a rather technical area of the law, depending as they do on a complex of definitions and fine legal distinctions. Unfortunately, one definition or distinction does not necessarily build on another, largely because of the piecemeal development of the law in this field.

Larceny

In practice, larceny[182] and theft mean the same thing, although their legal definitions may be distinctly different. Larceny is the traditional way of describing theft.

---

181 For a useful discussion of this see C. R. Williams, *Property Offences*, Law Book Company, Sydney, 1999.

182 In order to explore the law on larceny we draw on the legislative provisions of the NSW *Crimes Act* and consider the connections with English common law.

The common law of larceny as it still exists in most of the non-Code jurisdictions[183] of Australia has long been influenced by statutory modification. Most of the statute and code definitions are based on the common law as it existed in the old English *Larceny Acts*, and the interpretation of their terms therefore may depend on English case-law which now has no application in the United Kingdom.

Theft is committed as follows:[184]

> A person who steals, without the consent of the owner, fraudulently and without claim of right made in good faith, takes and carries away anything capable of being stolen with intent, at the time of such taking, permanently to deprive the owner thereof:
>
> Provided that a person may be guilty of stealing any such a thing notwithstanding that he has lawful possession thereof, if, being a bailee or part owner thereof, he fraudulently converts the same to his own use or to the use of any person other than the owner.

This definition is subscribed to in ***Illich v. R*** (1986) 162 CLR 231.

The expression 'takes' includes obtaining possession

- by any trick;[185]
- by intimidation;
- under a mistake on the part of the owner with knowledge on the part of the taker that possession has been so obtained; or
- by finding, where at the time of the finding the finder believes that the owner can be discovered by taking reasonable steps.

Taking must involve a trespass against the person in possession of the property, although that person may not be the owner (as in *Illich*). In addition it can involve taking property and contents, so in ***Garlett*** (1989) CLJ 13 at 16, the High Court held that there was an intent to steal where the accused took a taxi with the intent to keep any money found therein.

The expression 'carries away' involves the slightest movement with the intention permanently to deprive[186] and includes any removal of anything

---

183 Recognising the time at which the Queensland, Western Australian and Tasmanian Codes were drafted these still retain resonances of larceny. The Northern Territory Code and its offence of stealing in s. 209 is influenced by the *Theft Act* approach. The proposed Commonwealth Model Criminal Code, however, has recommended a *Theft Act* model (see S. Bronitt and B. McSherry, *Principles of Criminal Law*, Law Book Company, Sydney, 2000, Chapter 13).

184 The explanation in s. 116 of the *Crimes Act* that relates all larcenies back to the law of George IV.

185 See *R v. Ward* (1938) 38 SR (NSW) 308.

186 *Wallis v. Lane* [1964] VR 293.

from the place it occupies, but in the case of a thing attached to real property, only if it has been completely detached.[187] Property which has been abandoned cannot be stolen.[188]

The expression 'owner' includes any part owner, or person having possession or control of, or a special property in anything capable of being stolen. A person lawfully in possession of something cannot be guilty of a larceny.[189] For larceny, property must be taken without the consent of the owner.

The elements of the offence are therefore:

Prohibited conduct:

Anyone (1) without the consent of the owner (2) takes and carries away (3) anything capable of being stolen;

Mental state:

(4) fraudulently (5) without claim of right (6) with intent at the time of taking to permanently deprive.

Elements of the prohibited conduct for theft

Without the consent of the owner:

The absence of the owner's consent[190] is crucial for the common law offence of larceny. Consent may be express, implied, continuing, or conditional. For example, a person may have been given property for a specific purpose, such as where a person leaves his or her car at a garage for mechanical repairs and the mechanic subsequently steals it. This situation would be covered by the statutory provisions which govern the rights and duties of a 'bailee' (a person who holds property belonging to another on condition that he or she deal with the goods according to specific conditions).

In *Croton* (*supra*) the accused had formed an association with a woman to whom he was not married. He did not mention to her that he was already married. They made an arrangement that they would live off his wages and bank her wages for a honeymoon or a house. A joint bank account was opened by them for the purpose. The accused took a large amount of money out of the account without her knowledge and opened up another account in his name. He was convicted of larceny for this. The High Court allowed the appeal on the basis that the money was not stolen from the victim because at the relevant time it was not in her possession, and it was not stolen from the bank because it transferred possession to the accused. Regardless of whether he obtained money by deceit, a chose in action (which is the debt owed by the bank once the money has actually been

---

187 *R v. White* (1904) 21 WN (NSW) 104.
188 *R v. White* (1912) 7 Cr App R 266.
189 *Illich* (*supra*).
190 See *Croton v. R* (1967) 117 CLR 376.

deposited) cannot be stolen. At the time she parted with the physical money, the victim had agreed to this.

Consent must be actual, and if it is implied, the nature of the implication may be limited to a certain purpose or under certain conditions. In **Kennison v. Daire** (1986) 160 CLR 129, a customer of a bank in South Australia was convicted of larceny by virtue of having dishonestly drawn money from an automatic teller machine at a time when it was off-line from the computerised account system. This the customer did at a time when he did not have a corresponding credit balance in his account (in fact he had closed the account). The High Court upheld the conviction, rejecting the argument that the bank had consented to the withdrawal of cash via its machine. The machine, being non-human, was incapable of giving such consent. The facts did not otherwise disclose any consent, implied or otherwise, on the part of the bank. In these circumstances the bank never intended ownership in the money to pass via its machine or by any other means to persons not entitled to it.

There must be an owner of the goods before the person can be convicted of theft.

Theft by finding may arise where a person finds goods that are apparently lost, and takes them away for his own use. At the time of the taking, the accused must believe that the true owner could be found by taking reasonable steps, but intends to keep the property from the true owner. For instance, in **MacDonald** [1983] 1 NSWLR 729 it was determined that such a belief can be inferred from the facts of the finding. The intention to keep the goods from the owner must exist at the time of taking. This intention can arise at any time during a continuous trespass. For example, a decision to keep a wallet after the finder later looks at it and discovers it contains money was the situation in **Mingal v. McCammon** [1970] SASR 82.

In *MacDonald* (*supra*) the court held that if at the time the finder takes possession he believes that the owner can be found, larceny has been committed. In inferring the finder's belief the jury can take into account not only what the finder does in relation to the goods but also what he doesn't do that might be consistent with the acts of an honest person. In determining whether the defendant took reasonable steps to find the owner, it is important to consider the factors from which the necessary intent to permanently deprive may be inferred. These are narrowly drawn: for example, was the owner known to the finder? Were there identifying marks on the article?

In **Thompson v. Nixon** [1966] 1 QB 103 it was confirmed that it is necessary, even for larceny by finding, that the *actus reus* and the *mens rea* of larceny should be contemporaneous at the time of finding. Therefore if the accused at the time of finding does not think that by taking reasonable steps the owner can be found, then he does not commit larceny.

There may also be a problem where an owner consents to the taking of his or her property because of a mistake as to the identity of the taker.

The coincidence between the taking without consent and the intention to permanently deprive has been assisted by the presumption of continuing trespass against the owner's property as set out in **Riley's** case [1853] 169 ER 674. In this case the accused had driven a flock of lambs from a field, supposing all of them to be his. One of the lambs was in fact the property of another farmer and had joined the flock without the accused's knowledge. The next day the accused discovered the additional lamb and decided to sell it as if it was his. His conviction was upheld even though the trespass against the victim's property, and therefore the taking, was complete once the flock was driven from the field. This was also a time at which the accused did not have the intention to permanently deprive the owner of his property. The court here proposed the fiction that the accused continued to be a trespasser from the time the lamb left the field and until the lamb returned to the rightful owner, if ever it did. At the time the accused decided to sell the lamb he became a thief. It should be remembered that the *Riley* principle only applies in situations where the original taking was trespassory, and not where the property originally was transferred with the consent of the owner. In the Code jurisdictions where taking and carrying away is seen as continuing, such a 'legal fiction' is no longer necessary.

In **Ruse v. Read** [1949] 1KB 377, the accused took the victim's bicycle to his home, kept it there overnight, and the next morning, after removing the dynamo and the pump, consigned it to himself to await collection at the railway station. There was evidence that when he took the bicycle he had been too drunk to form the intention to steal but the court found it unnecessary to go into this. Whatever his state of mind, the accused's original taking was a tort against the victim, which his subsequently manifested intention to steal converted into larceny.

Takes and carries away

In **Walsh** (1824) 168 ER 1166, the accused was charged with larceny of a bag from the boot of a coach. He had succeeded in only lifting the bag from the floor of the boot, but not removed it outside, when he was detected and dropped the bag. The mere lifting from the floor was held to be sufficient for taking.

Difficulties arise with the proof of the 'taking' component again if the accused is in lawful possession of the goods.

Sometimes determining when taking and carrying away occurs may be difficult (for example, taking products from shelves in a self-service supermarket—what difference is there between this and shoplifting?). Mistake is also an important issue when examining taking and carrying away. What about the situation where due to some prevailing mistake on the part of the owner of the property or her agent, the accused is presented with possession of the goods, allowing him to carry these away—apparently minus the 'taking' component? For instance, in **Middleton** (1873) LR 2CCR 38, the accused presented his savings passbook and a withdrawal form for 10 shillings at the post office, the total credit to his name in the account being 11 shillings. The counter clerk confused the accused's withdrawal with another and wrote 8 pounds against his account book, and placed the money on the counter. The accused realised the error but said nothing and took the money away. Here a majority held that the conviction should stand because at the time the accused took the money from the counter, he knew that it had been placed there for him by mistake. The law was established that there was a taking sufficient for larceny if at the time the accused received the property he knew that the victim was acting under the influence of a mistake. The difference here between the law as it had existed up until then on larceny by trick, and the law on false pretences, was that for larceny by trick it was not required that the mistake should have been induced by the accused. This was the first major decision that larceny had occurred where the property had passed voluntarily from the victim without the inducement of the accused.

The misdelivery cases also provide an interesting dimension of this element of the offence. In **Hudson** [1943] KB 458, the Ministry of Food intended to send a cheque to someone whose surname was Hudson, but by mistake made it payable simply to 'Mr Hudson'. Presumably the same mistake was made in addressing the envelope in which the cheque was sent out, for the letter was delivered to the defendant, a 'J. Hudson' who lived near enough to the actual person intended to receive the cheque that their addresses might be confused. There was no indication in the facts whether the accused should have known the cheque was not for him. Three weeks later the accused returned the cheque to the ministry, informing them that his initial was J. The cheque was duly reissued and the accused opened a bank account in order to deposit the cheque. The Court of Criminal Appeal upheld his conviction for larceny. The court took as irrelevant all events prior to the time that the accused knew that the cheque was not for him, and yet did not deal with the difficult issue that nothing that he did thereafter could be considered a 'taking and carrying away' in the traditional legal sense. There seemed to be situations of both larceny and obtaining by false pretences here, depending on the time the cheques were sent to the accused, and these are alternative offences and cannot stand together. The court did not seem to indicate at what stage the larceny occurred. By implication here the case principle might be that larceny occurs when, owing to the mistake of the victim, the accused innocently receives property to which he is not entitled, which he converts to his own use or that of anyone other than the owner after he discovers the true state of affairs. This is similar to the rule about continuing wrongful possession.

In **Moynes v. Cooper** [1956] 1 QB 439, the accused asked for an advance on wages from his employer, which he was given. Later he was paid the full week's wage, the earlier advance not having been deducted. When he opened the pay packet and realised the mistake he appropriated the full sum. The court in deliberation distinguished *Middleton*, where the accused knew of the error as soon as he received the wrong sum. Here, at the only time at which there could be said to have been a physical taking, the accused had an innocent state of mind. Therefore he did not take the money within the meaning of the definition of larceny. *Hudson* was also distinguished: in that case neither the cheque nor the envelope was intended for Hudson and in that case he took it knowing the taking to be without the consent of the victim. But these grounds of distinction are not necessarily convincing, as they do not go to the heart of the matter.

In **Illych v. R** (1986) 162 CLR 110, the appeal dealt with a definition of theft where a fraudulent taking or conversion would qualify as an element of the offence. Again the central issue was whether the handing over of property from the victim to the accused under the influence of the victim's mistake could be considered as non-consensual because of this mistake. This was another case of the overpayment of earnings the accused came to know about subsequent to the time of payment. In quashing the conviction the court said that the mistaken payment did not prevent the property passing to the accused. He did not fraudulently take it nor did he subsequently fraudulently convert it. A person cannot take or convert what is his or her own. The English authorities determined that mistake would vitiate consent provided the mistake is of a 'sufficiently fundamental type'. The identity of the transferee, or of the thing delivered or of the amount, would account for such a mistake. There was no such mistake here of a fundamental enough kind that would prevent property from passing. The court stated that what was being attempted here was to criminalise a dishonest failure to return property in excess of the accused's legal entitlement.

Anything capable of being stolen

At common law for larceny only moveable, tangible things were capable of being stolen. The property had to be capable of being taken and carried away. Land and things attached to land could not be stolen unless the chattel had 'been completely detached'. Common property such as wild animals and game also could not be stolen. The issue of value and possession is again important here. Therefore animals in the custody, control, or possession of some person may be stolen.[191]

However, one of the biggest problems with 'modernising' the definition of what could be stolen is what do you do with intangible things such

---

191 *Gadd* [1911] QWN 31—where the property was bees.

as shares, wills, credit, electricity, rights to land, computer time, etc. A large number of specific offences in the regional legislation deal with these sorts of intangibles along with chattels such as fences, trees and plants, and otherwise 'common' property such as fish and cattle. For general larceny the property must be tangible and thus information cannot be the object of a general larceny.[192]

Fraudulently

The word 'fraudulently' has caused great difficulty in the law of larceny. For instance, if an accused obtains money by false pretences, he does not commit the offence unless he does so with intent to defraud. Usually the intent to defraud will consist of an intention to steal, but not always. With false pretences it is the 'obtaining' of the money which is crucial and not so much what the defendant does with it afterwards. There is an intent to defraud if a defendant intends to deal with the victim's property in a manner inconsistent with the details of the representation. Thus in **Denning** [1962] NSWLR 175, the accused received deposits from a number of people on the understanding that he would obtain finance for the building of dwelling houses, provide the land on which the dwelling houses were to be built, and build the houses. He was convicted of obtaining money by false pretences, the evidence being that the state of his companies was such that he could never be in a position to fulfil his commitments. The accused appealed on the grounds that he did not intend to defraud the victims, but rather eventually intended to furnish them with houses as they had expected. Despite what he had told the depositors he intended to use all the deposits to build a small number of houses, sell them, and use the profit to build more houses. Whether this could work or not, it was fundamentally different from the details of the scheme as he had originally represented it to the defendants and therefore a fraudulent misrepresentation. The appeal court suspected that the accused was suffering under the misapprehension that for the misrepresentation to be fraudulent it must also be malicious, mischievous, or wilful to rob the victims. This was not so. Once a false statement is made by a person with knowledge that the statement is false, and the victim parts with money on the strength of the false statement, then the fraud is complete. The court also said here that the test for intention in false pretences was an objective one (that is, would a reasonable man in his circumstances have intended to act in the same way?). This position was based on authorities which have since been rejected. Now it seems enough to prove a general subjective intent to defraud on the part of the accused.

---

192   See *R v. Lloyd* [1984] 3 WLR 30.

In **R v. Weatherstone** (1987) CCA 20/8/97, the court held that the intention to permanently deprive must be accompanied by some dishonesty or moral obloquy attaching to taking the property.

Under the English *Theft Act* the word 'dishonestly' has been used to replace 'fraudulently' in the definition of theft. 'Dishonestly' is defined in that Act in terms of the standards of the community. Therefore, as discussed in **R v. Ghosh** [1982] 2 ALL ER 689, the test for dishonesty is: 'How would the ordinary member of the community assess the accused's intentions with respect to the "dishonest" transaction?' In addition, in *Ghosh* the Court of Appeal also held that in determining whether someone acted dishonestly the court should also take into account whether that person realised subjectively that his actions were dishonest by community standards. If he did not, his conduct could not be regarded as dishonest.

In the English decision of **R v. Feely** [1973] QB 530, a community standard for dishonesty was advanced. However, the earlier pre-*Theft Act* English common law meaning of 'fraudulently' accepted that the expectation or hope of repaying the money unlawfully taken was no defence to a charge of acting fraudulently. This is consistent with s. 118 of the *Crimes Act* (NSW), where even an intention, at the time of appropriating the property to the accused's own use and benefit, to return the goods eventually does not deny the necessary *mens rea* for larceny.

Without claim of right

In **Walden v. Hensler** (1987) 163 CLR 561 it was held that claim of right protected an accused if he takes or converts property with an intention which is prima facie fraudulent, if he is acting under the influence of a belief that he has a right to the property or to take or convert it. The right need not be one which is only recognised at law.

It should be said that in **Williams'** case [1953] 1 QB 660, the words 'without claim of right' were not limited to the definition of 'fraudulently', and that they added to the separate components of the *mens rea* for larceny.

Where the defendant has an honest belief that he has a legal right to take the goods in question, there may be a defence to a charge of theft. The 'claim of right made in good faith' provision is similar to the defence of mistake of fact. The belief does not need to be reasonable provided that it is honestly held.[193]

Alleging that there is a legal right to claim the goods does not preclude raising the defence of mistake of fact. For example, a person may take money from an employer's cash register expecting that it would cover

---

193 *R v. Nundah* (1916) 16 SR (NSW) 482.

unpaid wages. If, however, the wages had been paid into the employee's bank account without his knowledge, he could raise mistake as to the fact that he had not been paid.

It is sufficient that the accused believes that he is entitled to possession, although he believes in addition that he is not entitled to take and carry away the property, or to do so by deception.[194] Therefore, the *mens rea* for larceny is not present if the accused person genuinely believes that he is asserting a lawful claim to something.[195] Whether the absence of a claim of right is essential to the mental state required for larceny, it could as well be conceived that the claim of right negates dishonesty and therefore fraud is not present. What about, therefore, the belief that the right is morally rather than legally based? Might this also deny dishonesty? In **Lowe** (1989) 17 NSWLR 608, under a charge of dishonest obtaining by deception (s. 178BA), it was held that a claim of right should succeed provided the defendant had a belief in the legal right to obtain the property, even if he had no belief in the legal right to practise the deception to get it.

With the intent at the time of taking to permanently deprive the owner

There are two principal parts to this element:

- permanent deprivation, and
- at the time of taking.

Section 118 of the *Crimes Act* (as divined in **Foster** (1967) 118 CLR 117) deems the accused to possess an intention to permanently deprive where he intentionally subjects the property to a condition which, irrespective of his expectation, may result in the property never being returned. In this case it was held that the accused stole money even though he intended to return to the owner the value of the money. The distinction between money as an object and as a denominator of value is emphasised here.

The requirement of permanent deprivation is beyond situations of borrowing and temporary possession, which may not come within the definition of general theft and therefore are sometimes covered by the provision of specific offences (such as the 'unlawful use of a motor vehicle'). As in **Garlett** (*supra*) the intention might have been merely to take the taxi temporarily in order to steal any money it contained. That would satisfy the requirement of permanent deprivation.

In **Lloyd's** case [1985] 3 WLR 30 it was held that the provision did not apply to a situation where a projectionist took films to be shown at a cinema without the knowledge or consent of his employer, to give them to another

---

194   *R v. Langham* (1984) 36 SASR 48.
195   *Cooper* (1914) 31 WN (NSW) 164.

for the purpose of making pirate videos. The films were then returned undamaged to the original cinema. After noting the difficulties associated with the interpretation of the provision, the court concluded that such a temporary removal would not amount to theft because

> the goodness, the virtue and the practical value of the films to the owner has not gone out of the article (by virtue of the unauthorised borrowing). The films could still be projected to paying audiences ...

The fact that the ultimate owners of the films would be damaged in their commercial interests seemed not to be considered by the court as an outright taking or disposal.

It was said in this case that 'mere borrowing is never enough to constitute the necessary guilty mind unless the intention is to return the thing in such a changed state that it can be said that all its goodness and value are gone'.

In **R v. Beecham** (1851) Cox CC 181 the accused took railway tickets intending that they should be returned to the railway board only after the journeys had been completed. Clearly the 'borrowing' here is for a period and in circumstances equivalent to an outright taking or disposal because if and when the tickets are returned as intended, all their goodness and value is gone.

Larceny by a bailee

Section 125 of the *Crimes Act* creates the offence of larceny by a bailee. Here the central conduct is the taking and converting of goods to one's own use, or the use of another, beyond the terms of the bailment. The elements of the offence are:

- the accused possesses the goods in question as a bailee;
- he took or converted the property to his own use or the use of another; and
- he acted fraudulently.

Conversion involves dealing with the goods in a manner inconsistent with the rights of the true owner with the intention to deny the owner's rights or assert rights which are inconsistent with those of the owner.

There is some doubt whether it is necessary for the prosecution to prove the intent to permanently deprive the owner of the property or whether it is sufficient that there merely be a dishonest breach of bailment. Fraud may be proved through establishing dishonesty.

Fraudulent appropriation

Section 124 of the *Crimes Act* (NSW) has introduced the concept of appropriation into larceny. Appropriation overcomes the need to establish taking and carrying away. It also applies to objects which might not be appropriate objects for conventional larceny.

CONTEXT OF THE PROBLEM

These problems extend the situations in which we have considered mistaken belief. The manner in which mistake relates to the formulation of fraud and dishonest possession and retention of property is revealed.

The limitations of the definition of property, and the manner in which it can be possessed are at issue. What happens when ownership appears to pass through qualified or unfounded consent?

Should borrowing present an excuse to larceny and if so are there other offences that might cover this situation?

PROBLEM

Analyse the following facts, apply the law on theft to these, establish what offences may have been committed, and discuss the issues involved in successfully establishing criminal liability:

Sarah Thompson receives her weekly pay-packet and takes it home without opening the envelope. When she does open it up she realises that they have paid her $2000 instead of $200.

Also, in the envelope she finds a cheque for a Ms S. A. Thompson in the amount of $200. Sarah's initials are S. Q., and she knows that the cheque is not meant for her. Even so, she goes to her bank and deposits the cheque in her account.

To complete a very lucky day Sarah uses the ATM outside the bank. Instead of withdrawing $400 as she intended, she types in an extra zero by mistake. The computer system that operates the ATM is down at that moment for its routine upgrade. The $4000 is produced by the machine even though Sarah's account is only in credit for $500.

Sarah goes to the pub to celebrate. After a few drinks she leaves the bar and notices, resting outside the door, a bicycle belonging to her friend Martha. She decides to use the bike to get home. On arriving at her house she puts the bike in the garage in case Martha comes by and scolds her for using the bike without permission.

ENGAGING THE PROBLEM

In determining whether there was theft or misappropriation here it is essential to examine the coincidence between the prohibited conduct and the criminal mental state within the environment of charges which are defined in terms of multiple elements. Mistake may tend to challenge this coincidence. The nature of the acts required by each offence and the connection between fraud and dishonesty will also be challenged by a claim of right. Borrowing, after all, is really a justification based on consent, claim of right, or mistake. How do these issues combine to deny criminal liability?

ADDITIONAL RESOURCES

Brown, D., Farrier, D., Egger, S., and McNamara, L., *Criminal Laws*, Federation Press, Sydney, 2001, paras 10.1, 10.2.

Fisse, B., *Howard's Criminal Law*, Law Book Company, Sydney, 1992, pp. 197–215, 246–60.

Rush, P. and Yeo, S., *Criminal Law Sourcebook*, Butterworths, Sydney, 2000, Chapter 2.

Garlett (1989) CLJ 13:67

Croton v. R (1967) 117 CLR 326

Kennison v. Daire (1986) ALJR 249

Walden v. Hensler (1987) 61 ALJR 646

Foster v. R (1967) 118 CLR 117

TOPIC 21

PROPERTY OFFENCES: DISHONEST ACQUISITION II

Continuing the discussion of property crime commenced in Topic 20, the conversion of the law on larceny by trick into the offences of fraudulent appropriation and fraudulent misrepresentation is discussed here. The other significant offences of burglary, robbery, false pretences, demanding money by menaces, obtaining property by deception, and receiving stolen goods are examined.

Introduction

Beyond the law of larceny are a range of offences that involve the illegal acquisition, appropriation or conversion of property outside the definitional limitations of larceny. These generally must be fraudulent and may arise from misrepresentation or misappropriation.

In addition to these, the other common property crimes to consider are those with an assault or trespass dimension such as robbery, breaking and entering, receiving stolen property, and demanding money with menaces.

Each of these other offences has been created in order to account for situations in which an essential element of the conventional larceny offence might otherwise be missing (e.g. where the consent on the part of the owner is induced through fraud).

In these offences it is often useful to distinguish the offence being proven on the basis of where either possession or ownership is gained. For instance, under the *Crimes Act* (NSW):

	possession gained	ownership gained
mens rea at taking/handing	Larceny by trick (s. 117)	Obtaining property by false pretences (s. 179)
subsequent *mens rea*	Larceny by bailee (s. 125)	Fraudulent misappropriation (s. 178A)

For larceny and the specialist property offences there exists the possibility of alternative verdicts. For instance, alternatives to larceny (including by a bailee) could be embezzlement, fraudulent misappropriation, obtaining by false pretences, or fraudulent appropriation. For embezzlement, an alternative charge is larceny by trick.

Fraudulent misappropriation[196]

On a charge under s. 173 it is said that 'fraudulently' is equivalent to 'dishonestly' and it is not necessary for the judge to define dishonesty.[197] The jury should apply the current standards of 'ordinary decent people'.[198]

Mere unauthorised use of property is not enough for it to be fraudulent. There must be some degree of moral abuse. Section 178A of the NSW *Crimes Act*, for instance, is a general provision covering all types of fraudulent misappropriation. It does create several specific offences within its terms. The difference between this offence and theft by a bailee is that in misappropriation the accused may obtain ownership as well as possession.

Fraudulent misappropriation under s. 178A (interference with money or valuable securities) is an alternative charge to false pretences (s. 179). For misappropriation there must be proof of a fiduciary element in the relationship of the accused to the property concerned. The receipt of property must be for another or another's purpose. The offence covers situations in which both ownership and possession are transferred. It may be seen to overlap with larceny by trick, and false pretences.

Obtaining property by deception (by false pretence)

The offence of obtaining money by deception[199] relies on the accused engaging in a deception dishonestly in order to obtain money, valuable property, or 'a financial advantage of any kind'. The *Crimes Act* defines deception as deliberately or recklessly committed by words or conduct, including a deception as to a present intention, and as to an act or an omission producing an unauthorised mechanical response. Essential to the offence is that the property or thing of value is handed over as a consequence of the deception.[200] It does not matter that the person deceived is not the person from whom the property is obtained.

It is the concept of obtaining, and the object being a thing of value, which set the offence apart from larceny. It is necessary that both possession and ownership pass; otherwise larceny by trick might be the appropriate alternative charge. The relationship between larceny and misrepresentation or false pretence is discussed in ***Croton*** (1967) 117 CLR 326.

---

196 See s. 173 *Crimes Act* (NSW) (by directors); s. 178A (of moneys collected or received).
197 *Glenister* [1980] 2 NSWLR 597.
198 *Feely (supra)*.
199 See ss. 178BA 178BB; s. 178BC; s. 179 of the *Crimes Act* (NSW).
200 *R v. Ho* (1980) A Crim R 145.

Dishonesty in this context was discussed by the High Court in **Peters v. R** (1998) 151 ALR 51, where it was held that if the act of the accused is to be considered dishonest according to ordinary notions, it is sufficient for the trial judge to instruct the jury that the accused's actions are to be considered according to the standards of ordinary decent people.

Section 178BA offences are designed for situations of obtaining 'financial advantage' by deception. Financial advantage is to be taken as its plain meaning and not narrowly construed. This would now also cover obtaining an unauthorised response from an ATM.

Section 178BB extends these offences to obtaining money or valuable things or financial advantage through making or publishing misleading statements, which the accused person knows to be misleading. It also covers a situation where the statement is false or misleading and the accused person makes or publishes the statement with a reckless disregard as to its veracity.

The mental state for this offence does not require fraud or dishonesty. Intent to obtain money and so on must be proved. An offence under this Act is now deemed to be of specific intent.

Section 178C is the offence of obtaining credit by fraud. It envisages incurring any debt or liability by false pretence or wilful false promise.

Section 179 creates the general false pretences (wilful false promise) offence. Here there must be an intent to defraud. Obtaining property by means of a false pretence with intent to defraud occurs when the owner or the bailee is induced by the fraud of another to part with a possession, and the trickster at the time of taking the property intends to misappropriate it to his own use. It is misappropriation if the owner intends to part with the property as a result of the false pretence offered.

Statements of present intention or opinion cannot form a false pretence or promise.[201] A wilful false promise occurs even in situations where there are no false statements regarding the present, but promises for the future are false. A promise, the fulfilment of which is outside the reach of the promisor, is within the section.[202] This is also an offence of specific intent.

It is necessary to prove an intention to defraud. It may be enough to show an intent to obtain money by deceit. It is not necessary to show that money or property obtained would be used for purposes other than what was represented. There must, however, be a causal connection between the deception and the obtaining of the property.

In **R v. Clucas** [1949] 2KB 226, the accused induced a bookmaker to bet with him by falsely representing that he was acting as an agent for many

---

201   *R v. Dent* [1955] QB 590.
202   *R v. Freeman* (1981) 2 NSWLR 686.

people at his place of work. The bet was successful and the accused was paid the winnings. He was convicted of obtaining money by false pretences. The court posed the question: Is it obtaining money by false pretences when the capacity under which someone makes a bet is misrepresented to a book-maker before the winning bet? The court held that the money was obtained not because of the people whom the punter falsely pretended to represent, but rather because the winning horse was backed. The bookmaker paid because the horse had won. It was true that the bookmaker might never have opened an account with these people if he had known the true facts, but the court distinguished between contributing and effective causes of obtaining. The false pretence which obtained the money was not the false pretence which made the bookmaker accept the bet.

In *Petronius-Kuff* [1983] 3 NSWLR 178, it was agreed that the false pretences offences have now taken over most of the ground once covered by larceny by trick. This is so under s. 179 where possession or ownership passes. 'Obtaining' in this offence therefore covers either possession or own-ership. As well, by reason of s. 180 (where the offender is not required to take physical custody of the property) the false pretences offence will hold even if only possession passes (not limiting it to larceny by trick).

How can one distinguish between false promises and broken promises? A statement of intention about future consequences, whether or not it is a statement of existing fact, is not a statement that can amount to a false pre-tence in criminal law. A false promise can be associated with a false represen-tation of fact so as to make it a false pretence (e.g. a promise to marry and a false statement about being unmarried).

Receiving and handling stolen goods

The essential issue for the receiving offence[203] is knowledge, at the time of the handling, receipt, or disposition of the goods (or the attempt to do so), that they were stolen. Here knowledge involves an 'actual belief of the accused that the property was stolen in the sense of the believer accepting the truth in that he believes as distinct from having a mere suspicion'.[204] The belief must be actual and recklessness or negligence is not sufficient.[205] The existence of a suspicion on the part of the accused, and a failure to take steps to alleviate that suspicion, may be evidence towards knowledge, but wilful ignorance alone is not the same as actual knowledge. The circumstances in which the accused received the property may be sufficient to prove that the

---

203 Sections 188 and 189.
204 *R v. Raad* [1983] 3 NSWLR 344.
205 *R v. Parker* [1974] 1 NSWLR 14.

accused knew they were stolen. In **Griffith's** case (1974) 60 Cr App R 40 it was suggested that in addition to actual knowledge of these facts, or belief in these facts, an accused may be convicted in the light of evidence disclosing that the accused knew of circumstances arousing suspicion of the existence of these facts and that he wilfully closed his eyes to this (constructive knowledge). More recent authority has held otherwise.[206]

In **R v. Creamer** [1919] 1 KB 564, it was confirmed that there must be theft before there can be receiving. Thus, as with **Walters v. Lunt** (*supra*), and **Haughton v. Smith** (*supra*), the goods must have been stolen and remain so until the time they were received, and the acquirer must be to some extent implicated in the theft through the receipt of the goods.

In **Re Attorney-General's Reference (No. 1 of 1974)** [1974] QB 744, it was clarified that for police officers merely to observe the property believed to have been stolen without resolving to take it into their control or return it to the owner or agent may not reduce the property into lawful possession. In such circumstances the goods may remain 'stolen' when they come into the possession of the accused. Despite the fact that the police officer had found stolen property in the car, immobilised the car, and kept the car under observation until the accused returned to the car and tried to start it, this situation was sufficient for a charge of handling stolen goods. The police officer had not taken possession of the goods. The court here accepted that the police officer had not decided to take the goods into his possession until he had the benefit of the accused's explanation of what he was doing with the goods. Once an implausible explanation was given, then the police took the decision to restore possession in the goods to a lawful authority and not before. Therefore the issue of possession is crucial to charges of receiving and handling.

The *mens rea* for receiving and handling offences is the intent to receive and handle. Receiving must be into the possession of the accused. Therefore he must intend to control the goods. As such, control is one of the elements of possession. Recent possession of stolen gods may be evidence that the accused is guilty either of larceny, or of receiving.

Malicious damage to property

What is required in the offence of malicious damage to property[207] is that the accused person damages or destroys property belonging to another, and does so maliciously (with intent or subjective recklessness).

---

206 See *R v. Anderson* [1978] Cr LR 223.
207 Sections 195, 196 of the *Crimes Act* (NSW).

Robbery

Robbery[208] is an aggravated form of theft in that violence is used or threatened in order to obtain property. It combines the offences of larceny and assault. Robbery itself can be aggravated by acting with others, and by the use of weapons (see s. 95 for circumstances of aggravation).

Essential to the offence is an intent to steal, some degree of threat or force putting the person in fear, and taking from the person. Section 94 of the *Crimes Act* (NSW), for instance, also creates the offence of an assault with intent to rob, where the stealing may not actually be carried out.

It has been said in cases such as ***Pollock*** [1967] 2 QB 195 that the threat involved in common law robbery might go as far as to accuse the victim of being involved in an unnatural crime, and to that extent to obtain money or property in a similar situation to extortion. It is also not essential that the assault or threat actually frightened the victim but that it is calculated to do so.

In *Pollock* it was also decided that the accused must possess the *mens rea* for robbery, which is an intent to obtain property by resort to violence or the threat of it, at the time of applying force or making the necessary threat of it. The threat must coincide with the stealing.[209]

Obviously it is necessary that the person assaulted is also the person robbed, and the person doing the assaulting is also the person carrying out the robbery. Further, it is required that the assault should be carried out in the presence of the victim, and the property that is taken should also be in the victim's presence and control (though it does not necessarily have to be taken from the victim). In ***Smith v. Desmond*** [1965] AC 960, the notion of presence was given a fairly wide interpretation (that is, where presence meant immediate control in order to resist taking). For the purpose of determining presence, the time to be considered is the time when the victim is assaulted rather than when the property is taken.

A claim of right may stand as a defence to a robbery charge but would not excuse the commission of an assault.

Section 96 offences require the additional proof of wounding or grievous bodily harm to the victim of the robbery. Wounding involves the breaking and cutting of the exterior and interior layers of skin.

Burglary and housebreaking[210]

Burglary is more serious than theft in that it involves the breaking into (or out of) a house with the intent to commit a felony.

---

208 Sections 94, 95, 96.
209 *R v. Emery* (1975) 11 SASR 169.
210 Sections 109–15.

The components of the offences of burglary and housebreaking are discussed below.

Breaking and entering

Minimum interference with the building constitutes breaking, for example pushing open an unlocked window. However, entering by going through an open door is not breaking.

Entering is complete when any part of the body or an instrument is inserted into the building.

A building is a dwelling or other building as defined under the legislation. It may be a house, school, shop, factory, store, garage, or workshop.

Trespass

Obviously the offence can only be committed by a trespasser and not by an invitee. Whether someone is a trespasser where the invitation to enter is founded on a mistake was examined in **R v. Collins** [1973] QB 100. Here the defendant was convicted of burglary with intent to commit rape. The facts were that the accused had followed the victim one evening after she had been out with her boyfriend and came home intoxicated. The victim went to bed naked and slept by an open window near a lattice. She saw a naked blond man with an erect penis at the windowsill. Thinking he was her boyfriend, she sat up in bed, he descended from the window, and they had full sexual intercourse. Something about him was 'not like her boyfriend', the victim later stated. When she turned on the light and saw it wasn't the boyfriend, she slapped his face, and he left. No force was involved in intercourse but she said she would not have allowed it if she had known he was not her boyfriend. Throughout the sexual activity the accused wore his socks in order to 'effect a fast escape' if necessary.

The court held that the crucial fact for burglary was whether he was in the room before she beckoned him to enter, and whether she beckoned him. It had to be proved by the prosecution that he entered the room, that he entered as a trespasser, and that he entered with the intent to rape. It was necessary to show that he knew that he was entering as a trespasser and continued to do so, or at the very least was reckless as to whether he was a trespasser. Because the jury was never invited to consider whether he entered as a trespasser, the appeal was allowed. It doesn't matter that he intended to trespass anyway; the question is whether in these circumstances he actually trespassed, intended to, or was reckless as to whether he did. In this case it appeared that the accused was an invitee.

Certain of these offences may be committed with aggravation, including being armed. Circumstances of aggravation and special aggravation are listed in the definitions section for this part (s. 105A). These include the deprivation of liberty of the victim, and grievous bodily harm.

Section 114 creates the offence of being armed with the intent to commit one of these offences. This also includes being in possession of house-breaking implements.

Blackmail and demanding money with menaces[211]

These offences relate to uttering or writing threatening correspondence, knowing the contents of the correspondence, without any reasonable or probable cause, to demand property or money with menaces. The *mens rea* for the offence is the intent to extort with knowledge of the threat, demand, or menace communicated for that purpose.

Menace is said to mean a demand

> of such a nature and extent that the mind of an ordinary person of normal stability and courage might be influenced or made apprehensive so as to accede unwillingly to the demand.[212]

Under s. 104 it is immaterial whether the menace is constituted by violence, injury, or an accusation to be caused or made by the accused person or others.

In **R v. Boyle** [1914] 3KB 339, where there was a threat, published in a newspaper, to attack a company, it was held that the menace was sufficient to demonstrate an intent to steal even though this would not have satisfied the general requirements for larceny.

Thorne v. Motor Traders [1937] AC 797 presents the traditional definitions of demanding money with menaces. This case involved a friendly action in which a member of a trading association wished to test price maintenance arrangements imposed on members. If a member was found to be discounting relevant stock it was proposed to put the member's name on a 'stop list' unless the member paid a fine to the association. If sending a letter regarding the fine amounted to demanding money with menaces, then the rule would be *ultra vires*. The House of Lords held that given that price maintenance arrangements of this type were legal at that time, to send a letter in these terms would not amount to blackmail because the communication would be with reasonable cause, that is, in the furtherance of legitimate business arrangements. 'Menace connotes threats of violence and injury to persons and property, and a contrast might be made between menaces and threats.' But in other case-law, menace has been given a meaning equivalent to threat.

Blackmail under s. 100A additionally includes the procurement of office as a valuable thing against which the demand is directed. It includes

---

211   Sections 99, 100, 100A, 101.
212   *R v. Clear* [1968] 2 WLR 122.

unwarranted offers to publish, refraining from publishing, and an offer to prevent publication.

Additional offences relate to an intention to defraud where a person is forced to alter, destroy, or execute a document or valuable security (s. 103).

CONTEXT OF THE PROBLEM

These scenarios identify offence situations where the larceny definition, or a crucial component of larceny, may not hold. They also demonstrate the case for codification. The confusion in *mens rea* caused by borrowing, the challenge to establish coincidence, questions of what is possession and what is appropriation, and conversion to use were all reasons for law reform in those jurisdictions such as Victoria, where a consolidated theft act approach has been preferred. Look at the Victorian legislation and compare it to the range of supplementary offences in this area within the NSW *Crimes Act*, and argue for a preference.

PROBLEM

Discuss any offences against property that may have been committed in each of the following situations:

1   A takes $100 from her employer, B's, cash register intending to 'lend' it to a needy friend, C, for a few days until C comes into funds to repay it, at which time A intends to return an equivalent amount to the cash register. B has given instructions to A never to borrow money from the cash register.

2   Same facts as in Problem 1 except that A receives the $100 from a customer, puts it in her pocket and then 'lends' it to C.

3   D believes, unreasonably, that E owes him $100. He corners E at knifepoint and takes E's watch, worth $200. He tells E that he will keep the watch until E pays him the $100. D knows he has no legal right to use a knife like this.

4   F agrees to repair the motor of G's car for $500. F has told G that he is a qualified motor mechanic but he is not. He has, however, some experience as a motor mechanic and believes he can repair the motor. G pays F the $500 in advance. F tries to fix the motor but is unable to do so. F refuses to refund the $500.

5   E enters a milk bar and asks for 'a cup of coffee and a slice of plain cake'. E and the server behind the bar know that a cup of coffee costs 50 cents and so does a slice of plain cake. When the server gives E her order, he hands her an extra slice of cake without realising it. E does not point out the mistake. She simply pays the $1.00 and walks away with the order.

ENGAGING THE PROBLEM

Once the appropriate offence has been settled on, the issues in these scenarios relate to justification or excuse. Is there a claim of right justifying the appropriation or taking? Does borrowing vitiate *mens rea* for theft? What if the required *mens rea* for appropriation is not present when possession passes? What impact does a mistake have on consent to pass possession, or the taking of possession? What are the limits to lawful possession for a bailee?

ADDITIONAL RESOURCES

Brown, D., Farrier, D., Egger, S., and McNamara, L., *Criminal Laws*, Federation Press, Sydney, 2001, paras 10.3–10.9.

Rush, P and Yeo, S., *Criminal Law Sourcebook*, Butterworths, Sydney, 2000, Chapter 3.

Fisse, B., *Howard's Criminal Law*, Law Book Company, Sydney, 1992, pp. 215–45.

Lanham, D., Weinberg, M., Brown, K. and Ryan, G., *Criminal Fraud*, Law Book Company, Sydney, 1987, Chapters 2, 3, and 4.

Andrews v. R (1968) 126 CLR 198

R v. Freeman [1981] 2 NSWLR 686

DPP v. Ray [1974] AC 370

R v. Denning [1962] NSWLR 173

TOPIC 22

SENTENCING AND PUNISHMENT I

In this topic and the next we will be looking at various issues concerning sentencing and punishment.[213] What are the various justifications offered for punishment by the criminal justice system? Which do you find the most compelling? What are the sentencing principles which guide judges in the exercise of their discretion? Do judges need further control on their sentencing? If so, how? Can preventive detention be justified? Can we predict who will be dangerous?

Punishment?

In his marvellous analysis of punishment, David Garland proposes a definition of punishment as 'a complex set of interlinked processes and institutions, rather than a uniform object or event'.[214] In this respect punishment is more convincingly viewed as:

- stages of a multifaceted process;[215]
- governed by ideological forms of and responses to the criminal law;
- presented in condemnation rituals; and
- confirmed by institutional routines.

---

213 For a more expanded discussion of my views on punishment, see M. Findlay et al., *Australian Criminal Justice*, Oxford University Press, Melbourne, 1999, Chapter 7.

214 D. Garland, *Punishment and Modern Society*, Clarendon Press, Oxford, 1990, p. 16.

215 In this respect punishment can occur at any stage of the criminal justice process.

Punishment is a process which reveals much about the dynamics of principle and practice in criminal justice, their motivations and justifications. In this sense punishment, while contextually relevant, is not spatially or temporally bound.

Punishment needs to be considered well beyond a natural outcome of crime and struggles for justice. It is important to recognise the relationship between punishment and social solidarity. Punishment is viewed as the embodiment of social and moral order (pointing to the moral content of instrumental action). Garland emphasises the relationship between punishment and constructs of social theory, the symbolic meaning of penal rituals, the important role of onlookers, and the relationship between penal ritual and public sentiment.

Prison as the ultimate punishment in Australian jurisdictions remains the paradigm of an organised and institutionalised collective penal response. It has come to represent and enact links with crime as 'moral circuitry in motion'.

Punishment cannot be wholly explicable in terms of its purposes because no social artefact can be explained in this way. It is useful to distinguish between the nature of punishment, its character as a social institution, and its role in social life. In so doing, the link between the nature of the outrage and the nature of the response connects crime and state intervention on behalf of the victim and his or her community. Why does the state have a monopoly over penal violence?

But punishment is not only about intent and form. The severity of punishment proportional to the intensity of collective conscience speaks of the quality rather than quantity of punishment. Conventional explanations for punishment, which dwell on pain or unpleasant consequences as the required response to offence against legal rules, tend to diminish the role of punishment as a social destinguisher—a mechanism for maintaining difference. Punishment is the ultimate identification of an offender and the intentional administration of authority by those in authority.

Principles of punishment

It is perhaps more convincing to view what are commonly termed the principles for punishment[216] as relative justifications (sometimes ex post facto) for what sentencers decide to do. These justifications, rather than demonstrating or arising out of pre-existing and informed theory, help give substance to the sentence imposed, and reasons for it.

Justifications for punishment are often directed towards the nature of punishment and its distribution. They appear in sentencing statements as a

---

216 See, for instance, P. Bean, *Punishment*, Martin Robertson, Oxford, 1981, Chapter 2.

compromise between distinct and partly conflicting principles. Even so, they are advanced as part of a cohesive strategy for sanctioning offenders.

The search for general aims of punishment is a thing of fashion. It is heavily influenced by political expectations for criminal justice and as such can swing wildly. This is what Stan Cohen refers to as constructing criminal justice policy on failure theory.[217]

As Garland observes, philosophies of punishment are traditionally based on idealised, one-dimensional views of crime, justice, and punishment. In this respect they sit well within classical notions of criminal responsibility.

Aims

Blame-based aims

Retribution places limits on the distribution of punishment in terms of liability, location, amount. Under this principle, punishment is restricted to the offender and the offence. Also, retribution limits the extent to which general social aims of punishment may be pursued at the cost to the individual and his or her rights, or the community and its legitimate expectations. Punishment must be deserved by voluntary offences and rational offenders.

Just deserts emphasises the necessity of guilt. This principle has strong ties with justice and puishment as the consequence of crime. Just deserts relies on the potential to calculate and compare proportionality in punishment with the harm caused by crime. It relies on measures of seriousness in both crime and punishment that are quantifiable and comparable. Just deserts suggests a potential for rectification or compensation, but the question in practice remains: is equivalence possible?

Reform-based aims

Rehabilitation: If punishment entails suffering and compulsion, how can it equate with rehabilitation, which suggests therapy and compliance? Particularly in the confines of the prison, how can reform be ensured through a deprivation of liberty and choice?

Rehabilitation demonstrates a close connection with causal theory. Indeterminacy in sentencing and the open-ended nature of the treatment models within punishment compete with determinate and certain sentencing commitments.

Deterrence connects the threat and danger posed by crime to the threat and sanction of social control. Deterrence is linked to 'pleasure–pain' balance argued for by the utilitarian reformers when considering the rationales

---

217 S. Cohen, *Visions of Social Control*, Polity Press, Oxford, 1987.

for punishment. Through deterrence, punishment must be grounded, efficacious, and profitable.

Deterrence is concerned with consequences, both of crime and punishment: (1) to prevent individuals from committing crime, (2) to minimise mischief, (3) to influence offenders and offences as directly and cheaply as possible, and (4) to influence and control the individual and the community. Deterrence, therefore, is both general and specific, directed towards the free-willed individual and the rational community.

Each of these rationales exhibits the strengths and weaknesses of punishment strategies within criminal justice. Further, the contradictions they present in combination mirror some of the profound ethical and operational dilemmas for criminal justice.

Sentencing theory

If one considers that the sentencing process is a logical distillation of consistent and rational sanctions, then the conclusion must follow that the principles of punishment are enunciated through sentencing. Consider occasions in your examination of sentencing policy and practice where this may not be the case.

A single and unassailable theory of sentencing informed by principles does not exist and is not apparent in any Australian jurisdiction. As we examined in an earlier topic, looking at discretion in criminal justice, sentencing policy is not so much driven by theory but rather is the consequence of, or a reaction to, political agendas and policy formulation for particular forms of criminal justice.

Conventional sentencing processes are said to involve the determination of tariffs, primary tariffs generally being pre-defined by legislation, and secondary tariffs constructed around policy considerations, legislative ranges, and the concern for consistency and certainty in sentencing.

Factors which influence sentencing are:

- indeterminacy
- consistency
- certainty
- precedent
- appellate structures, and
- the independence and political power of the judiciary.

Regulating sentencing discretion

As examined in earlier topics, sentencers have discretion over: (1) conducting the sentencing process, (2) applying the principles to the facts, (3) determining the range of sentence, (4) giving effect to mitigating factors, and (5) choosing the appropriate sentence and its consequences.

A sentence is based on different forms of judgment: about the facts, the statements of principle, explicit applications of principle, the weighting given to factors influencing the sentence, and finally the sentence.

Regulators over sentencing discretion include:

- individual experience and discretion (within the ideology of independence);
- legislation (range, limits on sentencing power, framework for sentencing);
- judicial decisions and principles (precedent, guidelines);
- techniques of guidance (appeal decisions);
- guideline judgments, general policy judgments, rules and principles; and
- relevant factors in each new case.

Operating as the sentencer does within a political framework of the separation of powers, where the judicial officer is independent and accountable to the law but in reality subject to political influence and community opinion, conflict will emerge over the distinction between certainty (uniformity) and discretion (individuality). Recent attacks on lenient sentencing in Australia are evidence of this tension.

Dangerousness?

Determinations of dangerousness have become a central element in the predictive function of criminal justice. Police employ them in stereotyping, probation officers use them in preparing pre-sentence reports, and judges are supposed to be mindful of them when exercising the protective dimension of penalty.

But the calculation of dangerousness is far from an exact science. What is it to be measured against?

- Risks of re-offending?
- The nature of the offence?
- Concerns of the victim?
- Public outrage?

There is considerable debate about the most suitable forms of predictors for dangerousness (legal, psychological, personality, statistics).[218]

CONTEXT OF THE PROBLEM

Determinations of early release (or the determination of indeterminate sentences) tend to throw into stark relief the legitimate expectations for a penalty, and the anticipated effect of that sentence on the offender. In addition,

---

218 J. Hinton (ed.), *Dangerousness: Problems of Assessment and Prediction*, Allen & Unwin, London, 1983.

a variety of competing and sometimes opposed interests are publicised in order to lay claim to their share of the decision. What does this say about the life of punishments such as imprisonment?

PROBLEM

You are the Chair of the Parole Board. Before you for consideration is an offender who some 25 years ago committed a vicious murder of a child. There was a sexual dimension to the killing. He was originally sentenced to life imprisonment, and later had the sentence redetermined to 20 years. He has spent 25 years in jail.

While in prison, except for some periods of depression, and an occasion where he walked away from a medium security environment, the prisoner has engaged in all the educational, work and welfare programs made available to him. Even so, the Commissioner of Corrective Services refused to grant the prisoner day release or work release, for fear of a media backlash.

Recently both the Government and the Opposition have tried to pressure members of the Parole Board to keep the offender in prison. They have even threatened special legislation to keep him inside.

The majority of the psychiatric reports say that the prisoner is fit for release. The parole officer supports release, and the Serious Offenders Review Council, after years of opposing this man's release, now thinks the time is appropriate.

The parents of the victim are enlisting community feeling against release. They are supported by many victims' organisations. They say that the prisoner has not reformed, that he remains a danger to the community, and that research shows that persons committing such offences are more likely to re-offend than other criminals. The media are right behind this argument.

Your primary concern is to balance the issue of justice for the inmate against community safety. What would be your decision on this application for parole and how would you answer those opposing your decision?

ENGAGING THE PROBLEM

Obviously the responsibilities of the Parole Board in your jurisdiction are set out in legislation. First consider this. Then relate the original aims of the sentence in question to the prison history of the offender. Reflecting on these issues, how do you balance community protection against predictions of dangerousness? Is there any place in the determination of the board for considerations of adverse publicity?

In balancing the legitimate conflicting interests in this scenario, what weight should be given to the victim's views (both specific and general)? Does revenge have any place here? How do you reconcile the anticipated determination of a sentence against the view that no reduction or termination of sentence in such a case is satisfactory?

How do you know when an offender such as this one has served his time? What of the offender's legitimate interests here? Should the media and the community have the opportunity to continue his punishment after release or how might he be protected from this? Why is it rare for long-term offenders to adjust to society successfully after release?

ADDITIONAL RESOURCES

Brown, D., Farrier, D., Egger, S., and McNamara, L., *Criminal Laws*, Federation Press, Sydney, 2001, paras 12.1, 12.2–12.3.2, 12.3.6–12.3.8, 12.4–12.5, 12.6–12.7, 12.8, 12.11.

Craze, L. and Moynihan, P., 'Violence, Meaning and the Law: Responses to Garry David' (1994) 27(1) *ANZ Journal of Criminology* 30.

Fairall, P., 'Imprisonment Without Conviction in New South Wales: *Kable v. DPP*' (1995) 17(4) *Sydney Law Review* 573.

Findlay, M., Odgers, S., and Yeo, S., *Australian Criminal Justice*, Oxford University Press, Melbourne, 1999, pp. 212–18, 222–30.

Johnson, A., and Spears, D., *The Sentencing Act 1989 and its Effect on the Size of the Prison Population*, Judicial Commission of NSW, Sydney, 1996, pp. vii–viii.

Shea, P., *Psychiatry in Court*, Hawkins Press, Sydney, 1996, Section D.

Spiegelman, J., 'Sentencing Guideline Judgments' (1999) 11(1) *Current Issues in Criminal Justice* 5.

Zdenkowski, G., 'Contemporary Sentencing Issues', in Chappell, D. and Wilson, P. (eds), *The Australian Criminal Justice System: The Mid 1990s*, Butterworths, Sydney, 1994, p. 171.

Kable v. DPP for NSW (1996) 138 ALR 577

TOPIC 23

SENTENCING AND PUNISHMENT II

What role or roles does the prison play in society? Do you think these are achieved? Has the prison always played such a central role as a mode of punishment? What are the primary alternatives to custody available? Consideration might also be given to new sentencing options such as family group conferencing.

Prison and alternatives

Origins of the prison

The historical interconnections between the birth of the prison, the factory, the asylum, the reformatory, the hospital, and the workhouse are replete in the literature concerning the prison.[219] In the development of the penitentiary and regimes such as solitary confinement and systems of silence, the emphasis was on the discipline of the mind, rather than discipline of the body as with corporal and capital punishment.

Following on from classical notions of criminal responsibility and attendant theories of punishment which were utilitarian, a relationship between the prison and the concept of *less eligibility*[220] became essential to the status of the prisoner. The prison regime and its design (physical and human) relied on the control over time, space, and the *habituating of labour*: surveillance, power and the organisation of space (*government of populations*).[221]

As both a social and a penal institution, the prison is about reproducing and distorting social relations. Through confinement, environments of power and dominance are generated within the prisoner and prison officer community and their interconnection; drug abuse is rife and drugs serve as currency for power and dominance; sexuality is distorted through homosexual contact in a heterosexual symbolism.

The history of the prison has demonstrated the inextricable link between the development of the corporate state, the industrial revolution, the criminal justice 'profession', and the penitentiary. Labour and obedience to the demands of capitalist industry were the original stimuli for the transition from the workhouse to the penitentiary.

Ironically, the prison as the symbol of enlightenment in the reform of punishment in the nineteenth century has now become a feature of penal repression and the expansion of state punishment. It is the distorted rhetoric of 'hope' within a failed reform agenda.

Perpetuation of the prison

As Garland argues, since its inception there has been a connection between welfare and discipline in the prison.[222] This is obviously a by-product of the commitment to reform behind the development of the original penitentiaries. In the twentieth century the push for rehabilitation and treatment within prison fostered this connection. In reality it was to create an atmosphere of greater repression and loss of liberty in the name of welfare.

---

219 See M. Foucault, *Discipline and Punish: The Birth of the Prison*, Penguin, London, 1979; M. Ignatieff, *A Just Measure of Pain: The Penitentiary in the Industrial Revolution 1750–1850*, Macmillan, London, 1978; D. Melossi and M. Pavarini, *The Prison and the Factory: Origins of the Penitentiary System*, Macmillan, London, 1981.

220 Where the poorest free person exists in better conditions than the prisoner.

221 The prison is for classes of people as well as for individuals.

222 D. Garland, *Punishment and Welfare*, Gower, London, 1985.

Due to concerns for the economic and social cost of the prison, and the fact that it seemed not to attain any of its objectives beyond incapacitation, there was a decline in resort to the prison in the late nineteenth and mid twentieth centuries. New forms of intervention in terms of public health, psychology, psychiatry, and welfare followed along with the decarceration and deinstitutionalisation projects.[223] This was not accompanied by any decline in the significance of incarceration, but was rather a redefinition of its purposes. The prison came to link treatment to reform outcomes and was doomed to failure, as was the earlier connection between religious enlightenment and reform in prison.

Prison represents the institutionalisation of class division. Prison statistics in any Australian jurisdiction demonstrate communities of inmates as evidence of warehousing social division and inequality.

In Australia, historically the prison has been shored up through periodic outbreaks of reform.[224]

The prison exists now not so much as a testament to its utility but as to the failure of the decarceration movement. In addition, the explosion of the drugs and crime control agenda, and the restoration of retribution as the primary sentencing principle for conservative politics have seen an explosion in prison populations throughout the world.[225]

Paradox of prison

Prison life is full of paradox:

- *The reality of prison labour:* In most Australian prisons there is little valuable or marketable occupation or industry. Since the inception of the penal colonies, forced labour was a futile feature of penal servitude. Today the forms of labour within prison tend to increase marginalisation and decrease real access to employment on release.
- *The reality of individual liability:* The prison creates, sustains, and vindicates a particular image of the criminal (and of criminality) which is class-determined, drug-dependent, and habitual.
- *The perpetuation of prison populations:* The prison is meant to deter, reform, and punish, but its population is a revolving one.
- *The arbitrary nature of the custodial environment:* Rather than regulated and disciplined, prison communities tend to be lawless, and reliant on terror.

---

223 A. Scull, *Decarceration: Community Treatment and the Deviant: A Radical View*, Polity Press, Oxford, 1977.
224 For instance, see M. Findlay, *The State of the Prison: A critique of reform*, Mitchellsearch, Bathurst, 1982.
225 See N. Christie, *Crime Control as Industry*, Routledge, London, 1993.

- *The prison as a means of addressing the social cost of crime:* The economic cost of imprisonment to taxpayers—including the victim—makes a joke of this supposed role, and the fact of recidivism might suggest that the prison exacerbates the social cost of crime.
- *The prison as a way of protecting the community:* A period of imprisonment transforms offenders into re-offenders and therefore tends further to endanger the community and to fragment that danger.

Alternatives?

As many sentencing options are not, in reality, alternatives to prison, viewing the notion of penalty as 'prison and its alternatives' is somewhat misleading. One thing is certain: options for penalty surrounding imprisonment tend to emphasise the importance of the prison as the ultimate penalty.

What follows is a discussion of sentencing options. These may or may not be alternatives or staging posts on the way to a prison sentence. They may represent alternative control models or simply invite imprisonment as a consequence of their failure.

Sentencing options

Imprisonment

Prison environments focus on the deprivation of individual liberty. Prisons are classified on the basis of the security in which inmates are contained, and the manner in which they are integrated within the community (such as with day release centres).

Periodic detention

This is a special form of imprisonment usually catering for prisoners with strong community and employment ties, and who have committed offences which are likely to occur over identified periods (e.g. drink driving offenders who are detained over the weekend).

Home detention

This is confinement within the offender's home. This form of house arrest is monitored in certain jurisdictions with the use of electronic tracking devices.

Suspended sentences of imprisonment

Here the sentence of imprisonment is deferred for a designated period, during which certain conditions may be stipulated through a behaviour bond. At the expiration of this period and the satisfaction of these conditions the imprisonment term will lapse. Should the conditions be violated or a further crime committed, a part or all of the original term may be activated.

Fines

This is the most popular form of sentence in Australia and involves monetary confiscation by the state. It may be designated in terms of dollars or penalty units, which can be regularly revised in value. The amount of the fine is determined under the jurisdictional limit and within the range set for the offence. Ability to pay is sometimes a sentencing consideration. Fines may sometimes be issued automatically in terms of infringement notices.

Community service orders

Community service orders (CSOs) are court orders that an offender perform unpaid work or service in a designated form and for a nominated community organisation (or in some cases for the victim), over a period of hours. If the offender fails to comply with the order the breach will result in a period of imprisonment. Along with probation, CSOs are the most popular order after the fine.

Probation orders

With probation orders, the court requires an offender to enter into a bond or undertaking for supervision with the probation service, during which the offender must comply with certain nominated conditions and be of good behaviour. A breach will usually result in imprisonment.

Compensation or restitution

In conjunction with other penalties the court may award compensation for loss and injury to be paid to the victim by the offender (or through a state compensation fund).

Confiscation of assets

Though more a form of a civil remedy than a criminal penalty, the criminal courts can confiscate the assets of an accused person where it is suspected that those assets are the proceeds of crime. Usually the onus of proof rests with the accused to prove that the assets are legitimately obtained.

Attendance Centre orders

Attendance centre orders are imposed on juveniles, usually requiring that the offenders attend an activity centre either before or after school, or at other times when crimes are likely to be committed, for designated hours of the week.

Good behaviour bonds

Similar to a suspended sentence or probation, good behaviour bonds are conditional orders, but do not have the automatic consequence of imprisonment on breach. Nor does the bond require supervision. The conditions of the bond are generally that the offender should keep the peace and be of good behaviour.

Admonish and discharge

The court, without the imposition of further penalties, may publicly remonstrate with the offender for the crime. This option is usually reserved for minor offences.

Juvenile conferencing

On a plea of guilty and evidence of contrition a court (such as in the ACT) may order that the offender attend and participate in a conference with the victim and with his own supporters, perhaps his family and others significant in his community. The experience is designed to shame as well as to reintegrate. This can also be used in certain jurisdictions (such as New South Wales) as a diversion from trial and sentence.

Finding of fact but no conviction

Commonly known as a first offender provision, for a minor offence and usually on a plea of guilty the sentencer will find the facts of the offence proved but will not proceed to the recording of a conviction or the imposition of any other sentence. It may in certain circumstances attach to a good behaviour bond or probation.

Consider the following diversion strategies as they influence sentencing practice in your jurisdiction:

- Pre-trial, pre-sentence and pre-release diversion
- Police cautions
- Screening of the mentally ill
- Drug court
- Screening of low risk or non-violent offenders
- Screening of vulnerable offenders (e.g. juveniles)
- Screening of protection offenders
- Screening out offenders for special reform programs.

Remember that punishment in criminal justice may precede the sentence of the court. Consider these examples:

- Punishment without trial
- Summary justice
- Police cautions
- Infringement notices.

CONTEXT OF THE PROBLEM

Prison and its alternatives are intended to address the circumstances of the offence and the offender, and the interests of the state, the community and the victim. In your decisions below, how do you recognise and realise these interests? Pay conscious attention to how you make your determination, for whom, and why.

PROBLEM

Sentencing exercise

Reflecting on the sentencing options discussed in this topic, determine what sentence you might consider to be appropriate in each of the following situations and why.

1 First offence, drink-driving, upper limit reading, several speeding violations
2 First offence, shoplifting, youthful offender, law student
3 Shoplifting, middle-aged offender, second offence, medical treatment for depression
4 Malicious damage to property, third offence, graffiti
5 Offensive language, Aboriginal offender, previous convictions for assault, resists police arrest
6 Embezzlement, middle-aged bank employee, gambling addiction, no prior offences
7 Assault occasioning actual bodily harm, prior convictions for domestic violence, already on AVO
8 Possession of 20 marijuana plants, one previous conviction for possession of drugs
9 Attempted murder, in company with others robs a garage, cashier shot by accomplice, previous property and drugs offences
10 Breach of bail, child abuse charge, previous sexual assault offences

ENGAGING THE PROBLEM

How much did the social context of the offence, the offender, and the victim influence your decision? Discuss the variations in approach among the class and reasons.

ADDITIONAL RESOURCES

Biles, D., 'Crime, Custody and the Community' (1996) 7(3) *Current Issues in Criminal Justice* 325.

Brown, D., 'Prison Policy: Where To Now?' (1995) 17(1) *Current Issues in Criminal Justice* 68.

Brown, D., Farrier, D., Egger, S., and McNamara, L., *Criminal Laws*, Federation Press, Sydney, 2001, paras 12.2.3–12.2.5, 12.5, 12.9, 12.10.

Cohen, S., *Visions of Social Control*, Polity Press, Cambridge, 1985, Chapter 4.

Cunneen, C. and Morrow, J., 'Alternative Penal Sanctions', in Tay, A. and Leung, C., *Australian Law and Legal Thinking*, Sydney University Faculty of Law, Sydney, 1994.

Foucault, M., *Discipline and Punish: The Birth of the Prison*, Penguin, London, 1977, Part 3.

Garland, D., *Punishment and Modern Society*, Clarendon Press, Oxford, 1990, Chapters 9 and 10.

Hampton, B., *Prisons and Women*, UNSW Press, Sydney, 1993, Chapter 1.

Hogg, R., 'Policing and Penalty' (1991) 4 *Journal for Social Justice Studies* 1.

Ignatieff, M., *A Just Measure of Pain: The Penitentiary in the Industrial Revolution 1750–1850*, Macmillan, London, 1978, Chapters 2 and 7.

Polk, G., Hayes, H., and Prenzler, T., 'Restorative Justice and Community Conferencing: Summary of Findings from a Pilot Study' (1998) 10(2) *Current Issues in Criminal Justice* 125.

Bibliography

Antrum, M., 'Frisky Business: Police Search Powers and Young People' (1998) 10(2) *Current Issues in Criminal Justice* 197.

Ashworth, A., *The Criminal Process: An Evaluative Study*, Oxford University Press, Oxford, 1998.

Australian Institute of Criminology, *Report No. 148* March 2000.

Australian Law Reform Commission, *Equality Before the Law: Justice for Women*, Report No. 69, Part 1, 1994.

Bargen, J. and Fishwick, E., *Sexual Assault Law Reform: A National Perspective*, Office of the Status of Women, Sydney, 1995.

Bean, P., *Punishment*, Martin Robertson, Oxford, 1981.

Biles, D., 'Crime, Custody and the Community' (1996) 7(3) *Current Issues in Criminal Justice* 325.

Blazejowska, L., 'Sorting the Myths and Reality of Domestic Violence' (1994) 32(11) *Law Society Journal* 41.

Braithwaite, J., *Crime, Shame and Re-integration*, Cambridge University Press, Cambridge, 1989.

Breckenridge, J. and Carmody, M. (eds), *Crimes of Violence: Australian Responses to Rape and Sexual Assault*, Allen & Unwin, Sydney, 1992.

Brereton, D. and Ede, A., 'The Police Code of Silence in Queensland: The Impact of the Fitzgerald Inquiry Reforms' (1996) 8(2) *Current Issues in Criminal Justice* 107.

Bronitt, S., 'Rape and Lack of Consent' (1992) 16(5) *Criminal Law Journal* 289.

Bronitt, S. and McSherry, B., *Principles of Criminal Law*, Law Book Company, Sydney, 2001.

Brown, D., 'The Royal Commission into the NSW Police Service: Process Corruption and the Limits of Judicial Reflexivity' (1998) 9(3) *Current Issues in Criminal Justice* 228.

——, 'Prison Policy: Where to Now?' (1995) 17(1) *Current Issues in Criminal Justice* 68.

Brown, D., Farrier, D., Egger, S., and McNamara, L., *Criminal Laws*, Federation Press, Sydney, 2001.

Brown, J., Collins, A. and Duguid, P., 'Debating the Situation: A Rejoinder to Robinson and Weinberg' (1989) 18(4) *Educational Researcher* 10.

Carlen, P., *Magistrates' Justice*, Martin Robertson, Oxford, 1976.

Carrington, K. et al. (eds), *Travesty: Miscarriages of Justice*, Pluto Press, Sydney, 1991.

Chan, J., *Changing Police Culture*, Cambridge University Press, Melbourne, 1997.

Chappell, D. and Wilson, P. (eds), *The Australian Criminal Justice System: The Mid 1990s*, Butterworths, Sydney, 1994.

Christie, N., *Crime Control as Industry*, Routledge, London, 1993.

Chunn, D. and Menzies, R., 'Gender, Madness and Crime: The Reproduction of Patriarchal and Class Relations in a Psychiatric Court Clinic' (1990) I *Journal of Human Justice* 33.

Clough, J. and Mulhern, C., *Criminal Law*, Butterworths, Sydney, 1999.

Cohen, S., *Visions of Social Control*, Polity Press, Oxford, 1987.

Corns, C. 'The Liability of Corporations for Homicide in Australia' (1991) 15 *Criminal Law Journal* 351.

Coss, G., 'Revisiting Lethal Violence by Men' (1998) 22(2) *Criminal Law Journal* 5.

——, 'A Reply to Tom Molomby' (1998) 22(2) *Criminal Law Journal* 119.

Cotterrell, R., *Sociology of Law*, Butterworths, London, 1992

Craze, L. and Moynihan, P., 'Violence, Meaning and the Law: Responses to Garry David' (1994) 27(1) *ANZ Journal of Criminology* 30.

Cunneen, C., 'The Report of the Inquiry into the Death of David John Gundy; Royal Commission into Aboriginal Deaths in Custody' (1991) 3(1) *Current Issues in Criminal Justice* 143–7.

——, *Aboriginal Perspectives on Criminal Justice*, Institute of Criminology, Sydney, 1992.

Cunneen, C., Findlay, M., Lynch, R., and Tupper, V., *Dynamics of Collective Conflict: Riots at the Bathurst Bike Races*, Law Book Company, Sydney, 1989.

Cunneen, C. and Libesman, T., *Indigenous People and the Law in Australia*, Butterworths, Sydney, 1995.

Cunneen, C. and Morrow, J., 'Alternative Penal Sanctions', in Tay, A. and Leung, C., *Australian Law and Legal Thinking*, Sydney University Faculty of Law, Sydney, 1994.

Davies, M., *Asking the Law Question*, Law Book Company, Sydney, 1994.

Davis, K., *Police Discretion*, West Publishing Company, St Paul, Minnesota, 1975.

Dixon, D., 'Reform of Policing by Legal Regulation: International Experience in Criminal Investigation' (1996) 7(3) *Current Issues in Criminal Justice* 287.

Downes, D. and Rock, P., *Understanding Deviance*, Oxford University Press, Oxford, 1998.

Duff, P. and Findlay, M., 'The Jury in England: Practice and Ideology' (1982) *International Journal of the Sociology of Law* 253.

Duff, P. et al. (eds), *Juries: A Hong Kong Perspective*, University of Hong Kong Press, Hong Kong, 1992.

Eames, G., 'Aboriginal Homicide: Customary Law Defences or Customary Lawyers' Defences', in Strang, E. and Gerull, S. A., *No. 17 Homicide: Patterns, Prevention and Control*, Australian Institute of Criminology, Canberra, 1993.

Edwards, A., and Heenan, M., 'Rape Trials in Victoria: Gender, Socio-Cultural Factors and Justice' (1994) 27(3) *The Australian and New Zealand Journal of Criminology* 213.

Fairall, P., 'Imprisonment Without Conviction in New South Wales: *Kable v. DPP*' (1995) 17(4) *Sydney Law Review* 573.

Felson, M., *Crime and Everyday Life*, Pine Forge Press, Thousand Oaks C. A., 1994.

Findlay, M., *The State of the Prison: A critique of reform*, Mitchellsearch, Bathurst, 1982.

——, 'Acting on Information Received: Mythmaking and Police Corruption' (1987) *Journal of Studies in Justice* 19.

——, *Jury Management in NSW*, Australian Institute of Judicial Administration, Melbourne, 1994.

——, 'The Ambiguity of Accountability: Deaths in Custody and the Regulation of Police Power' (1994) 6(2) *Current Issues in Criminal Jus*tice 234–51.

——, *The Globalisation of Crime*, Cambridge University Press, Cambridge, 1999.

——, 'Juror Comprehension and Complexity: Strategies to Enhance Understanding' (2001)(a) *British Journal of Criminology* 56.

——, 'Globalisation and Crime: Planning for Solutions' (2001)(b) unpublished conference paper.

——, 'Fair Trial and International Criminal Procedure' (forthcoming) *Criminal Law Review.*

Findlay, M. et al. (eds), *Issues in Criminal Justice Administration*, George Allen & Unwin, Sydney, 1983.

Findlay, M. and Duff, P., *The Jury Under Attack*, Butterworths, Sydney, 1988.

Findlay, M., Odgers, S. and Yeo, S., *Australian Criminal Justice*, Oxford University Press, Melbourne, 1999.

Finnane, M., *Punishment in Australian Society*, Oxford University Press, Melbourne, 1997.

Fisse, B., *Howard's Criminal Law*, Law Book Company, Sydney, 1992.

Fitzgerald, M., McLennan, M., and Pawson, D. (eds), *Crime and Society: Readings in Theory and History*, Routledge, London, 1981.

Foucault, M., *Discipline and Punish: The Birth of the Prison*, Penguin, London, 1979.

Fraser, D., 'Still Crazy After all These Years: A Critique of Diminished Responsibility', in Yeo, S. (ed.), *Partial Excuses to Murder*, Federation Press, Sydney, 1990.

Garland, D., *Punishment and Welfare*, Gower, London, 1985.

——, *Punishment and Modern Society*, Clarendon Press, Oxford, 1990.

Graycar, R. and Morgan, J. (eds), *Work and Violence Themes: Including Gender Issues in the Core Law Curriculum*, materials prepared for DEET, 1990.

Greer, P., 'Aboriginal Women and Domestic Violence in New South Wales' in Stubbs, J. (ed.), *Women, Male Violence and the Law*, Institute of Criminology, Sydney, 1994.

Hampton, B., *Prisons and Women*, UNSW Press, Sydney, 1993, Chapter 1.

Hawkins, K. (ed.), *The Uses of Discretion*, Oxford University Press, New York, 1992.

Hinton, J. (ed), *Dangerousness: Problems of Assessment and Prediction*, Allen & Unwin, London, 1983.

Hogg, R., 'Perspectives on the Criminal Justice System', in Findlay, M. et al. (eds), *Issues in Criminal Justice Administration*, George Allen & Unwin, Sydney, 1983.

——, 'The Politics of Police Investigation', in Wickham, G. (ed.), *Social Theory and Legal Politics*, Local Consumption Publications, Sydney, 1988.

——, 'Identifying and Reforming the Problems of the Justice System', in Carrington, K. et al. (eds), *Travesty: Miscarriages of Justice*, Pluto Press, Sydney, 1991.

——, 'Policing and Penalty' (1991) 4 *Journal for Social Justice Studies* 1.

Hogg, R. and Brown, D., *Rethinking Law and Order*, Pluto Press, Sydney, 1998.

Hood, R. and Sparks, R., *Key Issues in Criminology*, Weidenfeld & Nicolson, London, 1972.

Hubble, G., 'Feminism and the Battered Woman: The Limits of Self-Defence in the Context of Domestic Violence' (1997) 9(2) *Current Issues in Criminal Justice* 113.

Hughes, R., *The Fatal Shore: A history of the transportation of convicts to Australia 1787–1868,* Pan Books, London, 1988.

Hunter, J. and Bargen, J., 'Diminished Responsibility: "Abnormal" Minds, Abnormal Murderers and What the Doctor Said', in Yeo, S. (ed.), *Partial Excuses to Murder*, Federation Press, Sydney, 1990, p. 125.

Ierace, M., 'Acting for the Intellectually Disabled Offender' (May 1987) *Law Society Journal* 42.

Ignatieff, M., *A Just Measure of Pain: The Penitentiary in the Industrial Revolution 1750–1850*, Macmillan, London, 1978.

Indermaur, D., 'Public Perception of Sentencing in Perth, WA' (1987) 20(3) *The Australian and New Zealand Journal of Criminology* 163.

Johnson, A., and Spears, D., *The Sentencing Act 1989 and its Effect on the Size of the Prison Population*, Judicial Commission of NSW, Sydney, 1996.

Keyzer, P., *Legal Problem Solving*, Butterworths, Sydney, 1994.

Lacey, N. and Wells, C., *Reconstructing Criminal Law*, Butterworths, London, 1998.

Lansdowne, R. and Bacon, W., 'Women Homicide Offenders and Police Interrogation', in Findlay, M. et al. (eds), *Issues in Criminal Justice Administration*, George Allen & Unwin, Sydney, 1983.

Latham, M., 'An Unreliable Witness? Legal Views of the Sexual Assault Complainant', in Breckenridge, J. and Carmody, M. (eds), *Crimes of Violence: Australian Responses to Rape and Sexual Assault*, Allen & Unwin, Sydney, 1992.

Laurillard, D., *Rethinking University Teaching: A Framework for Effective Educational Technology*, Routledge, London, 1993.

Leader-Elliot, I., 'Battered but not Beaten: Women Who Kill in Self-defence' (1993) 15 *Sydney Law Review* 1.

——, 'Sex, Race and Provocation: In Defence of Stingel' [1996] 20 *Criminal Law Journal* 72.

Leal, S., and Robson, S., 'The What, Where, When and How of AVOs: A Step by Step Guide' (1994) 32(11) *Law Society Journal* 30.

Leaver, A., *Investigating Crime*, Law Book Company, Sydney, 1997.

Lincoln, R. and Wilson, P., 'Aboriginal Offending: Patterns and Causes', in Chappell, D. and Wilson, P. (eds), *The Australian Criminal Justice System: The Mid 1990s*, Butterworths, Sydney, 1994.

Mahoney, M., 'Legal Images of Battered Women: Redefining the Issue of Separation' (1991) 90(1) *Michigan Law Review* 1.

Manning, P., and Redlinger, L., 'Invitational Edges of Corruption: Some Consequences of Narcotic Law Enforcement', in Rock, P. (ed.), *Drugs and Politics*, Transaction Books, London, 1977.

McBarnet, D., *Conviction: Law, the State and the Construction of Justice*, Macmillan, London, 1981.

McConville, M., Sanders, A., and Leng, R., *The Case for the Prosecution*, Routledge, London, 1991.

McDonald, D. and Cunneen, C., 'Aboriginal Incarceration and Deaths in Custody: Looking backward and looking forward' (1997) 9(1) *Current Issues in Criminal Justice* 5.

Melossi, D. and Pavarini, M., *The Prison and the Factory: Origins of the Penitentiary System*, Macmillan, London, 1981.

Model Criminal Code Officers Committee of the Standing Committee of Attorneys-General, *Model Criminal Code Discussion Paper: Chapter 5, Fatal Offences Against the Person,* June 1998.

Molomby, T., '"Revisiting Lethal Violence by Men": A Reply' (1998) 22(2) *Criminal Law Journal* 116.

Murgason, R. and McNamara, L., *Outline of Criminal Law,* Butterworths, Sydney, 1997.

Naffine, N., 'Windows on the Legal Mind: The Evocation of Rape in Legal Writings' (1992) 18 *Melbourne University Law Review* 741.

——, 'Possession: Erotic Love in the Law of Rape' (1994) 57 *The Modern Law Review* 10.

Neal, D., *The Rule of Law in a Penal Colony: Law and Power in early NSW,* Cambridge University Press, Melbourne, 1991.

NSW Criminal Law Review Division, *A Review of the Law on the Age of Criminal Responsibility of Children,* Attorney General's Department, Sydney, 2000.

NSW Director of Public Prosecutions, Office of, *Guidelines for Prosecutors,* 1996.

NSW Law Reform Commission, Discussion Paper 33, 1996.

——, *The Jury in a Criminal Trial,* 1996.

——, *Partial Defences to Murder: Diminished Responsibility: Report 82,* 1997.

——, *Partial Defences to Murder: Provocation and Infanticide,* October 1997.

——, *The Right to Silence,* Discussion Paper 41, 1998.

Norrie, A., *Crime, Reason and History,* Weidenfeld & Nicolson, London, 1993.

O'Connor, D. and Fairall, D., *Criminal Defences,* Butterworths, Sydney, 1996.

Odgers, S., 'Regulating Police Interrogation: Back to First Principles', in Selby, H. and Freckelton, H. (eds), *Police in Our Society,* Butterworths, Melbourne, 1988.

O'Gorman, T., 'We Need to Know More' (1992) 27(3) *Australian Law News* 10.

Polk, G., Hayes, H., and Prenzler, T., 'Restorative Justice and Community Conferencing: Summary of Findings from a Pilot Study' (1998) 10(2) *Current Issues in Criminal Justice* 125.

Potas, I. et al., 'Informing the Sentencing Discretion: The Sentencing Information System of the Judicial Commission of NSW' (1998) 6(2) *International Journal of Law and Information Technology* 99.

Redfern Legal Centre, *The Law Handbook,* Redfern Legal Centre Publishing, Sydney, 1997.

Richardson, M., and Reynolds, S., 'The Shrinking Public Purse: Civil Legal Aid in New South Wales, Australia' (1994) 5(2) *Maryland Journal of Contemporary Legal Issues* 349.

Rock, P. (ed.), *Drugs and Politics,* Transaction Books, London, 1977.

Rush, P., *Criminal Law,* Butterworths, Sydney, 1997.

Rush, P. and Yeo, S., *Criminal Law Sourcebook*, Butterworths, Sydney, 2000.

Salmelainen, P. and Coumarelos, C. (1993) 2 'Adult Sexual Assault in NSW' *NSW Bureau of Crime Statistics and Research Crime and Justice Bulletin 2.*

Sapsford, R., 'Individual Deviance: The Search for the Criminal Personality', in Fitzgerald, M., McLennan M., and Pawson, D. (eds), *Crime and Society: Readings in Theory and History*, Routledge, London, 1981.

Schneider, E., 'Equal Rights to Trial for Women: Sex Bias in the Law of Self-Defence' (1980) 15 *Harvard Civil Rights–Civil Liberties Law Review* 623.

Scull, A., *Decarceration: Community Treatment and the Deviant: A Radical View*, Polity Press, Oxford, 1977.

Selby, H. and Freckelton, H. (eds), *Police in Our Society*, Butterworths, Melbourne, 1988.

Sharpe, A., 'The Precarious Position of the Transsexual Rape Victim' (1994) 6(2) *Current Issues in Criminal Justice* 303.

Shea, P., *Psychiatry in Court*, Hawkins Press, Sydney, 1996, Section D.

Sheehy, E., Stubbs, J., and Tolmie, J., 'Defending Battered Women on Trial: The Battered Woman Syndrome and its Limitations' (1992) 16(6) *Criminal Law Journal* 369.

Sinclair, K., 'Responding to Abuse: A Matter of Perspective' (1995) 7(2) *Current Issues in Criminal Justice* 153.

Skolnick, J., *Justice Without Trial*, John Wiley & Sons, New York, 1966.

Smith, J. and Hogan, B., *Criminal Law*, Butterworths, London, 1992.

Spiegelman, J., 'Sentencing Guideline Judgments' (1999) 11(1) *Current Issues in Criminal Justice* 5.

Strang, E. and Gerull, S. A., *No. 17 Homicide: Patterns, Prevention and Control*, Australian Institute of Criminology, Canberra, 1993.

Stubbs, J., 'Self-defence and Defence of Others', in Graycar, R. and Morgan, J. (eds), *Work and Violence Themes: Including Gender Issues in the Core Law Curriculum*, materials prepared for DEET.

Stubbs, J. (ed.), *Women, Male Violence and the Law*, Institute of Criminology, Sydney, 1994.

Stubbs, J., and Tolmie, J., 'Battered Woman Syndrome in Australia: A Challenge to Gender Bias in the Law?', in Stubbs, J. (ed.), *Women, Male Violence and the Law*, Institute of Criminology, Sydney, 1994.

——, 'Defending Battered Women on Trial' (1995) 8(1) *The Canadian Journal of Women and the Law* 122.

——, 'Feminism, Self-defence and Battered Women: A Response to Hubble's "Straw Feminism"' (1998) 10(1) *Current Issues in Criminal Justice* 73.

Tay, A. and Leung, C., *Australian Law and Legal Thinking*, Sydney University Faculty of Law, Sydney, 1994.

Travis, G., 'Police Discretion in Law Enforcement: A Study of Section 5 of the NSW *Offences in Public Places Act 1979*', in M. Findlay et al. (eds),

Issues in Criminal Justice Administration, George Allen & Unwin, Sydney, 1983.

Trembath, O., 'Judgement by Peers: Aborigines and the Jury System' (1993) 31(15) *Law Society Journal* 44.

Trimboli, L. and Bonney, R., *An Evaluation of the NSW Apprehended Violence Order Scheme*, NSW Bureau of Crime Statistics and Research, Sydney, 1997.

Vold, G., *Theoretical Criminology*, Oxford University Press, New York, 1998.

Walker, C. and Starmer, K., *Miscarriages of Justice: A Review of Justice in Error*, Blackstone Press, London, 1999.

Wallace, A., *Homicide: the Social Reality*, Bureau of Crime Statistics and Research, Sydney, 1986.

Waller, L. and Williams, C. R., *Criminal Law: Text and Cases*, Butterworths, Sydney, 2001.

Wayne, V., 'Rape and the Unconscionable Bargain' (1992) 16(5) *Criminal Law Journal* 94.

Wells, C., 'Swatting the Subjectivist Bug' (1982) *Criminal Law Review* 209.

White, R. and Alder, C. (eds), *The Police and Young People in Australia*, Cambridge University Press, Melbourne, 1994.

Wickham, G. (ed.), *Social Theory and Legal Politics*, Local Consumption Publications, Sydney, 1988.

Williams, C. R., *Property Offences*, Law Book Company, Sydney, 1999.

Williams, G., *Textbook on Criminal Law*, Stevens, London, 1983.

Yeo, S., 'The Threat Element in Duress' (1987) 11 *Criminal Law Journal* 165.

——, (ed.) *Partial Excuses to Murder*, Federation Press, Sydney, 1990.

——, 'Native Criminal Justice After *Mabo*' (1994) *Current Issues in Criminal Justice* 26.

——, 'Criminal Cases in the High Court of Australia: *Walker v. NSW* (1994) 69 ALJR 111' (1995) *Criminal Law Journal* 160.

——, 'Sex, Ethnicity, Power of Self-Control and Provocation Revisited' (1996) *Sydney Law Review* 304.

Young, J., 'Thinking Seriously about Crime: Some Models of Criminology', in Fitzgerald, M., McLennan, M., and Pawson, D., (eds) *Crime and Society: Readings in Theory and History*, Routledge, London, 1981.

Zdenkowski, G., 'Contemporary Sentencing Issues', in Chappell, D. and Wilson, P. (eds), *The Australian Criminal Justice System: The Mid 1990s*, Butterworths, Sydney, 1994.

——, 'Limiting Sentencing Discretion: Has There Been a Paradigm Shift?' (2000) 12(1) *Current Issues in Criminal Justice* 58.

Index